THE HEYDAY OF THE

FOOTBALL ANNUAL

YIPPEE!

All the thrills in a boy's world are summed up in this picture of happy Leicester youngsters as their team scored against Spurs.

THE HEYDAY OF THE

FOOTBALL ANNUAL

Post-war to Premiership

by Ian Preece & Doug Cheeseman

CONSTABLE

First published in Great Britain in 2015 by Constable

Copyright © Ian Preece, 2015
1 3 5 7 9 8 6 4 2

The moral right of the author has been asserted.

A CIP catalogue record for this book is available from the British Library.

ISBN 978-1-47211-494-5 (hardback)
ISBN 978-1-47211-495-2 (ebook)

Design by Doug Cheeseman
Imaging by Jörn Kröger
Printed and bound in China

Constable is an imprint of
Little, Brown Book Group
Carmelite House
50 Victoria Embankment
London EC4Y 0DZ

An Hachette UK Company
www.hachette.co.uk

www.littlebrown.co.uk

Endpapers: WBA's Tony Kaye duals with Derek Dougan of Wolves, *Topical Times Football Book* **1970 Previous page: Jubilant Leicester fans in** *Charles Buchan's Football Monthly* **1963**

Right: Tony Brown and Jeff Astle of WBA, after the winning the 1968 FA Cup, in the *Midlands Soccer Annual* **the following year Following: A pre-photoshop age montage from** *Charles Buchan's Soccer Gift Book* **1963**

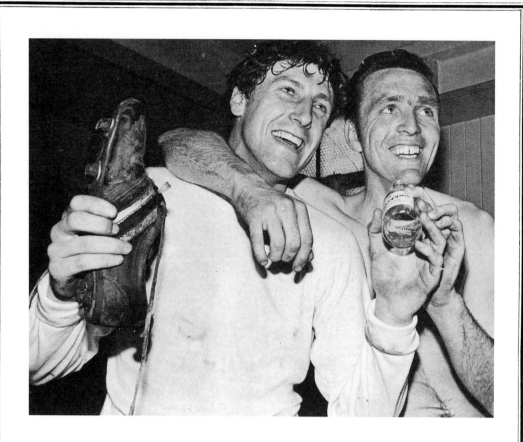

For Neil (Woollatt)
January 1967 – January 2014
RIP

(This book is also written for everyone struggling to stay awake
for *The Football League Show* on a Saturday night)

CONTENTS

12/6

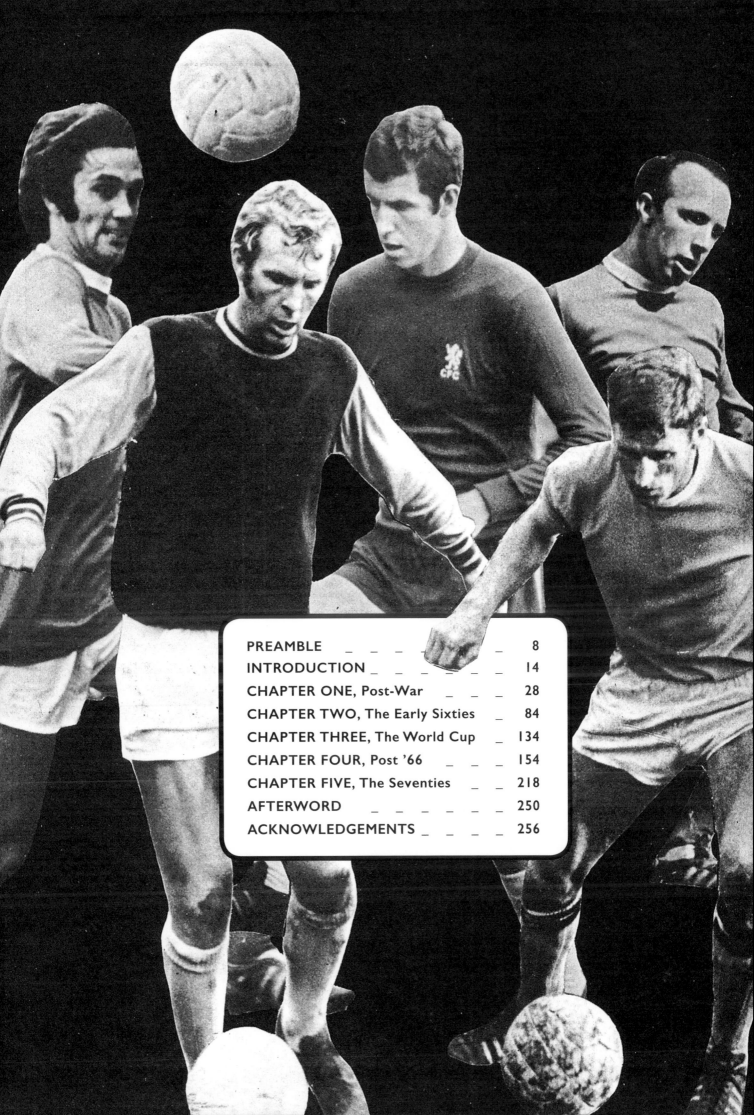

PREAMBLE _ _ _ _ _ _ 8

INTRODUCTION _ _ _ _ _ _ 14

CHAPTER ONE, Post-War _ _ _ 28

CHAPTER TWO, The Early Sixties _ 84

CHAPTER THREE, The World Cup _ 134

CHAPTER FOUR, Post '66 _ _ _ 154

CHAPTER FIVE, The Seventies _ _ 218

AFTERWORD _ _ _ _ _ 250

ACKNOWLEDGEMENTS _ _ _ _ 256

Preamble

||||||||||||||||||||||||||||||||||||||||||||||||||||||||||||||

In deference to the style of the annuals we are celebrating, 'Welcome to our book!' Calling it *The Heyday of the Football Annual* (having rejected *Smells Like Charles Buchan's Soccer Gift Book*), does invite the question, 'When was that, then?' The simple answer is: 'The year you can first remember watching the FA Cup final.' That tends to be when you were aged seven – the year can vary slightly, but that was normally the moment your football antennae became tuned and ready to receive further information. Invariably, at Christmas time in the same season, a pristine football annual arrived. Unwrapping it would usher in an overwhelming feeling that all was well with the world. Of course – as all football fans painfully discover – this is not always the case, but by then it's too late: you are hooked.

At this early stage in our lives, football, like pop music, is not a particularly cerebral thing, it's all about the adrenalin rush of youth. In keeping with all good pop ephemera, photos from our annuals were often torn out with reckless abandon and stuck into scrapbooks or onto bedroom walls. I can clearly recall my bedroom adorned with pictures of my first football idol, Tony Currie, and Spurs 'stars' Colin Lee and Ian Moores. (I switched my football allegiances from Sheffield United to Spurs after United were relegated in 1976. Spurs duly followed them down in 1977. There's a moral in there somewhere . . .)

After a few short years gazing longingly at these exotically colour-rich images, other interests enter our early teenage lives. The accumulated cultural debris of our childhoods is deposited at a church jumble sale or, if we're lucky, consigned to the loft where they can be retrieved in future decades. However, those annual covers and the images inside them, like fading family photos from our childhoods, somehow stay with us in a compartment of our subconscious marked 'Keep'.

My own annuals followed the jumble-sale route sometime in the early 1980s but they returned, in a roundabout way, later in the decade. I was a student dropout living in London when I first picked up the football fanzine *When Saturday Comes*. At last, here was a football periodical that seemed to say exactly what I was thinking – only written in coherent sentences with good jokes. I learnt more in one article by Andy Lyons (editor then and now) about football in Chile than I did in a year at university. In it he brilliantly asserted that the country was so narrow that all the football pitches had to be laid out vertically north to south.

I liked it so much I pitched up at *WSC*'s offices as a volunteer and didn't budge until they felt sorry for me and said I could stay. There were a number of office-cum-publishing duties performed, as best they could, by the two-strong full-time and assorted part-time staff. Cut and paste magazine layout was one such task but the then publisher John Duncan's attempts to hastily change a scalpel blade often ended with blood on the Letraset. I had a CSE grade 1 in art so I said, 'I can do that . . . ' From then on I was an unstoppable magazine paste-up artist. Completely unskilled and untrained, but unstoppable.

The magazine was growing fast and needed pictures every month. Stacked around the *WSC* office were piles of football annuals. There were the ones you'd expect – such as *Charles Buchan's Soccer Gift Book*, *Topical Times*

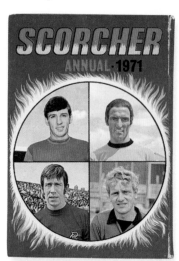

What finer example of the designer's art could there be than the cover of Scorcher 1971?

||||||||||||||||||||||||||||||||||||||||||||||||||||

Above: The 1971 *Scorcher* annual cover blazes a trail for seventies graphic design
Right: Sheffield United's undisputed star of the decade Tony Currie, pictured in *Tiger* annual 1976

8

TIGER PORTRAIT

Tony Currie

Now here's a jolly lot... a jolly, jolly lot!

Scene: White Hart Lane. Time: Last winter's big freeze. Occasion: Spurs v. Blackpool. Wonder if those policemen were thinking of their warm station, a big mug of hot tea—and a message to the sergeant... "Wish you were here!"

If you can't beat it, use it! Someone at Halifax got his skates on and came up with a very bright idea during last winter's big freeze. He thought, if there is so much ice on our pitch that we can't play football, why not use it as an ice rink? And they did. And this was the result. Full marks!

Football Book and *Shoot!* – but less common titles too: the *Big Book of Football Champions*, *Football Parade*, the *Northern*, *London* and *Midlands Soccer Annuals*, books dedicated to blue-chip stars of the seventies like Brian Clough and Lawrie McMenemy, and one-offs like *Football Stars*. Many of these books were barely more than a decade old but they already seemed to belong to a different age. I immersed myself in their pages and it kindled a love for esoteric design and documentary photography.

Foremost for me was the imagery. I grew to love the epic landscape shot of fans ice-skating on the frozen pitch at the Shay, Halifax, that fell out of a broken hinged copy of *Charles Buchan's Soccer Gift Book*, and a huddle of policeman in the snow at White Hart Lane from the same title. In fact, I would venture to say *Charles Buchan* annuals from the 1960s are football's very own *Picture Post*. And where else, before the advent of the Google image search, could you be introduced to the concept of the footballing nun?

When Saturday Comes plundered the annuals for photos (retrospective apologies to any uncredited sources back in the day . . . we've cleared them all this time) armed only with a faulty photocopier. The magazine ran a photo series called TENDER MOMENTS FROM THE LIVES OF THE STARS that lampooned the cheesy photo-ops the annuals were prone to include, and there was no shortage to choose from. Even allowing

> I would venture to say Charles Buchan annuals from the 1960s, are football's very own Picture Post

for the indulgences of the period it's hard to imagine how Dave Webb agreed to a request to cut comedian Marty Feldman's hair, or why, at a *Shoot!* photographer's behest, Howard Kendall dressed up in a wig while his wife Cynthia wore one of his shirts. (A Football League representative team one since you ask.)

All this and more lay within the annuals' pages. They were not just great picture resources, they were a history lesson and a cultural studies course all rolled into one. They may not be generally regarded as design classics but they also contain many a graphic delight. *Charles Buchan's* design and typography was precise and considered, while *Topical Times* carried a weighty tabloid punch with its big red headlines and double-page spreads of dynamic photography. With its 'scorching' motif and a deft selection of players of contrasting positions, all from different regions of the UK, what finer example of the designer's art could there be than the *Scorcher* annual cover, 1971? (Though why they blacked out Derek Dougan's eyes is less immediately obvious.)

Other highlights included: the endpapers of *Topical Times* (see our own inside covers); the bizarrely retouched colour photos in *Big Book of Football Champions* (see p. 43 and 51), and the dramatic colour and scale of *Tiger Book of Soccer Stars* (see chapter 5). Going back further to the early 1950s, *Tommy Lawton's Football Book*, in its rare early colour interior pages,

Left: Slices of football life courtesy of the *Charles Buchan* photographers, none of whom were credited for their work in the books, both from the 1963–64 annual
Above: Sister John Gabriel shows a good touch for a cloistered nun, *Charles Buchan's Soccer Gift Book* 1966–67; Dave Webb asks Marty Feldman if he's going anywhere nice on holiday this year, *Football Star Parade* 1970; Howard Kendall and wife Cynthia sacrifice their dignity to the whims of *Shoot!* in 1976

featured meticulously hand-cut-out player profiles. The *FA Book for Boys* used fine spot-coloured illustration, while *David Coleman's World of Football* led the way with brash seventies-style graphics. Colour print was a premium product right up until the 1990s, so the annuals depicted a largely monochrome world, occasionally interrupted by a riot of colour as the designers sought the best possible value from their colour pages. Often they used only primary print colours in their graphics (cyan, yellow, magenta) to avoid badly registered colours on press (print aficionados see p. 188).

A popular feature which endured throughout the annuals' heyday was the photographer's home visit to the stars. In the fifties *Charles Buchan's* OFF THE FIELD feature would snap players doubling up in a small bath, or capture a scene of domestic bliss in their tiny kitchens. By the 1960s just about every first division footballer had moved into a new-build semi with a medium-sized garden; come the seventies,

> ## The annuals depicted a largely monochrome world, occasionally interrupted by a riot of colour

ornate fireplace surrounds and furry rugs had crept in but, generally, furnishings and lifestyle trappings were reasonably restrained.

The *WSC* office annual collection, though never complete, was always growing in new and unexpected directions – this was a time when you could pick up an annual for 5 pence in a charity shop. When I found a 1973 *Football Facts* annual in a book exchange in Stratford it was like finding an old friend (but without having to ask, 'What are you up to these days?') As *WSC* developed, Andy hatched a plan to produce a book, essentially a long-form version of the magazine. It was a given that it should be a parody of the hardback A4 annuals. Published for Christmas 1989, it was called *Offside!* (in deference to *Shoot!*, naturally) and carried spoofs of the features we knew from the annuals, the moody endpapers, the cheesey photo-ops and the slightly stilted articles about the birth of the game. I took up the task of gluing it all

Above: Period design classics from *Tommy Lawton's Football Book* 1950, the *FA Book for Boys* 1959, *Topical Times Football Book* 1971 and *David Coleman's World of Football* 1974

into place and became a DIY graphic designer, of sorts, in the process. My 'technique' was pretty much based on copying the layouts and fonts from the annuals. A limited technique, agreed, but as on-the-job apprenticeships go, it was a half decent one.

The opportunity to compile *The Heyday of the Football Annual* with writer Ian Preece came about after we produced a supplement on the annuals for *WSC* in 2013. There was so much good stuff that ended up on the cutting-room floor (owing to lack of space) that we decided to keep going. In the process of sourcing the material for this book we have revisited all the annuals in our possession again. The pictures and layouts still seem fresh, and though that can't be said of the musky smell of old books that now lingers in my office, that in itself is reassuring. It's a tangible reminder of when we were young and blissfully ignorant of the world around us. The annuals recorded that moment for posterity, packaged it all in a hardback book with the year on the front and, for good measure, threw in some big colour pictures you could stick on your wall. They were educational and entertaining but, moreover, they were the backdrop to our lives at a time when our cultural senses were most receptive.

A nice thing about finding annuals in second-hand shops and car-boot sales today is that they always look strangely familiar. You're almost disappointed to see the inscription on the inside front – usually along the lines of 'Happy Christmas, Johnny, love from Auntie Jean XXX' – dedicated to someone else. (You don't often find them for 5 pence these days, but I can offer you this second-hand football-annual buyers' guide: less than £1, buy it anyway; over £1, check the pictures haven't been cut out; more than a fiver, don't buy it, you'll find it cheaper somewhere else one day.)

In short – well, with relative brevity, I hope – this preamble is how we arrived at *The Heyday of the Football Annual*. From here I'll leave you in the capable hands of Ian. We hope you enjoy our book and, lastly, in the words handwritten in the back of our copy of *Charles Buchan's Soccer Gift Book* 1954, remember:

SOCCER IS OUR NATIONAL GAME PLAY IT CLEAN AND ALWAYS DO YOUR BEST

Doug Cheeseman
April, 2015

Above: In a feature that has endured throughout the heyday of the annual, *Topical Times Football Book* 1967 invites itself into assorted footballers' family homes

GORDON BANKS
Leicester City and England

Introduction

||||||||||||||||||||||||||||||||||||||||||||||||||||||||||||||||||||||||||||||||||

There is a scene in Ken Loach's *Wednesday Play* from 1968, *The Golden Vision*, where the young lad Johnny Coyne (played by Ian Doran) is sitting on a park bench, being tested on his football knowledge by an old fella from down the street. Mr Hagan (Sammy Sharples) doesn't really have much else to do, other than look back fondly at the past and cultivate a proper sense of history in young Johnny's mind of the club they both love.

'Easy one this time,' says Mr Hagan. 'Name the 1939 Everton football team.'

'Easy,' replies Johnny. 'Mercer, Lawton, Thompson, Stevenson . . .' He reels them all off, before old Mr Hagan interjects: 'I don't suppose you know when Dixie Dean scored his sixtieth goal?'

'In 1927–28 we were playing Arsenal, the score was 4–3,' Johnny pauses – 'You've given me an 'ard un here, 'aven't yer?' – but then he smiles as he remembers it was eight minutes from the end, and from a corner kick. Winger Alec Troup took the corner.

'En't you good, aye?' nods Mr Hagan, approvingly.

It's a scene from a black and white world of short back and sides, flat caps and overcoats on a chilly day; corporation flower beds in the park, awaiting the first bloom of spring; the rumble of traffic in the background. It's also a scene from the world of the football annual. The chances are that Johnny – if this had been real life – would have unwrapped the *Big Book of Football Champions*, or maybe the *Topical Times Football Book* or *Charles Buchan's Soccer Gift Book* on Christmas morning.

That was certainly the case for Labour politician Alan Johnson, who, during the course of his childhood, graduated from the *Hotspur* annual in the late fifties to the *BBC Grandstand Book of Sport*. He wrote in his autobiography, *This Boy*, of one sad Christmas Eve (1963, his dad long gone; his mum in hospital again)

when he wrapped up his *Grandstand* annual himself so he'd have at least one present to open in the morning[1].

In many homes, from the 1950s onwards, the football annual was an ever-present under the Christmas tree, sharing space with selection boxes, book tokens and WH Smith's gift vouchers. The chances were it had been picked up in a Smith's book department, or from the newsagent's, by a harassed aunty or a pipe-smoking, travelling salesman uncle. Virtually every annual we've read for this book has a handwritten dedication scrawled on the inside front – something like, 'To Barry, from Nan & Grandad, Christmas 1969.'

No one ever really bought a football annual for the writing alone. 'Football is very much of the moment. If you're playing football or watching football, you look forward to it then you have a post-mortem in the pub, and that's pretty much it,' says Derek Hammond who, having written several fine volumes on retro football paraphernalia[2], is perhaps surprisingly less than dewy-eyed when considering the football annual. 'The trouble with those early football annuals is that they are talking about football – "he kicked the ball to Charlton who swung the leather over to Viollet who volleyed it into the lobster pot, over the outstretched hand of Hopkinson" – it's just dull. Football writing is hobbled by the fact that it's very difficult to whip up the same excitement of the moment.'

That said, some of Britain's best-known football writers cut their spurs writing for annuals, or at least contributed to them back in the day: Brian Glanville in the *International Football Book*, Bernard Joy in the

'There was Gordon Banks, the coming man, terrific . . .'

|||||||||||||||||||||||||||||||||||||||||||||||||||

---

1 His mum had ordered it, along with his sister's 'pop-music annual', from the newsagent's before being admitted to hospital. Despite them not having been paid for, the newsagent passed the books on anyway. Another world . . .

2 *Got, Not Got, The Lost World of Football, What a Shot!*, and *Shirt Tales & Short Stories*, all with Gary Silke. See chapter 5.

Left: Gordon Banks resplendent in yellow shirt but with mildly unsettling red eyes in *Charles Buchan's Soccer Gift Book* 1964–65

Topical Times, John Thompson, Pat Collins and his son Patrick Collins in *Charles Buchan's Soccer Gift Book*; and Desmond Hackett, the 'wise-cracking, widely travelled columnist of the *Daily Express*, the man in the brown bowler hat . . . flamboyant but intensely readable', cropped up in Peter Dimmock's *Sportsview* annual. 'Why no Soccer Hazlitt?' wondered Fleet Street veteran John Macadam in *Charles Buchan's Soccer Gift Book*. 'You can read Hazlitt on boxing, and writers of the quality of Cardus on cricket, and Bernard Darwin and Henry Longhurst on golf. But where is the man who will catch the romance of big-time football? The romance of the pit-boy who pulls himself up by the laces of his football boots to a home and a security for life, to a position of esteem in his community?' Macadam, and other *Buchan* writers, as discussed in chapter 1, did a fine job of that themselves.

'I really miss [when you go to a match] those placards they used to attach to lampposts – "Desmond Hackett is here"; "Bernard Joy is here" – all those big Fleet Street names,' says Richard Williams of the *Guardian*. 'It was a big thing, you know, "Desmond Hackett is here" – so we're going to get something about the "strolling

soccer seňors".' Richard was a childhood reader of general sports annuals rather than specifically football – the *Eagle Sports Annual*, with its tips on how to look after your bike, the correct grip for an approach shot with a wooden club, and features on ice-skating, boxing and rally driving – as well as motor-racing annuals. The sporting heroes of the day were characters such as Stirling Moss, Reg Harris and the snooker player Joe Davis. 'It was sort of the pre-visual information age, really. My heroes were people I never even saw, even on telly – Fangio or Neil Harvey [the cricketer] or Puskás. By the time I saw them they were retired.'

It's hard to envisage in today's media-saturated world, but when *Charles Buchan's Soccer Gift Book* took you behind the scenes into the dressing room at Roker Park – the players standing around drinking 'pop' after training – it was genuinely revelatory. The same applied even as late as 1969, when *Kenneth Wolstenholme's Book of World Soccer* not only visited the Football League headquarters in Lytham St Anne's but also unveiled the stylish new interior of Tranmere Rovers' ultra-modern dressing room ('showers' were visible, and much was made of the steam extractors – no more 'climbing into

Above: Behind the scenes at Roker Park, Sunderland, and the Victoria Ground, Stoke, *Charles Buchan Soccer Gift Book* 1954–55. The early annual photoessays were always sublimely shot and edited Right: Brash typography and dynamic photography, a *Topical Times* trademark, 1965

a large bath with ten other mud-spattered characters bathing in filthy water').

Access to players was not a problem back then. Patrick Collins, who today is a senior football writer for the *Mail* group of papers, recalls the time when granting an interview to Charles Buchan's stable of publications was seen as novel, a genuine pleasure: 'At this distance, it seems curious to remember how luxurious the *Gift Book* felt. The quality of the colour was much better than anything else around, and Dad [Pat Collins, the editor from the mid-sixties onwards] would make a summer tour of pre-season training and stock up with dozens of player articles. There was no question of payment to players, they were genuinely delighted to feature in the book. They used to ask Dad: "When can I buy it?"'

In the *Soccer Gift Book* the use of full colour – albeit of a faded 1950s vintage – and the low-key layout of straightforward magazine columns and photography matched the simple kits and basic appearance of the grounds. There would be no cropping out of a sponsor's logo, or protracted negotiation around terms of use – not least because there was barely a club badge, never mind a sponsor . . . There might be an advert for pale ale or Mahogany Flake tobacco painted across the corrugated roof of a stand, or Johnny Haynes holding a can of Brylcreem, but that was about as busy as things got.

Topical Times led the way in superimposing a jazzy riot of headlines over a cloudless sky

As the sixties moved on the *Topical Times* led the way in superimposing a jazzy riot of tabloid headlines over a cloudless sky, or even cutting out figures and captions and placing them against a white background. While *Buchan* devotees might have sniffed at the *Topical Times*' red-top approach, compared with the horrible riot of desiccated blocks of primary colour and Photoshopped, cauterized, freeze-dried bullet points that scream of 'star men', 'Prem super league' matches, number of appearances and 'transfer values' which are splashed all over a *Match* annual today, the *Topical Times* of mid-sixties vintage stands up well. It's bit like comparing the Blue Note record sleeves of Sam Rivers or Ornette Coleman with the Thompson Twins' artwork circa *Into the Gap*.

Flip through the annuals in the 'seasonal aisle' in Tesco today, and it's hard to find a single segment of text longer than forty words, as if the kids can't possibly take any more in – either that, or the average reader of *Match of the Day*, *Shoot!* or the *Official Manchester United Annual* is five years old. Back in these annuals' early-to-mid sixties equivalents three- or four-page articles on Benfica and the Portuguese first division, or football 'behind the Iron the Curtain' were not hard to come by; Charles Buchan's features on mastering aspects of positional play, working his way through the entire team, could reach double-figures in terms of pages.

The UPS AND DOWNS *of* FOOTBALL

GOAL! Manchester United have just scored against Birmingham. UP go the arms of Denis Law (No. 10) to hail the score. UP go the arms and legs of Noel Cantwell and scorer Bobby Charlton (No. 8) in a dance of delight. DOWN are three Birmingham defenders —floored in a desperate effort to ward off disaster. You can almost imagine the look on the face of the fellow on the left as he looks round and sees all the Manchester elation.

And be it photo-spreads of MEN OF BURNLEY, Kenneth Wolstenholme's detailed history of shirt numbering, moustachioed early TV presenters like Peter Dimmock taking you through the perils of sports reporting ('it's not all champagne and roses') or the humble player interview – Jimmy McGowan of Partick Thistle, say, balancing life as a goalkeeper at Firhill with being a coal delivery driver – the football annual was part of the fabric of the game. Issues of the day could vary: arguments raged over whether goal average was a satisfactory way to determine promotion and relegation; there was a fair bit of brouhaha over the advent of the 'tracksuit manager' – whatever next? Fancy Continental ideas about retaining the ball?; and, in the 1950s, there was reasonable concern with the appalling sanitary arrangements at most league grounds (in contrast to the tones of hushed awe displayed when discussing the dressing rooms at Ibrox, Highbury or the Bernabéu – all under-floor heating, plunge pools and chipped marble). I must have read half a dozen articles marvelling at the Needler family of Hull's innovative building of a railway platform to usher fans into Boothferry Park (and studied a dozen spectacular aerial photographs). The dominance of teams from the north, and accompanying disparaging comments about those

> ## Football annuals pretty much told it like it was when it came to a sense of place

from the south (London in particular) were pretty common in the fifties, and again by the mid-sixties[3]. Football annuals pretty much told it like it was when it came to a sense of place too: Kenneth Wolstenholme in his *Book of World Soccer* wrote of the life injected into Stoke City by Tony Waddington, who'd brightened 'a scene dominated by factory chimneys and slag heaps'; Peterborough was described in the 1969 *Midlands Football Annual* as 'a grey, flat town'.

In fact, plenty was just as it is today: ARE GOAL JUDGES NECESSARY? was a double-page spread from the 1960 *Big Book of Football Champions* that included a series of terrific did-it-cross-the-line? action shots. The only marked difference from the debate of recent times was that the photographic evidence was taken from the likes of Gillingham v Exeter and Partick Thistle v Falkirk, and the main objection to further

3 Roland Allen in the *Charles Buchan Soccer Gift Book* of 1959–60 questioned the need for Wembley and wondered, Herbert Chapman's Arsenal aside, 'How many of the all-time great professors of the game have been born within a London Transport trip of Bow Bells, let alone within their sound? . . . London crowds are the least knowledgeable and the most parish-pump-minded in the game.' A decade later, in Jimmy Armfield's *All Stars* annual, Alex Stepney was saying pretty much the same thing. A further ten years on, in the *Soccer Monthly Annual* of 1980, Don Revie gave it all another airing...

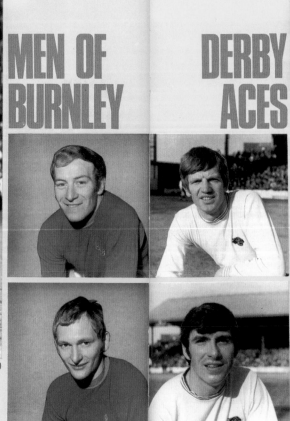

Above—Martin Dobson. Right—(top) Ralph Coates and Steve Kingdon.

Above—Terry Hennessey. Left—(top) Alan Durban and Kevin Hector.

adjudication seemed to be the 'extra cost of two or more officials'. There were periodic calls for a mid-winter close season (or 'sunshine soccer'), and plenty of debate over whether football was 'too rough'.

In the *Sun* annual of 1979 John Peel took an early swipe at the prawn-sandwich brigade, complaining about directors' wives in the box at Wembley for Liverpool's 1974 FA Cup final against Newcastle who knew nothing about football and who shouldn't have been there at the expense of disappointed ordinary fans – it was back to the Kop for him. Ten years earlier, in *David Coleman's World of Soccer* annual, Honor Blackman had made the same comments about the stuffy directors' box at Craven Cottage. Looking back through football annuals it's possible to see that Roy Keane was in good company.

There was a steady stream of articles about football in America – in the 1973 *International Football Book* Matt Busby revealed some hazy thinking, seemingly ascribing the failure of the first wave of league soccer in the States to society being too affluent and middle-class, with kids not getting hold of a football at a young enough age[4]. And right from the beginning the annuals were obsessed by television. In a thoughtful, 3,000-word piece in the *All Stars* annual of 1971, Leslie Plommer looked at how TV companies under pressure 'to provide entertainment do not always reflect the true nature of a soccer encounter'. He continued: 'No amount of clever editing can disguise a poor game; on the other hand it can make it appear considerably more interesting than it was in actuality,' and concluded that the camera was no substitute for the human eye, which *could* cover all angles of the pitch, sharpening our appreciation of tactics and the all-important build-up of a move. As late as the *Shoot!* annual of 1978, Manchester United's Gordon Hill and Jimmy Armfield went head to head about the merits of televised football. The gist of Armfield's argument was that *Match of the Day*, and especially *Football Focus* with its montage of goal highlights, whipped everyone up into a Saturday lunchtime frenzy of anticipation – everyone headed off to the match with their pockets full of Mars bars and their heads full of net-bulging, free-flowing football that, come 3 p.m. – given this was the seventies,

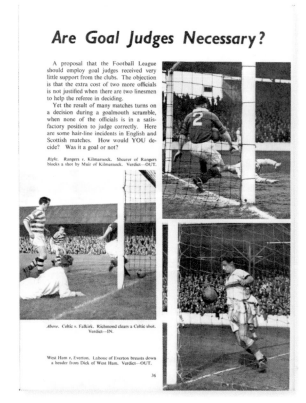

Are Goal Judges Necessary?

A proposal that the Football League should employ goal judges received very little support from the clubs. The objection is that the extra cost of two more officials is not justified when there are two linesmen to help the referee in deciding.

Yet the result of many matches turns on a decision during a goalmouth scramble, when none of the officials is in a satisfactory position to judge correctly. Here are some hair-line incidents in English and Scottish matches. How would YOU decide? Was it a goal or not?

Right. Rangers v. Kilmarnock. Shearer of Rangers blocks a shot by Muir of Kilmarnock. Verdict—OUT.

Above. Celtic v. Falkirk. Richmond clears a Celtic shot. Verdict—IN.

West Ham v. Everton. Labone of Everton breasts down a header from Dick of West Ham. Verdict—OUT.

with fair dash of negative football and plenty of 0–0 draws – could only result in disappointment. The arguments over whether televised football was actually killing the game stretched back (in the pages of annuals) to the days when Jock Stein was making waves in his first managerial job at Dunfermline and 80,000 turned up for the Amateur Cup final at Wembley – if you'd missed it there would be an accompanying match report in the *Big Book of Football Champions* – and goalkeepers had names like Gerry Cakebread (Brentford) and Arthur Lightening (Coventry).

And, of course, the annuals looked so good. It's probably best to turn straight to Chapter 5 for a homage to the *Tiger Book of Soccer Stars* and its ilk. Put simply, before the advent of the telephoto lens cropped everything bar Cristiano Ronaldo's head (and neck) out of the frame, there was a lot more in the picture: sunlight coming through grimy panes of glass at the back of the stand; blocks of flats, corners of houses, bedroom windows (trees, even) – all visible above the open terrace. Then there were the infinite hues of mud, all caught in rich monochrome; supporters packed on to terraces dressed in ordinary clothes for a normal Saturday (not fancy-dress or face-paint for some kind of dazzling spectacle). Put even more simply, the world seemed a better place back then.

---

4 Kids and 'soccer' has never really been the issue in the States, and by 1973 the NASL was about to experience its second coming. For a fuller analysis of the early faltering steps of the North American Soccer League see Ian Plenderleith's *Rock and Roll Soccer* (Icon, 2014); for Ian's views on selected football annuals of the 1970s, see Chapters 3 and 4 of this book.

Left: The designers on the *Topical Times* 1970 didn't hold back with the primary colours

Above: The *Big Book of Football Champions* ponders one the burning questions of 1960

There's no denying that the main, simple pleasure of flipping back through the pages of an old football annual is, basically, nostalgic. Take Johnny Steele, Barnsley's 'seen it all manager', looking back over his thirty-two years at Oakwell in the 1970–71 *Topical Times Football Book*, who was proud to belong 'to a generation more interested in the job than what you got for doing it'. While he didn't begrudge players a decent wage given their short careers, at the same time he believed 'the pendulum has swung too far in the other direction. Ninety per cent of clubs are struggling. They have to pay out every penny coming in at the gates in wages. It's short-sighted, to say the least.' Steele went on to grumble about the limited life-span of the modern, flimsy football boot, which had to be constantly replaced – not like in the old days when 'one pair used to last three or four seasons' – and fondly remembered when team talks used to consist of, 'Right, lads . . . out there and get stuck in,' rather than being an hour-long tactical deconstruction of the opposition. And despite what you might have heard (circa 1970) about the disreputable nature of modern-day footballers, Steele reckoned there were plenty of 'better characters' around in the game: 'For instance, we don't have more than three lads who smoke. And only a few light lime and lager drinkers – who cut it all out towards match day.'

Over the page Oxford United were busy spraying high-expansion foam – to a depth of six feet – over the pitch at the Manor Ground to beat the frost. And the following year's *Topical Times Football Book* reported on Halifax Town's plans to play a recording of the 'Wembley roar' over the Tannoy at the Shay to intimidate the opposition.

It goes without saying that there's a reasonable amount of guff to be found in the average football annual[5] – and that much of the joy of looking back is not easily corralled into a tidy, thematic account, but is simply stumbled across randomly in isolated, entertaining fragments of football's rich past – Pedro Richards being late back for pre-season training at Meadow Lane after being injured in the Pamplona bull run; the *Sportsview* annual caption writer who was a little hasty, or gambled with an early deadline, in claiming Real Madrid had bought Pelé for £150,000 in 1958; Brechin City's half-time cake raffle organized by their potato-merchant former chairman who, on a wet day, would cover seats in the old wooden stand with potato sacks[6].

But thumbing back through hundreds of old football annuals opens a fairly revealing window on to the (n)ever-changing world of football – one where the devil is in the detail.

And having ploughed through a multitude of dusty annuals published between 1950 and 1987, it's been an edifying experience to inhabit a world where Forfar Athletic, Blackpool, Coventry City and Shrewsbury Town have as much a claim on our attention as any of the habitués of Old Trafford, Anfield, Stamford Bridge or Highbury.

The simple pleasure of looking back ('the past') is something that grows more alluring with age – and every bit of found BFI footage (be that the opening of the M1, film of pre-war London flower markets, or just West Ham v Spurs from 1965) – and more powerful too. As you get older it becomes more difficult to fight back the tears that seem to well up from nowhere when you catch a glimpse of a faded family photograph, see another favourite old café torn down, another record shop shut, a pile of books from a closed-down library slung in a skip.

The writer Ian Penman co-presented a couple of *Wire* magazine 'charity case' radio programmes on the London station Resonance FM in 2013, talking of his (not inconsiderable) time spent hanging about in branches of Barnardo's or Help the Aged, picking

> 'Ninety per cent of clubs are struggling. They have to pay out every penny coming in in wages. It's short-sighted, to say the least'

---

5 Don Revie trying to make out England were one big happy family under him (*Topical Times*, 1976); Kevin Keegan's 'ones to watch' column (Mike Fillery, Steve Whitton, Mark Higgins); articles on 'soccer boffins'; by and large any attempt at light-heartedness from 1975 onwards . . .

6 Player bonuses included 'a dozen eggs for a draw, plus a chicken if two points were won'.

Above: Straight-talking Barnsley manager Johnny Steele confronts the ever prescient issue of players' wages in the *Topical Times* 1970

55

up old, forgotten, battered LPs left to gather dust, and playing numerous highlights. He was mainly interested in bits of discarded esoterica – compilation albums of exotica, ambient, even new-age LPs; records of field recordings from the Côte d'Ivoire, devotional music or 1980s science-fiction movie soundtracks dumped in a bargain bin somewhere. Many of the records thrown away were once a genuinely popular artform, part of everyday life. But, Penman claimed, 'There's nothing wrong with [charity-shop] melancholy.' The contents of that British Heart Foundation shop stand in proud defiance of the Blair/Cameron/Portas hygienic clean-up of the British high street where, generally, there's 'no dust, no leftovers, no melancholy, no slow time.' Penman saw a kind of beauty in 'low-level inconspicuous consumption . . . [finding] old dreams in a new context.'

All of which applies equally to the humble football annual. Judging by the numbers picked up for this book alone – not to mention misspent time hanging about in junk and charity shops in our twenties – it too has done its time as a leading unwanted Christmas gift, alongside those Robin Gibb solo albums, Top Trumps and cassette storage trays. That said, annuals from the heyday – very roughly the early 1950s to the

mid-1980s – are becoming increasingly hard to come by. Unable to resist a final pop into a local east London Oxfam, despite this book having been completed – but just on the off-chance someone had deposited a set of Peter Dimmock's *Sportsview* annuals, or a *Raymond Glendenning's Book of Sport for Boys* from the early fifties – all I could find (filed alongside Jeremy Clarkson) was a very slim-looking Arsenal annual for 2014. The spine-width must have been about 3mm; blink and you could have mistaken it for a calendar[7].

Anyhow, it's our hope that this book does a reasonable job of sifting through the murk to find the gems; finds some kind of beauty amongst the junk; distils the essence of various annuals; and shines a light on lost, forgotten or hidden aspects of the game – that maybe someone is even reading this introduction standing in a fusty-smelling branch of Help the Aged one wet afternoon, thinking back to a time when goalkeepers dressed in green and football was just something you did on a Saturday. Clearly it can't be definitive – there are just too many annuals, especially between 1966

---

7 Myself and Doug would say that not only the cheapest annuals but also the richest pickings are to be found in charity shops in coastal towns – or that was certainly the case in our experience, largely on the south and east coasts of Britain.

Above: The *Tiger Soccer Stars* annual 1971 gives bigger billing to Watford's Barry Endean – a former pub team player in the third division, than European Cup winner Brian Kidd

and 1974 – but we've taken our starting point, very broadly, from the moment when miniature publications like the *Littlewood's Football Annual*, the *Daily Worker Football Annual* and *Hill's Sporting News* and the original *Topical Times* – forerunners of the *Playfair* annuals and *Rothmans Football Yearbook*, and full of stats, 'honours', fixtures, adverts for Zetters 'the world's easiest pools', and headlines such as BRAZILIAN BOMBSHELL AND BOGOTA BEANFEST – began to cede ground to more feature-based publications, issued in the autumn for Christmas rather than August for the start of the season, and generally published between hard covers.

Laurie Rampling is West Brom's official photographer and archivist, and his old darkroom and garage, attached to his house on the outskirts of Southend, are both crammed to the ceiling with shelves, filing cabinets, piles of books and bundles of cuttings. Laurie agreed that 'the precursor of the football annual was the football handbook – it all started off with the *Athletic News* football magazine-cum-programme, around 1910–11 or 1912. The first club annuals were around the turn of the century, though, rounding up all the info from the previous twenty or thirty years. The roots of the football annual go back as far as that. The very famous *Book of Football* – if you buy it now, it'd cost you nearly a thousand pounds – was also a kind of round-up. It heralded football from its earliest beginnings – you know, teams from the late 1800s, with your standard plate-glass footballer negative, such as Billy Bassett standing there in his England kit, leaning on the wall, or something – that was your very first football annual. I saw it at a book fair in London going for £600 for an original, first edition. I could've afforded it, the bloody great thing . . . value for money, yes, but have I got other things to buy for that? Where are you going to put it . . . something that thick?

'It's criminal,' continued Laurie, 'that we've never actually sat down with some of these footballers and said, "There's a tape recorder, just speak into it, for as many hours as you can." But we do have the football annual . . .'

I mention to Laurie a story Tommy Lawton recounted in his own 1950 annual, the then Burnley youngster worrying on a long bus journey back north

from an away match about being seen as conceited (he'd scored a couple but had been chided by a team-mate for possibly over-celebrating, or at least being pleased with himself – see Chapter 1). 'Stuff like that is absolute rocking horse,' reckoned Laurie. 'Because they're all dead, they're long gone.'

Steve Smith, who has written comprehensively on football annuals and paraphernalia for the Bristol Rovers programme and the local Saturday evening paper the *Green 'Un*, is also something of a hoarder-cum-archivist and collector. Crammed into his spare room in a terraced house on the outskirts of Bristol are nearly 3,000 football books, including hundreds of annuals, all lining the walls, protruding from every available piece of wall-space. There are so many books in the room there is nowhere to sit down; in fact, the three of us couldn't all stand in the room the same time, and I had to keep backing out of the door while Steve calmly retrieved another annual so that Doug could scan its cover, all the while providing a typically accurate summary of the contents within: 'Ummm, the *Sun*, first annual, 1972 – the last two came twenty years later and were large paperbacks. [Plenty of] quizzes, word searches, duotone colours of pink and green. [But the] first and last of any run . . . you can't compare them.'

Where Laurie passionately rails at and works himself into a lather over the corporate modern game that thinks football history commenced in 1992, Steve, while sharing the same views, seems to radiate a supreme calmness, as if having ingested the entire contents of his football library – packed with Kupers, Winners, Wilsons and Glanvilles, alongside twenty- or thirty-year runs of annuals and statistical histories – can't be fazed by anything the modern world, or the modern game, has to throw at him. Where Laurie, you suspect, pines for a simpler time – when West Brom's Derek Kevan was in contention for an England place and Scunthorpe had just erected the first cantilever stand – Steve, given his impeccable recall of football detail from any given year (and the exact place on his extensive shelving where he knows there's a relevant article), is actually living in 1976, or 1982[8].

---

8 A fine way to be. Immense thanks to both Steve and Laurie for sharing their daunting collections of annuals.

Above: Small format statistical guides, like the *Littlewoods Football Annual* 1936–7, were annuals in name – but were distinctly not the full cultural package that emerged from the 1950s onwards

Right: Moody black and white photography was a hallmark of the mid-sixties annual. Blackburn's Johnny Byrom walks the streets of his home town in *Charles Buchan's Soccer Gift Book* 1965–66

STREET OF GOALS!

A street in Lancashire. No pomp. No trees. No side. But a leaning lamp-post— and John Byrom, centre-forward of Blackburn. It is his home, and was the home of Fred Pickering, of England. It is (aptly) John Bright Street, Blackburn.

Both Laurie and Steve fear for the future of not only the football annual but also the book itself, citing a generation possibly growing up without a deep love for books – or at least one inhabiting the throw-away society of recent years. Steve had recently been dismayed to find a 2012 *Match* annual going for 50p on a car boot sale: 'Someone had that only a couple of Christmases ago . . . ' When Steve was growing up, 'A football gift book was one of your main presents for Christmas. That, or maybe a train set.'

For Laurie there's no question *Charles Buchan's Soccer Gift Book* was 'the Bible'. Although younger, Steve recently pulled off 'a swap deal-cum-price reduction with a charity shop' that involved a hasty trip back home to retrieve an almost complete set of *Soccer Gift Books*, which Steve then, having sped back to the charity shop, traded up for their set, ' . . . complete with dust-jackets – the spines are a bit sun-faded, but the fronts are perfect.'

Johnny Green, author, Gillingham fan and for-mer road manager of The Clash, was a *Buchan* man too. Fittingly, for a future punk, he was happy to deface his *Soccer Gift Books* with player-autographs, and even hacked apart his *Football Monthl*ies to make his own scrapbooks. 'I loved flair players,' says Johnny today, 'but I always liked dirty players too, because I wasn't very good – I was a clogger. I liked centre-halves and full-backs that used to kick people in the air, and I never saw that as bad form, I always thought that was pretty cool, you know – Chopper Harris, a bit of a role model . . . At Gillingham the players I really liked were the cloggers, who no one else liked. There was a man called Dennis Hunt, and Roy Proverbs, who looked like a psychopath, possibly was one, but my true all-time favourite foot-baller was a centre-half, Mike Burgess. He was quite a big man with one of those crinkle-cuts that the late great Ray Lowry always called "a cantilever haircut". People don't seem to have that any more – Douglas Hurd, maybe – but in 1964 we won the fourth division

'I loved flair players, but I always liked dirty players too, because I wasn't very good – I was a clogger'

with very few goals scored[9] and Mike Burgess was the centre-half in that team. A brute of a man, and I loved him for it, because off the pitch he was typically quiet, mild-mannered, and came off the bus with his gabar-dine mac over his arm [with a cheery] "How are you, lads?" [to the assembled autograph hunters]. He had a northern accent and one time in the Cup we were drawn away at Leicester City, and I couldn't go – it was midweek – and I made a special scrapbook up out of my *Charles Buchan* pictures in a school exercise book, very thin and pliable.

'There was Gordon Banks, the coming man, terrific – there must have been others . . . ' The Saturday before the game young Johnny approached the crinkle-haired centre-half: '"Excuse me, Mr Burgess, would it be too cheeky if I gave you my little auto-graph book, would you be able to get one or two Leicester players, because I can't go to the game?" "Well, I'll try, son," and he took the book off me, and we got beat, and the next week I went down to the Gillingham home game and he went, "'Ere you are, son," and he gave me the book and it was signed right across. He said, "I took it in the Leicester dressing room, son". And I was just over the moon, I thought, "What a kind man." The kindest of men is known as the most brutish – he was known as "the Spider" at Gillingham because he seemed all arms and legs[10].'

John thought the *Topical Times Football Book* 'a bit

9 59 to Carlisle's 113; Gillingham still topped the division on goal average!

10 Johnny Green's book *Push Yourself Just a Little Bit More*, on the Tour de France, was shortlisted for the William Hill Sports Book of the Year award in 2005, alongside (eventual winner) Gary Imlach's *My Father and Other Working Class Heroes*. The Halifax defender who ended his father, Stewart Imlach's career? Mike Burgess. John spent much of the awards ceremony trying to convince Gary Imlach that his hero wasn't all bad: 'He gave me a very strange look . . . Imlach [Stewart] also had a remarkable buzz cut that stood out a mile. "Great hair begat great art," as the great artist Raymond Lowry used to say.'

Above: A spate of injuries to goalkeepers begged the question 'Is Football Too Rough?' in the The Big Book of Football Champions 1960. The answer, according to the managers consulted, was 'no'

red-top; *Buchan* was more authentic'. (For a full consideration of both annuals, see Chapter 2.) He regarded the *Topical Times'* penchant for cartoons on their end-pages as 'flippant. I'd moved on from the *Beano*.' But opening up the same 1960 *Topical Times Football Book* in his office at William Hill, Sports Book of the Year co-ordinator Graham Sharpe's eyes lit up at the cartoon street-scene – a riot of kids, dads and dogs in a street game; someone brewing half-time tea, someone mowing a front lawn; factory chimneys belching out black smoke at the end of the road. 'That's the same artist as the *Beano*, isn't it?' wonders Graham. 'This is how I learnt to play football – "gate football" as we called it. There was a factory down the road too – Whitefriars glass works in Wealdstone. The majority of people worked there – or at the Kodak factory. There was a hooter that went off.' At the other end of the road, on Cup final day, the respective team coaches, in the days before the M1 had opened, would weave their way down Wealdstone High Street, past the fishmonger's, the ironmonger's and Woolworth's *en route* to Wembley. 'I should have picked the other team [in 1959], but for whatever reason I went for the black and whites. I'd

never seen them play live, and I haven't lived to regret it.' Luton Town and two annuals, the *Topical Times* and the *Big Book of Football Champions* – both renowned for their coverage of the amateur game – formed, along with local team Wealdstone, a kind of holy triumvirate in Graham's childhood.

Ros Pedley speaks on the phone in a lovely, thick, Black Country accent. Today she writes for *BackPass* magazine, but as a youngster she collected players' autographs and *Charles Buchan's Soccer Gift Book*s in particular, back in the days when she used to hang about outside Wolves' training ground. 'They'd come out [the players] and sign whatever you wanted to get signed, and then we would accompany them, on foot, into the Lyons Corner House in Wolverhampton, and we'd sit with them. Billy Wright – wonderful – everything they say about Billy Wright was true. He was down to earth; a lovely, lovely man. He never forgot you. "When they stop asking me to sign, that's when I've got to start worrying," he used to say. So modest and unassuming. They were all the same – Bert Williams, Jimmy Mullen – footballers were just down to earth then, just from the local area. They had to rent houses; they didn't have cars . . . '

Above: Football annual endpapers were always a graphic delight; in 1960 the *Topical Times* used a *Beano*-style illustration of *Turnstile Terrace*. Both titles were published by DC Thompson, based in Dundee

Following pages: Another typically glorious endpaper design from *Tiger Soccer Stars* annual 1970. Note the editor carefully pre-empting the risk of players being transferred while the book was at the presses

MAN. UTD.
EUROPEAN CUP WINNERS

SPURS

EVERTON

LIVERPOOL

PORTSMOUTH

CARDIFF

STOKE CITY

PLYMOUTH

NEWCASTLE

CELTIC

BURY

HULL

BURNLEY

BLACKPOOL

IPSWICH

SOUTHAMPTON

LEEDS UTD.

CHELSEA

ASTON VILLA

ARSENAL

BRISTOL CTY.

WOLVES

DERBY COUNTY

W. B. ALBION

MILLWALL

FULHAM

LEICESTER

MIDDLESBROUGH

HUDDERSFIELD

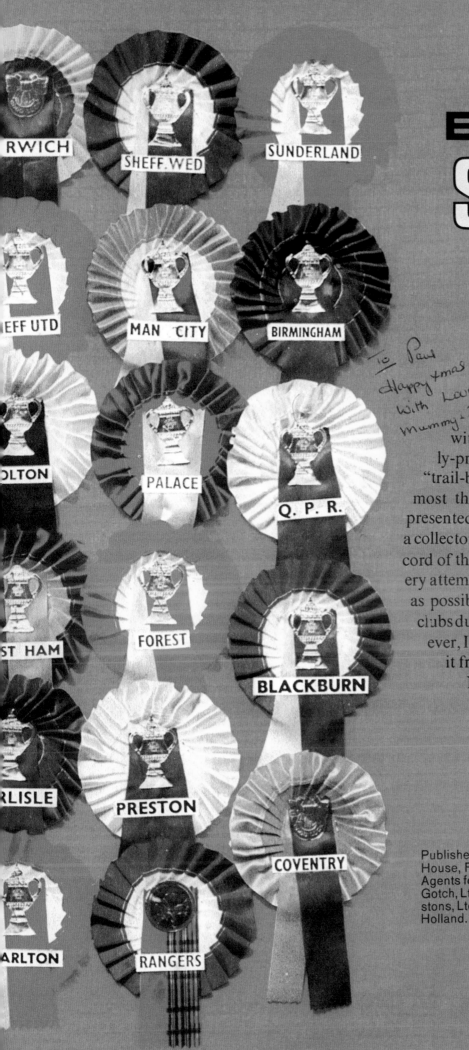

RWICH

SHEFF. WED

SUNDERLAND

EFF UTD

MAN CITY

BIRMINGHAM

OLTON

PALACE

Q.P.R.

ST HAM

FOREST

BLACKBURN

RLISLE

PRESTON

COVENTRY

ARLTON

RANGERS

TIGER
BOOK OF
SOCCER
STARS
1970

To Paul
Happy Xmas
With Love always
Mummy & Daddy.

It's always a great thrill to be first with something—and this superbly-printed book is truly a football "trail-blazer". For the very first time, almost the entire galaxy of British stars are presented in magnificent full-colour photos—a collector's item for all fans keen to own a record of the current soccer scene. Although every attempt has been made to be as up-to-date as possible, some players will have changed clubs during the printing of the book. However, I am sure that this will not prevent it from being a real soccer success. Now I'll leave you to enjoy the book!

The Editor

900376-66-X

© IPC Magazines, Ltd., 1969.

Published by IPC Magazines, Ltd., Fleetway House, Farringdon Street, London, England. Sole Agents for Australia and New Zealand : Gordon & Gotch, Ltd.; Rhodesia, Zambia and Malawi : Kingstons, Ltd. Printing and binding by Jan de Lange, Holland.

12/6ᵈ

'WOULD YOU LIKE TO PLAY FOR WOLVERHAMPTON WANDERERS?'
'I WOULDN'T MIND'

POST-WAR

In 1959 Grove Press in New York announced plans to publish an uncensored edition of *Lady Chatterley's Lover*, the same year Jack Kerouac wrote an introduction for Robert Frank's *The Americans* – Frank 'sucked a sad poem right out of America on to film'; half a million American women were on the pill; Miles Davis and John Coltrane were recording *Kind of Blue* in an old church in Manhattan; the space race was hotting up; there were queues around the block at the Museum of Modern Art; and an early screening of the world's first independent film, John Cassavetes' *Shadows*, took place in Greenwich Village. To paraphrase John Cage in Fred Kaplan's sweeping account of *1959: The Year Everything Changed*, Americans began to wake up to the life they were living.

In England, we were preparing for another night in.

Although that perhaps wasn't the case if you were a member of the great and good in the Black Country, where that summer the mayor of Wolverhampton hosted a banquet for Billy Wright, in honour of his hundredth cap. A vast number of diners crammed into trestle tables in the civic hall, presumably for roast beef and two veg. The speeches and presentations made, the England captain rose to his feet but, before he could embark on his own roll-call of thanks, the audience broke out into a verse of 'For he's a jolly good fellow'. Wright – neatly brushed hair and a nice suit the veneer over a hardened, flat Shropshire growl – made a couple of jokes at the expense of his disciplinarian bosses at Molineux, Major Frank Buckley and Stan Cullis, and

his famous sisters-in-law. Then the camera panned back to Joy, his glamorous wife and third member of the Beverley Sisters, capturing an expression of affection mixed with a faint hint of boredom as she looked up at her husband talking. Wright is presented with a couple of rose bowls on behalf of Wolverhampton Corporation and a silver salver from the FA. Sir Stanley Rous leads the applause, as the Pathé News commentator breezily suggests, 'Mrs Wright is never going to be at a loss for something to polish,' before concluding, 'every football lover wishes well to a great sportsman, one of nature's gentlemen – a prophet very much with honour in his own country – Billy Wright!!'

Wright, along with the likes of Stanley Matthews, Tommy Lawton and, unusually for a goalkeeper, Bert Williams, had fronted a couple of football annuals in the fifties. There had been his eponymous *Football Album* in 1954, and then, four years later, the first in a regular series of *Billy Wright's Book of Soccer*. But at Christmas that year, as the decade drew to a close, legions of schoolboys up and down the country discovered a new football annual wrapped up beneath the tree: the very first *Topical Times Football Book*. The hardback had a dust jacket: Bobby Charlton smacking a leather ball out of a brilliant-red pillar-box background, England playing beneath an Archibald Leitch stand; above the kop, red-brick chimneys are visible against the blue sky.

Inside, a feature entitled TRAMPOLINES, ROUGH-HOUSES AND MID-WINTER SEA BATHING catches the eye: it's a sprightly whip through various 'progressive' club training routines – climbing a rope in the gym at Ayresome Park; playing rounders at Old Trafford; hanging upside down from a crash barrier at Scunthorpe; and a plunge in the icy North Sea at Sunderland. And at the Hawthorns, ' . . . maybe you've seen the US Marines marching to the "St Louis Blues"! The Albion

Left: Billy Wright, captain of Wolves and England, in *Charles Buchan's Soccer Gift Book 1955–56*

lads carry out this routine to orders – but without the music.' The article goes on to reprimand Nottingham Forest manager Billy Walker for his old-fashioned methods of 'sprinting, lapping and ball work'. Never mind that Forest had just won the FA Cup, such a routine was deemed 'not good enough' to produce players able to match the world's best. What was lacking was an embrace of new methods, or fancy gimmicks, in order to 'make our players athletes first and footballers second'. Such skewed logic certainly helped write the rest of English football history – we definitely took on board the athletic part – and had its roots not only in Hungary's 1953 demolition of England, something which hung like a cloud over a decade's worth of writing in football annuals, but also Spartak Moscow's trip to these shores the following year. Warming up before a game at Highbury, Spartak raised the home crowd's eyebrows during a forty-minute display of loosening-up exercises, laps of relay races, short bursts of sprinting and running – 'knees up until they are almost touching the chin' – all conducted with a trainer tooting vigorously on a whistle. The routine also included 'two players. One ball. Passing to each other.' That, clearly, was not quite how things were done. (Although Moscow Dynamo had behaved in such an eccentric fashion on their 1945 tour too.)

'Make our players athletes first and footballers second'

Subsequently West Ham brought in a trampoline, and manager Ted Fenton introduced stamina and high-jump tests; Chelsea had their players lifting logs, and Arsenal's squad were also 'having a go at Russian-style athletic preparation', which presumably didn't interfere unduly with the half-time fags at Highbury – manager George Swindin, when asked in the same annual if he'd prefer it if players didn't smoke, replied, 'Not really – providing it's only in moderation.' Falkirk decided to paint the outline of a goal on a brick wall: 'Looks a bit strange, doesn't it?' observed the *Topical Times*. 'But this was a stunt to try to improve the shooting of the forwards – and give them a bit of fun at the same time.'

The *Topical Times*, in particular, was quite hooked on a sense of progress – the coming modern world – allied to glorious, nitty-gritty detail from behind the scenes. A year later, in the 1960–61 annual, a double-page spread pours through the contents of Bolton trainer Bert Sproston's 'hamper . . . a cross between a doctor's surgery, a chemist's shop and an operating theatre' and regales readers used to seeing just a bucket and sponge with tales of rubbing in soap to unclog studs for better grip on a snowy pitch, and moistening socks with the same soap 'to help take some of the jar out of contact with the ground' on a frozen pitch. A good trainer is

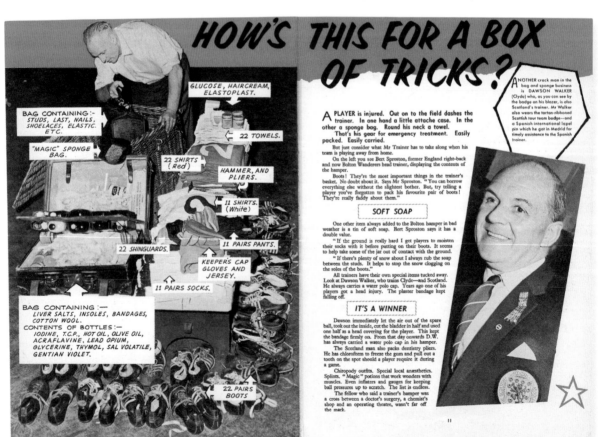

Stadium of the Future

HERE'S how Wolves propose to give the biggest face-lift in football to their ground at Molineux — as shown in the architect's model.

Capacity will be increased from 55,040 to 74,444. At present there is room for 48,900 standing customers, with 6140 seated.

The new Molineux stadium budgets for 55,518 standing and 18,926 seats.

The four stands will all be double-decker cantilever type, with no pillars to obstruct the view. In each will be top-class refreshment and toilet facilities.

Entrances and exits will be highly

organised for slick and efficient ground control, and the floodlighting system will be the last word. All in — as modern a stadium as you could imagine. Making most of the Continental and South American grounds look pretty old-fashioned.

Lucky Wolves fans!

also something of an improviser. Dawson Walker, the Clyde physio, tells the annual of the time he attempted to treat a player with a head injury, only for the plaster bandage to keep falling off: 'Dawson immediately let the air out of a spare ball, took out the inside, cut the bladder in half and used one half as a head-covering for the player. This kept the bandage firmly on.'

A player running around with half a ball-bladder on his head feels decidedly old world, but away from the football pitch Britain's towns and cities were being redeveloped at a considerable pace. Slums were cleared, concrete tower-blocks and super-highways – well, the M1 at least – began to appear, and a few pages on from Bert Sproston's kit bag the *Topical Times* reproduced an architects' scale model of a newly developed Molineux featuring a double-decker cantilever stand complete 'with top-class refreshment and toilet facilities', and floodlights! Sadly it never came to pass, and the Molineux faithful were left inside the gold-gabled Molineux Street Stand for the best part of another thirty years.

Left: Bolton trainer Bert Sproston reveals the contents of his kit bag. Essentials included haircream, liversalts and 11 pairs of pants, *Topical Times* 1960

The *Topical Times* in 1960 revealed the Molineux that never was. 'The plans hit the buffers because we couldn't finance it,' remembers long-time Wolves fan and *BackPass* writer Ros Pedley. 'There was a big upheaval and it went pear-shaped because the directors pulled out – it wasn't a successful period for the club.' Ros recalls that the facilities for ladies tended towards the basic at Molineux, probably because football 'wasn't considered a thing that ladies did. There were no loos – or, rather, there was no roof on 'em. I can remember in the winter they put the paraffin lamps in there to stop 'em freezing up. It was like a concrete shack you went into, separated from the ground, and if you went you had to say the bloke standing by you on the terraces, "Will you keep my place, please, so I can get back in where I can see?"

'Mind you,' continues Ros, 'the worst ground I ever went to was Blackpool. Bloomfield Road – a real shocker; corrugated iron everywhere. Northampton was another one that was pretty awful; Derby, the Baseball Ground, that was dire.' At Molineux in the seventies during an evening game she can also recall a power cut. The solution: 'They lit candles stood in beer bottles on the wooden bar, which was in a wooden stand. The stairs that you went up, the floor in the old stand – all wood.'

But those were happy days. 'You couldn't buy it now: corrugated iron roofs, and if it rained you were unlucky if you were sitting on the end row because it blew in. Great. You wouldn't swap it for the world.'

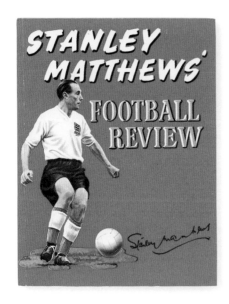

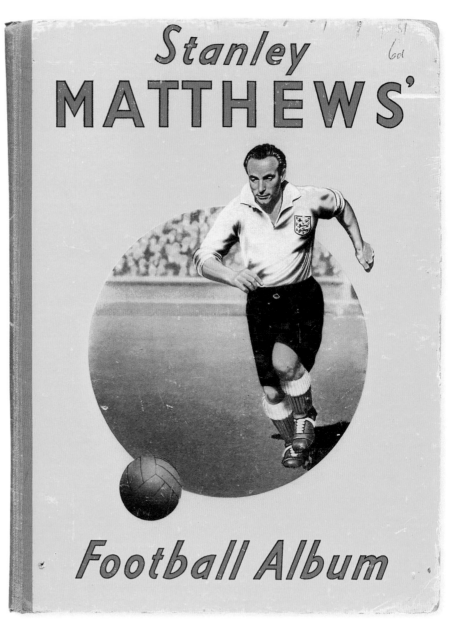

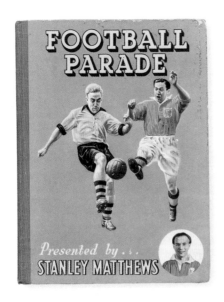

Only A-list footballers merited their own annual in the 1950s. Stanley Matthews led the way with his *Football Album*. He also fronted *Stanley Matthews' Football Review* and 'Presented' *Football Parade*, both sold by exclusive arrangement with Marks & Spencer's, no less.

Billy Wright was close behind with his *Football Album* and *Book of Soccer*; pictured is no.5, published in 1962. The series ran for seven years, 1958 to 1964, when it was duly passed on to the next England captain, Bobby Moore. He continued the series until 1972.

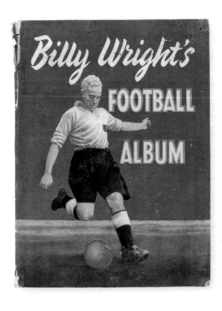

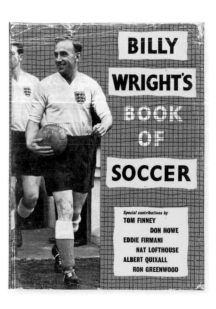

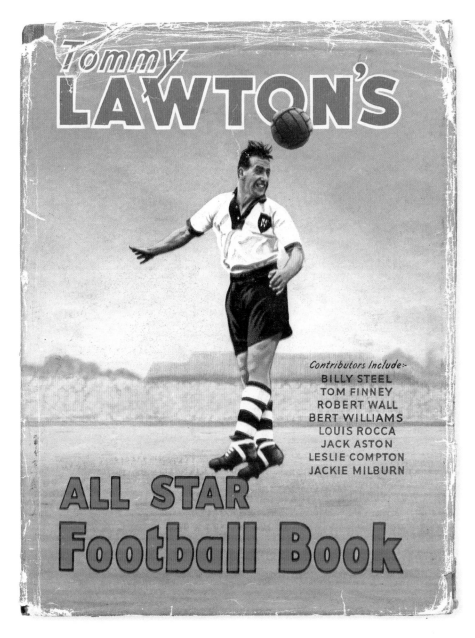

Also in the leading pack of '50s stars was Tommy Lawton, pictured left on the cover of the beautiful *All Star Football Book*. The equally fantastic back cover design is below. A sister publication in the same style was dedicated to England goalkeeper Bert Williams. Keepers enjoyed hallowed status in the annuals of the period, arguably second only to centre-forwards in football's positional pecking order.

Williams emphasised the importance of the role in the introduction to his book: '…the position gives a detached viewpoint, which is denied to others who are in the thick of things. Add to that the philosophical outlook which comes from being the lonely last line of defence and you can see why I feel that I can bring a balanced judgement to the game.'

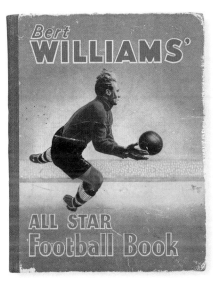

Stanley Matthews' Blackpool colleague Stanley Mortensen also chipped in with his *International Soccer Book*. A pleasing and economic design feature of this title was that the striking cover design was repeated on the back. Better still, though, was the approach of Tommy Lawton's book. His back-cover design was a variation on the cover, effectively creating a double-fronted jacket.

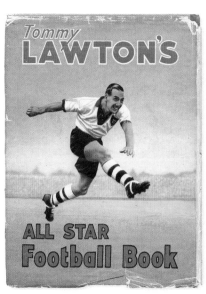

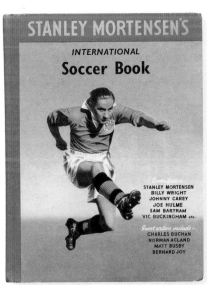

North of the border, in 1963 Dundee United unveiled their beautiful new cantilever stand, and there it is, in its full glory and stark relief as featured in the *Eagle Football Annual* of that year. Again, though, the old world is still with us: reassuringly manager Gerry Kerr smokes a pipe, and the training ground shot of United players 'with a ball apiece' features the obligatory terraced housing bordering the recreation ground.

But the football environment was slowly changing: according to Kenneth Wolstenholme, in his 1963–64 annual, Everton's refurbished changing rooms at Goodison Park wouldn't have looked out of place in a Hollywood club: baths, showers, and even an ice-cold plunge pool (the latter the scene of particularly brutal initiation ceremonies for new recruits to the first-team squad). New supporters' club lounges, pleasure domes of Formica tables and moulded plastic beer pumps, were proudly unveiled at Oldham and Crystal Palace (the former the doing of a young go-ahead chairman, Ken Bates). And in their '63–64 annual the *Topical Times* ran a WHAT'S NEW? feature: all-seater stadia could be on the horizon, it seemed; Burnley, league champions in 1960 – 'the small town club which thinks so big' – had plans for 'a double-decker stand complete with private boxes similar to those in the recently completed grandstand at Royal Ascot. These private boxes would be big enough to seat three or four people – man, wife, and his children, for instance.' Bob Lord, Burnley chairman, was also toying with heated stands: blowing hot air down over the occupants – an idea similarly under consideration at Highbury. At Loftus Road and Stamford Bridge slap-up meals in adjoining first-class restaurants were applauded, Peterborough had included plans for a dance hall in their new stand, while 'drama . . . cabaret . . . bingo . . . that's the dream-child of fourth division Rochdale', who were busy pondering demolition of their existing changing rooms at Spotland and replacing them with a 400-seat theatre to be shared with a local drama society – potentially bringing in 'over £100 per week!'. At Rugby Park, Kilmarnock, huge Tannoy speakers had been erected, constructed with the same technology – no distortion; huge wattage – as those used on NATO airfields. And, finally, Fulham plugged in

a pioneering electric scoreboard, a three-sided affair that could be seen clearly from all four corners of the ground: 'Only six half-time scores are flashed on the board at a time. Six matches are covered by letters from A to F. This happens five times with different coloured lights – red, amber, green, white and pink – to indicate the particular series of scores.' It's not clear if printed instructions were provided in the programme, but no doubt the Craven Cottage faithful were left pining for the old flap-over card and letters along the side of the pitch. Flashing coloured lights and rapidly changing luminous scorelines cutting through the misty dusk by the Thames? It must have seemed like something borrowed from down the road at the Ealing Studios, where the BBC were filming a new Saturday evening series, *Dr Who* – on at 5.15, just in time for those out of the ground early, with not too far to trudge home.

While the *Topical Times* was busy embracing the new Ballardian world of electronic scoreboards – a decade and a half on and they were equally excited about Meadowbank Thistle's new model – and cantilever stands, three years earlier, the *Big Book of Football Champions* had hit the nail on the head. 'As a nation we do not take kindly to new ideas,' so began the first line of an article, WHAT THE FUTURE HOLDS. The piece went on to chronicle the unstoppable dawning of the floodlight – apparently early advocates of such technology were dismissed as 'wild dreamers' ('Grimsby v Scunthorpe, on a Tuesday night?! Don't be such a wild dreamer . . . ') – as well as regular 3 p.m. kick-offs, 'with the lights being switched on in the second half when the days are short'. The establishment of an England under-23 side was mooted; along with the adoption of lightweight kit and low-cut boots 'favoured by Continentals'. And early FA president William Pickford's vision of the FA Cup final in the first decade of the twenty-first century, from Pickford's vantage point in the 1930s, was reconsidered:

Although flying was still a pipe dream Pickford foresaw "air motors, great and small, electroplated, red-cushioned, swift, noiseless and crowded, converging towards the spot" [presumably a future Wembley]. A Department of State had succeeded

IT may look like a "secret weapon." It's simply the perfectly harmless, but rather novel, loud-speaker at Rugby Park, Kilmarnock.

Costing £600 it is the same as in use on NATO airfields. There is no distortion and the speaker has enough power to carry the "message" or music to all parts of the ground.

Above: Kilmarnock's eye-catching, and by all accounts ear-splitting speaker system, revealed in the *Topical Times Football Book* 1963–64

Right: Floodlight technology was amongst the futuristic innovations predicted in *Big Book of Football Champions* 1956

What the Future Holds

the FA, refereeing was a branch of the Civil Service and a football tax raised money to run the game. The pitch was made of rubber at the mighty Stadium holding 500,000 spectators where the Final was played. The referee controlled the match from a hover-plane, which flew immediately above the ball, and a loud speaker broadcast his decisions. When a man was ordered off he was whisked away by another hover-plane.

If that dystopian vision wasn't enough to give 1950s schoolboys nightmares, the FA secretary, Sir Stanley Rous, was proposing an even darker notion. Change was on the way, the 'top of the football structure will probably be a Super League composed of the leading eighteen clubs in Britain . . . which would bring us in line with foreign countries like Hungary, Russia and Uruguay, where international football can have a more important role as a result.' The freedom of movement for players, the abolition of the maximum wage, and a mid-winter break were all mooted, and 'tactics will change so that craft and intelligence will play a bigger part than speed and brawn'. *The Big Book of Football Champions* was on a roll: interfering directors with no experience of football would be banished to the sidelines, experienced players would become coaches, tactics would be underpinned with a scientific approach to the game, refreshment bars and covered seating would be provided for fans, and . . . Pickford again, who foresaw a stadium of the future where 'there rose tiers upon tiers of magnificent polished oak and mahogany seats splendidly upholstered and fitted with every convenience, like stage boxes of a West End theatre'.

Over in the Peter Dimmock-edited *Sportsview Book of Soccer* in 1958, Danny Blanchflower opened their inaugural Christmas annual with a similar fusion of science fiction and football. In a satire that perhaps hasn't dated too well, and is full of contemporary jokes at the expense of Chelsea ('a music-hall joke') and Notts County (unable to stop firing their manager), the Spurs captain did predict that we'd be watching future FA Cup finals on six-foot television screens (albeit as soon as 1975) and that tickets for the Cup final would be really hard to come by, largely because the game would 'become such a social occasion that only Royal Dukes and true blue debutants could apply'.

But this was the 1950s, numbers through the turnstiles were plummeting and, torn apart by the Hungarians, English football was suffering a crisis of confidence. A couple of years later in the *Sportsview* annual Billy Wright admitted to David Coleman that 'the Continentals' had surpassed us in terms of skill. His solution to England falling behind echoed Rous' proposition: an eighteen-club 'Premier League', with smaller clubs reverting to amateur status. 'That would mean fewer professional clubs, and they would, of course, attract the best players,' objected Coleman. 'Yes, indeed,' replied Billy. Slightly incredulous at this tampering with the foundations of the home football, and the likely amassing of wealth and power in a few hands, Coleman returned to Wright's proposition no less than five times during the course of the interview,

'Grimsby v Scunthorpe, on a Tuesday night?! Don't be such a wild dreamer . . .'

as if to check the England captain actually meant what he was saying.

Back on planet Earth, in the *Big Book of Football Champions* you could read Sunderland's Ernie Taylor imploring his England team-mates to 'stick to our game' and stop faffing about trying to adopt the Continental short-passing method. Football is a simple game, stressed Taylor: get the 'cross pass from the inside-forward to the other wing man' and pump it back over the far post (this from a man whose only cap came in the 3–6 mauling at the hands of Hungary in 1953). Similarly, in *Charles Buchan's Soccer Gift Book* you'd find Arsenal keeper Jack Kelsey *defending* the old-fashioned shoulder charge on the grounds that a good keeper should be able to stand his ground.

R efreshment bars and stands with toilets may have been opening left, right and centre, half the league grounds had floodlights, but on the pitch Wolves' and Newcastle's long-ball game dominated, and the few foreign fixtures that took place were often 'marred by roughness' – stitches to a nose wound here, a broken jaw there, swollen ankles forever being cut from boots[11]. Worse still, a cruciate knee injury spelled the end of a career, a broken leg meant you'd be out for a year. In a brisk, no-nonsense piece on players' pain thresholds in the *Soccer Gift Book*, Southampton physiotherapist Don Featherstone[12] pointed out that it was often the tough men who couldn't deal with a needle – not surprising given the gory details he revealed of wiring together

They said he had everything—well, nearly everything. Trouble was his lack of inches. But there had been mighty little men like Hughie Gallacher and Alex James, and he took his courage in both hands and set out to prove that good stuff very often comes in small bundles. So—

Don't worry if you're small...

By RON WYLIE
Notts County

the bones of Charlton centre-half Derek Ufton's shoulder (three times – it kept re-dislocating). Plates under the skin and light plastic supports and splints were the way forward, proposed Featherstone, ruing the fact that plaster of Paris was unfortunately still banned on a football pitch.

The Saints physio somewhat conformed to stereotype by suggesting that wingers tended to be 'poor pain reaction types', unsuited to 'demanding endurance or frequent knocks' that are part and parcel of life in the centre. In the early days of the football annual there was a near obsession with height, or lack of it. DON'T WORRY IF YOU'RE SMALL ran the headline of a 1954 *Charles Buchan* piece on Ron Wylie of Notts County, who, despite his lack of inches, was a well-regarded midfielder, but was still sent to work on a farm one summer to bulk him up after someone spread rumours about him being 'choosy' with his food and not eating heartily enough.

Ron Wylie was a Glaswegian, who moved down to Nottingham with his parents after a childhood at Clydebank Juniors. Two *Soccer Gift Books* later, another pint-size attacker, Bobby Collins of Celtic, really got to grips with the size issue north of the border. In an evocative article entitled DON'T WORRY IF YOU'RE WEE Collins wrote of how every time he was on the team bus on his way to Hampden he hoped they'd pass Cathkin Park, Third Lanark's ground, or, rather, the waste ground opposite where he used to play for junior side Polmadie Hawthorn, listening to the roar of the crowd at nearby Hampden (and sometimes even Cathkin Park), and dreaming dreams of 'one day being responsible for some of that wonderful noise'. In the fifties he worried that all the scrubland he played on in the South Side of Glasgow – places like Glasgow Green by the Clyde – was being built over too quickly for new housing projects, and there'd be no place left for the 'scheming and ball trickery like you've never seen'. Back in the days when he was knocking about on the waste ground, Collins became slightly obsessed with reading about the

---

11 Examples taken from an account of a violent Wales v Austria fixture in the *Big Book of Football Champions* 1957. Mel Charles departed with torn knee ligaments; Alfred Wagner, Austrian inside-left, succumbed to a fractured shin bone. There was bad bruising for players on either side. John Charles mentioned that the French ref couldn't speak a word of English, which didn't help.

12 According to a recent obituary on Southampton's website, Featherstone, a columnist for the original *Topical Times* paper, got the job after the editor passed him the Southampton advert in advance of publication.

Above: Ron Wylie reassures those who may be deterred by their dimunitive stature in *Charles Buchan's Soccer Gift Book* **1954–55**

Facing: The *Big Book of Football Champions* **goes big on the 1959 FA Cup final between Nottingham Forest and Luton in 1960**

A Magnificent Cup Final

Nottingham Forest open the scoring. Roy Dwight comes into the middle to meet a centre from Imlach and sends a first time drive crashing through the Luton defence.

Forest two up. A header by centre forward Tommy Wilson (not in picture) to a diagonal pass from Gray goes across Baynham and lands in the far corner of the Luton goal.

The moment of tragedy. Dwight is carried off on a stretcher after breaking a leg in a collision with Luton right back McNally. He watched the rest of the match on TV in hospital.

46

Despite facing ten men for most of the game, Luton could manage to score only one goal. Here it is, Pacey (not in the picture) beating Thomson and Whare. The other players are Burkitt, Whitefoot, Brown, Morton and McKinlay.

The Nottingham Forest defence came under heavy pressure in the second half, but stood up to it magnificently. Thomson and McKinlay deal with a raid by Morton, the Luton centre forward.

47

THE F.A. CUP—THIRD ROUND TO FINAL

52

53

Football annuals of the fifties and sixties majored on the FA Cup. *The Big Book of Football Champions* has a lovely report of the 1959 final: 'Tranquilliser pills were available in the dressing room before the match for the Nottingham Forest players. They were not needed. This elegant and unfashionable club went out right from the opening whistle as though they had been playing on the Wembley turf all their careers . . . Forest made football look easy. They kept the ball moving from man to man, and Luton were chasing shadows . . . it was the football of the Hungarians of 1953 and the "push and run" Spurs of ten years ago.' The splendid FA Cup 'Third Round To Final' double-page graphic more than compensates for the photographer having only been able to capture one of the three goalscorers in any of the frames featuring the ball in the back of the net.

More interesting, perhaps, is the fairly prominent theme of a crisis stirring in Scottish football

diminutive stature of his football heroes, not least as he kept being assured he was the next Hughie Gallagher: 'I loved to hear about the little men who had made good in senior football . . . the Scottish game [had] many of them . . . Alan Morton, Hughie Gallagher, Alex James, Patsy Gallagher, Jimmy McMullan . . .' In the article, he takes you through them one by one; but his heart sank a little every time 'I found out that each of them could beat me by an inch or two'. Nevertheless his passion for the game remained undimmed, and at Pollok Juniors scouts began to take notice, but 'my height was debated for weeks and months'. The 'rummle-them-up' school of thought was prevalent at the time in Scottish football, with its emphasis on strength, height and getting stuck in, but Everton soon showed an interest in wee Bobby, which prompted Celtic to weigh in . . . ultimately to much muttering about the gamble the hoops

had taken. 'That sort of talk just riled me. I was what a Scot would say "fair boiling".' So now he felt duty bound to write a piece for the 'little chaps' out there who were thinking they might not be able to make a difference – it doesn't matter if you're five-foot-two wearing size four boots: work hard, enjoy it, don't play with fear, don't be afraid of making mistakes.

Ten years on in the *Soccer Gift Book* the same cast of characters crop up – Bolton's Johnny Hancocks (size three boots) and the Spurs pair Terry Dyson and Tommy Harmer ('the Charmer') joining the Scottish gems – as Bryan Douglas asks: ARE YOU A MEMBER OF THE TIDDLERS CLUB? Don't worry if so: if you're good enough you're big enough is the message from the Blackburn Rovers and England winger. There are not many instances where the modern-day annual triumphs over those from the heyday, but it's progress of a sort that Aaron Lennon, Nathan Dyer or Jack Wilshere are probably not be found addressing this issue in their respective club annuals today.

More interesting, perhaps, is the fairly prominent theme in annuals of the day of a crisis stirring in Scottish football. This at a time when all the leading lights north of the border were heading south – a *Topical Times* of the mid-sixties reproduced a team photograph of all sixteen Scottish players in Preston North End's squad, and a cover detail from the same annual

SIXTEEN SCOTTISH PLAYERS — ALL WITH *ONE* ENGLISH CLUB

IN days of old, Preston North End were often called "Preston Scottish". Because they had so many Scotsmen on their books.
But the Deepdale club have never been more Scottish than they were last season.
Just look over this 16-strong line-up of players on their books.
All are Scotsmen. And there are two more "in the backroom"—Manager Jimmy Milne from Dundee, and second team trainer Willie Cunningham, from Hill of Beath.
With Invernessian right-back George Ross getting into Highland rig to add a touch of tartan, names and home towns are (left to right):–

Standing— Alec Dawson (Aberdeen), Ernie Hannigan (Glasgow), Stan Lapot (Edinburgh), Bill Cranston (Kilmarnock), John Donnelly (Glasgow), Gerald Stewart (Dundee), George Ross (Inverness), Billy Watt (Aberdeen), John McNamee (Coatbridge), Dave McDonald (Bo'ness), Ian Marshall (Tain), Jim Smith (Arbroath).
Kneeling — Ron Selway (Dundee), Bert Patrick (Twechar), Abe Spark (Stenhousemuir), Tommy Ure (Linlithgow).
How appropriate it is that Preston's No. 1 Scottish scout should be called — Jimmy Scott.

featured action from Celtic v Motherwell.

To kids reading *Match* annual today, the weaving of Scottish football into the very fabric of a generic football annual published in London would be mind-boggling – as mind-boggling as a lengthy feature on third division north side Port Vale's captain Tom Cheadle (who reveals his team-mates have nicknamed him 'Wooden Head' due to the twenty-two stitches he's had sewn in – 'proof indeed that toughness must be one of the first essentials of the centre-half' – and who goes on to equate Vale manager Freddie Steele, in terms of influence in the Potteries, with the writer Arnold Bennett[13]); or as puzzling as a piece celebrating the comeback from injury after a lengthy lay-off, in front of a crowd of 30,000, of Bristol Rovers centre-forward 'big' Geoff Bradford.[14]

In fact, most twenty-first-century youngsters south of the border probably have only a very sketchy idea of how many divisions there are in Scottish league football.[15]

Whereas back in the sixties and seventies, every schoolboy and girl worth their salt knew the story behind THE DAY THE RED LICHTIES MADE HISTORY, in other words Arbroath's record 36–0 win over Bon Accord. A re-telling in the *Eagle Football Annual* of 1963 describes Arbroath – the 'crack club of Forfarshire' from 'the bonny fishing town' north of Dundee – as being apprehensive before the 1885 Cup fixture, having never heard of Bon Accord, from Aberdeen. But little did they know that full-back Andrew Lornie had never played in goal before being pressed into emergency action for the Cup tie, which took place in a downpour. Arbroath's '62–63 trainer, John Martin, recounts, 'They do say that Lornie retired right after the game and never set foot on the field again . . . As

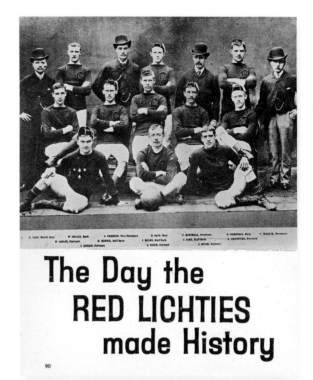

The Day the
RED LICHTIES
made History

90

for Milne, the Arbroath keeper, he didn't touch the ball once throughout the ninety minutes' and apparently a thoughtful spectator passed him an umbrella to stand under, while doing nothing between the posts. 'Still my stories are just hearsay,' said Martin, and pointed the *Eagle* in the direction of ex-Arbroath player Willie Rae, who was in the crowd that day. Hot-footing it down the high street, the *Eagle* found ninety-year-old Mr Rae in his daughter's house, 'sitting up in bed reading a Western'. He told them it actually wasn't much of a game, Bon Accord 'didn't know anything' and appeared on the field in 'ordinary shirts, long working trousers and . . . most of them wore carpet slippers.'

The piece is illustrated with a quintessential 1960s football-annual shot, of present-day Arbroath captain Jimmy Fraser, running with a leather ball, quiff ruffled by the sea-breeze, resplendent in the maroon jersey, white collar and cuffs, and framed against a pebble-dash council house-cum-terraced cottage at the back of Gayfield. That the photo is in black and white, dotted with hickeys, makes it all the more evocative.

Another photographic staple of any football annual from the 1950s to the 1970s was that of a rammed Hampden Park on a Saturday afternoon, fans packed into the vertiginous slopes of the bowl – a breath-taking spectacle in the days before a proper roof and stands were erected; like the Hampden roar, something

13 How many third-division centre-halves today would be responsible for the line, 'For to know Bennett is to know the Five Towns'? The article also features some fine slapstick: Ronnie Allen falling backwards over a dog-track fence when pacing back to take a corner; and, at the same (sadly unnamed) third division south ground Billy Pointon, noted for his long runs 'and unusual habit of running with his head down, gathered the ball on the halfway line, and made off, as he fondly imagined, goalwards.' But he overshot the touchline and ran straight into a trap on the dog track. 'Always the comedian, Billy poked his head out of the dog-trap amid roars of laughter from the rest of the crowd.'

14 According to *the Big Book of Football Champions*, 'The crowd were so emotional at this fight against the odds that even policemen had tears in their eyes.'

15 This is not to say youngsters today have lost their astonishing sponge-like ability to soak up football facts, statistics and trivia . . . it's not their fault they've been born into a media world where Rochdale, Millwall and Shrewsbury don't exist any more.

Left: 'Preston Scottish' as they were known; pose for a team picture in the *Topical Times* 1966–67. Only Inverness-born full-back George Ross is wearing a kilt and sporran

Above: The *Eagle Football Annual* 1963 tells the story of Arbroath's record Scottish Cup victory. Annuals saw it as their proud duty to keep the past alive for future generations

BRITAIN'S GREATEST STADIUM

You can almost hear the mighty roar of the crowd so vivid is this picture of the vast concrete bowl of Hampden Park. It was taken during the semi-final between Celtic and Motherwell on March 27, 1954.

to make the hairs on the back of your neck stand up. The same *Eagle* annual of 1963 noted that Hampden is a natural bowl – a river running underneath means drainage has never been a problem – and that a survey once found that 163,000 people could feasibly 'get in': 149,547 watched England v Scotland in 1937; 134,000 saw Real Madrid beat Eintracht Frankfurt in the European Cup final of 1960. Queen's Park, the amateur side whose home is the bowl, have survived on their share of such gate receipts over the years – a good thing: at the time of writing 351 folk turned up to see Queen's Park, bottom of Scottish league division two, beat Albion Rovers 4–0 (albeit at the less romantic Excelsior Stadium, home to Airdrieonians, under a temporary ground-share arrangement while Hampden was redeveloped for the 2014 Commonwealth games[16]).

A *Charles Buchan's Soccer Gift Book* feature described a typical international at Hampden, circa 1959: 'About three or four hours before kick-off the ground starts to fill. Out come the sandwiches, flasks and half-bottles, to the chorus of "Sally" and other familiar songs in the organised community singing. The tension mounts as the massed pipe bands parade around the track to the cheers of the crowd as they pass each section of terracing. At 2.50 the roar starts to grow, and with the teams running out from the tunnel it reaches a deafening pitch which sends the pigeons streaking out from the rafters of the stands. After the introductions, the game is on. With every Scottish attack the roar breaks out again, echoing round the basin and heard two miles away . . . '

Jack Harkness, former Scotland keeper and now 'one of Britain's leading sportswriters' (he must have been: the *Topical Times* photo has him in regulation Trilby, smoking a pipe and wearing a checked sports jacket–loud tie combination) was there in goal for the men in blue when the Hampden roar was born, in April 1929. The score stood at 0–0 as a last-minute corner was awarded to Scotland. The crowd sensed an unsettled English defence, and the roar steadily grew louder. Harkness, in goal at the other end, 'got the feeling the heavens would split at any moment'. Over came the slow inswinger, and this was possibly the very moment the phrase 'the crowd sucked the ball into the net' was

coined too. Delirium was heightened as Scotland had been reduced to ten men for much of the game: winger Alec Jackson, who departed with a broken arm, came round from his anaesthetic in a nearby hospital having heard the roar, exclaiming, 'Nurse, nurse. We've won. Take it from me that noise couldn't be anything but a last-minute goal for Scotland.'

Whether it's Bobby Collins dreaming dreams on waste ground by Cathkin Park, legendary keeper Jimmy Brownlie bemoaning the lack of characters in the modern Scottish game (over three pages), or the numerous photo action spreads of present-day keeper Jocky Robertson[17] and his receding hairline, the ghost of Third Lanark (Scotland's own Workington, Accrington Stanley or Barrow) floats through the pages of many a late-fifties, early-sixties football annual.

'Nurse, nurse. We've won!'

Third Lanark were named, Kenneth Wolstenholme informs readers of one of his early books of *World Soccer*, after the army battalion that later morphed into the Territorial Army, hence the old regimental war cry 'hi, hi, hi' that was used by Third Lanark fans (not forgetting the Hi Hi bar in the Gorbals[18]). Wolstenholme goes on to roll some other Scottish fancies off his tongue: Heart of Midlothian 'which brings a breath of Sir Walter Scott's famous novel into football', and plenty of Scottish non-league gems: Ormiston Primrose, Irvine Meadow, Maryhill Harp and, of course, the Glenbuck Cherrypickers: 'Glenbuck is a bleak Ayrshire mining village,' writes the BBC man. 'The last thing one would expect to see growing there is a cherry tree, the least likely occupation for any of its inhabitants would be cherrypicker.'[19]

Other accounts of Third Lanark's hi-hi's nickname

---

16 Not enough to prevent them finishing bottom of the Scottish league altogether.

17 Robertson looks like more like the proprietor of his own ice-cream parlour. For atmospheric footage, there's a short, silent, hypnotic 1960 film by Enrico Cocozza, *Meet the Stars* (easily found on YouTube), of leading Scottish players of the day demonstrating their skills inside an eerily empty Cathkin Park. In the middle of a sequence Jocky Robertson, slightly weirdly, plucks a ball from the air then pulls out a box of cigarettes from his shorts and proceeds to light up.

18 The club lost their last league game 5–1 to Dumbarton, in April 1967, and were liquidated that summer.

19 Leyton Orient legend Tommy Johnston played for a few attractively named Scottish amateur and junior sides too: Loanhead Bluebell (who played at the Bonnyrigg Rose Athletic Ground); Loanhead Mayflower and Peebles Rovers (where he crushed his left wrist in a pit accident, before returning to football with an aluminium splint and being signed by Kilmarnock).

Previous page: Hampden Park, Glasgow, in all its glory, *Charles Buchan's Soccer Gift Book* 1954–55. Right: The hand-tinted colour photographs in *The Big Book of Football Champions* were an art form in themselves. By the time the retoucher had finished they could look more like a gouache painting than a photograph. This scene is from an Old Firm game in 1956

The match of the Scottish year, the ' blood battle ' at Ibrox Park between Rangers and Celtic. Billy Simpson, left, in a midfield duel with little Bobby Collins. Simpson, an Irish international has been playing at inside forward for Rangers. Collins is Celtic's Scottish international inside-right. Result was 0—0.

point to a high-clearance from a Lanark defender as being responsible – no doubt raising a disapproving eyebrow or two in the homeland of the passing game. In the 1960 *Big Book of Football Champions* Dave Mackay laments the Scots abandoning the true spirit of their play – the Scots 'were renowned all over the world for their craft' – in favour of a high-pressing power game, clearly visible in the shift away from the progressive passing academy of Hearts to the 'apostles of power football from Ibrox', as Mackay grudgingly acknowledges Rangers' thirty-first league title in passing.

Reading the annuals today, there's no question the Scots knew their football, and historically indulged in a rich exchange of ideas.

In the 1960 *Topical Times* George Herd of Clyde thanks the 'old timer' in the crowd who, after a bitter derby with Partick Thistle, proffered a bit of advice because he hated 'to see any player not making the best of himself.' The old fella (a Jag at that) told Herd, 'Look, son, if you want to get to the top, you'll have to cut out a lot of that useless dribbling and learn to pass the ball at the right time. Just think back on the number of times today that you were robbed of the ball . . . ' Herd pondered the advice all week and the next Saturday saw him spraying passes here there and everywhere; six weeks later he was playing for a Scottish representative XI.

But the problem was the world could now not only out-pass Scotland but also outmuscle them at their own game of 'rummle-em-up'. So, while a *Charles Buchan's Soccer Gift Book* article in 1959 appears to be celebrating a new generation of Scottish young talent – 'let's pop in at Fir Park and visit Motherwell. They produced the boy with the Monroe wiggle on the field, Ian St John'[20] – it isn't long before the shameful swiping of Denis Law ('the Tommy Steele of football') from under Aberdeen's noses by another Scot in exile, Bill Shankly at Huddersfield, crops up, and, in turn, the darker prospect of restructuring the league is mooted.

---

20 Along with Pat Quinn, another one initially dismissed as 'too wee [a] mite'. Joe Baker 'the centre-forward with TNT in his boots' at Easter Road, deemed a suitable replacement for the glory-days forward line of 'gay Gordon Smith', Bobby Johnstone and the rest, is featured; as is Douglas Baillie, the 'lusty babe who swopped his running shoes for a pair of Airdrie's boots'.

'Look, son, if you want to get to the top, you'll have to cut out a lot of that useless dribbling'

'Our domestic football will soon be reorganised,' writes James Sanderson. 'Our division one must be streamlined. There will be tears, wailing and cries of distress. But the strong will live and the weak will go. Our second division is a mockery. The French, the Brazilians, the Swedes and Italians . . . yes, even our oldest soccer enemy England . . . laugh at our puny weakling . . . just as they admire our new found "babes". We must cut and prune ruthlessly. The Brechins and the Forfars cannot live in the jungle that is football now. And the sooner we realise that the better . . . it may sound harsh, but in one or two or three years we will undoubtedly have a "bloodless" execution of the weakling clubs.'[21]

Five years on, and while Scots such as Busby, Shankly and Law were running riot in the English game, according to the *Soccer Gift Book* of 1964–65 little had changed north of border. W. G. Gallagher's response to the perpetual sense of crisis in Scottish football was to look back to the golden age, to a time when the likes of legendary scout Sammy Blyth – 'he needed to have only one look at a kid on his first pram outing and he could tell whether or not the wee laddie were destined for football greatness' – reckoned that only unless Scots were once again swept by hard times, depression and, presumably, were to be seen scrabbling about for food on slag heaps, would God's own country regain its football greatness: '"Just like the boxers," he used to say, "a' the guid yins came oot o' hungry hames."' Then there was Frank Thompson, Irish outside-left who went on

---

21 Dave Mackay reached more or less the same conclusion in the *Topical Times* of 1960–61, claiming the problem with Scottish football was that the top teams had too many games against the likes of 'Arbroath, Stirling Albion, Dunfermline and one or two others'.

ONE THEY HAVE ◀ CAUGHT

Jimmy Gabriel of Dundee— destined to become a power in Scottish football.

ONE THAT GOT AWAY ▶

Denis Law — taken from under Aberdeen's nose to delight Huddersfield fans.

to manage Clyde and Ayr: "'Give me a team of miners,'" he emphasised with a thump of the table, "and I'd lick the world.'"

All of which set W.G. Gallagher off on his round-up of great personalities north of the border from back in the days when 'characters were as rich in numbers as the Carse of Gowrie with strawberries in June.' Fellas like Jacky Robertson, the Rangers and Scotland half-back who was hauled before the SFA for using ungen-tlemanly language. "'I admit to swearing," he said, "but I was only cursing myself for having a bad game." [And] another Ranger, a Scotland player, inside-forward or wing-half, Tommy (Tully) Craig who was second to none at giving a dummy. In one match the dummy was completely unsuccessful against an opponent. Dispossessed time after time, Tully turned to his tor-mentor, exasperated to the full, and demanded: "D'ye no recognise a dummy when you see yin?'"

Gallagher fondly recalled Partick Thistle goalkeeper Rab Bernard 'as hairy of body as a gorilla, and as strong as that citizen of the jungle', who'd make a save then stand on the goal-line, ball firmly clutched, and roar at the opposition forwards: "'Come on, have a go, or are ye a bunch o' fearties?'" (Bernard also scored more than forty penalties for the Maryhill Magyars.)

What's more, railed Gallagher, there was no *bonho-mie* left in the game. Gone were the days when, after a match, ' . . . time was when the chairman of each club made a little complimentary speech [even toasting the gentlemen of the press] . . . now the boardroom gathering, with few exceptions, is a cold, formal affair. The dram is hurriedly swallowed, the departure of the visiting officials is a hasty one.' It was win at all costs.

Still, for English editors of football annuals, there was nothing like a thrashing handed out to the old enemy to avoid having to talk about Hungary and 1953. Don Revie's and Stanley Matthews' frying alive of Clyde left-back Harry Haddock during England's 7–2 thrashing of Scotland in April 1955 is re-lived in luminous detail in *the Big Book of Football Champions*. And for the Scots, well, there was always more raw tal-ent to be hauled up from that rich vein underground.

George Young, formerly of Kirkintilloch Rob Roy, now captain of Rangers and Scotland, was of the view that OUR YOUNGSTERS NEED MORE COACHING but, in the 1957 *Big Book of Football Champions*, he praised another Young – Alex – for his 'speed, ball control, eye for an opening, balance and springiness'. The Hearts youngster had started out on the wing to ease the hard knocks and pressure of an inside-forward's lot, and where

PATSY GALLACHER

THE BEST FOOTBALLERS LIKE THE BEST BOXERS . . .

were the hungry ones !

ultimately he 'displaced another of Hearts' future hopes, John Hamilton, who works in the mines at Stepps Colliery and is up every morning at 4.45 to reach the pits.'

Part-time down the pit; training in the afternoons. That wasn't an unusual way to make a living in the central coal-belt of Ayrshire and Fife. South of the border, as recently as the mid-1960s, Scunthorpe's Ray Clemence was collecting deckchairs on Skegness beach during the summer months in order to bump up his pay. And back at the dawn of the football annual, players were, of course, of humble origin. Charles Buchan, a lanky and prolific inside-forward for Sunderland and Arsenal in his day, set up *Charles Buchan's Football Monthly* in the autumn of 1951. Two Christmases later, in the inaugural

Left: *Charles Buchan's Soccer Gift Book* 1959 tracks the progress of Jimmy Gabriel and Denis Law, two Scots who both ended up in England in the end

Above: W.G. Gallagher laments the loss of footballing talent drawn directly from the Scottish coal mines in *Charles Buchan's Soccer Gift Book* 1964

Charles Buchan's Soccer Gift Book, he wrote of racing the horse-drawn tram to school to save on the fare, and of splitting his one-penny pocket money between a bag of broken biscuits and comics. Unable to pay at the turnstile, he stood around outside Highbury until the gates were flung open ten minutes before the end, then rushed in with his mates to enjoy the finale.

This was also a time when players routinely used public transport to get to training, matches or even for an initial meeting with a club. Even as late as the eighties, Stan Bowles famously caught the Central Line on a Saturday lunchtime on his way to play for Orient at Brisbane Road, chatting with fellow tube travellers.[22] In the *Topical Times* of 1960–61, Jack Harkness, the Scotland goalkeeper-cum-reporter, recalled his time with 'Edina's darlings' (Hearts, a club whose popularity remained undimmed, even if their boardroom sideboards remained empty), and specifically the tram conductor taking him back into Edinburgh city centre after his interview at Tynecastle (this was 1928) asking him if he'd signed – 'Aye' – then the conductor telling him, 'I've followed Hearts all my life. And I'll keep on doing so. Yet, it's like being a follower of Bonnie Prince Charlie. A great cause, but no hope of victory at the end.' (Hopefully the conductor, probably having hung up his ticket-machine by 1958–1959, was still around

to enjoy Hearts' consecutive titles.) Harkness goes on to tell the story of the club who lost so many in the First World War and recalls a time when the club's seasonal bonus consisted of a turkey per player on Christmas Eve: 'One or two of the players who were travelling a distance opened their parcels in the dressing-room to re-wrap them in greaseproof paper. It was then that one player noticed his bird was ever so much smaller than another's. In a flash he picked up his turkey, stamped through to the manager's office, threw the bird on the table and demanded a transfer. "I've suspected favouritism all along," he said, "but now I have proof of it."' He got his transfer, but that was the end of turkeys at Christmas for the rest of the squad.

In the second *Soccer Gift Book*, unwrapped at Christmas 1954, Forest's Billy Walker reminisced about his furious dad hiding football-mad Walker jnr's boots, as he thought there was 'no future in the game' for a son of his. But fortunately nature took its course for the young Billy and he was soon sacked from his West Midlands' engineering works for kicking a tin can around, and ended up scoring twice on his debut for Aston Villa in a January 1920 Cup victory over Queens Park Rangers. And even back in the fifties it seems the elder generation considered the subsequent crop to have it all too easy: with their 'chicken and fish, perhaps a steak, with toast and tea' Walker considered the modern 'big-time players'[23] pampered. What was wrong with 'a chop and new-laid egg? In my day,' Walker continued, 'when we played away we always had to walk from the station to the ground. Taxis and buses were frowned upon ... in places like Everton and Manchester it was a damned long walk!' It was also seen as a 'privilege' to talk to directors, who travelled on a separate train. So maybe changes in the new world weren't all for the bad, but the Forest boss still placed his faith in youth who just play for the love of the game, and was suspicious of the coming generations of Arthur Seatons. He was also worried that rival attractions such as ice hockey, dog racing and the cinema would all make a further dent in gates that were declining after a post-war high. Football had to sharpen its act up in a world where money was not so easy to come by, and housewives had more of a say in the spending of the family budget: 'I know plenty of instances where the "old man" is having to cut out his beer and football to

---

22 A year earlier, while playing for Forest, Bowles claimed to have rented a place in Bulwell, just north of Nottingham city centre. I grew up in Bulwell, but today it would be surprising if you bumped into Britt Assombalonga doing his shopping in the Co-op on the Vale.

23 If this had been the *Topical Times* or *Big Book of Football Champions* I suspect the word 'Charlies' would have been retained from the original draft.

Left: Ray Clemence doing his summer job stacking deck chairs in Skegness, as featured in *Shoot!* two decades later in 1983

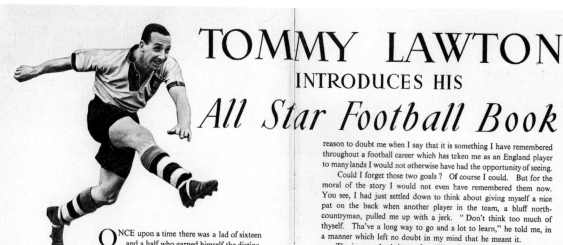

TOMMY LAWTON
INTRODUCES HIS
All Star Football Book

Once upon a time there was a lad of sixteen and a half who earned himself the distinction of being the youngest centre forward ever to play in a Football League game. On his second senior side appearance he scored two goals, one in each half. The team won by 2—0 and earned two precious points which set them on the road to avoiding relegation, most dreaded word of all in football.

You couldn't have a more romantic start to a fairy story, could you? But this one happens to be true. The date was April, 1936: the team Burnley, playing against Swansea Town at Vetch Field: the player, young Tom Lawton.

Can you imagine the pride with which my young heart was bursting? Of course you can. You probably wouldn't have any

10

reason to doubt me when I say that it is something I have remembered throughout a football career which has taken me as an England player to many lands I would not otherwise have had the opportunity of seeing.

Could I forget those two goals? Of course I could. But for the moral of the story I would not even have remembered them now. You see, I had just settled down to think about giving myself a nice pat on the back when another player in the team, a bluff north-countryman, pulled me up with a jerk. "Don't think too much of thyself. Tha've a long way to go and a lot to learn," he told me, in a manner which left no doubt in my mind that he meant it.

The journey back home from West Wales was a long one. All the way to Burnley, every time I felt pleased with myself, I found these words running through my head. That, however, was just as it should have been, probably just exactly how the self-appointed moralist had intended it.

He had taught me soccer's greatest lesson—that one player doesn't make a team, however outstanding his performances may be. In fact, that everything in this great national game of ours, which has by this time almost encircled the globe, depends on eleven men pulling their weight all the time and, if necessary, giving themselves beyond the limits of human endurance to achieve the desired result—for each other, for the TEAM.

11

---

pay for the television set,' said Walker ruefully.

Tommy Lawton, as a youngster, probably wouldn't have spoken to a director either. In the introduction to his 1950 *All Star Football Book* he's feeling pretty pleased with himself having scored two crucial goals for relegation-threatened Burnley in only his second appearance. But then a big fella, a Burnley team-mate, 'a bluff north-countryman', strolls over: 'Don't think too much of thyself. Tha've a long way to go and a lot to learn,' he chides. And Lawton takes it all on board, remonstrating with himself on the long journey back from the Vetch Field for the slightest lapse into self-congratulatory mode – it's the team that matters, not the individual.

That was April 1936, but fifteen years later the same principles held true. In *Charles Buchan's Soccer Gift Book, 1955–56*, Jimmy Seed, Charlton 'secretary–manager', quoted Rudyard Kipling to get his point across: 'The game is more than the player of the game, and the ship is more than the crew.' A few pages on and *Gift Book* readers learned it was the same at Goodison Park, where

Everton were 'taught to play as a team . . . no big stars or individuals' – in fact, Everton, 'home to the Irish', were so much of a closely knit team it played havoc with their promotion campaign in 1954, as Ireland went all out to reach the World Cup.

Team spirit was perhaps not so difficult to forge at a time when players, by and large, shared similar backgrounds. Time and again in the football annuals of the 1950s players recount childhood tales of being too poor to pay at the turnstile. Frank Blunstone of Chelsea is one of numerous footballers who 'fess up (here in *Charles Buchan*, 1957–58) to scrambling over barbed fences and walls[24]. At Gresty Road,

> ## 'What was wrong with a chop and new-laid egg?'

---

24 Manchester United's Johnny Berry did the same, wriggling under a fence at Aldershot's Recreation Ground. Flipping through an old annual, Johnny Green came across a picture of Frank Blunstone. He remembers him playing like a kid too. 'He used to kick the ball and run after it like a school-kid would: kick, then run like fuck to catch up with it, none of this trap, control and pass. He was a little man, who used to put his head down. He was a fast runner; it worked for him: kick it ten yards then go hell for leather from a standing start.'

Above: *Tommy Lawton's All Star Football Book* opens with a flourish in 1950

JOHN ATYEO
Bristol City

for Blunstone and his pals, ' . . . half-time was quite a caper. The ball was left on the centre spot, but as soon as the players left the field about fifty of us used to scramble over the barrier for a free-for-all kickabout. We were hustled off when the teams returned, and had the ball not been taken off at the finish, we would have all swarmed over for another session.' And Blunstone, like so many future pros, was eventually taken on by the groundstaff: 'Each Friday afternoon Mr Turner [Arthur Turner, the Crewe manager] gave me the money for an ice cream, and half a crown to go to the pictures. It was a delightful personal gesture on his part.'

The early years of the football annual are also full of testimonies from players who one day arrive home from their apprenticeship, in a nearby shop or factory, to find their local club manager having a cup of tea with their mum. In Derek Tapscott's case, his boss at Barry Town was to accompany him to Highbury the very next morning. In the Black Country, one keen young football student was already assistant manager of a grocer's shop at sixteen when 'one evening, he folded his apron and went home to supper and his father said, "How would you fancy joining Wolverhampton Wanderers?" "I wouldn't mind," said Stanley Cullis.' Although in those days, as John Thompson wrote in the *Soccer Gift Book*, 'the prospect of becoming a football star did not excite him very much. His placid reply to his father reflected that.'

In the same 1955–56 *Charles Buchan Gift Book* Huddersfield's Ron Stainforth provided an entertaining account of being sacked from his job as a milkman for tearing through his round in record time so that he could attend a trial at Stockport County. 'You must have flogged the horse to death,' noted his boss, surprised at Stainforth's early return to the dairy, but whose mood darkened when he learnt of the trial. 'Anyway to cut a long argument short, I was out of work when I left the dairy a few minutes later,' added Ron. 'I went home to break the news to my wife and then set off for Stockport. The trial by this time had become a lot more important to me . . .'

And, even though by 1962 the maximum wage had been abolished, you get the sense that football was not necessarily a career to be leapt at: Mick McNeil, the Middlesbrough defender, enjoyed chemistry at school, and implied that he only took up a contract at the club

'My luck changed. I scored four goals in six minutes and the match was won!'

so that he could help his dad with his market-garden business on the outskirts of town, 'especially during the summer months'. Ron Wylie took advantage of afternoons off from Meadow Lane to learn the textile trade as an apprentice in a Notts County director's lace factory. Bert McCann of Motherwell, a student of languages at Edinburgh University, was portrayed by the *Big Book of Football Champions* as a 'lonely man', a solitary figure spending his evenings training in a empty gym, having resisted the lure of a career in England so he could continue his studies (he subsequently spent nine years at Fir Park and played twenty-six times for Hamilton Academical). And John Atyeo resisted overtures from high-flying Portsmouth and threw his lot in with third division Bristol City as a part-time pro so he could work at his job in quantity surveying. He was duly accused of lacking ambition, but 351 goals in over 600 appearances for the Ashton Gate club, six England caps (and five international goals), then a life as a maths teacher after retirement from the game feels like a life lived to the full. Charles Buchan would have undoubtedly approved.

But the hardy perennial of these annuals is a tale that's told repeatedly: local boy overcomes the odds, the little gem with the quick feet shines through the murk. Atyeo used to cut a lonely figure, kicking a ball about in a local orchard until dark, then playing for Westbury United, in the Wiltshire league aged fifteen, he was seventy minutes into his debut. At 1–1, 'I was playing centre-forward, trying really hard to succeed and somehow feeling I wasn't quite making it! Then my luck changed. I scored four goals in six minutes and the match was won!'

And if you were anybody in the north-east in the early twentieth century, it seems you played for Hylton Colliery Juniors in Durham mining country: Harry Hooper of Wolves, Tommy Cummings of Burnley; and Allenby Chilton, part of the bedrock of Matt Busby's first title-winning team – but praised by Charlie Buchan for achieving the extraordinary ability to run backwards at high speed by 'hard and patient practice' – all learned the ropes there. In the same *Buchan* editorial Albert Quixall is commended for always carrying a tennis ball about with him to keep his footwork sharp; and Duncan Edwards achieved his huge levels of sustained

Left: John Atyeo, quantity surveying's loss was Bristol City's gain. *Charles Buchan's Soccer Gift Book 1955–56*

concentration from . . . well . . . 'Ask the modest Duncan and he'll reply, "Well, I do quite a bit of fishing."' Practise, practise, practise – hard work – and more practice: it's a mantra repeated throughout early editions of the *Soccer Gift Book*. One afternoon *Buchan* scribe Roland Allen comes across 'a bright, chirpy chap, one of those to be found on the fringe of cockneydom' at a north London cricket-school practice session. He seems quite useful with the bat, but his school master sighs, 'He'll never make it as a cricketer.' The reason: he'd rather be in the kids' enclosure at White Hart Lane watching Spurs. Get out there with a ball, and work at it, chides Allen, pointing out that that's how the legendary England captain and centre-half Billy Wright overcame his early 'sacking': 'the basic skills of football cannot possibly be instinctive, any more than the mechanics of the great artist can be acquired without slogging study and infinite patience and, indeed, mental courage.'

The Big Book of **FOOTBALL CHAMPIONS**

For more detail on Billy Wright's 'sacking' we have to turn to the *Big Book of Football Champions*, a fine annual that ran from the early fifties to the early sixties. Its hand-tinted colour illustrations may have been on the basic side (but they look utterly beautiful today), and there was a strong emphasis on the FA Cup and events of the previous season, but it offered a comparatively down-to-earth view of the game, often taking a more critical look at football in Britain than *Buchan*.[25]

25 Wales' performance against Scotland in the 1959 Home International at Ninian Park was described as 'pathetic . . . the wingers, Len Allchurch and Phil Woosnam, were the chief weaknesses', in a game where Matt Busby's Scots, chiefly eighteen-year-old Denis Law, ripped the men of the principality apart; England's chances at the forthcoming 1960 Olympics: 'a hopeless quest'; Portsmouth's arrow-shaped attack, comprising three centre-forwards headed by Ron Saunders (recently of Gillingham), didn't function well because, according to the *BBoFC*, Peter Harris and Ron Newman, the wingers behind the spearhead, were ill-disciplined 'go-ahead types who favoured a personal strike at goal' over grafting to keep the shape and the supply line open from the back. (Portsmouth went on a twenty-four-game run without a victory and were duly relegated, ten points adrift at the bottom of the first division – only Leeds in 1947 had been relegated with fewer points); Sheffield United's right-back Cecil Coldwell is singled out as the weak link in a back five 'bolt plan' at Bramall Lane, and blamed for their Cup exit at the hands of third division Norwich in 1959.

In a feature entitled THE SPIRIT OF ENGLISH FOOTBALL from the 1960 edition, the Hungarian FA offered their compliments on Wright reaching his one hundreth cap: 'You have reached this rare jubilee as a player of such temperance, zeal and fairness as to set an example for every footballer in all parts of the world.' This, of course, was the same Billy Wright last seen charging about like 'a fire engine going to the wrong fire'[26] against the very same rampant Magyars of 1953–54. It turns out that Wright owed his career to Wolves secretary Jack Howley, who pleaded his case with manager Major Frank Buckley – the Major having decided to let the youngster go as he was 'not fulfilling his promise'. Wright was to be sent back to Ironbridge immediately. 'The bottom of the world dropped out. Young Billy ran from the office to the referee's room at the end of the corridor at Molineux and burst into tears', where Jack Howley found him and proceeded to take up the matter with the Major. Howley pointed out that Wright was 'such a good worker' when it came to the chores of the groundstaff boys, 'sweeping the dressing rooms and terraces and weeding the pitch. The Major relented and Wright stayed on.'[27] Later in the article Wright is self-effacing and aware enough to acknowledge the Hungarian massacre – and you can't help but wonder if Steven Gerrard would 'fess up to being kept on at Anfield as a youngster because he was handy at cleaning the toilets.

You also can't help but wonder if Allenby Chilton, rather than practising running backwards at high speed, shouldn't have been perfecting his ball work. And if Charles Buchan shouldn't have been using his 1954–55 editorial to deconstruct England's savaging at the hands of Hungary. Not a word of it: there's a lengthy account of Buchan dashing through traffic to get back to the BBC studios in Glasgow from Hampden in time to file his sports report, and the relating of another unfortunate mishap, this time concerning blowing his nose having already had make-up applied for a

26 Geoffrey Green in *The Times*.

27 Wright later claims in his own annual, and tells the guests in Wolverhampton Civic Hall, that it was because he was too small.

Above: The first *Big Book of Football Champions*, from 1950–51, featuring Newcastle's Jackie Milburn on the cover, in all its tattered glory

Right: Billy Wright performs international captain duties, as depicted in the *Big Book of Football Champions* 1960

The English and Italian captains, Wright and Segato, exchange pennants before the start of the England-Italy international at Wembley in May. The result was a 2—2 draw. This match was Billy Wright's 101st international.

television appearance.[28] It's left to Peter Wilson of the *Daily Mirror* to wring his hands concerning the precedence league football enjoys over the national team, dismiss the current crop of England internationals as not fit to share the same turf as Stanley Matthews, and to herald Moscow Dynamo's tour of 1945 as the moment English football's dominance was irrevocably shaken. Rather like on the pitch, where there was considerably more time and space on the ball, the football annuals of yesteryear tended to run articles over several pages, offering glimpses of atmospheric detail not always found in more concise, newspaper match reports. In fact, the heavily moustachioed Peter Wilson spends more time describing the mayhem leading up to Chelsea v Moscow Dynamos fixture than the thrilling 3–3 encounter itself:

> Householders near Stamford Bridge unsuspectingly answered their doorbells on the day of the match only to be swept aside by rabid fans who stormed through the houses, across the back yards and over walls to gain unwarranted admission to the ground.
>
> I well remember seeing one man crash through a glass-covered section of the stand. Mercifully he did not hurt himself, but he didn't exactly do much good to the fellow who was sitting underneath his unpremeditated point of entry.
>
> However, the original occupant of the seat treated this unexpected cuckoo in his nest with a typical British mixture of firmness and hospitality.
>
> Having picked himself up, assured himself of no broken bones or other calamities, he punched the intruder firmly and sharply on the nose, as though to teach him that such liberties were not lightly to be tolerated, and then obligingly hunched himself up so that the interloper could share his seat.

Ah, where would we be without that British 'firmness and hospitality'? Billy Wright, in his *Football Album* of Christmas 1954, related how the English XI remained calm in the face of Uruguayan thuggery in Montevideo – this must have been England's 2–1 defeat in May 1953 – and slowly won over the home crowd, who began to turn on their own team as the barbaric tackles continued to fly in: 'During this match our opponents had not been as sporting as we expected. To the credit of the Englishmen, however, they never once lost their heads ... Long before the end we were

---

28 Though to be fair to Buchan, he probably felt he'd already broadcast enough to the nation on this subject. For the return Hungary fixture, in May 1954, he commentated for the BBC from Budapest, where England lost 7–1. The official Buchan website reproduces a later quote from Charlie: 'I did not realise there was a double microphone in the booth and all my asides and groans were heard live throughout Britain.'

'As the coach moved off, all the lads sang Land of Hope and Glory . . .'

being cheered so much one might have thought we were Uruguay. Then, at the end of the match, thousands of spectators waited behind to cheer and applaud us for giving such a splendid display of sportsmanship, and, as the coach moved off, all the lads sang "Land of Hope and Glory" ...' Earlier in the same piece Wright had suggested that one of the main factors behind Portugal's recent ascent through the international ranks had been the laying of Cumberland turf in the National Stadium in Lisbon: 'It is watered twice a day and the result is a green jewel in the brown countryside and a pitch little if anything inferior to Wembley. On this lush stretch any team should be able to play good football.'

But to give Wright his due, he didn't shirk from expounding upon, in great detail, his own failings: he wrote of his fear of smacking a ball again with his right foot after months out with a broken ankle, something it

Above: Billy Wright opens his *Football Album* in 1954 and chooses recovering from a broken ankle, twice, as his toughest football assignements

seemed Major Buckley and half the Wolves team were all aware of (he kept using his left), and of the difficult road to overcoming a loss of form and the loss of his England place. Despite talking it through with his landlady and her son every evening – 'the harder I tried on the field the poorer I played' – something approaching the old Billy finally came back on a tour of South Africa. Only for the next 'assignment' to be none other than Puskás and his mates . . . Then suddenly a veil is drawn, and the article comes to a swift conclusion: Puskás is a 'great ball player, the complete artist. To play against him was a pleasure, an education, and a lot of fun.' A lot of fun? Really?

A few pages on, Newcastle and England's Ivor Broadis provided probably the fullest account of 'the Hungarian Rhapsody': 'Why, the man in the street who used to fight shy of the tongue-twisting names, now finds himself discussing the "Masterly Magyars" with the fluency of a would-be Glendenning![29] Practically everyone realises that we are now mere subordinates as far as this soccer game is concerned, and indeed opinions have been expressed that we are outclassed in all phases of the game . . . Looking back, I couldn't agree more.' He described a sense of being completely overwhelmed by the Hungarians' great skill and great intelligence in applying that skill. They hit the ball instinctively – even on the half-turn! – to where they knew a player would be. There was no need to look first. And, early on, there was no sparring, just straight out full-on attack: 'Anxiously you probe. Confidently they prance. You're struck by their speed, fitness and cleverness straight from the word go and then you're wrapped up in the game, and you've no time to wonder about anything except during the oh so long half-minute when you're moving toward the centre-spot for a fresh kick-off.' On calls for the English to up their training, Broadis believed: 'An abundance of ball-work would probably enable us to field eleven trained seals, while to resort to a Zatopek schedule would yield eleven ready-made contestants for the London to Windsor race . . . as TV chef Philip Harben would say: "It's in the mixing."'

By 1959, after another underwhelming World Cup and years of stagnating football on the home front played in the shadow of European giants such as Real Madrid, views were hardening. For the second edition of the *Sportsview Book of Soccer* Peter Dimmock remained on the cover – in a throwback to his RAF

29 Plummy-accented BBC Radio sports reporter with thespian roots (and extreme handlebar moustache).

days, the weekly TV sports presenter is photographed gazing to the horizon, neatly groomed with a clipped moustache, resplendent in a dashing leather jacket with a fulsome fur collar – but handed over the nitty-gritty of the editing to pioneering BBC sports journalists Paul Fox and Ronnie Noble. In turn they let ex-Arsenal winger and Middlesex batsman Denis Compton loose on the state of the game. 'WHERE ARE THE ARTISTS?' implored Compton, 'the real ball artist in football has become almost as rare as the genuine leg spinner in cricket.' There was Haynes, Blanchflower, Eastham, Charlton and Tommy Harmer, but not too many others. Too much emphasis was being placed on becoming a tireless worker; speed had taken precedence over skill or flair or real intelligence and ball control, complained the recently retired Middlesex man. What's more, simple possession was now seen as a bad thing; latent skills were

'We are now mere subordinates as far as this soccer game is concerned'

Above: Ivor Broadis, in the same annual, acknowledges England's inferiority to Hungary after the infamously heavy defeats in 1953 and 1954

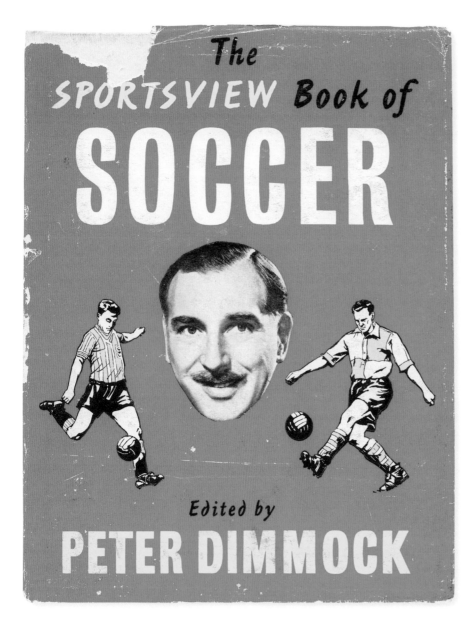

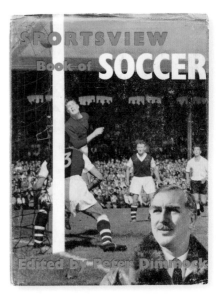

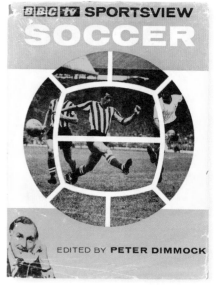

|||||||||||||||||||||||||||||||||||||||

The *Sportsview Book of Soccer* was a spin-off from the Wednesday night TV show broadcast by the BBC between 1954 and 1968. Eight 'soccer' annuals were published, fronted by the show's presenter Peter Dimmock, carrying some surprisingly forthright views on the game. While the interior pages were, on the whole, plain text-based layouts, the covers were a delight to the eye.

Pictured here, clockwise from top left, are the jackets from 1958, 1959, 1963, 1964 and 1966 respectively. From 1968 the TV show, Dimmock and the publications, were superseeded by David Coleman's *Grandstand*.

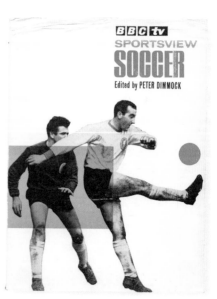

being coached out of youngsters, plenty of balls were launched forward '"hoping for the best". This, I think, is disastrously wrong.' And it wasn't just commercial forces bearing down upon a result-is-all professional game. Compton wrote of a recent trip to an Amateur Cup semi-final, which he found 'more than a little depressing. Frankly, I thought the standard of play was pathetic . . . the players lacked subtlety, they lacked ball control, they even seemed to lack any real intelligence. There was a vast amount of enthusiasm and ill-directed energy, but no one on the field seemed to play with any plan or job in mind, except to get the ball up the field – and once again to hope for the best.' Only Raymond Kopa of France and Didi of Brazil seem to have remembered the game should be a spectacle; as far as England was concerned, 'the pupils have gone very, very far ahead of the masters.'

The contrast with the world of *Charles Buchan* was striking. In the 1956–57 *Soccer Gift Book,* Roland Allen really got to the crux of what English football was all about: to hell with international football and all those baffling tactics . . .

> What we like is BREAD-AND-BUTTER FOOTBALL. We know we play too many league matches and Cups, we know all about the deplorable state of British Soccer in comparison with that of the rest of world . . . that we are in danger of becoming a fourth-rate footballing power, and that with all that hanging around us, here we are revelling in a little tin-pot Cup. We know there is not time before the next World Cup or the next match against the Ruritanians. We know we ought be doing something about it NOW.
>
> But this Cup competition is fascinating, isn't it; and we do want to see the little fellows get through another round – so long as they don't push our team out. And, to strike a serious note, it is from all these clubs that the men will come to uphold the honour of England . . .

Great players, Allen suggested, are forged in 'hectic Cup games and desperate struggles for points' in the 'parish-pump stuff that has to go on'. The article climaxed in a *Monty Python*-ish paragraph, italicized by the *Soccer Gift Book* for emphasis:

> *The Old Ship may be listing, but she is not sinking. We can afford to give a little of our time and thought then to other distractions besides foreigners . . . Cups and Things. So let's do just that, and wait for the return to our greatness of the past.*
> *Sure enough it will come.*

'What we like is bread and butter football'

Where the typical portrayal of Billy Wright in football annuals of the day is of the calm, affable, focused individual, valiantly helping those around him on the pitch, a fine ambassador for the originators of the game off it, the reality is more complicated.

West Brom photographer and archivist Laurie Rampling, whose vast collection of football paraphernalia includes several feet of shelving holding an immaculate collection of football annuals, can just about remember the England captain: 'He was the best centre-half in the country at the time by a mile; he could pass a ball second to none. He didn't boot it out, he was a footballing centre-half and, to be fair, he took that doctrine with him to Arsenal [as manager].' Rampling thinks the problems with English football lay elsewhere, namely with the FA, the selectors and the manager: 'Walter Winterbottom was a decent fellow, very laid back, and with no great affinity for football. He was an autocrat, brought in to [adopts a Raymond Glendenning tone] "Let's get the boys together . . . " Up to '53 we were of our time, then Hungary was the start of the continental revolution. We'd lost to the United States before that in the World Cup, of course: one or two warning signs had been there long before Hungary, but we wouldn't change. Everybody knew what was going on on the Continent, behind the iron curtain, and in South America. We'd beaten Brazil 4–2 at Wembley, but as far as the football was concerned, they played us off the park. And we still didn't tend to heed the warning signs.'

For Laurie, better players were often overlooked by the FA selectors and Winterbottom. John Kaye, 'a terrific centre-forward at West Brom', never played for England, and Tony Brown, Ronnie Allen, Derek Kevan and Jeff Astle garnered just a few caps between them: 'The selectors drove straight through the Midlands to the north, or just stayed in London. Bomber Brown was a goal-scoring phenomenon who played just once for England. And what did Alf Ramsey do? He played him out of position.' (Laurie acknowledges there was the small matter of Bobby Moore keeping him out of the team at wing-half too.[30] And things didn't get much better in the seventies: 'Cyril Regis was pulling up trees before he even got considered for England.')

---

30 Kevan also edged Brian Clough out of the 1958 World Cup squad.

A young Richard Williams (today of the *Guardian*) was also aware of strange, enticing forces from the east. Dynamo Moscow and Spartak Moscow were 'a wonderful rumour that you heard about, like beings from another planet. Like the Hungarians – of course I didn't see them either, but I was definitely aware, when I was 7 or 8, that there was this thing that was more advanced than we were. The metaphor for it was the boots. The first boots I had came up over the ankle, with an extra leather strap across the instep, they were hand-me-downs, good for wellying it – or buffing it, as we used to say.' The protective nature of the high top couldn't be underestimated: 'When the full-back came over – *phoom* – took you out over the touchline and probably took your ankles with you.

'We didn't have a lot of money, though for some reason, when I got my first pair of own boots they were dark red, a kind of burgundy colour, and they were cutaway – they were continental style, which was amazing. Those were what Puskás and the Hungarians wore! It was like, I dunno, your first bike with derailleur gears; those boots represented a completely different philosophy, even when you were 8 you knew that those boots really signified something.'

As for Billy Wright: 'You sort of accepted he was the captain of England, but he was not a remotely interesting figure. Bobby Moore, you knew he was a wonderful player, but you never really thought that about Billy Wright. There was something sort of stolid about him; even then you felt he was part of the past, he represented almost a pre-war ethos.

'Then there was the Beverley sister – I can't remember a football star being married to an entertainment star before, so I suppose that was the beginning of the meeting of those worlds, but even then it didn't seem very interesting because the Beverley Sisters weren't very interesting, they were like something from an earlier era of entertainment.'

Long before Billy Wright was receiving his rose bowls at the Wolverhampton civic hall banquet, John Graydon of the *Sunday Graphic* was writing about the Hungarians in his review of the 1953–54 season in the England captain's *Football Album*. But Graydon could also see the green shoots of progressive football in England: in Arthur Rowe's Spurs side – it's noted that it's no coincidence Rowe coached in Hungary – and in Duncan Edwards, spotted by Graydon reading a book on tactics while killing time on an England trip. The *Sunday Graphic* man also gives the thumbs-up to ball players Johnny Haynes and Albert Quixall, the latter 'with his flowing blond hair, and pants hoisted up so that they sometimes resemble a bikini, is a fantastic young character', who, like Haynes, espoused the virtues of constant practice. Quixall himself wrote a feature, lamenting the fact that youngsters don't seem to have the heart these days to keep going, endlessly practising, even under a lamppost after dark, or smacking a tennis ball against a wall, all of which stood him in good stead for life at Sheffield Wednesday.

Quixall added, ' . . . with a tennis ball, or small ball, I've seen many young fellows perform the most wonderful tricks – but once they get on to the field it is frequent to forget all about their artistry and become just straightforward players. Now this is all wrong. If a footballer has outstanding control of a football he should be encouraged to use his tricks during a match . . . when I've played against Continentals, you usually discover that all their players are craftsmen and artists. Abroad there is no such thing as a *forward* or a *defender*. Everyone is a *footballer*. Their sole objective is to gain complete mastery of a football. We too should try and achieve this ambition . . . '

Wright and his editors clearly saw Sheffield Wednesday as a progressive force. Wednesday trainer Allan Brown contributed a piece: 'For some time, and particularly since England's defeat by the Hungarians, it's been fashionable to decry the ability of coaching in England,' and then walked the reader through a studiously lengthy account of the intensive coaching regime employed to get the prolific but somewhat uncultured striker Derek Dooley to use his weaker foot – right back to the time when 'the mechanics of his kicking were the thing that needed tackling first' and Dooley was left to train alone, smacking the ball repeatedly against a wall with his left foot, through to when, weeks later, he was bringing it down and knocking it in with either foot and, surrounded by natural technicians like Quixall, Redfearn Froggatt and Alan Finney,

Above: Albert Quixall makes a radical suggestion in *Billy Wright's Football Album* 1954. A '50s and '60s annual mainstay, Quixall was transferred to Man Utd for a record fee of £45,000 in 1958

Portrait of a FAILURE?

Soccer's most misunderstood man

Above: *Kenneth Wolstenholme's Book of Football*
assesses England manager Walter Winterbottom's
tenure in the job, which ended in 1963

SOCCER'S MOST VITAL KICK IS JUST — BLUFF!

ALF RAMSEY

he went on to smash long-standing scoring records at Hillsborough.[31] (For the modern-day reader, of course, Dooley's subsequent, horrific leg amputation forever hovers in the background; for the schoolboys of 1954 it was touched upon lightly, a 'tragedy' buried in the smaller print of a caption.)

Charlton trainer Jimmy Trotter – 'Jimmy Trotter and Trotter's Travelling Surgery', as the *Soccer Gift Book* would have it – was a fixture of 1950s annuals, usually to be found espousing progressive stuff, such as using a ball to train with, and here he advocated ball-work as actually being the key to fitness itself – a radical proposition at a time when pre-season training consisted of running up and down a hill for three weeks. He also proposed that all footballers are different and should be treated accordingly as individuals.

But before we get too carried away, and start seeing an embryonic Barcelona in the pages of *Billy*

Wright's Football Album, it's worth noting the forces of ignorance and darkness were fully on display too. Alf Ramsey blithely claimed all penalties are just kidology and bluff – you could study the penalty-taker's previous form (left or right) but 'the actual technicalities of taking a penalty are few, and simple [always remember to place the lace of the ball facing away] and *no lengthy practice from the twelve-yard spot is necessary*.' Never mind the future ramifications for England, this was from a man who cheerfully admitted in the *Billy Wright* article that he once missed all three penalties awarded to Tottenham in a season (even if, overall, Ramsey had a good record from twelve yards).

And it's probably not too difficult to envisage what 'robustious' Trevor Ford of Cardiff City made of blond-haired, bikini-bottomed ball players and their bag of tricks: 'There is too much of a namby-pamby attitude on the part of soccer administrators today,' wrote the Welsh international. 'An honest to goodness shoulder charge used to be one of the features of British football. When one does it today frequently the referee's whistle goes for a free kick!' And this also had its roots in 1945:

---

31 It's a frequently told tale. Tommy Lawton thanks his old sports master at Tonge Moor Council School, Bolton, Mr 'Bunny' Lee, for making him wear a canvas shoe on his stronger right foot.

Ford blamed stipulations laid down by the touring Russians not to 'bump' any of their players for present day refs being soft on goalkeepers – Moscow Dynamo duly ran out 10–1 winners at Ninian Park, but Ford was having none of it: 'If Cardiff had played their normal league game,' he railed, 'they most certainly would not have lost by this margin.'[32]

All of this was taking place three years before Peter McParland's infamous shoulder charge on Manchester United keeper Ray Wood in the 1957 FA Cup final left Wood dazed and staggering around on the touchline[33], Villa with the Cup, and Busby's Babes without a league and Cup double. A year later, many of the Man Utd squad had died in the Munich air crash, and back at Wembley a United keeper was again involved in a controversial incident: Harry Gregg this time, being bundled into the net by Bolton's Nat Lofthouse. There's a frame-by-frame spread in the *Big Book of Football Champions* for that year. Nine-year-old future *Racing Post* writer and author Sean Magee can recall, like it was yesterday, tracing over a hand-tinted illustration of Gregg diving: 'Harry Gregg was my great hero – Doncaster Rovers, Ireland, Manchester United . . . what a man. I read somewhere (possibly in here[34]) that he carried on playing, but after the game he was sick in the dressing room.'

Munich led young Sean to become a Man United fan, but his first game was Arsenal v Burnley in 1958, a night match at Highbury: 'All lit up, to a nine-year-old, it was magical.' He also attended a schoolboy international at Wembley. At half-time out came the police dogs ' . . . called things like "Ripper". They'd rush out and run along a bar and we'd all cheer . . . today you'd get someone doing keepy-uppys.' Part and parcel of being a fan back then was the dead certainty that under the Christmas tree would be a neatly wrapped annual. For Sean it was the *Big Book of Football Champions*: 'My grandmother – Nana – bought it every year. Cousin

John in Shenfield had one too. It was inevitable I would get it: she knew I liked it. It was part of the fun . . . without sounding too prim, you were used to waiting for things back then, nowadays you just go on Amazon and buy it. You grew out of it quite quickly, though. I was very upset when it stopped, and was replaced by a packet of Senior Service or something, very disappointed . . . I was crushed . . . I got all my information from it – along with *Charles Buchan's* monthly magazine too.' He stresses how little information there was available back then. Today, 'bland headlines are everywhere: "I DON'T WANT TO GO ANYWHERE," SAYS ROONEY.' Back in the fifties the only live football was the FA Cup final, though Sean feels sure he remembers watching the 1958 semi-final replay on next door's television – Man United overcame Fulham 5–3 on a foggy Wednesday afternoon at Highbury. Given the scarcity of televised footage, and the fact that most annuals seemed to be aimed at schoolboys but written in a way so as not to patronise an older audience, I wonder if his dad ever disappeared with the *Big Book of Football Champions* to the outside loo or shed: 'Cockfosters in the sixties! By heck, don't make assumptions . . . we didn't have a telly never mind a shed – no, he used to watch rugby in a decrepit old stand at Saracens where a lady of a certain age used to bellow from the back of the stand, "Come on you Saris . . . "'

With its slightly surreal colouring of rough, hand-drawn copies of photographs, Magee considered *the Big Book of Football Champions* more downmarket than *Buchan's Soccer Gift Book*.

Johnny Green, author, ex-road manager of the Clash and Gillingham fan, also 'expected' to be handed a number of football annuals every Christmas morning. He also found the colour illustrations somewhat on the crude side. Flipping through an old annual he can recall instantly his teenage reaction: 'John Charles, *ugh!* He don't look like that – I've met him!'

Both Johnny Green's parents were teachers, originally from Irlham, a suburb of Salford, so the family

---

32 George Young, captain of Rangers, and no shrinking violet himself, took completely the opposite view in *Buchan's Soccer Gift Book*: Rangers were taken apart by 'the fabulous' Moscow Dynamos, and there had been 'some folk who suggested we might "get stuck in"'. What they did not appreciate was that the Russians did not hold the ball long enough for us to tackle them. It was tip-and-run soccer – played exceedingly well.'

33 McParland later revealed in the 1959–60 *Topical Times* annual that he'd received death threats.

34 *The Big Book of Football Champions*

'There is too much of a namby pamby attitude on the part of soccer administrators today'

Left: Alf Ramsey reveals his penalty technique in *Billy Wright's Football Album* 1954

Bobby Charlton, Manchester United, and Colin Bell, Manchester City

made the long journey north from Kent for most school holidays in the late fifties and early sixties: 'I saw Denis Law play one of his first matches for Manchester City after they'd signed him from Huddersfield Town, and he was a strippling of a kid [but] he seemed to cover every blade of grass.' His dad took him to Maine Road, but also 'to his great chagrin' (as a City fan) had taken his son to see the Busby Babes at Christmas 1957. The team in red flashed alive.

It was something John hadn't seen before: 'They passed the ball – even as a kid I could tell that. Teams like Newcastle and Wolves seemed old school, and probably still had toe-caps on their boots. Some players seemed to exude old-fashioned man-liness. Some blokes were like a throwback to my father's war-time colleagues, because, of course, that was still very fresh – you're talking only ten years after the war – whereas I was admiring the more youth-like men – well, they were men, but they didn't seem like it to me. Those big old players were still around, but somehow they were over there somewhere. Maurice Norman, Tottenham centre-half, a classic player from any era. Sure, I got his autograph, but he didn't interest me very much, you know, he was making up the numbers.'

Frantic Saturday mornings autograph-hunting, a subscription to *Charles Buchan's Football Monthly*, exposure to football in London, Manchester and at the Priestfield at an early age, and, of course, an immaculate collection of *Buchan's Soccer Gift Books* . . . all formed a heady brew for young Johnny.

'My annuals were all autographed – worth a fortune. I was an autograph-hunter. I got into that by hanging out by the players' entrance at Gillingham. It was very easily accessible. Aldershot, say, would park up; we would get there at twenty-to-two. I didn't have to worry about Gillingham – we'd got them on the training ground. We knew the players from *Charles Buchan's Football Monthly* and from newspapers.'

I express surprise that not only were Aldershot players featured frequently enough in the *Soccer Gift Book* for the mob of schoolboys to recognise the men from the Recreation Ground as they got off the bus – but also that Green and his mates would cut up the annuals.

'Nah, we cut the photographs from the monthlies. I kept great big hardback albums with each team on its page . . . not action pictures so much, more the portraits,

'My annuals were all autographed – worth a fortune'

or mug-shots, which were easily identifiable. I'd then hand it to the players getting off the bus, and hope they would pick themselves.'

Soon the gang got wind of bigger catches in London. With a bit of light Sellotaping and handy work with scissors 'you'd transfer your pictures into a portable scrapbook, take your Chelsea and Burnley pages, and join the milling crowds by the players' entrance at Stamford Bridge. A much bigger scale, a bit of security, but talking to the London kids you quickly realised there was life beyond the football stadium.' John puts it down to an early stirring of the 'fledgling road manager' within, but before long he was charting a whole radius around London, with one team arriving by train at Paddington, another being met by coach from Euston, a third departing St Pancras for the Midlands. 'London teams going to the Midlands, teams coming into London – you were running around like a manic. You'd work out the logistics, "OK, I can get Tottenham, they're playing at Wolverhampton, they're on the 11.10 to Snow Hill." You'd buy a platform ticket, a train would come in, there'd be a little sticker saying RESERVED FOR WEST BROMWICH ALBION FOOTBALL CLUB in the window. The players would be in relaxed mode on a Saturday morning. And there was a reservations room – you could go in there [beforehand] and they were very nice to you, they would show you the reservations list, and you'd be, "Ah, look, Birmingham City are coming in on the 12.30 . . . but, hang on, I'm round the corner from Russell Square: Manchester United are staying there, they're playing at Chelsea."

Northern teams would stay in a hotel. Once they'd had breakfast they'd be sent to train, which meant walking round Russell Square in blazers and flannels . . . and I'd be there. You'd know which hotel teams would be at.' And standing by the hedge in Russell Square would be Johnny with his satchel, containing that year's *Soccer Gift Book* ready for the '*crème de la crème*. You'd fill these up quite quickly then go back and resurrect old annuals [from previous years]. I always had with me the current year's *Charles Buchan*. *Topical Times* was a lesser book; *Buchan* seemed to have more gravitas, which was a strange thing for a thirteen-year-old kid to think. But *Topical Times* was a bit more red-top; *Buchan* more authentic. Nice pictures, a lot of sky, not touched-up.'

I wonder if he ever worried that he was defacing

Left: The highly coveted autographs of Colin Bell and Bobby Charlton, as inscribed on the *Football Champions* annual 1968

his *Soccer Gift Books* with players' signatures, especially as protocol seemed to dictate 'best wishes, Bobby Tambling' be scrawled smack 'over the face not to the side'. Wouldn't an autograph book have sufficed?

'I'd've regarded that as, er, amateur . . . "Ah, that's little Jimmy, with his autograph book . . . that's not real . . . ", he adds, disdainfully. 'If somebody really meant something to you personally that would be signed, "To John, best wishes, Denis Law." That's the apex of it all. *Charles Buchan* was great because of the large portraits. I knew that year's annual inside out, better than any school textbook . . . I could tell you where every pic was back in the day. That was the beauty of the book. It was very concise, it bestowed a sense of authority.'

Charles Buchan also had his eye on the likes of Johnny. Earlier in the 1950s the *Soccer Gift Book* had delved into the sweatily obsessive world of programme collecting (see page 130–131), but a feature in the '62–63 annual sought to explore a whole new area of obsessive fan behaviour. Dedicated autograph hunter Graham Ireland wrote about the 'thrill of the chase' and the studied art behind collecting 12,000 player autographs in six years. On one occasion he hung around the snooker room of Lancaster Gate, the FA's headquarters, 'hunting Manchester United autographs', and Duncan Edwards, Tommy Taylor and Roger Byrne happened to stroll by. Assuming he was staying there, the Busby Babes asked him 'to make up a foursome. Of course, I jumped at the chance. And afterwards had no trouble in getting them to sign.'[35] Then there was the time, after some quick thinking, that he managed to intercept the great Real Madrid side of Gento and Di Stéfano, stuck at fogbound London Airport waiting for a connection north to Manchester. And on the occasion of Yugoslavia's visit to London for a 1956 friendly the indefatigable Ireland somehow talked his way into the corridor behind the tunnel at Wembley, just by the visitors' dressing room. Again, we're not sure how he made it into the inner sanctum, but once there, 'I got into their dressing room and made for Boskov, the left-half, the only one still under the shower. Without

> '**Charles Buchan was great because of the large portraits. I could tell you where every pic was back in the day**'

thinking, he suddenly turned on the spray and I was soaked. The Yugoslavian players roared with laughter, then felt so sorry for me that they signed to a man.' Those were the days: you could just wander in, share a shower with international footballers, and no one would think to call security.

On yet another caper our man managed to attach himself to the touring Spanish national squad staying at the Park Lane Hotel. One evening the players piled out of the hotel into taxis for a night out at the cinema. Ireland quickly hailed a cab, jumped in and followed, making it out just in time to intercept Arieta I, the centre-forward, as he was being ushered into the cinema, and who 'still had my book [in his hand] as he went in . . . so I followed. Obviously it was thought that I was with the Spanish party. [Obviously!] I was given a seat beside Arieta, saw a first-class show and during the interval I went round and bagged the whole party.' In November 1953 he cornered the Hungarians Bozsik, Lorant and Kocsis in a lift in their hotel, but Puskás proved more elusive. Photographers and interviewers pursued him everywhere. But it would take more than a nascent media scrum to thwart an autograph-hunter of Ireland's pedigree. No doubt dodging traffic and hiding behind lampposts, he 'stayed on [Puskás'] heels and eventually landed him in a Hungarian hotel on Edgware Road. He signed.'

'Gold dust – that's class,' says Johnny Green, when I recount the adventures of Graham Ireland. 'The language of it . . . "I've got Ron Springett; I've got Jimmy Armfield, he was easy, a pushover" – you talked in those terms, who was easy who was hard. People would swap these stories: "I've got Bryan Douglas of Blackburn Rovers" . . . "He's easy, he'll sign 'em till the cows come home, but Jimmy Greaves . . . "

'Jimmy Greaves was a very hard player. I once walked down the platform with him at Paddington, and he had one of those brown, foam-backed Italian raincoats draped over his jacket, so the sleeves were empty. Dave Mackay was there alongside him, and he had a portable radio, and I thought, "That's wonderful," it really looked state of the art, and I remember the song that was playing – it was 'Eso Beso' [bursts into song], "*Ooh, that kiss, da da-dada-dah-da*," a Latin number that was big in the charts, and he was dancing like this [demonstrates a kind of bossa-nova

---

35 It's not clear how Mr Ireland got in there in the first place. (Nor how he fared on the baize.)

Right: Sam Bartram shows off his wonderfully white teeth in *Charles Buchan's Soccer Gift Book 1956–57*

SAM BARTRAM
Charlton Athletic
and York City

Graham Ireland (left) corners Di Stefano (centre) who obliges with his signature (see bottom of page 99).

shuffle] and signing everybody's autographs . . . Dave Mackay, man o' the people.' Young Johnny spotted his moment and sidled up to Greaves. 'I went, "Mr Greaves, can you sign this please?" and he went, 'I can't, son, I've got me arms in this jacket. I've got this coat on, son, I can't,' and he seemed to enjoy that – he was hard. But if he did sign one, then you'd flick through quick, coz you knew there was another one a page away, and you'd say, "Oh, and can you do . . . " and he'd look you in the face and say, 'I've just signed for you, son. One. That's enough.' You really relished Greaves because he was a hard man to get.

'I've had my run-ins with Bobby Charlton too – a very grumpy, gloomy man. Outside the Russell Hotel: the last chance, waiting around while they had their steak and salad inside. The hotel was off limits[36], we

> ## 'I've had my run-ins with Bobby Charlton too – a very grumpy, gloomy man'

didn't want to make a fuss, we were very polite – always "mister". The team came out in dribs and drabs, and the bags were loaded on to the bus by the trainers – and the entourage was small, by contemporary standards.' John spotted Denis Law, by now 'my hero. I walked alongside him, and he turned to me and he said, "Are you going to a match this afternoon?" And I said, "Yeah, I am, I'm coming to see you, Denis." And I think I called him Denis – as a sign of, you know, our eternal friendship [laughs] – and he said, "Look, do you want a lift, son?" You could have knocked me over with a feather. I got on the Manchester United team bus, and I sat next to him, and I was stuck for a word (which is a rarity), and I sat as the players filed in, and nobody really commented, a little card school set up. Then Bobby Charlton came on, late, and as he was walking down the aisle – it was just a charabanc, not like these big fuck-you tour buses with smoked glass that you get now; just a little coach with a plaque in the

---

36 John is equally perplexed as to how Graham Ireland got into the lobby at Lancaster Gate and the away dressing room at Wembley.

Above: Autograph hunter Graham Ireland reveals his signature-chasing skills in *Charles Buchan's Soccer Gift Book 1962–63*

window: MANCHESTER UNITED FC – he said, "What's the kid doing here? Get him off the fucking bus." And he swore. And Denis Law looked up from his seated position, where Charlton was looming over us, and said, "He's with me." It was quite confrontational and quite emphatic, and Charlton sat down: "Fuck's sake." I didn't speak to Denis Law, I just sat and glowed, really. We got to the gates at Stamford Bridge, and Denis Law said, "Hang on," and he got up and went to the front of the coach, to where the officials were, and came back and handed me a ticket: "Here you go, son, enjoy the game."

'I was aware, at an early age, of the disparity of the media presentation of sportsmen, and my reality as a kid, having to deal with 'em from a lowly footing.'

I f Gillingham were at home, John would be comparing notes with a couple of mates while speeding – rattling – back on the 2 p.m. train from Victoria (just in time for 3 o'clock kick-off, no Gills autographs to worry about). If travelling alone he'd flick through his *Soccer Gift Book* for the umpteenth time. '*Charles Buchan* was pretty serious stuff; well, the writing wasn't hard and it didn't challenge me, but the biographical stuff made me feel I was meeting people like Ron Flowers – I felt I knew him, but of course I didn't. Some of the writing was bland, because these were summaries, really. I was reading newspapers and football magazines all the time, so I'd already lived through that season. I knew it all: who was playing well, who'd done what, what was happening on the transfer market . . . So a little potted biography, or an article about someone's pet hobby of photography – I liked that – but I ain't goin' to read 'em very often. It wasn't the same as bread-and-butter, hard-arsed fact and reporting that I was up on through the football season. [The annuals were] a little bit of a sideshow, really, and quite a pleasant one at that . . . so therefore the only lasting power of the annuals are the photographs, not the articles – they're the mortar – the bricks of it are the photographs.'

By the simple dint of freeing up a full page, either a close-up portrait or a detailed action shot, the photography in the *Soccer Gift Book* does seem more impressive, less tampered with – strangely, closer to the action – than many of its rivals. The captions are minimal and seven-point in size, and run unobtrusively in the bottom corner. Spend any length of time contemplating the milky expanse of white sky and the brick chimneys behind Ron Davies' (of Norwich City) head; or the empty seats and white painted walls of the Filbert Street

JIMMY GREAVES
(Spurs and England)

Johnny Green did get Jimmy Greaves (pictured in *Charles Buchan's Soccer Gift Book* 1963–64) to sign autographs in the end. 'I once saw there was charity golf match on in Essex one Sunday. I caught the train into London and out of Liverpool Street, and I walked several miles to this golf course. I got his autograph eighteen – count 'em – times, which was unheard of. I got 'em all done. I was hoping for the moon and I got it. He was in a very relaxed mood, drinking at the bar, and I just shuffled in there. He was, "How far you come, son?" He was really chatty, and signing all my pictures. I had 'em all there, all my scrapbooks and *Charles Buchan* books.

Nobody – fellow autograph hunters – believed me. Nobody had heard of Jimmy Greaves signing eighteen autographs. But I went out there just to nobble him, because he was difficult. The ones everyone wanted – and it had nothing to do with their fame as footballers, more to do with their irascibility – were people like Willie Cunningham of Preston North End and Scotland, a left-back who worked in a sports shop in Preston.'

Johnny stayed at a friend's in Preston and caught the bus to the sports shop, where Cunningham 'did indeed prove to be a thoroughly curmudgeonly man, who did give us the autograph then shooed us out of the shop . . .' (They also took the opportunity to drop in at Tom Finney's plumbing shop, and the Preston winger signed the famous picture in the spray at Stamford Bridge, reproduced in the 1957–58 *Soccer Gift Book*. 'He didn't look like a plumber, I have to say. He had a suit on. I suppose he was running it.')

. . . long time passing! Centre-forward, Ernie Pythian, in the temporary role of goalkeeper (for Wrexham, against Altrincham), keeping a lonely watch.

PROBABLY WHOOPING IT UP LIKE THIS CHAP!

He is celebrating Oxford United's Cup victory over Blackburn Rovers

Soccer Gift Book was a gallery, a catalogue, a visual compendium rolled into one

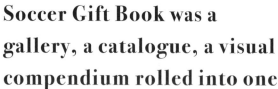

stand in front of which Bill McDerment is crouching . . . then flip open a *Topical Times* of the same mid-sixties vintage and the contrast is striking. It's like William Burroughs, Brion Gysin or the news editor of the *Daily Express* have seized control: why have a simple mass of cloudless sky, or a sea of faces high up in a triple-decker stand, when you can run the headline MEN OF ACTION in lurid red across it? In fact, why have any natural photographic background at all when you can just cut round the heads of a bunch of Glasgow Rangers players and stick them on a lurid yellow block of colour?

That said, in the fifties, the *Soccer Gift Book* had struggled with hand-tinting and colour reproduction as much as the best of them – witness the peculiar complexion of Hibernian's Lawrie Reilly arranging his

plastic flags on a coffee table (but nevertheless sporting a fine green-tie and beige-shirt combination, pigments of which haven't been seen since the heyday of the Lee Target knitting pattern).

In terms of composition, for the *Buchan* annual photographs it's definitely a case of less is more; in terms of the quantity of snapshots, head-shots and posed portraits, the *Soccer Gift Book* didn't hold back. It was a gallery, a catalogue, a visual compendium rolled into one. By the time young Johnny Green would have been thrusting his Coventry City page at Arthur Lightening on the platform at Euston, hoping the goalkeeper could find himself in amongst the numerous mug-shots and whirl of excited schoolboys, there were pages and pages of MEET THE PLAYERS photographs in the *Gift Book* – forerunners, in essence, of the football cards and sticker annuals to come. The photography was clear and largely unadorned, especially in black and white: Bill Griffin of Sheffield Wednesday had a terrific quiff; Jantzen Derrick of Bristol City had a future in Ingmar Bergman films; Bobby Craig, also of Wednesday, looks like Brad Dourief's Billy Bibbit after the wires have been removed; Derek Lampe of Fulham is London old-school; Brian Sawyer appears

Previous pages: Minimalist monochrome photography, thoughtful juxtaposition of imagery and somewhat cheesy captions. The *Charles Buchan's Soccer Gift Book* trademark, 1964–65

Above: Lawrie Reilly of Hibs and Roy Vernon of Everton, just two of the eclectic full-page colour portraits that adorned *Charles Buchan's Soccer Gift Book* in 1956–57, and 1963–64, respectively

too friendly and approachable to be playing centre-forward for Rotherham United (although at that point the Millers were hovering mid-table in the second division rather than scrapping in the basement).

Still, even in the *Soccer Gift Books* of the early-to-mid-sixties, there was something queasy about the colour tinting. John White's teeth were extremely white; Peter Dobing of Manchester City had eyes to match his kit – bluer than the pools swum through by Burt Lancaster in *The Swimmer*, and there was something very wrong with Newcastle's John McGrath, Coventry's Mick Kearns and Wolves' Dave Woodfield – a peculiar, psychopathic light shining through their eyes in shades of amber, green and ice-blue respectively. Everton's Roy Vernon probably didn't look like that in real life either.

Platform tickets for ha'penny, relaxed footballers dancing to transistor radios while signing autographs for kids . . . the rays of the morning sun shining through the glass roof at St Pancras or Paddington . . . chips for lunch, or a sandwich and lemonade; kick-off still a few hours away – what could be more idyllic? Sadly, it didn't last. Even during Johnny Green's brief stint scampering between London railway termini a kind of mafia protection racket developed: 'It was an early introduction to metropolitan crime,' recalls John. 'These older youths – early twenties, or late teens – they used to suddenly arrive and ask for "subs", and you had to pay them. They would chat affably to you – "Yeah, who have you got?" Have you got this boy? Have you got that boy? "Ah, Jimmy Greaves: *'ave you!*" – and they'd steal your book.'

It wasn't any old handmade scrapbook that the racketeers were after, of course: 'What they wanted was the *Charles Buchan Soccer Gift Book* – high currency – especially if you'd got the really top-notch names [signatures] in that. So you were caught in a sort of cleft stick,' remembers John. 'You wanted to take your book with you, but if you got it out and they saw it was a good 'un, they'd walk off with it. And there was nothing you could do – these were big kids. Often if you saw them coming you'd run – even if you were in a good vantage point to cop a good team, you'd leg it. You'd always be looking around, there was a strong element of paranoia: protect your books. If you'd paid your couple of bob, of course . . . they wouldn't nick your book for that.'

It hardly needs stating, but Charlie Buchan himself would have been appalled.

Leeds United and England men – *(left)* NORMAN HUNTER and JACKIE CHARLTON

Partners in a teenage beat club near Edinburgh are – COLIN GRANT, Hibs *(left)* and DENNIS SETTERINGTON, Rangers

The *Topical Times* may have been more tabloid in photographic style but as late as 1967–68 there is still plenty of fantastic photography. A colour spread of Norman Hunter and Jack Charlton, looking way too agreeable; across the page 'partners in a teenage beat club near Edinburgh', Rangers' Dennis Setterington and Hibs' Colin Grant, are both playing red electric guitars in an edgy-looking basement where someone has daubed 'The Beau Brummels' on the wall. Grant is wearing a slightly louche fur coat.

Right from the get-go, Buchan was very concerned with presiding over his boys' club – a coven of schoolboys across the world, numbering into the many thousands, many having discarded their silver *Eagle* badges, trotting to the newsagent's every month for the magazine; fishing the A4-shaped wrapping paper from under the tree every Christmas morning – and took a slightly paternalistic view towards his readers: 'Yes, this old game of ours certainly does form a wonderful fellowship!' wrote Buchan in his opening editorial of 1953. A year later he too was quoting Sir Walter Scott, 'Then strip, lads, and to it, though sharp be weather . . . life is itself but a game at football,' and infused his own standfirsts with such conquering spirit:

> Soccercraft is the heritage of every British boy. Like the ever-burning torch of Marathon each generation flings it to the host behind with the shout, "Go to it, lads!" With the undying love born of a glorious birthright, the Old Masters of the greatest game in the world pass on the trust. It is YOUR privilege to honour their faith.

Privilege is a word that crops up often in the early days of the *Soccer Gift Book*; sound principles of learning were grasped through listening to your elders and getting out there on the football field. Suffer setbacks and defeat with dignity; practise constantly; and don't throw your toys out of the pram when you're dropped. You will be dropped. What followed were pages and pages on where a wing-forward should stand (five in a line with the wingers 'level with their comrades'), where the centre-forward should be ('in the goalmouth when the attack is being pressed home. He should not be out on the wing at crucial moments'), how full-backs could work well in tandem with their half-backs, how to achieve good balance and control when crossing, etc, etc. It was pretty rudimentary stuff, and all geared towards a rigid 2–3–5 formation, though progressive-minded players like Danny Blanchflower were often cited as role models.

Where in the *Big Book of Football Champions* Billy Wright's ability to sweep out the changing rooms was noted, the same 1960 annual couldn't further resist recounting the time a Swedish XI gained the upper hand in cunning over the hapless Wright. Once the England captain had won the toss, ahead of a 1949 international at the Solna Stadium, just north of Stockholm, the home team told Wright to kick into the sun in the first half 'because it would be much worse in the second half'. Ted Ditchburn, blinded by the sunshine, duly conceded three first-half goals. Then, strangely, once the teams 'came out after the interval the sun had disappeared behind the terraces' and England lost 3–1[37].

Over in the *Soccer Gift Book*, meanwhile, there was certainly no talk of tears back in Ironbridge, Buchan merely referring to Wright's 'faltering steps at Molineux'; and the lasting image of the England captain as captured by Buchan is of the softly spoken – a quiet word of encouragement and a pat on the back rather than any histrionics – distinguished gent abroad: 'In Rio de Janeiro during the World Cup, I saw Billy Wright, the recalcitrant mop of hair carefully brushed, carry a bunch of red roses into the most palatial Embassy in the world, on his way to have tea with the British Ambassador and

---

37 There had been previous at that stadium. AIK of Stockholm played Charlton just after the war at the Solna. With just 20 minutes left, Charlton, who were prone to featuring in high-scoring games, were 1–7 up and, recounted the *Big Book of Football Champions*, Sam Bartram 'the flame-haired goalkeeper was yawning with boredom. Bert Turner and George Robinson had so little to do they started arguing between themselves and the Swedes took advantage to score a goal.' Then another . . . and another. 'It was like putting a match to hayrick in a dry August.' AIK got it back to 6–7 and, with seconds to go, equalised. 'If it had gone on for a minute or two longer,' said Bartram, ' we would have lost. The game was completely out of our control.'

Charles Buchan teaching boys the art of heading in one of the F.A.'s first instructional classes in 1933.

★ by **JOHN MACADAM**

Reflecting on the old days JOHN MACADAM, Britain's most popular sports columnist, tells you why

Boys then could really control a ball

THERE has been much talk to the effect that what is wrong with football today in Great Britain is the lack of facilities for youngsters to play the game.

There is talk of traffic and congested streets and rows of parked cars and constables with an undue regard for such valuable properties as windows and windscreens.

What a lot of nonsense it all is! What is wrong with football today is that there are not too few facilities—but too many.

When I was a boy, and that is around the time that Alex James was a boy and Hughie Gallacher was a boy, and David Jack and Charles Buchan and Jimmy Seed were little more than young men to whom we could look slightly up, there were no facilities.

You didn't have radio and television and enough pocket-money for cinemas twice a week.

What you did have was the freedom of the streets and you had a way with waste paper that produced in some tortuous fashion a paper ball.

This ball, properly wound and tied with string, would perform in an erratic way pretty well as an ordinary sixpenny rubber ball would, and it would last for at least an evening's street football.

It was the erratic performance that counted, for not only had the player to make the ball do the work after his agile feet had done with it, he had to use the kerb and, maybe the wall (in the absence of five or six of the eleven, this was important) and any passing stranger to get the return pass.

He had to kick it correctly when he had it in position for kicking, or he would have kicked up a heap of dirt or loose stones in the street.

He had to kick it not only correctly, but also hard because it had some of the lightsome quality of a shuttlecock.

He had to be able to use it or, by golly, he was out of a game!

And there is no shame to equal the shame of a kid turning up on the street and being ignored when there's a game in progress.

If you aren't automatically co-opted, then you aren't

36

Some of these kids have football boots, others ordinary shoes, others merely have slippers. But they all have one thing in common—eagerness to get the ball.

any good and you may as well go away and talk to the girls.

I know that James and Gallacher learned all their footwork and all their trickery with the ball this way.

They were boys in the same pit at the same time that Alex Jackson was a boy in the Vale of Leven (and you will excuse my references to these great Scottish players rather than English ones or Welsh ones; it is merely because I was a Scots boy of the same period and was going through the same things).

I have written about this before now, but I feel that it is worth repeating the thought: It was the great era of the paper ba' and I often have the feeling that it is a great pity that some physical thing could not happen to the world that would sweep away all the radio and television and cinema and general mechanisation and bring it back to us again.

Then, and only then, would we find the footballers—the natural ball-players of my youth.

With very few exceptions they cannot be manufactured, as they manufacture these so-called wonder teams from the Continent.

I read about these teams and I go to the ends of the earth to see them, and all that I feel, for all the mechanical brilliance of team-work and physical fitness and discipline they produce, is that they are Petrouchka and

WILF MANNION, former idol of Middlesbrough, joins in an alley kick-about with the local kids. *Picture Post Library*

37

'What is wrong with football today is that there are not too few facilities – but too many'

his wife.' In *Buchan* you're far more likely to read of solitary Union Jacks fluttering in the sunshine on a packed terrace in Arica than you are of Dave Mackay battling with his leg boils[38]. Tea and roses with the ambassador (and his wife), a world of Brylcreemed hair, wooden desks, that glorious 'little tin-pot Cup', Stanley Matthews entering a packed stadium like a gladiator, knowing your place, and perhaps not knowing a huge amount about football . . . it could be just be a reflection of the times,

38 According to *The Big Book of Football Champions* (1960) a fractured foot followed by a boil on his leg delayed Mackay becoming a regular for Spurs after his move from Hearts. Bill Spurdle of Man City also missed a Cup final 'owing to boils'.

but there was something a bit stilted and fluffy about the early days of the *Soccer Gift Book*.

'I think they pitched it pretty well perfectly for the public of the day,' says Patrick Collins, senior football writer for the *Mail* group of papers today. 'And the sales would seem to bear out that belief. Of course, newspapers did not attach any great importance to football in those days – certainly nothing like today's coverage – so both the *Monthly* and the *Gift Book* had a largely unopposed ride.'

As it moved through the fifties and sixties, though, there was a wonderful yearning for the golden age of football's past. Much of this sprang forth from the typewriter keys of Buchan's best writers: John Macadam, John Thompson and Peter Morris.

Simon Inglis, in his introduction to *The Best of Charles Buchan's Football Monthly*, describes John Macadam as 'a diminutive, feisty Scottish bachelor [who'd] always dreamt of becoming a great dramatist, but was happy in the end to help pay his bar bills by freelancing for Buchan'. In a fine rant entitled BOYS THEN COULD REALLY CONTROL A BALL Macadam, in the '56–57 *Soccer Gift Book*, dismissed talk of busy streets, traffic

Left: The man himself passes on his footballing skills, in the first edition of _Charles Buchan's Soccer Gift Book_ 1953–54

Above: John Macadam waxes lyrical, if somewhat tetchily, about what makes a good footballer in _Charles Buchan's Soccer Gift Book_ 1957–58

and parked cars, people moaning about broken windows and endlessly whining on about the lack of facilities and space for youngsters to play football properly: 'What a lot of nonsense it all is! What is wrong with football today is that there are not too few facilities – but too many. When I was a boy, and that is around the time Alex James was a boy and Hughie Gallagher was a boy . . . there were *no* facilities. You didn't have radio and television and enough pocket money for cinemas twice a week.' Football was all about controlling a 'paper ba' wound tightly with string; playing the 'ba' off the kerbstone developed you into a proper, natural ball player. 'I read about these teams and I go to the ends of the earth to see them,' sighs Macadam, referring to the big names of the mid-fifties, 'and all that I feel, for all the mechanical brilliance of team-work and physical fitness and discipline they produce, is that they are Petrouchka and Petrouchka and Petrouchka!'

As for today's youngsters: 'Oh! how I hate to see that little fellow, on a Saturday morning, go off by the tube or along a suburban street with a brown parcel under his arm. I know what it means. It means that he has his

by **JOHN MACADAM**

Britain's most popular sports columnist

You notice how they walk and run; you observe the tilt of their heads and the poise of their bodies; and you know that these are not ordinary mortals

The quality of a STAR

'Behind the outsized moustache Macadam had the "melancholy of a man looking for something he could not hope to find"'

strip – given him by his school – and his boots and he is going to take part in a form match and he is going to wear regulation colours and shorts and stockings (for which his fond parents have paid!) and he is going to be told things about team-spirit by some earnest young English teacher . . . **Oh dear! How much better he would be without all that clobber just running wild around the streets near his home!**[39] I see them as I move around, playing indifferent football on indifferent pitches and with indifferent instruction. I see them almost every Saturday morning in one place or another. But nowadays I never see them in the streets . . . let us please stop pampering these children with marked-out grounds and goalposts that aren't a heap of coats . . .'

The conciliatory tone of the picture captions was no doubt a belated in-house attempt to soften Macadam's invective . . . (see previous page).

In the 1962–63 *Gift Book* Macadam wistfully re-imagined Grimsby trawler men sailing up the Thames for the 1939 FA Cup final. Alas, it didn't happen, as Wolves had thrashed them 5–0 in the semi-final, but that trifling detail wasn't enough to stop Macadam [by now living on a Chelsea houseboat 'with bohemian friends'[40]] using Grimsby's recent promotion from the third division as an excuse to reminisce at length on the days when hospitality for the gentlemen of the press was a given. Especially at Grimsby, flying high in the first division in the thirties, where someone from the club would always greet thirsty press men straight from the train, and someone else would put you up for the night: ' . . . the social side of the game; Grimsby had it *in excelsis* . . . And when you did eventually return to London, you would be pursued by a box labelled "Assorted Rounds" which would turn out to be a collection of the most delectable fish from the North Sea.' On one occasion Macadam got off the train to be met by none other than the Grimsby manager himself: ' . . . dear old Frank Womack . . . we had a few drinks together and then he excused himself for he had to get to the ground to make sure that all was well for the match in the afternoon.' Frank tells Macadam to head down to the fish-quay for some lunch (presumably for some solids; fortification to allow him a sporting chance of filing a coherent match report) and where he'll be able to find the chairman and have a word.

Arriving at the quay, our man 'was faced with a

---

39 Macadam's rage is such he types in bold for emphasis.

40 Norman Giller in a column on the Sports Journalists' Association website is very entertaining on Macadam.

Above: 'Britain's most popular sports columnist' in rueful mode in *Charles Buchan's Soccer Gift Book 1957–58*

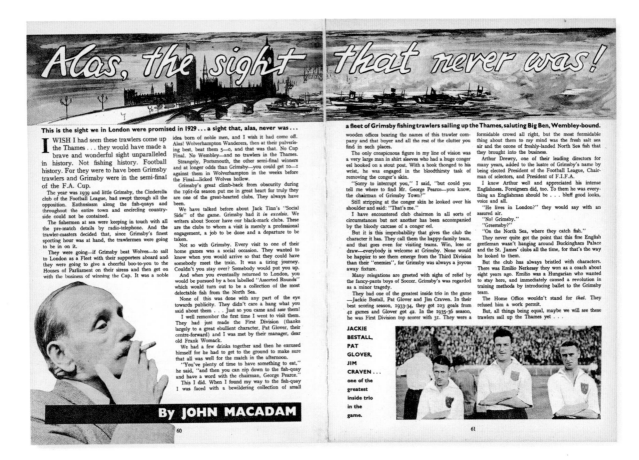

Alas, the sight that never was!

This is the sight we in London were promised in 1929 . . . a sight that, alas, never was . . .

a fleet of Grimsby fishing trawlers sailing up the Thames, saluting Big Ben, Wembley-bound.

I WISH I had seen these trawlers come up the Thames . . . they would have made a brave and wonderful sight unparalleled in history. Not fishing history. Football history. For they were to have been Grimsby trawlers and Grimsby were in the semi-final of the F.A. Cup.

The year was 1939 and little Grimsby, the Cinderella club of the Football League, had swept through all the opposition. Enthusiasm along the fish-quays and throughout the entire town and encircling country-side could not be contained.

The fishermen at sea were keeping in touch with all the pre-match details by radio-telephone. And the trawler-masters decided that, since Grimsby's finest sporting hour was at hand, the trawlermen were going to be in on it.

They were going—if Grimsby beat Wolves—to sail to London as a Fleet with their supporters aboard and they were going to give a cheerful boo-to-you to the Houses of Parliament on their sirens and then get on with the business of winning the Cup. It was a noble idea born of noble men. And I wish it had come off. Alas! Wolverhampton Wanderers, then at their pulverising best, beat them 5—0, and that was that. No Cup Final. No Wembley—and no trawlers in the Thames.

Strangely, Portsmouth, the other semi-final winners and at longer odds than Grimsby—you could get 10—1 against them in Wolverhampton in the weeks before the Final—licked Wolves hollow.

Grimsby's great climb-back from obscurity during the 1961-62 season put me in great heart for truly they are one of the great-hearted clubs. They always have been.

We have talked before about Jack Tinn's "Social Side" of the game. Grimsby had it *in excelsis*. We writers about Soccer have our black-mark clubs. These are the clubs to whom a visit is merely a professional engagement, a job to be done and a departure to be taken.

Not so with Grimsby. Every visit to one of their home games was a social occasion. They wanted to know when you would arrive so that they could have somebody meet the train. It was a tiring journey. Couldn't you stay over? Somebody would put you up.

And when you eventually returned to London, you would be pursued by a box labelled "Assorted Rounds" which would turn out to be a collection of the most delectable fish from the North Sea.

None of this was done with any part of the eye towards publicity. They didn't care a hang what you said about them . . . Just so you came and *saw* them!

I well remember the first time I went to visit them. They had just made the First Division (thanks largely to a great ebullient character, Pat Glover, their centre-forward) and I was met by their manager, dear old Frank Womack.

We had a few drinks together and then he excused himself for he had to get to the ground to make sure that all was well for the match in the afternoon.

"You've plenty of time to have something to eat," he said, "and then you can nip down to the fish-quay and have a word with the chairman, George Pearce."

This I did. When I found my way to the fish-quay I was faced with a bewildering collection of small wooden offices bearing the names of this trawler company and that buyer and all the rest of the clutter you find in such places.

The only conspicuous figure in my line of vision was a very large man in shirt sleeves who had a huge conger eel hooked on a stout post. With a hook thonged to his wrist, he was engaged in the bloodthirsty task of removing the conger's skin.

"Sorry to interrupt you," I said, "but could you tell me where to find Mr. George Pearce—you know, the chairman of Grimsby Town?"

Still stripping at the conger skin he looked over his shoulder and said: "That's me."

I have encountered club chairmen in all sorts of circumstances but not another has been accompanied by the bloody carcase of a conger eel.

But it is this improbability that gives the club the character it has. They call them the happy-family team, and that goes even for visiting teams. Win, lose or draw—everybody is welcome at Grimsby. None would be happier to see them emerge from the Third Division than their "enemies", for Grimsby was always a joyous away fixture.

Many relegations are greeted with sighs of relief by the fancy-pants boys of Soccer. Grimsby's was regarded as a minor tragedy.

They had one of the greatest inside trio in the game —Jackie Bestall, Pat Glover and Jim Craven. In their best scoring season, 1933-34, they got 103 goals from 42 games and Glover got 42. In the 1935-36 season, he was First Division top scorer with 31. They were a formidable crowd all right, but the most formidable thing about them to my mind was the fresh salt sea air and the ozone of freshly-landed North Sea fish that they brought into the business.

Arthur Drewry, one of their leading directors for many years, added to the lustre of Grimsby's name by being elected President of the Football League, Chairman of selectors, and President of F.I.F.A.

I knew Arthur well and appreciated his intense Englishness. Foreigners did, too. To them he was everything an Englishman should be . . . bluff good looks, voice and all.

"He lives in London?" they would say with an assured air.

"No! Grimsby."

"Greemsby?"

"On the North Sea, where they catch fish."

They never quite got the point that this fine English gentleman wasn't hanging around Buckingham Palace and the St. James' clubs all the time, for that's the way he looked to them.

But the club has always bristled with characters. There was Emilio Nerkessy they won as a coach about eight years ago. Emilio was a Hungarian who wanted to stay here, and immediately caused a revolution in training methods by introducing ballet to the Grimsby team.

The Home Office wouldn't stand for *that*. They refused him a work permit.

But, all things being equal, maybe we will see these trawlers sail up the Thames yet . . .

JACKIE BESTALL, PAT GLOVER, JIM CRAVEN . . . one of the greatest inside trio in the game.

By JOHN MACADAM

60

61

---

bewildering collection of small wooden offices bearing the names of trawler companies and that buyer and the rest of all the clutter you find in such places. The only conspicuous figure in my line of vision was a very large man in shirtsleeves who had a huge conger eel hooked on a stout post. With a hook thronged to his wrist he was engaged in the bloodthirsty task of removing the conger's skin.

'"Sorry to interrupt you," I said, "but could you tell me where to find Mr George Pearce – you know, the chairman of Grimsby Town?"

'Still stripping at the conger's skin he looked over his shoulder and said, "That's me."'

Macadam goes on to recall the days when the fine club was full of characters: Emilio Berkessy, the Hungarian who somewhat controversially introduced ballet to training at Blundell Park ('the Home Office wouldn't stand for *that*. They refused him a work permit'); the free-scoring inside trio of Jackie Bestall, Pat Glover and Jim Craven; and the sad end of an era: 'Many relegations are greeted with sighs of relief by the fancy-pants boys of Soccer. Grimsby's was regarded as a minor tragedy.' Macadam wistfully signs off, 'But, all things being equal, maybe we will see those trawlers sail up the Thames yet.' Sadly it wasn't to be, and Macadam never appeared in the *Soccer Gift Book* again.

He left an autobiography, *The Macadam Road*, of a childhood in a tenement overlooking the Clyde, full of tales of scalding porridge, escape from the Greenock shipyards, a heavy drinking grandfather prone to getting his banjo out when a certain boat berthed in the morning (a 'reunion' being on the cards with his old seafaring friends), and various cads, *flâneurs*, old timers and encounters from the sports writing life.[41] Inglis quotes John Thompson, who took over from Buchan himself as editor, writing on the Scotsman's death in 1964, that 'behind the outsized moustache he had the "melancholy of a man looking for something he could

---

41 As clear from Grimsby, Macadam was strongly of the opinion that real life seeping through or surrounding a major sporting event was of equal if not greater importance than any 'expert' opinion. When in Chicago for a Dempsey–Tunney fight, Trevor Wignall of the *Daily Express*, the high-practitioner of this art form in Macadam's view, 'would come home with his pockets stuffed with stories about Al Capone and Spike O'Donnell'. It's fair to assume Macadam would have detested this world of Prozone and *Moneyball*.

Above: Macadam, cigarette in hand, signs off from *Charles Buchan's Soccer Gift Book* in 1962–63 with a bizarre tale of football fiction

AMONG OUR MEMORIES . . .

One of the countless thrills that Soccer brings to its millions of supporters is captured by this picture of a raid on the Burnley goal. It was launched, as so many attacks were, by Roy Swinbourne of the Wolves. The ball has curled out of the grasp of Colin McDonald, the Burnley goalkeeper.

Wembley Hoodoo!

8 out of 10 Cup Finals ruined by injury

PETER MORRIS recalls some tragic moments
at the world's
greatest stadium

not hope to find". His ukelele would be much missed on foreign trips.'

Patrick Collins was too young to really know Macadam, but remembers he had been a big name in his day: 'He was genuinely famous, in a pre-television fashion. "A bit of a bon viveur",' says Collins, in response to my description, 'would be a very diplomatic way of describing him. In the manner of so many Fleet Street men of his day, he enjoyed a drink. They do say that, at his peak, he was a wonderful writer. He was also genuinely eccentric.' Patrick recalls his dad telling the story of the pair returning from a match he thinks was in Switzerland, Macadam and Pat Collins Snr, later to become editor of the *Soccer Gift Book*, 'taking the train to Calais for the cross-Channel ferry. Macadam saw another train in the station and asked where it was heading. "Milan," he was told. "Never been there," he said. Whereupon he caught the train to Milan. Nobody heard a thing from him for ten days, when he turned up, with no explanation, at the office of the *Daily Herald*.

That was the kind of gesture which the big names could expect to get away with. I believe the drink got to him at the end, which was sad. But they say that when he was on a good day, he was very good indeed.'

Reading back through the lengthier pieces in the *Soccer Gift Book* today it would seem sub-editor and feature writer Peter Morris, described by Inglis as 'a dour Midlander', slipped effortlessly into Macadam's Hush Puppies. Morris was a bird of different plumage, though. 'He was the polar opposite of Macadam,' remembers Patrick Collins. 'Not an unpleasant man, but distinctly joyless. Pedantic, stern, careful (I believe he carried a purse). As I say, not unpleasant, but he was rarely the life and soul of any party.'

But like Macadam, Morris, too, always seemed to be drawn outside the box, or to be placing football in the wider context of daily life, beyond mere events on the pitch – albeit in less theatrical, more down-to-earth prose, fitting for a monochrome Britain of newly set, pre-stressed concrete bridges and kitchen-sink dramas.

Previous page: The number of colour pages in
***Charles Buchan's Soccer Gift Book* were limited but**
those that were there went for the full effect, as
with this action spread from the 1955–56 book

Above: Peter Morris strikes a more sombre
tone in the first post-Macadam edition of
***Charles Buchan's Soccer Gift Book*, 1963–64**

Lugubrious he may have been, but in his writing Morris combined warm, resigned understatement with a slightly mordant humour and plenty of glances back over the shoulder, as if longing for happier times. In the first *Soccer Gift Book* post-Macadam, under the heading WEMBLEY HOODOO! 8 OUT OF 10 FINALS RUINED BY INJURY, Morris works his way, over three dense pages, through 'some tragic moments at the world's greatest stadium'. Between 1952 and 1961 there were only two FA Cup finals that passed without a serious injury to a player, and Morris walks us through Wally Barnes' wrenched knee ligaments that signalled the end of his career; Man City right-back Jimmy Meadows succumbing to a similar career-ending knee injury; Manchester keepers Bert Trautmann and Ray Wood (a broken neck and concussion in 1956 and '57 respectively); Roy Dwight's broken leg for Forest in 1959; Dave Whelan's broken leg for Blackburn a year later; and another wrenched knee, that of Leicester's right-back Len Chalmers. After the rainforests devoted to the Stanley Matthews final of 1953 it's good to hear Morris point out, 'few thought of the 15th minute leg injury to [Bolton] left-half Eric Bell' that necessitated a crucial defensive reshuffle at a point in the match when the team in white were on top. Surprisingly, there's no call for substitutes, or for a return to skill and technique at the expense of brawn, but, to be fair to Morris, he's more concerned with how the injuries affected the outcomes of a decade's worth of finals (once Whelan departed, the fight went out of Blackburn; the lustre

Writing as good as Peter Morris's is the reason a generation of middle-aged men clean up in pub quizzes today

went out of Forest's performance after Dwight departed on a stretcher, etc). It could be down to the 'thick, luxurious turf', or players tense with nerves, he speculates.

'The Wembley curse,' says Johnny Green today, by way of making the point that 'these patterns would be flagged up by the books. You had that wider knowledge and context that the football magazines and annuals taught you. It's a cliché, but it's true: you saw the bigger picture.'

Throughout the sixties Morris identified several 'patterns'; he would write lengthy but engaging features on the formation of the football league, Dynamo Kiev, why teams don't fare so well away from home, or 'the perfect life' of playing cricket in the summer and football all winter (a four-page marathon in the 1964–65 *Soccer Gift Book*, profiling just about every professional footballer who ever played cricket, from William Gunn, six-foot-three founder of Gunn and Moore cricket bats who played for Forest, Notts County and opened the batting for Notts, to Jim Standen of West Ham and Worcestershire; Bobby Etheridge and Ron Nicholls of Bristol City and Gloucestershire, etc, etc). Writing as good as Peter Morris's is the reason a generation of middle-aged men clean up in pub quizzes today. In fact, occasionally he would set the *Soccer Gift Book* quiz himself (sample question: 'the Football League was founded in 1888. Can you name the original twelve members?'[42])

Patrick Collins remembers that Morris 'believed the football world revolved around Villa and Birmingham'. Accordingly, in between checking copy for *Buchan* publications, he wrote the first serious club histories, in hardback form, of Aston Villa and then West Brom.

A GREAT LIFE IF YOU DON'T WEAKEN! says PETER MORRIS

42 Accrington (but not Stanley), Aston Villa, Blackburn, Bolton, Burnley, Derby, Everton, Notts County, Preston, Stoke, West Brom, Wolves.

Above: Morris extolls the virtues of football, and cricket, in *Charles Buchan's Soccer Gift Book* 1964–65

Press-box in Brazil! A Sao Paulo policeman looks over John Thompson's shoulder during one of Arsenal's matches on their first South American tour.

the corrugated roof of the old 'cowshed' at Molineux, where almost as much mud covered the terraces as the white shirts of the opposition, Swansea Town.

As a nipper he was consumed by the game, collecting football cards that came with sweet cigarettes (furtively rummaging through the boxes in the tobacconists' for new players before being apprehended) and reading anything he could get his hands on: 'Rod of the Railway Rangers . . . from Pitboy to pro' in the *Sports Budget* magazine; flicker books of Huddersfield and Chelsea winger Alex 'Skinner' Jackson taking a corner, or Hughie Gallacher scoring (he calls for a modern-day version featuring Johnny Haynes); and the 'old *Topical Times* [which] provided the best value. This publication included glossy full-length photographs of the soccer giants of the day and later offered them in colour. Many boys of my generation had a full set. I still have mine at home.' He even invented Subbuteo with his mates: 'One day a pal of mine was flipping through some of his cigarette cards of footballers and eating chocolate at the same time. When he finished he rolled the silver paper into a ball and flicked it with one of the cards. It happened to be a picture of Jimmy Trotter who, a few years earlier, had been Sheffield Wednesday's centre-forward. When that boy flicked his silver-paper ball with the card, it looked as though Trotter was shooting for goal! In next to no time we were flicking the ball about with our own cards and then someone made a goal from an old cigarette packet. That was the start. We rigged up goals from strips of Meccano and our sisters' hair nets and made up card teams from our sets. A league was formed and we took it in turns to play home and away games in our houses – to the scorn, and later, the annoyance of elder relatives.' The gang started fashioning their own cards, turning up the bottom edges of wingers so they could lob a ball in from the flank. But too many goals were being scored, so the keepers were widened and given arms: 13–8 soon became a more realistic 1–1 or 2–0.

Still, he drew comfort from the fact that 'today's crop of soccer-crazy kids [despite rival attractions] are just as much in love with the game as we were . . . I frequently see pick-up games in back yards and only the other day I stopped to watch a bunch of lads engaged in a fierce game on an open space between towering blocks of flats in south-east London. They were oblivious to my presence, they were in a Soccer world of their own.'

When I bring up his name in Laurie's garage, the West Brom archivist sighs, 'Ah, Peter Morris – long gone; he must have been dead twenty years. He was a prolific writer, very earthy. Peter was a football purist, there's no doubt about that whatsoever, and he wrote some terrific books – the finest Albion history in hardback was Peter's *Soccer in the Black Country* . . . [Laurie pulls out a mint, first edition of *West Bromwich Albion, Soccer in the Black Country, 1879–1965* from his safe, wrapped in a plastic sleeve.] OK, historically, in one or two places, it's not correct, but Peter was one of those people who'd go and research everything . . . he wrote it as it was, and it's still an entertaining read, and that's all you can ask for. We serialised it in the programme recently.'

Morris grew up close enough to Villa Park to hear the roar of the Saturday afternoon crowd. 'It was a strange and unidentified noise,' he wrote, in an article, BOYHOOD MEMORIES, in the '61–62 annual. 'When I asked my mother what it was she told me: "It is from the football match – that's where your father is."' Of his first game, young Peter couldn't remember the score, but he could recall Billy Walker leading the team out, resplendent in claret and blue, and Gordon Hodgson of Liverpool (later of Villa) 'in their colours'. He'd sometimes go with his dad to see Wolves, and stood beneath

Where Morris saw beauty in the ruins, or at least in the everyday and the humdrum, John Thompson

Above: **John Thomspon, in fetching Fedora, pitchside with his portable typewriter in Brazil, *Charles Buchan's Soccer Gift Book* 1956–57**

perhaps best carried the spirit of his old boss into the sixties. Even in his earliest pieces Thompson was quite keen to bottle the essence of football abroad, as witnessed in the lovely atmospheric attempt to capture the scene in grounds in Brazil and England, the first page of which was reproduced complete with a photograph of Thompson typing away at the side of the pitch, looking like a young David Goodis in a fedora. The ultimate sentiment of the piece – 'soccer knows no frontiers. It spans the world like a mighty handshake' – could have been written by the old man himself. Thompson also includes a fine trouser-ripping incident: witnessing a Vasco de Gama supporter in the mêlée outside a match against a touring Arsenal side, fighting to get in, he writes, 'I saw one man gripped by the trousers and pulled back by a police officer. The trousers ripped to pieces and the man delightedly shook himself free and dashed through the entrance in his pants!'

Later on the tour he was taken with the Sao Paolo fans' speciality – Chinese lanterns, or 'fire-balloons'; paper lanterns 'with the name of the team written across them. Cotton wool, soaked in paraffin, is placed in the bottom of the balloons and the hot air causes them to rise slowly over the heads of the crowd until the fire burns out.' Back in Rio, Vasco narrowly beat Arsenal and the crowd went bananas: 'Rockets flared into red and silver stars above the vast floodlit stadium. Women around me kissed each other and wept with joy. Men exploded fireworks. And on the field Vasco players rushed to congratulate Nestor, who had scored the winning goal. In their enthusiasm they knocked him out and jumped all over his prostrate body.' This was May 1949, and Arsenal paid tribute to the players who'd just lost their lives in the Superga air disaster in Italy – Thompson saluted Tom Whittaker for realising that many Sao Paulo building workers were Italian, and before the game 'a record played softly "Ave Maria" and the young men from London, their red shirts aflame in the floodlights against the green of the Brazilian field, stood stiffly to attention in memory of Italian lads who also loved football . . .'

In the last *Gift Book* with Buchan at the helm ('59–60), Thompson, by then 'joint editor' of the *Football Monthly*, considered the joys of being a sportswriter:

'Football,' Thompson noted, 'and Fleet Street too, are small and jealous worlds'

there's a bit of froth about Matthews and Finney, and those solitary Union Jacks 'fluttering defiantly', firecrackers and flocks of pigeons released in the Maracanã, Rio, and 'of all the Cup finals and the personalities who have played at Wembley I remember most vividly the copper-topped Irishman Peter Doherty, flashing his genius across Derby County's triumph. What a player he was, this hopelessly erratic ex-bus conductor. (They say that the bus would be kept waiting while he enjoyed a kickabout.)' Thompson also recalled an Eric Boon and Dave Crowley fight he saw with his wife at Harringay Arena, at which point his records his wife turning to him and remarking, '"Do you remember the first time you took me to see Boon fight?" I recalled a muddy field near Chatteris, sheltering under the ring to phone the story of one of Boon's first triumphs. "Yes," I said. "I remember." We had been married that day.'

But in amongst the recollections of good times are one or two small, buried asides to any budding sports writers. 'Football,' Thompson noted, 'and Fleet Street too, are small and jealous worlds,' and, more poignantly, 'There is the memory of Hughie Gallacher telling me: "When I quit playing I'll be quite content to take my place among the crowds on the terraces."' But still, 'you can at least be sure that the modesty of your bank balance will be compensated by the richness of your memories,' he offered in conclusion.

In another feature Thompson began by lamenting how swiftly sporting glory fades. The problem with the

Above: **Thomspon's photo byline which appeared above his writing for several years in *Charles Buchan's Soccer Gift Book***

The first *Soccer Gift Book*, published in 1953, featured Birmingham and England goalie Gil Merrick on the jacket, in keeping (as noted on p31) with the general deference to goalkeeepers of the period. In fact, nearly every cover in the title's first decade featured a keeper in some capacity – although the editors' liking for a picture of a goalmouth mêlée meant their presence was pretty much a given.

The designers' experimented with type and logos on an annual basis. Colours and fonts were tossed in with careless abandon, or, depending on your standpoint, with a refreshing disregard (by modern standards at least) for the principles of brand continuity.

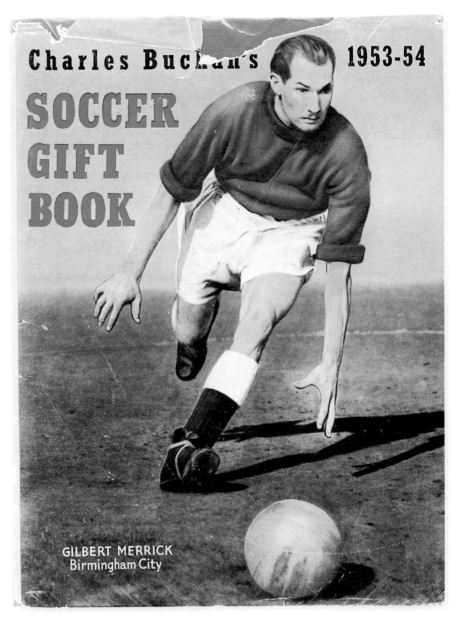

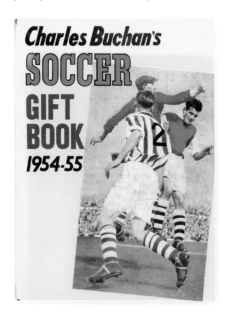

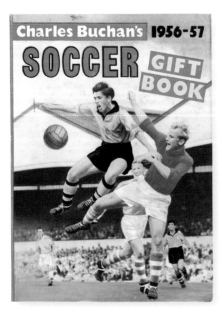

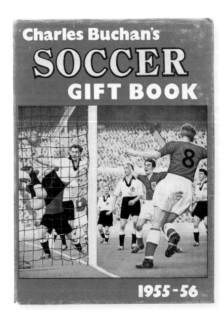

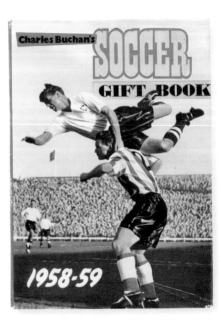

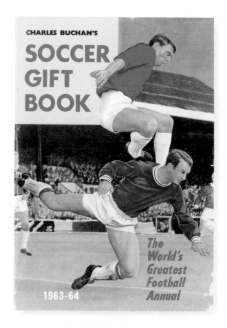

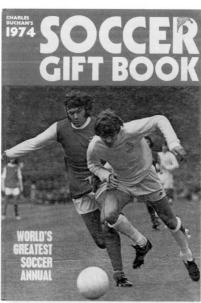

Even in the early sixties the *Gift Book*'s cover type was still subject to experimentation, while goalies, albeit to a lesser extent as the decade progressed, were still in vogue. The 1961–62 jacket (a personal favourite) features Ron Springett in a forlorn leap in his bright yellow shirt and matching gloves. The designers eventually settled on a red band for the masthead, deviating again, on occasion, to a yellow square. Rumbustious action shots remained the order of the day for the cover picture.

In 1966, 16 pages were held back for the 'World Cup Special' but press deadlines meant England's triumph came too late to get explicit billing on the cover.

In 1974 'The World's Greatest Soccer Annual' was published for the last time. It featured Arsenal and Leeds on the cover, aptly, some might contend, since both clubs' demeanour and playing style in this period didn't always hold up to the values that Charles Buchan and his editors once cherished. Or, you could argue, the *Gift Book* had finally fallen out of step with the prevailing trends in the game.

Either way, it was the end of a publishing era.

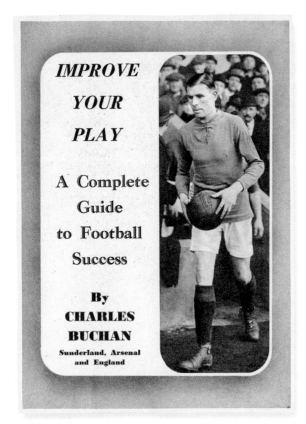

IMPROVE
YOUR
PLAY

A Complete
Guide
to Football
Success

By
CHARLES
BUCHAN

Sunderland, Arsenal
and England

Even late in life, just three years before his death, Charles Buchan chided himself for not practising more

crazed autograph hunters of today, he reasoned, was that they possessed no sense of history – and the same applied to many young players: 'In some cases I am afraid that a few hysterical headlines make them feel that they have arrived at the top. Then comes the sad, sickening plunge back to obscurity from which they came.' The piece morphs into a fine Buchanesque, fiery sermon aimed at youngsters who may stray from the path and start hanging around, drinking pop at the ice rink rather than putting in a decent shift on the training ground: Thompson proselytizes, relaying tales of the young Stanley Matthews dribbling between kitchen chairs in his back garden (a poisoned toe just meant he

wrapped his foot up with a tea-cosy and carried on); Puskás, 'a small and grubby boy', dribbling barefoot in a Hungarian meadow full of thistles with a ball made out of his mother's stockings; Peter Doherty the bus conductor (again) abandoning his ticketless bus passengers in Derry to shoot off to a game; Raich Carter 'striving to be good at games to overcome the handicap of a name like Horatio, using lampposts as goals, a bundle of newspapers as a ball' and, of course, Saturday afternoons spent standing behind a goal at Roker Park 'studying the science of Charlie Buchan's play'; future Charlton keeper Sam Bartram being considered ineligible for a schoolboy cap because poverty around the time of the general strike had forced him down the pit . . . '*All these and many others have the humility that makes for greatness,*' thundered Thompson ' . . . in the golden days of boyhood they marched steadily towards a dream that lay over the rainbow . . . *there is always so much new to learn.*'[43]

Even late in life, just three years before his death, Charles Buchan chided himself for not practising more, taking the time to become two-footed and devoting more thought to positional play – and perhaps this explains the thousands of tutorly words directed at 1950s youngsters in the pages of his publications. He further revealed that he would have preferred to play at centre-half (rather than centre-forward, where he scored a considerable number of goals for Sunderland and Arsenal[44]). He also confessed he wasted time not thinking through training routines properly, but just mindlessly following them. And 'more time was

43 John Thompson, along with fellow celebrated *Daily Mirror* writer Joe Sarl – 'J Maxwell Sarl, I believe was his full title,' says Patrick Collins – had been one of the original founders of the *Football Monthly* with Charlie Buchan. 'Thompson had real commercial flair,' remembers Patrick, 'and as the magazine went from strength to strength, he virtually stepped aside from active journalism and concentrated on the commerce. A pleasant man, he played a full part in the administration of the wider company when it was taken over by IPC. He once confided to my dad that, despite his business success, he was a fiercely committed Labour supporter. This was a result of his covering the Jarrow Crusade in the 1930s. "I remember that wonderful little woman Ellen Wilkinson [Labour MP and Jarrow March organiser]. And since I met her, I could never vote for any other party," he told Dad.'

44 Strangely another high-scoring forward, John Charles, in the *Big Book of Football Champions*, felt exactly the same, seeing greater ball-playing opportunities from deep. Major Frank Buckley, his boss at Leeds, dismissed this out of hand, believing the centre-half to be simply a stopper, and that 'anyone can play there'. Charles stuck to his guns, arguing he could dictate play from a deep position: 'I incurred the wrath of the major by asking if I could return there.' He did acknowledge he wasn't as good as a young Jack Charlton though.

Above: **More salient advice from Buchan,**
Charles Buchan's Soccer Gift Book 1954–55

squandered too, by the casual way I strolled through life. I made no effort to sharpen my mind or to think quickly. Once a master asked me to name the different streets in the order I passed them on my way to school. I failed.' No wonder, if he was racing the tram every morning, but the young dreamer Buchan came to rue, too late in life, that 'the ability to notice trivial things and to make a mental note of them is a valuable asset. It helps to sharpen one mentally and come to split-second decisions [that are] the hallmark of a great player'. And, finally, he regretted not learning a proper trade: 'With a trade at your finger-tips there is no need to worry about the future.' This sentiment would echo through various football annuals through the next decade.

Charlie died suddenly while on holiday with his wife, near Monte Carlo, in June 1960. There are some lovely accounts of office life at the Charles Buchan stable of publications on the Strand[45]. Not only was Buchan benevolent towards serving and ex-forces personnel, sending them copies of the monthly magazine, but also, according to the recollections of Mike Hayes (who obtained a position on the monthly magazine after persistently phoning the office up as a Soccer-mad youngster, wondering which players were going to be in colour the following month), he was forever

helping ex-convicts set themselves up with jobs too, as he 'never saw wrong in anybody'.

John Thompson rounded up the various tributes in the *Soccer Gift Book* and wrote of a late Saturday afternoon that brought back memories of his old boss: 'The game was long over and I looked across the muddy pitch to the empty terraces leaning back into the melancholy November mist. My work was finished and I picked up my typewriter and made my way along empty corridors to the players' and press entrance . . . ' where he came across three young boys waiting for autographs. The first player out of the ground brushed their pleas aside with a brusque, 'I've got a train to catch,' and Thompson was reminded of a similar scene in one of the cuttings he'd been trawling through, a piece headlined THE BUCHAN TOUCH AT MILLWALL, back from when Charlie was a player in his prime: 'The doors of the Den were locked, officials and players had gone. In the dimly lit thoroughfare stood a towering figure, encircled by ragged urchins. It was Charles Buchan, and though friends fumed at the delay, he signed his name over a hundred times. Even the youngster who admitted that his scrap of paper had been picked up (it looked as though it had been used for fish and chips) was not disappointed. "You can't disappoint them," said Buchan.'

45 See pieces by Mike Hayes and Roger White at www.charlesbuchansfootballmonthly.com

---

HITCH YOUR WAGON TO THE

STARS

by CHARLES BUCHAN

**Former captain of England,
Sunderland and Arsenal**

Every youngster can learn a lot from watching star players and studying the points that have brought them to stardom.

In this series, I have taken an international player for each position and pin-pointed the outstanding features of his play.

Study them closely and then practise them as much as possible. Remember, it is continual practice that brings success.

If possible, talk about these points with experienced players—men who, I am sure, will be pleased to pass on their knowledge to you.

You will notice I have not given any hints about the individual skills such as trapping the ball, heading, dribbling, tackling and the like. It is up to each player to perfect them in his own time and in his own way.

Team-work, of course, is of primary importance. When you next watch a big game, make a note of how the stars position themselves to help their colleagues. Do not be afraid to discuss their moves with your team-mates.

Simultaneously romantic and pragmatic in his 1956 *Gift Book*, Charles Buchan suggests would-be football stars of the future talk to 'experienced players – men who will be pleased to pass on their knowledge to you', which indicates the players of this era were a good deal more approachable than their modern counterparts, or at least that's the impression they gave him.

JOHNNY HAYNES, Fulham

"World Sports" colour photograph

'I PREFER TO THINK OF JOHNNY AS A PERFECTIONIST'

THE EARLY SIXTIES

While Peter Dimmock's *Sportsview Books of Soccer* were as capable as any 1950 or '60s annual of supplying overlong, fluffy player profiles, there was a pleasing edge to this yearly publication. As early as 1960, in a stars-of-the-future piece, they'd spotted 'a brilliant teenager' in West Ham's youth ranks – in fact, Bobby Moore could be an eventual 'long-term successor to Billy Wright'.

Four years before his eventual departure from the England job, BBC man Paul Fox was grappling with the problem of Walter Winterbottom, and suggesting names for his likely successor. And, as we've seen with Denis Compton's outburst, the *Sportsview* team didn't hold back when it came to just causes – the same 1959 annual featured a piece on Brian Clough, THE FORGOTTEN CENTRE-FORWARD, railing at the England selectors for failing to pick him despite his fine goal-scoring form for Middlesbrough. The feature dismissed out of hand the usual Middlesbrough-in-the-second-division argument, citing the likes of Johnny Haynes and Jim Langley at Fulham, Ronnie Clayton at Blackburn, and Alan A'Court at Liverpool, all of whom had had a run in the England side while playing in the second division – even keeper Reg Matthews won a cap while playing for third division Coventry. It was also noted that Clough might have been overlooked because 'he said something to

1958-59 Football League top scorer (43 goals) Brian Clough (Middlesborough).

upset selectors' as well as observing: 'and this, from an England player, he's not a good mixer!'

'It's obvious that the people who advance these theories do not know Brian Clough,' countered the piece. 'He is a frank, straight-talking lad, who manages to be pleasant and unassuming at all times. Looking at some of the brash young men who have worn the England shirt in the past few years, the thought that Clough could be excluded for his behaviour or his manners becomes laughable or tragic. England players are, or ought to be, picked on merit. And in this department, Clough is very long-suited.' This article, and another one gently sifting through Charlie Mitten's troubled reign at Newcastle, weren't ascribed an author. Jonathan Wilson in his 2011 biography of Clough pointed to the young centre-forward embarrassingly contradicting Billy Wright in an England training session as a possible factor in his sudden ejection from the squad for the World Cup in Sweden. And, viewed through modern eyes, the *Sportsview Book of Soccer*'s exemplary PR job of an article can't quite mask the roots of the bitterness that would later come to define Clough's relationships with (and views on) directors, 'selectors' and the FA. 'He plays football like a pianist who has not been taught to read music,' wrote either Dimmock, Ronnie Noble or Paul Fox – in other words he was a great improviser able to adapt to any team. England were crying out for him; Clough, for his part, learned early not to suffer fools.

By Christmas 1963 Clough's career had been tragically curtailed, England had been thrashed 5–2 in Paris

Left: The effortlessly elegant Johnny Haynes in the *Topical Times Football Book* 1959

Above: The young and brash Brian Clough pictured in the *Sportsview Book of Soccer* 1960

by France in Alf Ramsey's first match, then 'humiliated by the ten men of Scotland at Wembley' in the Home Internationals – and they hadn't exactly shone in Chile. The *Sportsview Soccer Book* team had had enough. In a couple of paragraphs that could have been written at any point in the subsequent half century, they felt it necessary to remind English readers that FOOTBALL IS A PASSING GAME:

> The morale of the English players slumped to zero and almost every reason possible was given for our team's dismal performances. It was even suggested that England lost to Scotland because the England supporters at Wembley had not shouted loudly enough! The critics sharpened their claws and trotted out all the old complaints. Lack of preparation; lack of fighting spirit; lack of cohesion. The old familiar words like shambling, fumbling, stereotyped and disjointed, were dusted off and brought back into use.
>
> But the critics missed the point. No one mentioned passing. Yet the greatest single factor in England's poor rating in world class football and the real reason we trail so far behind the foreign countries, is because our players are not able to pass with anything like the consistency, accuracy and technique of the players from other countries.

We were still, essentially, a long-ball nation, launching balls in desperation over the heads of retreating defenders – for the attacker, head down, sprinting into space, this made it 'a question of retrieving the pass rather than receiving it'. The best passers of the day were Danny Blanchflower, Jimmy McIlroy and Dave Mackay, none of whom were English. But one English ball player was held up as positive example: Johnny Haynes, photographed in an earlier *Sportsview* annual teaching his budgerigar to say, 'Come on, Fulham.'[46]

If the world of the 1950s annual had been broadly about hard work, relentless practice, 'Balls,' that, according to Sean Magee, 'you couldn't bend, caked in mud, just booted up the field', and the sublimation of the individual into the team effort, then, come the early sixties, individual characters, and the notion of the rebel, began to surface in the pages of the humble Christmas annual.

There's a point in Lindsay Anderson's 1963 adaptation of David Storey's novel *This Sporting Life*, where Richard Harris's doomed character, Frank Machin, tells the chairman's wife, 'We don't have stars in this game, Mrs Weaver, that's soccer.'

'Well, what do you have, then?' she asks.

---

46 For budgerigars and footballers, see chapter 4.

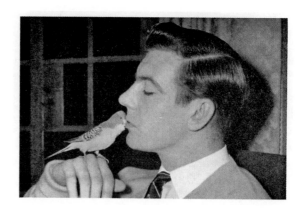

'People like me,' replies Harris, to the patronising laughter of the boardroom cronies. 'I've got a thirst: I think I'll be off.' And he stalks away towards the pub, the rugby league ground behind him, empty in the gloom.

But if rugby league players were pawns in the game, in the opening two pieces of the very first *Topical Times Football Book*, both Mel Charles and Albert Quixall revealed they were unaware of their (respectively) high and record-breaking transfer fees. Quixall reproduced pages from his rather minimal diary, which if not quite reaching the Kafkaesque heights of 'Germany has declared war on Russia; went swimming in the afternoon' certainly gave a sense of the unempowered realities of a footballer's lot:

1954
November 6 – v Manchester City. League match. Picked for right-half. As we lose 4–2 I guess it's goodbye to the no.4 shirt for me. It was!

1955
January 15 – demobbed.
May 12 – With England team to France, Spain and Portugal. Not picked for the game v France. We lose 1–0.
May 18 – v Spain at Madrid. 1–1. It was fiesta time. Maybe that's why the crowd were so frantic. What a match. Nat Lofthouse gets his shirt ripped off; Bentley brought down very heavily. Back to the team. I can't get going at all.

1956
February 8 – v Scotland Under-23. Sheffield Wednesday ground. Win 3–1. Hit it off with Johnny Haynes.
April 25 – v Irish League, Belfast. We lose 5–2 – and get a roasting from the critics!
September 19 – v League of Ireland, Dublin. Draw 3–3. Another roasting.

1958
February 19 – v Manchester United. First game after Munich. An unforgettable memory. Never have I played before such a hysterical crowd. The atmosphere is almost frightening. United win 3–0.

Above: 'My budgie is a smart bird' confides Johnny Haynes in *Sportsview Book of Soccer* 1960

April 26 – v Wolves. Beat Wolves 2–1. We're relegated, they're the champs. Not looking forward to League 2.

Still, not long into the new season Quixall was called into Harry Catterick's office – a move to Old Trafford was in the air, and he went home to discuss it with his wife:

September 17 – Wife not too keen to leave Sheffield. Tell the boss I'll join Manchester United if they want me.
September 18 – Matt Busby comes through. I sign. Only when I read the papers do I realise it's a record fee.

The further thoughts of Albert Quixall's wife weren't recorded, sadly, but the same 1959 *Topical Times Football Book* focused on how Quixall's new mate Johnny Haynes seemed to divide opinion. Haynes, you got the sense, did not suffer fools gladly either. Critics at the time pointed to his Berbatov-like 'drop of the shoulders when a colleague does not make the best of a Haynes pass.' Worse still, the be-quiffed playmaker 'hangs his head and throws up his arms when a lesser player fluffs an opportunity. Johnny is accused of petulance, irritability, peevishness. Frank Osborne, the Fulham general manager, gives it another name: "I prefer to think of Johnny as a perfectionist".'

Osborne had been worried about losing Haynes as a schoolboy to the north London 'glamour clubs' of his neighbouring Edmonton, Spurs and Arsenal, and even high-flying Wolves were interested too. But on a trip to Craven Cottage Osborne played up the picturesque sweeping views of the Thames from the top of the terrace: 'It's wonderful to look out on the river. You can see the start of the University Boat Race from the ground.' Unfortunately, when he took the young fifteen-year-old Haynes up to the back corner of the ground to enjoy the view, 'the TIDE WAS OUT.' To the manager's dismay, 'Instead of a lovely stretch of water we saw a series of pots and pans – all the flotsam and jetsam you get on a beach at low tide. Not an impressive sight.' But maybe the rubbish in the Thames added to the 'homely' aspect of the club the future England captain cited favourably on signing (more prosaically in *Buchan's Soccer Gift Book* it's claimed he put pen to paper in SW6 because he had a friend on the groundstaff).

Kenneth Wolstenholme's 1963 *Book of World Soccer* also featured a portrayal of Johnny Haynes, the bad-tempered perfectionist who became 'really annoyed when things go wrong. He is annoyed with himself

if he makes a bad pass or gets caught out of position. He just cannot bear failure.' Wolstenholme pointed to a north-south divide as far as the England captain was concerned. In the south, and especially at Fulham, he was idolised, 'one of the all-time greats'; in the north and Midlands he was considered over-rated, a bit of a southern fancy-dan.

The car crash on Blackpool promenade in August 1962 (late at night with a lady passenger) that effectively ended Haynes's England career wasn't mentioned, surprisingly enough, in any annuals of the day. While recovering from that serious knee injury and broken leg, Haynes told Charlie Buchan's *Soccer Gift Book* that he received letters of support from all over the country, ' . . . even from the north, where they are supposed to have a "thing" about me and the way I play football'.

Laurie Rampling, in his old darkroom on the east London–Essex borders, believes Haynes 'reinvented the inside-forward role. Johnny Haynes had a vision – an eye for a pass and an eye for a goal – he could read a game as well as anybody of his time. When he got the

> ## WE WERE STILL, ESSENTIALLY, A LONG-BALL NATION

Albert Quixall, of Manchester United, doesn't use his head only for thinking. When he has the ball on it, it is as good as another pair of feet to him.

Above: Albert Quixall shows off his ball-balancing skills at Old Trafford after his record £45,000 transfer, in *Charles Buchan's Soccer Gift Book* 1962–63

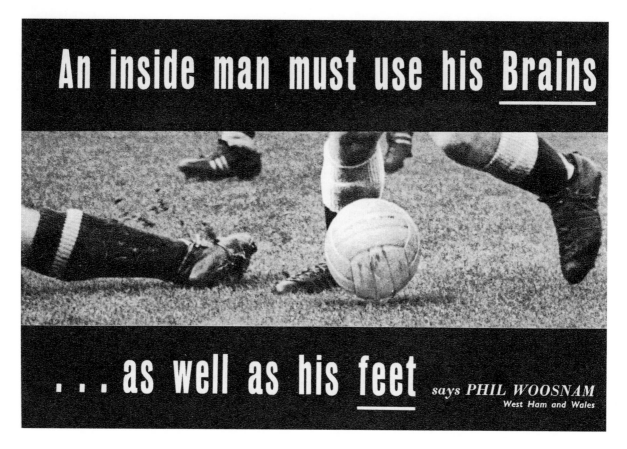

An inside man must use his Brains
. . . as well as his feet *says PHIL WOOSNAM*
West Ham and Wales

ball he wasn't necessarily thinking about the next ball he was going to play: he was thinking about what ball the next player would play, and what the next after that was going to do.'

Which was exactly how West Ham's Phil Woosnam saw him in *Charles Buchan's Soccer Gift Book* of 1961–62. Woosnam believed there were two types of inside-forward: goalscorers and schemers. He modelled himself on that latter; Haynes, with his ability to slow a game down like Di Stéfano, being his guiding light: 'Not enough players today are able to read the play. The accent is so much on speed that forwards tear up and down without giving a thought to what they are going to do with the ball.'

Not the Fulham captain. 'Johnny Haynes changed the game for ever when he was paid that £100 a week,' reckons Laurie Rampling. 'A great player; he wasn't posh, but he sort of played in that idealistic posh way – very fancy. He was football's first aristocrat, and everybody wanted to knock him down a peg or two – and one or two in the game tried. Maurice Setters [a West Brom then Man United wing-half] will tell you how he wanted to knock him down, this swaggering £100 a week player. But Maurice Setters will also tell you

how he couldn't get near him. Instead of engaging with the beauty of what he did on a football park, it was all about the negative: "How can he be worth £100 a week?".'

Haynes, of course, didn't see it quite like that. He was paid what he felt he was worth.[47] 'Bobby Robson was of the same ilk: a rebel, at least as far as wages were concerned, at the Albion,' continues Laurie. 'George Eastham was the same too – not as good as Johnny Haynes, mind. Johnny Haynes took football from a very, very earthy time – the doldrums of the 1940s and '50s – into its sexy period. Back in 1959 a fan on the park was earning £8 a week if he was lucky. I started for the Exchange & Telegraph press agency up in London in 1962, and was paid £5 a week.'

---

47 As England captain Haynes wrote that he wasn't quite the speech-maker that Billy Wright had been, but he still stressed, to *Charles Buchan's Soccer Gift Book* readers, the importance of the team over the individual: 'Hint to youngsters: always try to play as a team. You don't have to be an individual to be noticed. You may think the fellow who beats two and three players is something of a player; most times the team would have been better served by an earlier pass to a better-placed colleague.'

Above: Phil Woosnam of West Ham suggests footballers should think more creatively in *Charles Buchan's Soccer Gift Book* 1961–62

And there was Johnny Haynes, in all the Brylcreem adverts too, raking it in. It's not hard to see how resentment might have built on the terraces at Millmoor or Turf Moor. And what Haynes and Fulham team-mate Jimmy Hill started, through the PFA-assisted abolition of the maximum wage, looks to have reached some kind of apex today: 'Look at Wayne Rooney,' says Laurie, '£300,000 a week – that gap [in player–fan wages] is now so stretched . . . football is an obscene industry.'

Still, Laurie says that Haynes 'probably was a Winterbottom boy . . . the epitome of the establishment in some ways'.

From a distance of fifty years, misreading the quiff[48], the haughtiness, night-time entanglements on Blackpool promenade, and the fact that Irish footballer-turned-author-and-pundit Eamon Dunphy noted

---

48 'Haynes? We're talking pre-Hoxton quiff there' – Johnny Green.

'HAYNES WAS FOOTBALL'S FIRST ARISTOCRAT, AND EVERYBODY WANTED TO KNOCK HIM DOWN A PEG OR TWO'

in his autobiography[49] that Haynes and Denis Compton used to drink in the same pub (the Queen's Arms in Chelsea, 'frequented by poets, writers and assorted bums'), I put it to Richard Williams that Haynes was the first rebel.

'I never thought of Haynes in those terms,' he says, 'although there was the wage thing. He looked like a very conservative player, there was nothing extraordinary about him, visually; as a footballer he was very neat, very economical, and, of course, brilliant – fantastic. He had that terrific accuracy about him. It was very much about individuals in those days – each team had a creative player (maybe there was one other player approaching his level, like Tony Currie and Geoff Salmons [at Sheffield United], for instance) so you'd go and see whoever the visiting team was, looking forwards to whether it was George Eastham, at Newcastle or Arsenal, or later on Stan Bowles with QPR. Those kind of players . . . very often they seemed to stand out in the team in a way that generally wouldn't be so now – you know, in the way that you get full-backs bending the ball up the line . . . that would have taken three or four passes fifty years ago.'

Kenneth Wolstenholme's *Book of World Soccer* often took an interesting thematic approach to the game: Haynes was featured in an article that sought to assess how the tricky inside-forwards of England shaped up against their European counterparts: 'men like Dragoslav Šekularac, the stormy petrel of Jugoslavia' and other glittering stars of Europe and the 1962 World Cup.[50]

A few pages further on and Villa Park favourite, Derek THEY CALL HIM CHEYENNE Dougan was cited as proof that 'soccer today is not absolutely devoid of personalities'. Named after Cheyenne Bodie, TV hero of the aftermath of the Civil War, 'always on the look-out for fights, women and bad guys to beat up'[51] Dougan 'played with spirit and energy. He was never short of

---

49 *The Rocky Road*, published by Penguin Ireland in 2013.

50 Puskás, Eusébio, Rivera and János Göröcs, 'the pride of Hungary . . . a gipsy-looking frail inside-forward' are all discussed, along with John White of Spurs, spookily nicknamed 'the Ghost' – 'small, pale and frail' he kept popping up, unannounced, to score. He cropped up in numerous annuals of the time, but was famously killed by lightning while sheltering under a tree on a golf course in Enfield, aged only twenty-seven, six months or so after the Wolstenholme annual would have appeared.

51 imdb

Above: A schoolboy puts a few pertinent questions to Johnny Haynes in *The FA Book for Boys* 1959

a gesture to suit the occasion. A goal brought super celebrations from Dougan. A miss brought an equally super display of annoyance. Nothing is calculated to get the spectators more on edge than that,' concluded Wolstenholme, sounding every bit a BBC football commentator making something of an understatement, 'and so Derek Dougan often became the butt of supporters of opposing teams.' His chutzpah in submitting a transfer request hours before the 1960 FA Cup final was re-lived: Blackburn subsequently lost, 'and no one played worse than Dougan'.

Charles Buchan's Soccer Gift Book wasn't really known for focussing on hell-raisers, but in 1959 it did run an interview with another 'stormy petrel', Birmingham City's Bunny Larkin, whose crimes to date included a bit of a ruckus with Chelsea's Tony Nicholas – 'I admit then when I tackled him I might have been behind him' – and missing a Spanish tour because he overslept as 'my parents were away'. And a couple of seasons later, Calvin Palmer told the *Gift Book* he was 'a wild boy, a tearaway' and was accordingly sacked by Nottingham Forest at fifteen for indiscipline and sent back to playing with his mates on the field by the pier in Skegness. Subsequently he was picked up by Skegness Town, and Forest relented, giving him a second chance – although even then he missed out on the FA Cup final squad for failing to report to the City Ground in time prior to a league match ahead of Wembley. Unbeknown to Palmer he was to be an emergency replacement for injured skipper Jack Burkitt. With typical teenage nonchalance he just about made it to his seat in the Main Stand for kick-off, but failed to hear a Tannoy announcement asking him to report to the dressing room. A couple of fellow trainees just stared at him: 'I have an idea I wasn't too popular as a result of that,' he added, ruefully.

And, of course, it wasn't long before one George Best began to garner column inches in football annuals. In the 1965–66 *Topical Times* Best wrote of how, as a boy, he would be heartbroken for a week if his side lost; but today, ' . . . it's not the end of the world. Don't get me wrong, I hate losing . . . but when you can't do any more about it, why worry?' Then, rather poignantly, he added, 'When you're playing two or three games a week it's got to be the quiet life off the field. That doesn't bother me. I don't think I'll ever go mad for late

> 'I DON'T THINK I'LL EVER GO MAD FOR LATE NIGHTS AND BRIGHT LIGHTS'

nights and bright lights. Saturday and Sunday nights are my playtime. Usually I head for some club or coffee bar to catch a beat group or folk show. By eleven o'clock I'm drifting home.' And staying in the rest of the week, apparently, trying to deal with all the fan mail. There's a sense the endless letters from the teenage girls and 'the nut-cases', and people going on about his long hair, were beginning to get him down. But, he reflected, football had made him more outward going: 'It isn't so long ago I was short-changed five bob in a shop. I was too shy to go back and complain . . . Ach, it's all part of this mad football world. And I wouldn't change it. All the talk of tension and strain is so much baloney as far as I'm concerned. To me football with United and Ireland is laughs all the way.'

For Graham Sharpe, today of William Hill, but back in the sixties a tricky inside-right, resplendent in all-black Wealdstone Athletic kit[52] (the white boots a nod to Derby's Alan Hinton), it was another inside-right, 'an archetypal goal-sniffer of unconsidered trifles', who was a hero of sorts: 'I was always more drawn to the individuals, as characters. Haynes was an establishment-type player; Greaves and Best were what you wanted to be like.' Up until roughly the mid-sixties, Graham notes, 'everyone was an identikit version of their mums and dads – unless you were really rebellious. Jimmy Greaves, you got the impression from the way he played that he was different. But there was no *HELLO!* magazine type coverage then; [even in the annuals] there was more focus on the games than the personal lives of the players, so you imposed your own feelings of what they must be like because of the way they played.'

Choosing not to reflect on any personal World Cup disappointment in 1966 – although that perhaps was more likely a consequence of mid-sixties print deadlines – Jimmy Greaves went all out in the following year's *Topical Times* to emphasize the lighter side of being on tour with England. He talked of his inability to recall individual goals but, happily, was more concerned with relaying tales of listening to Ella Fitzgerald in a plush New York club; playing impromptu matches with Bobby Moore and Johnny Byrne and a bunch of 'street urchins in tattered pants and bare feet' along Copacabana beach;

---

52 All black with a white, trim collar. 'Referees went mad when we turned up . . .'

Right: A typically diffident George Best in *Topical Times Football Book* 1965

MY MAD, MAD, FOOTBALL WORLD

By GEORGE BEST

Manchester United

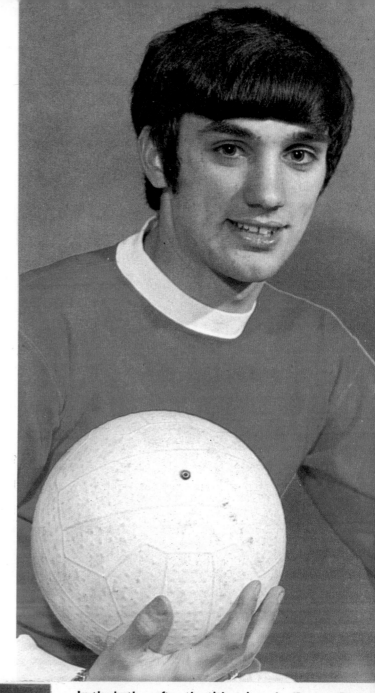

EVERYBODY asks—what's it like playing for United? The champions of England. I could never put it in words. Not till I saw a poster advertising a film. It said—"It's a mad, mad, mad, mad world."

For a while last season I hardly knew what day it was. Cup-ties, vital championship games. I never seemed to shut my eyes in my own bed. And the world got madder still when Ireland called on me.

One night I was supposed to be at Windsor Park

In the bath — after the title triumph. George Best *(also above)* in foreground facing camera. Clockwise, others are — Tony Dunne, Pat Crerand, David Herd, Denis Law, Nobby Stiles, Shay Brennan.

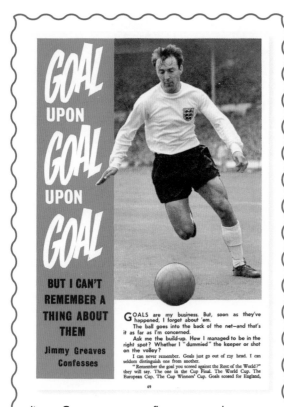

GOAL UPON GOAL UPON GOAL

BUT I CAN'T REMEMBER A THING ABOUT THEM

Jimmy Greaves Confesses

GOALS are my business. But, soon as they've happened, I forget about 'em. The ball goes into the back of the net—and that's it as far as I'm concerned.

Ask me the build-up. How I managed to be in the right spot? Whether I "dummied" the keeper or shot on the volley?

I can never remember. Goals just go out of my head. I can seldom distinguish one from another.

"Remember the goal you scored against the Rest of the World?" they will say. The one in the Cup Final. The World Cup. The European Cup. The Cup Winners' Cup. Goals scored for England,

69

Jimmy Greaves, a nervous flyer, recounted, at considerable length in the *Topical Times* 1966–67, an agonising journey home from South America. Despite Dr Bass, the FA doctor, slipping him a couple of travel pills and tranquillisers ('they don't seem to make any difference') Greaves became increasingly agitated as a routine stop in Recife turned into an engine overhaul, and the flight was diverted from Lisbon to Dakar, Senegal, because of strong headwinds. Eventually they reached Lisbon, though someone tells Greaves they have been losing oil while crossing the south Atlantic – 'hardly the stuff to calm a bad flier,' he deadpans – and, via Paris, a wrecked Jim, hours late, staggered through his front door . . . 'and there [in true *Carry On* style] was my wife, Irene, saying, "Hello, Jim! Had a nice trip?" I ask you!'

and with sharing the antics of Charlie, the Rio police motorcycle escort who 'looked like something straight out of a dictator's personal guard. A black uniform, leather riding boots, rakish peak cap, white leather gauntlets, belt full of bullets and massive revolver. A formidable-looking bloke.' Charlie, cruising ahead of the coach on the way to a ground, soon started riding side-saddle. On a second trip he stood on the saddle, eventually 'turning round to face backwards as his bike sped along'. The England

squad applauded this display of motorcycle gymnastics. 'Progressively he got more daring,' continued Greaves. 'He even balanced himself head down on the saddle. Riding along with arms and legs outstretched and siren screaming. The traffic stopped and we sailed through Rio – motorists pulling up in amazement. Some, no doubt, wondering if they were seeing things.'

The football fan of the early 1960s would most likely not come across the England team breaking out into 'Rule Britannia' in the annuals of the day, but, nevertheless, if there was an increasing fixation on Johnny Foreigner, there was still a deep ambiguity – and plenty of the writing is wince-inducing when viewed from the distance of today.

LET'S CHECK ON CHILE: HOT STUFF AHEAD screamed the *Topical Times'* World Cup '62 preview. Fans in Chile are generally well behaved, the piece observed – no 'wire fences to keep warm-blooded crowds at arm's length from the teams' required. The Port of Arica stadium left a little to be desired, though: 'The present pitch is pure dirt, but experiments are going on to see if grass can be coaxed to grow.' And despite West Germany having yet to qualify, 'Two thousand Germans have already made arrangements to hire a ship. This will sail from Germany and the fans will be able to live aboard and travel to any part of Chile. Remember it is a country that is mainly coastline.' 'Food problems' were also a concern: 'Little water is drunk in Chile. All tap water has to be boiled. Normal drink with meals is red wine. And food is very spiced . . . usually team manager Walter Winterbottom makes the fixing of as English a menu as possible his first duty on arrival in a foreign country.'

A couple of *Topical Times Football Books* later, ten years on from Hungary at Wembley, Sir Stanley Rous, the new English president of FIFA, had a revelation: 'World football is gaining strength with every moment that goes by. I have become very much aware of that in the past year.' He went on to back South Africa, the United States, Australia, Thailand, Indonesia, Egypt, Ceylon, Malaya, Japan, Thailand and Southern Rhodesia (as well as unspecified 'new African countries') to 'most certainly make an impact on world football'.[53]

53 Four years prior to that Rous had been tipping China for the top in the *Topical Times*, and predicting that artificial pitches and ground sharing would soon be commonplace. He also believed 'basic skills such as ball control and ability to use both feet' would be rectified in the English game in the near future. He was correct when he speculated that 'FIFA will cover the world'.

Right: FIFA President Sir Stanley Rous discovers football in the rest of the world, to the apparent surprise of FA director of coaching Alan Wade, *Topical Times Football Book* 1963

And in the *Topical Times* '65–66 annual, there was a lengthy account of the Albanian national team's trip to Windsor Park (BELFAST WILL NEVER FORGET THEM), which, despite obvious language problems, featured an evening at a local cinema: ' . . . not as daft as it sounds. They picked an Elvis Presley movie. No plot, just music and scores of bathing beauties.' There was a bizarre misunderstanding over refreshments at the interval, however, involving mass gurning and a request for chewing gum, and some of the players took to the field the following day wearing old-style high boots. And the bizarre behaviour didn't stop there. 'At free-kicks they solemnly counted out the paces before running up to have a bang. It was more like a rugby conversion than anything else. One chap fooled everybody – including his mates – by jumping over the ball. Unfortunately nobody had followed up . . . ' Apparently the Albanians would always immediately crowd around an injured player: 'no doubt about it, these chaps knew their first aid . . . they were as eager to practise as all amateur ambulancemen . . . so much so that the trainer Jimmy McCune had to fight his way to his patient.' Also, when booked or ticked off by the ref, the visitors would stand 'rigidly at attention for a second then [perform] a smart about turn so that the whistler could note their number.' The crowd, understandably, warmed to them no end.

A decade on from the United States doing away with England in the World Cup, the *Soccer Gift Book* was still chortling about the game in North America, or

These new boys will make their mark in world football, says Sir STANLEY ROUS, C.B.E., president of FIFA.

(in an interview)

★

THEIR STADIUM HAS A BUILT-IN HOTEL FOR INTERNATIONAL TEAMS

★

WORLD football is gaining strength with every moment that goes by.
I have become very much aware of that over the past year.
In it, I visited countries that, from a football viewpoint, are beginning to make their presence felt.
The United States and Australia. South Africa . . . Indonesia . . . Egypt . . . Ceylon . . . Malaya . . . Japan . . . Thailand . . . Southern Rhodesia . . . the new African countries.
All these " new " football nations will most certainly make an impact on world football.
Many are in the same position as was Russia at the

This is Mr ALAN WADE, the Football Association's director of coaching.

85

specifically in Canada, where a ref was a 'whistletooter', a player embarking on a dribble would be 'dipsy-doodling' or having a 'razzle-dazzle', and if that culminated in shooting wide of the open goal, said player would have 'flubbed' his chance.

All innocent fun, of course; but that seemed to sit cheek-by-jowl with a notion that money was an all pervasive and unwelcome foreign influence on the beautiful game, especially on the Continent. The same *Buchan* annual that linguistically deconstructed Canadian soccer also featured a piece on how 'an obsession with money' and the wealth of Barcelona, Real Madrid and Bilbao had distorted the true picture of Spanish football – not a healthy one elsewhere in the league, and certainly not at international level, where Spain were nothing if not underachievers. One the one hand, by 1961, most players in Britain would still be earning a wage comparable to that down the pit; but on the other, these articles seemed to be saying, such a tawdry state of affairs would never be allowed to happen here, home of 'playing the game for the game's sake'. Oh, no.

That's not to say there wasn't respect for the game abroad. The first edition of the *Topical Times Football Book* ran a slightly awed piece on life at the Bernabéu: 'How colourful the scene on match days! Scores of flags flutter from almost every point of the stadium. Nearly everyone wears a sun hat. Outside the ground there are water sellers. You pay 2d a swig – from big, ice-cool jars . . . the players are treated like Hollywood film stars'. It was noted that Di Stéfano planned to have a white marble statue of a footballer erected in his back garden, with the inscription 'thanks, Old Man'. And in the *Big Book of Football Champions* Bishop Auckland wing-half Bob Hardisty bemoaned the lack of preparation, comfort, professionalism in the amateur game here. Whereas in Sofia, ahead of a Bulgaria v England fixture in 1956, the dressing-room 'floors were carpeted, we had a locker each, with our names already on them, hanging in the lockers were bathrobes, clogs

IT'S SIMPLY FANTASTIC!

REAL MADRID F.C.

*T*HEY comb the world for talent... Their ground will soon hold 200,000 fans...

Their players get £100 a week — with £500 match bonuses

and there were flowers, boxes of cigarettes and bowls of fruit.' *That* was hospitality . . .

In the 1960 *Sportsview Book of Soccer* (Peter Dimmock now sporting a cravat on the cover) there was a profile of the 'Futbol Club de Barcelona [who] have found their twinkling feet and have joined soccer's goldrush.' Their new stadium, however, was so impressive that by comparison Wembley looked 'like a mining prospector's shack in the wilds of the Yukon'. There was a huge circular bath in the dressing room, big enough to swim in, 'surrounded by chip-marble flooring in exotic colours'. Boss Helenio Herrera had dossiers on the opposition – maybe Don Revie was reading the *Sportsview* annual after training at Elland Road – which worked through the opposition one by one. Herrera had travelled to the Black Country the Saturday before Wolves were to meet Barcelona in the first leg of the 1960 European Cup quarter-final. Watching the Molineux side against Blackpool, Herrera noted how the wing-halves liked to attack. Come Tuesday night at the Estabio Gamper and Ron Flowers and Eddie Clamp were sucked high up the pitch, before Luis Suárez and his team-mates counterattacked devastatingly. 'It was like a boxer who draws his opponent on and then, at the very moment when it counts, delivers the knock-out punch,' wrote Ronnie Noble in the *Sportsview* annual. 'That's how the Soccer

Señors plan, and execute their plans, to annihilate the opposition . . . tactics, tactics, tactics . . . they expect to score from pre-conceived moves, which are adapted to situations on the field.' Noble profiled a team of fluid, quick thinkers, proper students of the game who lived and breathed soccer theory all day long, concluding 'as much thought and planning goes into an individual's football as goes into a stonemason's mosaic'. Wolves were torn apart 4–0 in Spain, then 2–5 in the second leg in the Molineux mud.

The Chile World Cup, at least in advance, had caught the imagination of football annual feature editors. Ken Aston, England's appointed ref for the following year's tournament, wrote good-naturedly about his foreign travels for *Charles Buchan's Soccer Gift Book*. Once, when reffing a fixture in the Central American

Above: The *Topical Times Football Book* visits Madrid in 1959 adding: 'When Pelé ends his army service he is expected to join for £100,000'
Right: Ken Aston enthuses about reffing around the world in *Charles Buchan's Soccer Gift Book*

1961–62. This may have been dampened a year later when he officiated at the 'Battle of Santiago', the 1962 World Cup game between Chile v Italy that was marred by violent tackles and players exchanging punches

Games in Caracas, fifteen minutes prior to kick-off neither linesmen had turned up, ' . . . then an official appeared followed by six men. Their names were put into a hat and two drawn out. One of them towered well over six feet; the other a comparative midget. I soon had a row with the latter.' Aston looked to the diminutive fellow's flag for a difficult offside, but 'to my amazement he was standing with his back to the field of play, smoking a big cigar and talking to spectators . . . ' He also recounted the time he officiated the 1960 Independence Gold Cup clash between Ghana and Nigeria and was 'jostled and hooted by angry spectators because I had given several controversial decisions', but he still considered most foreign players (and fans) to be respectful of British refs. Hindsight, of course, can't help but recall the Battle of Santiago, which was about to blow up in Aston's face a year later.

> 'THAT'S HOW THE SOCCER SEÑORS PLAN, TO ANNIHILATE THE OPPOSITION – TACTICS, TACTICS, TACTICS . . . '

Despite unfortunate references to 'dusky followers of the game' in Ghana, and life in Kuwait, where apparently it wasn't unusual to see 'a bunch of Bedouin boys kicking around an inflated goat's bladder, with piled up sand for goalposts!' there was a sense of excitement in the *Topical Times* 1960 annual at the opening up of world football, a welcoming of life beyond our meat and potatoes game: floodlights were in their infancy, home nations were qualifying for the World Cup, there were even international managers (harbouring ideas about tactics!), ball-juggling South Americans . . . suddenly there was a hell of a lot to grapple with: 'The

rapidity with which Continentals and South Americans have made themselves known to us is quite remarkable.' Forget Home Internationals, the *Topical Times* suggested, 'the games that will tickle the palate in the future are the "world" clashes.'

Looking forward to Chile, they were very taken with the fiery Italian-Argentine Enrique Sívori who 'juggles the ball like a music artist [and] always plays to the gallery.' His refusal to wear shinpads cost him an Italy cap for a long time, and his superstitious nature was also noted: ' . . . like most of the South Americans. He won't come on to the field, for instance, without singing his "theme" song – "Sunday Is Always Sunday".' Sandro Mazzola, Di Stéfano, 'film star' Ladislav Kubala, Barcelona's former 'bare-footed back-street youngster' Luis Suárez, and another one who was always being sent off, Yugoslavia's Dragoslav Šekularac, all featured: ' . . . they're wonderful characters, these fellows. And wonderful players. They'll be welcome on the British football stage.'

The Eagle Football Annual, a year later, in their guide to WHO'S WHO IN WORLD SOCCER described Sívori as 'an accomplished oil painter' and profiled everyone – from Yugoslav keeper Vladimir Beara to Luiz Bellini (a tough Brazilian centre-half who was 'planning for the future and has opened a ladies shoe shop in Rio de Janeiro') to Rudolf Kučera (Czech inside-left), Ivan Kolev (Bulgarian inside-left), 'new discovery' Eusébio, and French centre-forward Just Fontaine, a recording artist who 'occasionally sings in clubs' – over the course of a lengthy twelve pages.

But Chile was ultimately a disappointment for England – 'crap' was the one word Johnny Haynes used to describe England's tournament in a 1998 *Independent* interview with Ken Jones. Brian Glanville, in his *Story of the World Cup*, quoted a Yugoslav coach considering Haynes: '"Number 10 takes the corners! Number 10 takes the throw-ins! So what do we do? We put a man on number 10! Goodbye, England!"' In his 1963

THE ADVENTURES OF AN ENGLISH REFEREE ABROAD

as told by

KEN ASTON

Book of World Soccer Kenneth Wolstenholme was already looking forward to the 'big jamboree' to be staged in England in three years' time. Unfortunately the under-23 side tipped as being full of the coming men featured only Martin Peters and one B. Moore of West Ham (visible in the team photo but not mentioned in the article) of the final squad, and the focus was on bright young things like the Swindon Town pair Norman Trollope and Bobby Woodruff, Mansfield's Ken Wagstaff, Neil Young and David Wagstaffe of Man City, Fred Hill of Bolton, John Sleeuwenhoek of Aston Villa (known as 'Tulip' because of his 'unpronounceable name') . . . 'so although the pessimists shake their heads, even a quick look around shows that there is ample promising talent in English football. So we could shock the world in 1966.'[54]

In early editions of *Kenneth Wolstenholme's Book of World Soccer* it's still possible to come across the old-school antics of England abroad. The 1963 annual features a marathon article on amateur side Middlesex Wanderers' early foreign tours, where it wasn't unusual for the opposition to line up in 'stockinette caps, with tassles such as fishermen wear', and on one occasion a player on the Continent appeared in a bowler hat. On a tour of East Africa, locals took to removing 'Mary the lamb', the Wanderers' mascot, from the goal, as when this once happened in Uganda the hosts immediately scored . . . cue a couple of reserve players guarding the back of the goal and the impromptu rendition of the insane club song, which featured an unorthodox rhyming scheme:

```
"Verrou" formations :
        ATTACK
          G
   RH     RB     LB
      CH  IL  LH
OR    IR       CF    OL

        DEFENCE
          G
          RB
   RH     CH     LB
      IR  IL  LH
      OR  CF  OL
```

. . . Hurrah for Mary,
Hurrah for the lamb,
Hurrah for the boys who didn't care . . . a little bit,
And everywhere the Wanderers went that lamb was
    sure to go,
Shouting out the battle cry of freedom.
Hurrah! Hurrah! Rah! Rah! Rah!

Away from the sinister public-schoolboy whiff of empire, the same annual did feature a detailed article

on Béla Guttmann's Benfica, a comprehensive appreciation of the contribution (and tragically early demise) of the Just Fontaine–Raymond Kopa partnership up front for France (albeit strangely illustrated with an accompanying photo of Ron Flowers of Wolves), as well as four pages on Josef Masopust of Dukla Prague and Czechoslovakia – all-round action man, defender, powerhouse, Czech army officer, opera lover and, having edged out Eusébio, winner of *France Football*'s poll of European Player of the Year (later more widely known as the Ballon d'Or) – and a pretty complex three-page article on tactics, calling for fluidity in systems (ultimately realised in the '*Verrou*' or 'bolt system' rather than a rigid application of 4–2–4), illustrated by an account of Milan ruthlessly employing *catenaccio* to overcome Ipswich at Portman Road after a first-leg victory in the San Siro. Wolstenholme lambasts hard-done by Ipswich fans for moaning that their boys did more of the attacking: ' . . . "more of the attacking" is a meaningless phrase in modern football. The team that wins is the team that does more of the important attacking . . .'[55]

A year on, and the 1964 *Wolstenholme Book of World Soccer* might as well have a come with a plastic View-Master and stereoscopic cardboard reel of colour slides, such was the global reach contained within its pages. There was a mini-directory of leading international clubs; a thoughtful appreciation of the recently retired Sepp Herberger, including his great ruse of playing the German reserves against Hungary in the group-stage game of the 1958 World Cup so that the first team could sit in the stand and watch, carefully noting down every Hungarian move for when they'd meet later in the final; an account of Lev Yashin's and Gianni Rivera's battle for the Ballon d'Or (Yashin, the Black Octopus – an imposing and athletic keeper – it was noted, picked up modern jazz records wherever he was playing, and listed photography and reading as his other interests); a condensed, seven-page history of football in 'soccer mad'

---

54 A Leyton Orient scout quoted in the *Topical Times* nails Moore fairly early on: 'That fellow Moore will be playing until he is 92. He doesn't break a sweat – yet he doesn't miss a thing.'

55 At the time of writing, the press was full of Brendan Rodgers bemoaning José Mourinho 'parking two buses' at Anfield in a game that could be considered to have cost Liverpool the 2013–14 title. Chelsea still scored twice – a trawl through the annuals of yesteryear reveals nothing if not the rock-solid fact that nothing changes in football.

Above: The subtleties of the 'Verrou' formation explained in *Kenneth Wolstenholme's Book of World Soccer* 1963

Right: European Player of the Year Josef Masopust shows off his postcard collection to his mildly disinterested kids, in the same annual

Europe's No.1 Footballer

Josef Masopust and his two children.

29

Milan (which included a player-by-player break-down of the two Milan teams: Giovanni Trapattoni, at twenty-five, was singled out as such a good marker that he'd twice snuffed Pelé out of a game); and a feature on the elegant and tricky Belgian wunderkind Paul Van Himst.

And if that feels a lot of ground to cover, by 1964 the Souvenir Press were into the sixth edition of their *International Football Book*, a somewhat dense, 144-page volume, packed with lengthy articles, plenty of monochrome photography and a detailed appendix of the previous year's European and South American international fixtures. Ian Ure, in the sixth volume, reckoned, 'You still meet the British football fan whose knowledge of football begins and ends in England and Scotland, but most have now been converted.' He mentioned televised highlights of the 1958 World Cup (still the only tournament where all four home nations have been present) as the key factor responsible for turning most heads in the football community, but his own personal epiphany occurred under the floodlights at Ibrox in 1957, as Milan dismantled Rangers

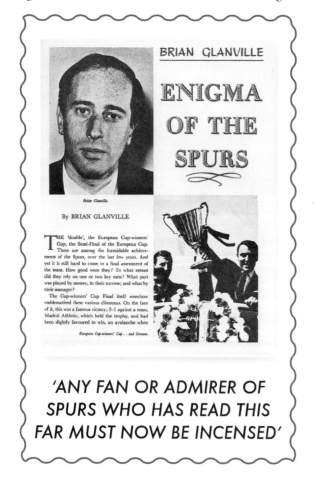

'ANY FAN OR ADMIRER OF SPURS WHO HAS READ THIS FAR MUST NOW BE INCENSED'

1–4, and the passing of the tall, skinny Juan Alberto Schiaffiano, combined with the general inventiveness of Milan's play, so enthused the young Ure that he even spent a train journey home discussing the match with his French master, 'himself a thoughtful football man', whom he'd bumped into.

Richard Williams, though he frowns at the mention of Ure, alludes to another occasion in Scotland – Real Madrid v Eintracht Frankfurt, the 1960 European Cup final, broadcast live on TV – as being a revelatory moment for British football fans: 'That match was like the light coming on . . . that was when you saw what you'd imagined people were doing. I can still remember the sound on the television of the intake of breath as Gento spun and went up the touchline . . . incredible.'

A staple of the *International Football Book* would be a young Brian Glanville's TOP TWENTY – MORE PLAYER SKETCHES. A typical entry would read:

> One of the outstanding young forwards in Europe, Peter Ducke, like his brother, works in the factory at Jena . . . Slim, a beautiful mover, quick to go to the wing, and the possessor of a fine burst of speed. Ducke was capped in his teens. The East Germans feel he is even better than Uwe Seeler.

Which, in its economy and authority, said it all, really. In the same volume Glanville was struggling to assess the current Spurs side – 'How good were they? To what extent did they rely on one or two key men? What part was played by money, in their success; and what by their manager?' He deconstructed Tottenham's 5–1 triumph over Atlético Madrid in the European Cup Winners' Cup – 'Spurs, though they won splendidly on the day [a sentiment which has the ring of a qualifier inserted by the editor back in the office] were just a little lucky to win at all, let alone by such a margin' – pointed out that other factors had a strong bearing on their Cup victories over Leicester and Burnley, and criticized the ferocity of their tackling against Slovan Bratislava in a European Cup Winners' tie (the men in white only easing up after being considerably ahead and 'playing with the fluent brilliance of which we knew [they] were capable; but this was like the repentance of a spoilt child, after it has got its own way'). There had been further ill discipline in a Cup fixture – 'the cup tie with Burnley was, of course, a disgrace' – and their dodgy away form was also noted. 'Any fan or admirer of Spurs who has read this far must now be incensed,' he added not unreasonably – a situation no doubt exacerbated should the reader have been

Above: Brian Glanville airs his mildly controversial views of Spurs' 1961 Cup Winners' Cup win in the *International Football Book* 1964

aware of Glanville's early life as an Arsenal fan.[56]

Despite Ian Ure's assertion that we were all international football fans now, Willy Meisl, writing in the same *International Football Book* on the European Cup final held at Wembley in 1963, as part of the FA's centenary celebration, expressed his disgust that while AC Milan and Benfica clearly rose to the occasion, 'England's soccer fans did not. Only a miserable 45,000 turned up at Wembley. The same stadium would have been sold out four times over for an English Cup final between Peterborough and Ipswich.' That was the game where a twenty-two-year-old Eusébio Da Silva Ferreira revealed himself to the world, in front of plenty of empty seats, but Meisl was surprised to read a leading English newspaper making a reference to Milan's 'English-style team-work' as being the factor that allowed them to dominate, eventually overcoming the Portuguese 2–1: 'Milan employing "English-style team-work" indeed! A fantastic idea, almost megalomaniacal.'

Meisl applauded the appointment of Alf Ramsey, mainly because of his links with the progressive Arthur Rowe and his Hungarian coaching, but in 1964, the contributors to the *International Football Book* were more than aware of the long road ahead. A few pages on, Tony Pullein of the National Federation of Football Supporters wrote of the problems of ordinary fans trying to afford tickets for a Cup final at Wembley: 'The only people who get them at face value are the socialites, the business executives . . . and the spivs.' Like Meisl he expressed dismay at the number of empty seats at England matches. The forthcoming World Cup, he believed, would herald a new era of international interest – 'the Cup final will soon be just another match to all but interested parties. Of that I am quite sure. It will happen in 1968.'

The same annual also featured Adansi United inside-forward Elliot Tenkorang writing to dispel the myth of superstition currently wrecking the image of the game in Africa. Most players had just a rabbit's foot for good luck (nothing more than Bobby Moore putting his shorts on last), and Tenkorang believed the deep enthusiasm for the game in Ghana pointed to the likelihood of the 'Black Star Group' being the first

ELLIOT TENKORANG WROTE TO DISPEL THE MYTH OF SUPERSTITION CURRENTLY WRECKING THE IMAGE OF THE GAME IN AFRICA

African nation to win the World Cup. (Sadly this was a bit premature, Ghana failing to qualify for another forty-two years.) There was also a slightly dense four-page history of Russian goalkeeping: from Nikolai Sokolov 'the Leningrad Eagle' (who saved fourteen penalties in 1924–25, became an office worker, was awarded the coveted Merited Master of Sport, became an accomplished skier and, aged sixty-three, was still employed as a forester's mate), through to Lev Yashin.

Laurie Rampling looks at me slightly blankly when I bring up the *International Football Book*, and ask him if he remembers buying it and reading it in the sixties, brushing up on his knowledge of János Farkas[57]

---

56 Eventually Glanville did put himself forward as one of Spurs' most ardent admirers – 'the memory of their football at its best, wonderfully varied, mobile, rapid, penetrating, graceful, will remain with all of us who have ever seen it' – and reserved his greatest praise for Danny Blanchflower: Greaves might receive all the plaudits for goals, but the Irishman 'steadied the defence, linked admirably with [John] White [and] imposed on the team a philosophy of movement, permutation, skilful football almost for its own sake, which caused the players to rise above themselves.'

---

57 Hungarian striker who updated 1968 *International Football Book* readers with tips on how to unpick *catenaccio*-type defences (see chapter 4), and on how the marriage of Hungarian skill and flair with the more physical game played in England, Germany and Russia was progressing: 'It isn't easy for players, who until now have usually done all their training with the ball . . . ' Found playing England 'interesting but not enjoyable'; Bychevetz was a talented Soviet winger of the 1960s.

Above: The future of African football gets an early serious appraisal in the same *International Football Book* 1964

DAVE MACKAY, Tottenham Hotspur

and Anatoli Bychevetz. 'I wouldn't have thought so (but I buy 'em for tuppence ha'penny now). I know, pretty boring, really. I've got a dozen in the loft, but that's where they are. I didn't particularly want to see Uwe Seeler. I'd rather have seen Johnny Haynes playing against West Brom, or Dave Mackay getting stuck in for Tottenham.'[58]

If by the early sixties it was commonplace for the likes of *Wolstenholme* and the *International Football Book* to take in broad, thematic round-ups of the international scene, traditionally annuals had tended to focus on the capers of touring sides, or individual players plying their trade abroad.

Charles Buchan's Soccer Gift Book looked back at Neil Franklin's move to Bogotá, and considered this the moment that 'set English players free', but that was a full fourteen years after Franklin's move from Stoke to Santa Fe, and so a fairly uncontroversial statement by 1964. As far back as the 1957 *Big Book of Football Champions*, Eddie Firmani, 'the 70,000,000 lira footballer from Charlton', spilled the beans on the gravy train that was the European signing-on fee, letting readers know how much several of his colleagues had raked in – £25,000 in the case of ex-Charlton colleague Hans Jeppson – compared to rainy old England, where league bonuses usually amounted to £2 for a win, £1 for a draw. In Italy you'd as likely get £36 for an away win, and then there was the drive home in the sunshine, in Firmani's case 'along the wide, palm-studded road to my marble-floored flat in Genoa'.

Things soon turned nasty for Firmani, however, as the goals dried up, the language proved difficult, and his grandfather's Italian nationality began to be questioned (due to the flood of South Americans after the war Firmani, a South African by birth, had made it in only because he was of Italian extraction). But eventually the goals came back, the crowd would yell '*cannioniere* [Bombardier]' when he left the pitch and harmony was restored, especially in the opulent Geona clubhouse where there were 'luxurious lounges equipped with deep armchairs, a TV room, billiard tables and refreshment bars. White-coated waiters are around to serve us with coffee or meals. We have a plenty to entertain us

The 70,000,000 Lire Footballer from Charlton

EDDIE FIRMANI

tells us all about his transfer to Italy

MY grandfather Pietro Cleito Firmani was a fisherman from Ortona-Mare on the Adriatic coast of Italy. Little did I realise the importance of that fact when I landed in Southampton from South Africa on a cold day in February 1950, to start five happy and eventful years with Charlton.

The "accident" of my grandfather's birth brought me to the luxury soccer land of Italy. As I drive along the wide, palm-studded road to my marble-floored flat in Genoa, I often think that but for grand-dad, who now lives in South Africa, I would still be in English football, tied to the regulations and wage restrictions of the Football League.

Italy is not entirely a soccer paradise. It has snags. But they are more than compensated by the fact that the clubs treat the players royally and much better than in England. My basic wage is not much more than the £15 a week in the Football League, but bonuses jump far beyond the £2 a win and £1 a draw. For an away win we get 64,000 lire (£36 10s.), for an

'IN ITALY YOU'D GET £36 FOR AN AWAY WIN, AND THEN THERE WAS THE DRIVE HOME IN THE SUNSHINE'

between games. A lift sweeps you upstairs to the main lounges, and the dressing rooms underneath are equally well appointed. I cannot help comparing it with some of the dingy club headquarters in England, the home of the game.'

Still, seven years later, Firmani was back at the Valley and writing in the *Soccer Gift Book* that, while he was far better off in Italy, he'd tired of his life in a Fellini film, and, in fact, blamed bad habits picked up at Sampdoria, Inter Milan and Genoa for making him moody and temperamental.

'Eddie Firmani was a complete joke,' asserts Johnny Green, then laughs – for a second I'd forgotten the intense rivalry between Gillingham and Charlton. 'I saw Eddie Firmani at the Valley, my uncle Stan used to take me – he lived near there – he [Firmani] looked like a fish out of water to me . . . but one of the virtues of an annual, as opposed to just weekly news, was

---

58 'Russian football took a lot from our game and put it in their game,' Laurie says later, and it transpires he follows the game in Russia. The touring Moscow teams in the forties and fifties 'gave us a footballing lesson . . . totally outplayed us'.

Previous pages: The *Topical Times Football Book* graphics department get creative with an image of Dave Mackay bursting through a tartan background in 1960; Bobby Charlton sets off

**on his world travels in 1965 in the same title.
Above: Charlton's Eddie Firmani relates his experiences of playing abroad in the *Big Book of Football Champions* 1956**

that I was aware that football was wider than England, or the UK. I was open to Real Madrid and Benfica: there was a world out there, and the books helped me understand far more. I was excited, it was quite exotic, and they played differently to us. It was covered by the fact that Jimmy Greaves, Law, Gerry Hitchens, had gone out to Italy and were successful – or appeared to be successful. As a kid in the fifties I was always aware of the shadow of Hungary, that we'd been outclassed, and we always might be somehow. I've never understood why my parents bought me a Hibernian shirt [in 1958], but I told everyone it was Northern Ireland [during the World Cup]; an Umbro with the white "v" – terribly modern, you know. The books [thumps the stack of annuals] were really useful for the international aspects of the game, and that continued into the sixties. And I didn't see that as a negative thing – to me *catenaccio* is a very positive word. "That's stylish," is what I thought, in the same way I was looking at mod clothes, seeing Ravel shoes . . . so I didn't see any disparity between Italian-style football and Italian-style footwear in Carnaby or Kingly Street.[59] Garrincha against England in '62. I think I found that exciting – South American football seemed wildly exotic. I liked all that, certainly didn't see it as a threat; I saw it as integral. I didn't see it as they were out to do "us" – I never saw it as "Garrincha is taking *us* apart". I saw it as Garrincha is showing us new ways of playing football. And I wouldn't have known it meant "Little Bird" without Charlie Buchan either.'

Jimmy Greaves, son of the Central line tube driver, cropped up frequently in early sixties annuals talking about his unhappy time in Italy. At Milan, he told the *Eagle Football Annual*, he didn't get on with the Jack Hawkins-like Nereo Rocco, was lonely, frequently late for training (on one occasion this was down to driving his mother-in-law to the airport – 'Excuses, always excuses,' said a club official), and confessed that he didn't really want to be there in the first place: he only went for the money, then the sudden abolition of the maximum wage left him high and dry, Greaves having already signed on the dotted line at the San Siro.

The canvas was definitely widening, wages were increasing, and there was an inkling of the 'professional' game to come, but there was absolutely no indication in the football annuals of the day that England would

---

59 I point out that he only read about it though – English football was barely on TV: 'That's right, you can't overestimate that lack of television, and so the emphasis on these [annuals]'.

be under pressure to put on a decent show in their own backyard come 1966, World Cups being a fairly muted presence in most annuals, until at least 1970.

In the pages of most yearbooks, though, there was an underlying feeling that the wind of chance, or fate, still blew strongly through football in the early sixties.

That could often be an ill wind. Just pulling out a sample selection of annuals from a three-year period, 1959–62, there's Roy Dwight's broken leg, knee-ligament trouble, broken arm and subsequent release from Forest which meant that, according to the *Big Book of Football Champions* in 1961, 'in 21 months Dwight slipped from Cup final hero to soccer's scrapheap'. There's Derek Dooley's aforementioned leg amputation; and the Sheffield Wednesday Boxing Day coach crash of 1960, described by Peter Swan in the 1961–62 *Soccer Gift Book* as his worst experience in football – inside-right Dougie McMillan, standing in the stairwell, retuning the radio as the coach failed to navigate an icy double-bend on the A1, lost a foot in the wreckage. Equally, though, there was plenty of

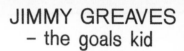

Jimmy in action for Milan against Rome

GREAVES ONLY WENT TO MILAN FOR THE MONEY, THEN THE SUDDEN ABOLITION OF THE MAXIMUM WAGE LEFT HIM HIGH AND DRY

Above: Jimmy Greaves during his short stay in Milan, featured in *Eagle Football Annual* 1963

Douglas McMillan of Sheffield Wednesday had his
right foot amputated after a coach crash.

was a renewed sense of hope and progress – in the country at large a post-war consensus sought education and a health service for all, and this optimism, combined with a liberation from a life down the pit, lent a celebratory, almost carefree (there-but-for-the-grace) edge to a footballer's existence. Or at least that's how it comes across in the annuals of the day. The hours were good – Mick McNeil could still help out his dad after training with his market garden business in Middlesbrough – and the darkness of war and mass unemployment in the thirties were firmly in the past (if never to be forgotten). In this light, football was . . . just football, and perhaps shouldn't be taken too seriously.

'Don't forget [throughout this whole period] you're not far off the war,' says Graham Sharpe, in his office at William Hill. 'I was effectively a war baby, born in 1950, and growing up, everything was still the war. The media wanted to be upbeat, we'd just come through the war and we were still struggling. We'd been through

good fortune, or happenstance: if, as the first *Topical Times Football Book* recounted, Jimmy Porter, Bury scout, hadn't been out driving in the countryside with a pal and stopped to light up a cigarette opposite a football field, he'd have never looked up and spotted Eddie Kilshaw, soon-to-be Bury stalwart, later sold on to Sheffield Wednesday for the princely record sum of £20,000.

The war played havoc with the careers of Kilshaw and his generation[60], so a decade or more later there

---

60 Manchester United's Johnny Berry, a former cinema projectionist at the Ritz in Aldershot, toured India during the war with the Army Kinematograph service, the travelling film unit, and played in the same army team as Fred Harris, 'Birmingham's star right-half'; Tom Cheadle crossed paths with a P.T. instructor, one Busby, M. during the war; Ivor Allchurch and Terry Medwin were just two others who wrote of their war-time life in various football annuals.

Above: Douglas McMillan of Sheffield Wednesday pictured after the coach crash that ended his career in *Big Book of Football Champions* 1961

The early annuals are full of tales of luck intervening in a player's career: 'If the Bluebirds, my local Welsh League club, had not been short in a six-a-side practice game, I would now probably be working at the coal-face in my native Blaengarw,' wrote Billy Rees (above), of Cardiff then Leyton Orient, in the *Soccer Gift Book*. Ron Yeats informs the *Topical Times* that if a Celtic scout, very keen to sign him for Celtic reserves, hadn't been killed in a fatal car crash on his way back to Parkhead, he wouldn't have signed for Dundee United, who plunged him straight into the first team, from which he never looked back on his way to Anfield (and never once played a reserve game).

rationing but you don't want to be giving people bad news, you want to be trying to uplift them. It wasn't till the Beatles arrived that the war began to disappear into the background, and people thought, "OK, we've burst into the sunlight now." And football *was* just football, because these guys weren't earning that much more money than the plumber and the baker. They were getting the odd under-the-counter payment, I'm sure, but by and large they lived in the community, were part of the community. You'd see players in the pub, they didn't have airs and graces.[61] It was Johnny Haynes who was to blame for it in a way.'

If the players were growing to see football as an easier way of life, at least they still retained a refreshingly down-to-earth view of things. 'I can't understand the moaners,' wrote Tony Kay in the 1962–63 *Soccer Gift Book*. Keeping fit and playing football, was, reckoned Kay, 'not much to do for the money we get! . . . we have our playing kit provided free; we get the best medical attention; we live in club houses at a ridiculously low rent, and when we travel at home or abroad we dine and wine [*sic*] like film stars in the best hotels. Anyone who complains about that sort of life wants their head examining!' For Kay, the footballer's life 'beats the daily grind in the factory or office, day in, day out, year in, year out.' Which reads all the more poignantly with hindsight, as Kay (like Peter Swan earlier) was only a few months away from his part in a match-fixing ring being exposed.[62]

Fittingly, high jinks and a sense of fun were slowly percolating through the pages of the annuals of the early sixties: where else would you learn that Donnie Mackinnon, Partick Thistle centre-half,

He's always around . . . yet seldom seen . . . his knowledge of what it takes to make a star player can mean a smash-hit attraction for the fans . . . maybe thousands of pounds for the club he works for.

MEET – MR FOOTBALL SCOUT

STOPPED TO LIGHT A FAG – AND FOUND A £20,000 PLAYER

was once bitten by a dog at Firhill; that Manchester United's hard man Maurice Setters spent many an evening talking to his pet African grey parrot; and that Kilmarnock, in their 1964–65 Scottish championship-winning season, had a club mascot, Wilma the sheep, who was fond of eating cigarettes lobbed at her from the crowd, and was 'so confident of Killie's defence that, during one game she strayed on to the pitch and started cropping the goal area' before being ushered off the grass?

This was also a time when a little over-exuberance on the terraces was seen as nothing to worry about, no more than a light-hearted distraction. A beer bottle thrown from the crowd at a St Etienne match hit the ref, and the French football authorities ordered bars to be closed unless paper cups could be used; at a match in Livramento, Brazil, a fan attacked the ref, before another fan appeared on the pitch with a gun and shot the attacker – both incidents were recounted in a 'funny old world'/THE STRANGEST THINGS HAPPEN IN FOOTBALL round-up

---

61 This still went on as recently as the mid- to late-eighties. As a student I remember several members of the Cardiff City first team, led by Terry Boyle, perm and all, suddenly appearing in a slightly tacky, half-empty city-centre wine bar one Saturday night. There was certainly no roped-off VIP area, just a sticky dancefloor.

62 'The heyday of fixed-odds football betting was in the early sixties, and I don't recall seeing a lot, if anything, in any of these,' says Graham Sharpe, nodding at the pile of annuals on his desk. 'Pools football as well. There was the huge scandal – Sheffield Wednesday, Bronco Layne – and stuff was buried, wasn't it.' As far as the annuals of the day were concerned he seems to be correct.

Above: Bury scout Jimmy Porter spots a star of the future during a cigarette break in the *Topical Times Football Book* 1959

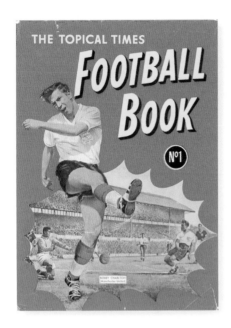

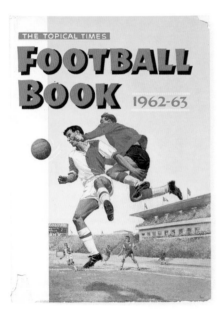

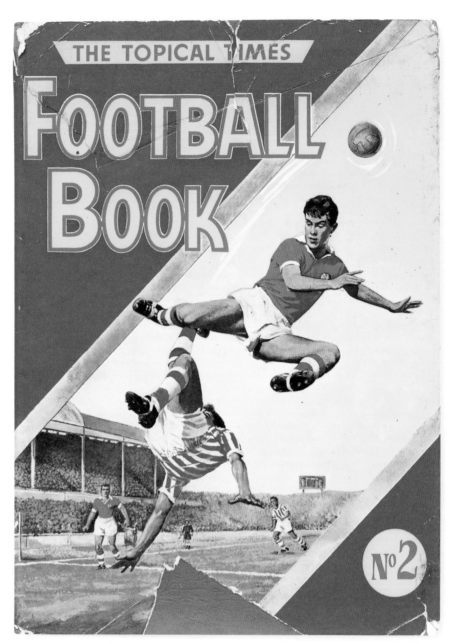

The *Topical Times Football Book* launched in 1959 with a big red splash and a photo of Bobby Charlton superimposed over what looks to be an English league XI playing Scotland. Publishers were ever careful to satisfy readers north and south of the border and Kilmarnock keeper Jimmy Brown adorned the back cover. Early '60s editions settled into a pleasing rhythm of finely illustrated high-impact goalmouth action and bold type.

In 1965 there was a shift away from illustration to photography, but the graphic formula remained the same: combative action photos cut out, retouched and overlaid on colourful blocks.

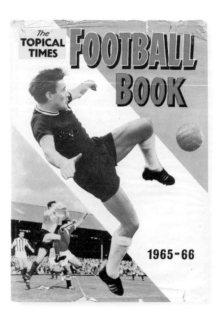

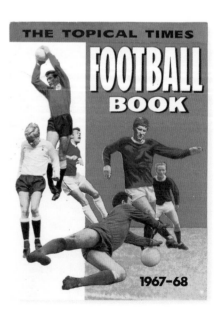

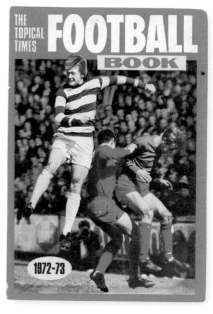

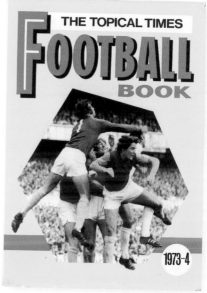

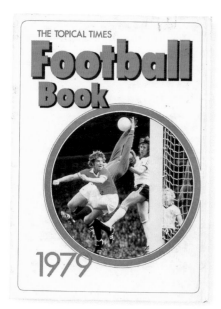

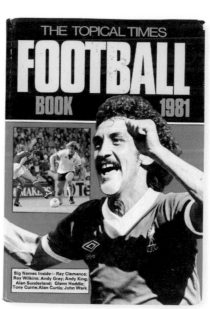

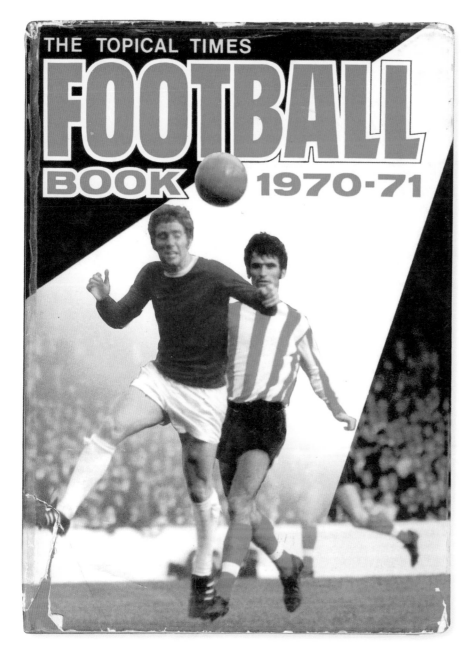

By the '70s *Topical Times* jackets were typically structured around one photo – the tried and tested impact action scene, of course – and a background colour. The 1972–73 cover featured a photo of QPR's Rodney Marsh rather heavily retouched. At least we think it's Rodney, such is the extent of the physical alteration.

By the late '70s and early '80s the publishers had settled, for the most part, on a white background, though there was occasional use of a red masthead and a deviation to black in 1981. *Topical Times* defied our loosely defined 'heyday' by publishing on throughout the 1990s before the presses finally stopped on this enduring title in 2000.

of entertaining shorts in the *Topical Times* of 1960.[63]

Later editions of the *Topical Times* STRANGEST THINGS collection included a photograph of a psychopathic looking Norwich City fan who lost a work-place bet over Norwich topping the table, and subsequently had to shave his head; and another Norwich fan in a mac, snapped launching a kick at the groundsman's salt bucket at Portman Road, having run on to the icy pitch in protest at the salt-spreading having taken place *only* in the Ipswich keeper's goalmouth. Then there was Southend's bid to increase noise at Roots Hall by handing out war-time rattles, formerly issued to air-raid wardens; the goat that ate the ref's clothes – shirt, tie, socks and underwear – left in a barn during an Irish league game; 'football players with adverts on their backs! Yes, it's happening – in Belgium'; photos of fans precariously crowded on the roof of St Luke's church on the corner of Goodison Park, studiously ignoring police pleas to come down; a ref officiating Port Vale v Torquay with a small dog tucked under his arm (the

> FOOTBALL, LIKE LIFE,
> WAS BRUTAL, BUT YOU
> JUST GOT ON WITH IT

dog had invaded the pitch three times prior to ref Les Haines of Bolton getting hold of it for good); before and after shots of Mr Arthur Holland of Barnsley, blacked-up with coal dust and wearing a pit helmet having just surfaced from his shift, then resplendent with Brilliantined quiff, sporting his FA Cup final referee's outfit; the tale of the railway engine driver who stopped his engine on a siding to catch Greenock Morton v Cappielow, but caused the match to be temporarily halted after smoke from the engine wafted down on the pitch thickening 'the already foggy air' (before the police were called to have a word); and the story of Vittorio Casa, a winger whose car was machine-gunned by the Argentine army on manoeuvres – twenty-five days later, after having his arm amputated, he presented himself at the training ground, and was soon back in the San Lorenzo first team.

Football, like life, was brutal, but you just got on with it.

I'M LUCKY TO BE ALIVE was the headline of a piece by Mansfield's Colin Askey in the 1963–64 *Soccer Gift Book*. Askey had an old Port Vale team-mate, Len Barber, to thank for diving in and saving his life after he got into difficulties with cramp in the local swimming pool one day after training. If it hadn't have been for the casual look back from Barber as headed towards the cubicles, Askey would have 'bought it'.[64]

---

63 The same feature informed us that 'spivs in South America sell rotten fruit to fans for pelting players'; Airdrie's Tommy Duncan could walk around the perimeter of Broomfield Park twice without stopping – on his hands; in a lower-league fixture between Malfetta and Martina Franca in Italy, only one fan turned up in a snowstorm and was applauded by both sets of players at the end of the match; and also in Italy, Roberto 'Bob' Lovati, Lazio's keeper, was so disgusted at the last-minute awarding of a penalty to the opposition, Bologna, that he turned his back on the ball 'only for the spot-kick to hit him on the posterior'. Overjoyed at his 'save' Lovati threw himself on the ball and promptly broke a finger.

---

64 The article then recounted several escapades involving the misplacing of Vale trainer Ken Fish's false teeth.

* * *

◀ This is PETER COOPER

A RED-HOT Norwich City supporter. And why Peter is so nearly hairless in our picture is—because of super-confidence in the "Canaries". He bet his workmates Norwich would be leading the League around the middle of last season. "I'll shave all the hair off my head if they aren't," he said. Well, they weren't! So Peter spent a cold week or two.

74

BOBBY SMITH says "Boy, isn't it tough in League 4!"

THERE'S a world of difference between the glamour of Division 1 and the hard world of Division 4.

I managed to switch from the high-up to the low-down in a matter of months.

In October 1963, I was leading the England attack against the Rest of the World. On the same field as big name men like Puskas, Di Stefano, Yashin, Santos, Eusebio, Masopust, Charlton, Law, Greaves, and Baxter.

I was then a member of the outstanding Spurs side that won the "double"—League and F.A. Cup, in the same year—were Cup winners in two successive seasons, European Cup semi-finalists, European Cup-Winners' Cup winners.

What a difference. Playing against Arsenal, Manchester United, Everton, and Sheffield Wednesday, compared with turning out against Crewe, Halifax, Hartlepools, and Rochdale.

Yet I don't regret the switch one little bit.

When Spurs put me on the transfer list I could have gone to any one of a dozen clubs. For instance, I could have stayed in London and the First Division with Fulham. Instead I decided on Division 4—with Brighton and Hove Albion.

I thus became part of a club determined to put

DOPED!

South Coast football on the map. A club that still thought hard about getting into Division 1. when they were in Division 4. Who have ideas of building the club up into a super South Coast sports centre.

7000 extra fans packed into the ground every week last season—because they really thought the club was doing something about getting right to the top.

Climbing with Brighton has been every bit as exciting as being with Spurs in their great days. As exciting as playing all over the world with England.

Naturally there is not so much glory. Missing, too, are the crowds and the excitement of Division 1. Playing in front of 60,000 fans the roar doesn't mean a thing. You simply don't hear the crowd.

Playing away from home in Division 4—with perhaps only two or three thousand fans—every remark is heard. Some of them pretty fruity, too.

Physically it is much harder in Division 4. There is much more physical contact. But then I was always prepared to give and take.

And if there are a few more knocks, there's also more time. Things don't move as quickly as in the First Division. A player gets that split second longer in which to decide on the next move. It all helps.

Being able to take in your stride anything in the way of ups and downs is an essential in the make-up of a footballer. And I don't think I need many for a set.

I joined Chelsea as a 15-year-old, but got so homesick in London I soon went back to my family in Redcar.

Then I decided to give it another chance—and got into the Chelsea League side at 17. I reckoned I was in the business. But it was in one week and out the next.

I didn't really settle until I moved across to White Hart Lane in December 1955—to eventually become part and parcel of all Spurs success.

Same with England. When the 1958 World Cup came around I never thought I had a chance of being in the party. When the twenty-two were named I reckoned Brian Clough was a certainty. Instead I went. I didn't play. But I went.

In 1962, just the reverse. I was established in the England side. We lost 2-0 to Scotland at Hampden. And I was the only man in the side left out of the party for Chile. Gerry Hitchens and Alan Peacock went instead.

I blew my top then because I was looking forward to Chile. But I got back again. And I suppose it's a good way to end an International career with a last match against the Rest of the World at Wembley. That was the one that was part of the celebrations in connection with the Centenary of the English Football Association.

One of the greatest of Spurs great moments I almost missed. Indeed I should have missed it. The final against Leicester City in 1961. The League and Cup "double".

I had an injury. No one knew about it. Not even manager Billy Nicholson. In fact, I've never mentioned it before now.

— SO I COULD PLAY IN THE FINAL AT WEMBLEY...

During the week leading up to the final I could hardly walk. A nerve was touching the cartilage of my right knee. Every movement was painful. I had been to my own doctor for pain-killing injections. With these I could play without feeling it too badly.

On the day before the final we had to turn out for the TV cameras. I jog-trotted around White Hart Lane. Trying to keep out of the camera's eye and praying that no one would ask me to kick a ball. They didn't, and on Saturday morning no one knew about the injury but myself.

If I had told Mr Nicholson I wouldn't have played at Wembley. And how I wanted to play.

On the morning of the match I went to my own doctor. He gave me an injection in the knee. I reported back to him again at 1 p.m. He gave me still another.

"That will last you until about 3.45," he told me.

He was five minutes out. 3.45 was half-time, and five minutes before this I felt the pain come back. I could hardly stand. Back in the dressing room I asked the club doctor for another pain-killing injection.

In the 66th minute I scored a goal. Spurs were on their way to the double. I also crossed the ball for Terry Dyson to head our second goal.

Five minutes before the finish I could hardly walk. But we won. The risk was justified.

In the close season I went to an osteopath. He clicked back into position a bone in my spine. This had

caused the nerve to cause trouble in the knee. It's never bothered me since.

We still talk about that wonderful Spurs side which owed so much to Dave Mackay and Danny Blanchflower.

Dave got the side going. He never stopped working. Chasing and shouting at everyone on the field. Never contemplating defeat. Always giving that little bit extra for a win.

But it was Danny who made things tick. Always planning. Always looking to give something to the game. On and off field for ever thinking about it. Searching and probing every weakness of the opposition. Setting

Scoring a goal — for Spurs

things up for the forwards. His approach to the game is something Spurs have never really replaced.

Blanchflower, on and off field, was always one move ahead of the opposition. It's a pity he decided to have no part of football management. He would have been outstanding.

But we all go our own way. As far as I'm concerned the main aim is to be a success at Brighton. The club is progressive. Look how we made Division 3 last season.

We could become the Blackpool of the South Coast—with the support and the enthusiasm to put us in Division 1.

Training on the beach — in Brighton's colours

66 · 67

And you wonder what Barrie Jones of Plymouth Argyle left out of his *Topical Times* account of the Pilgrims' initiation ceremony for an excited young player about to make his debut: 'I was all keyed up. Then someone said, "Step under the shower." Not a warm shower. Not even a tepid shower. But a shower of Arctic coldness. By jove – that cooled me down, for there's nothing like it to get the butterflies out of the system and make you feel all tingly.'

In the same 1965–66 *Topical Times Football Book* bustling centre-forward Bobby Smith put a brave face on his drop down the divisions, from playing in front of 60,000 fans at White Hart Lane, where you couldn't hear a word of abuse from the crowd such was the general roar, to 'playing away from home in Division 4 [with Brighton, at the likes of Crewe or Halifax] with perhaps only two or three thousand fans [where] every remark is heard. Some of them pretty fruity too.' It's unlikely an annual today would interview Freddie Sears about swapping life at Upton Park for Colchester, nor, for that matter, have a headline along the lines of – DOPED! SO I COULD PLAY IN THE FINAL AT WEMBLEY. Smith, a marauding centre-forward in his day, failed to

inform Bill Nicholson ahead of the Double-winning Cup final of '61 that he had a trapped nerve 'touching the cartilage of my right knee . . . I could hardly walk', preferring to keep it under control with regular, furtive visits to, and painkilling injections from, his own doctor. The gamble paid off though – despite the pain seeping back in the second half at Wembley he scored one and laid on the other as Spurs beat Leicester 2–0.

There was a similar by-the-seat-of-your-pants feel to a feature by England trainer Harold Shepherdson, as he relayed to *Topical Times* readers tales from behind the scenes with the national squad. These typically involved: flying lubricant out to Sweden for Nobby Stiles, who'd forgotten his contact-lens fluid (Shepherdson gets his revenge in by adding that Stiles also 'collects miniature dolls in national colours'); George Eastham getting his nose trapped in a lift-door in Leipzig; the same George Eastham who caused panic, the England squad nearly missing the plane to the Chile World Cup because George was having a haircut in the airport barber's; and Bobby Moore, strolling around various dressing rooms in his underpants, superstition dictating that he liked to put his shorts on last. Shepherdson noted that

---

Left: A typically quirky entry in the
***Topical Times Football Book's* Strange, and**
sometimes Odd things spread 1965

Above: Spurs' Double-winning striker Bobby
Smith adjusts to life on the south coast in
the *Topical Times Football Book* 1965–66

TRAINER TO ENGLAND

by

Harold Shepherdson

DURING all my spell as trainer of England's international team, I lost count of the times I have been asked what my biggest thrill has been.

But I always give the same answer to the question. The big thrill was getting the job in the first place.

That was 'way back in 1957. And I got a kick every time I got the familiar note from the Football Association telling me I was to be trainer for England's next match.

The job took me to countries all over the world—21 in all. Places as far apart as Russia and Mexico, Peru and Czechoslovakia, Luxembourg and Brazil.

Players who have been in my care, some as widely travelled as myself, make up a wonderful galaxy of stars. Bobby Moore, Tom Finney, Bobby Charlton, Jackie Charlton, Johnny Haynes, Duncan Edwards, George Eastham. And many, many more. It would need a computer to reckon their worth in transfer fees.

Like everybody else, I suppose, they are all a little

'last-minute Moore' had nearly been caught out a few times, the dressing-room bell having sounded and, ball in hand, England's captain had been on the brink of stepping out into the tunnel in just his boots, socks and shirt.

In Scotland there was horse-play behind the scenes too. Rangers' Billy Ritchie remembered (in a '66–67 *Topical Times* article) the time 'Wee' Willie Henderson, in a Monaco hotel for a European Cup tie, showed his new pair of fancy, Continental shoes to Jim Baxter: 'What d'ye think of these, Surr?' asked Henderson. Baxter's response, demonstrating admirable foresight of future footballer-behaviour, was to throw them out of the open window on to the street below. (Wee Willie tore downstairs, only to be told that a French gentleman had scooped up the loafers and made off with them. While Willie, 'in his pure, thick Lanarkshire', was down the road imploring a complete strange to open up his briefcase, another teammate fished the shoes out of a bush.) On another European date, Ritchie got himself locked inside the San Siro following a spot of sunbathing after training. And on his first trip abroad he recalled how he was given a new club blazer with red and white piping – fine braiding all over the cuffs, lapels and handkerchief pocket – 'All the other players had blazers of a different vintage – without the braiding.' As a result of this handsome blazer, everywhere they went everyone assumed Ritchie was '*Le Capitaine*'. Presumably having been asked to one interview or press conference too many, the actual captain intervened: 'Naw, he's no' the captain, he's our ice-cream man,' growled the imposing George Young to one official.

The supply of footballers-larking-about-abroad anecdotes was plentiful. In 1957 Arsenal's Joe Haverty contributed his reminiscences of an Eire youth-team tour of Germany to *Charles Buchan's Soccer Gift Book*. One afternoon the lads were making their way to a local shop to pick up some soft drinks, when someone yelled, 'Last man in the shop pays.' In the headlong sprint to avoid forking out for the refreshments one unnamed youth-team player mistook an open door for a plate-glass window . . .

HAROLD SHEPHERDSON'S, TALES INVOLVED FLYING LUBRICANT OUT TO SWEDEN FOR NOBBY STILES AND BOBBY MOORE STROLLING AROUND DRESSING ROOMS IN HIS UNDERPANTS

A few years later Bill Holden, Burnley (and future Stockport and Bury) stalwart, and centre-forward for England's Young Lions – the u-23s – filed a similar piece for *Buchan* concerning a recent tour of Italy under Ron Greenwood. England took Italy to the cleaners, and if that wasn't surprising enough, Holden was aghast at how the Italian fans turned on their own team, throwing cushions on to the pitch in disgust and screaming, '*Bidoni! Bidoni!*' (which, Holden informed us, means 'dustbins') before charging the team coach and sparking a near post-match riot: 'I shall never forget the wild picture afterwards as jeep-loads of police, armed with revolvers, tommy guns and truncheons, forced a way through the waiting mob of derisive fans . . . ' On another Young Lions tour the team manager and officials were out for the evening, and the players couldn't sleep because of the sweltering heat, when some bright spark remembered the swimming pool in the hotel grounds. 'Someone found a football – and at midnight a party of naked young Soccer stars were staging a water polo match in a cool pool,' relayed Holden. Suddenly, there was panic as the figures of the selectors, VIPs and team management were silhouetted in the hotel grounds, and, without time to dash to the lobby, the players all huddled under the pool's ornamental bridge as the team officials made their way over the water and back to their rooms, apparently none the wiser . . .

'At Upton Park – or the Boleyn Ground as it really is – if you hear anyone talking about "Muffin" you can be sure it's me they're referring to,' wrote John Bond, THE MAN WITH A KICK LIKE A MULE, in *Buchan's Gift Book* of 1959–60. Bond seemed considerably more happy-go-lucky and laid-back than most; his early footballing career had been disrupted by National Service rather than the actual war. Running at full pace, he once boarded a moving train out of King's Cross (having made the earlier mistake of going to neighbouring St Pancras) but atoned for his late arrival by scoring the winner at Hull. Yet despite West Ham boss Ted Fenton having had words, Bond was adamant he was going to stick with his casual style – a renowned penalty taker, in the article he relived taking a crucial

Left: Laughs aplenty for England trainer Harold Shepherdson and the squad in the *Topical Times Football Book 1966–67*

"MUFFIN" — the man with a kick like a mule

JOHN BOND

(West Ham)

free-kick on the edge of the box against fellow promotion rivals Liverpool, a couple of minutes from time: 'I wasn't nervous – I'm not the worrying kind.' He fluffed it, trudged back to his position, thinking, 'Well, that's torn it,' when the ref blew for another free-kick in exactly the same place. 'Muffin' got the nod, scored and West Ham went up.

The agonies of being late for games, or missing them entirely, were not an uncommon story in fifties annuals. Eighty thousand fans turned up at Wembley for the FA Amateur Cup final in 1956, which finished 1–1 between Corinthian Casuals and Bishop Auckland. After the final Corinthians summoned Mike Stewart, the England opening batsman, by telegram from a cricket tour of the West Indies, for the replay at Ayresome Park. A madcap dash involving a charter plane landing at Prestwick and 4,500 miles on the clock ended with a half-changed Stewart missing the kick-off by three minutes. This was in the days before substitutes. 'Citron continued at inside-left,' the 1957 *Big Book of Football Champions* coolly noted, the Casuals no.10 no

> 'WHERE TA FUCK HA' YOU BIN? YOU'D MADE THE STARTIN' LINE-UP . . . '

doubt aware of the half-changed Stewart glaring at his back from the shade of the tunnel. (Gerry Citron actually opened the scoring, but to no avail as 'cock of the north'[65] Bishop Auckland won the replay 4–1.)

Five years later and Rangers' Willie Henderson (again) was writing about exactly the same thing in *Buchan's Soccer Gift Book*, albeit this time it was heavy traffic in Glasgow coming to a standstill that made the young winger fume. But that was nothing to when it finally began to move, and Billy's mate's car wouldn't start. In a fury, he left his pal, managed to find a taxi, made it to Ibrox, by which time the teams were walking out on to the pitch. In a curious echo of the 1959 Calvin Palmer episode at the City Ground, some of his fellow trainees made noises along the lines of, 'Where ta fuck ha' you bin? You'd made the startin' line-up . . .' Rangers beat Standard Liège 2–0 but it wasn't enough to overturn an earlier deficit, and Henderson was disconsolate on the touchline: 'I only know that nothing worse could possibly happen to me . . . I failed my team . . . and myself.'[66] That was written a year after the match, in

---

65 Pathé News description of the north's most successful amateur side.

66 There's an alternate version of this story in the *International Football Book* of 1964 involving a four-mile sprint to the ground rather than a taxi, and culminating in him sitting disconsolately on the marble steps of the main Ibrox entrance, surrounded by concerned fans. No mention of Baxter in the context of footwear though.

Above: John Bond's attributes revealed in *Charles Buchan's Soccer Gift Book of 1959–60*

Right: Willie Henderson's tale of being late to a match in *Charles Buchan's Soccer Gift Book 1963–64*

the '63–64 *Soccer Gift Book*. These days there'd be a safe enough distance from such a fuck-up before it was relayed in a football annual – or it'd be all glossed over, swept under the carpet for ever.

Journeys from games could be equally as eventful. In the very first *Topical Times Football Book*, skipper Ronnie Ashman recounted third division Norwich's happy-go-lucky route to the FA Cup semi-final. Before an early round at Swindon wing-half Roy McCrohan had so much 'dope' pumped into a septic arm 'they had to call a halt – because the jabs were upsetting him more than the infection'. Needless to say, he played a blinder; as did striker Terry Allcock at Bramall Lane in the quarter-final, seemingly unaffected by having had his toe lanced just before the game; and keeper Ken Nethercott played in that match too (which turned out to be his last for Norwich) – with a dislocated shoulder. The Canaries had done away with Danny Blanchflower's Spurs in the fifth round (having already disposed of Man United), and skipper Ashman fondly recalled the 'Norwich roar' which 'seemed to build up in the covered area behind one of the goals. Sometimes it got so loud we could hear it crack as it whipped around the stand, just like a plane breaking the sound barrier.'[67]

---

67 Barrie Jones experienced something similar at Plymouth: 'Maybe one of these days the "Devon sound" will rival the Spion Kop scream in Liverpool, the Hampden roar, the Everton chant, or the Spurs "Glory, Glory—"'

The full lyrics of 'On the Ball, City' are reproduced, and the tale climaxes as the lights go out on the train back to Norwich following a narrow defeat in the semi-final replay at St Andrew's. Stuck on a dark train at Rugby the squad, players' wives and officials clean out the buffet-car bar of its six bottles of champagne, drinking by candlelight. 'At Peterborough we stopped again,' continues Ashman. 'As they tried to fix the lights I asked if I had time to nip up to the hotel near the station. "We'll hold the train," said an official. So I ran to the hotel and said, "Six bottles of port, please." A man offered to show me a shortcut back to the station. It was quicker but it meant a ten-foot drop down on to the track – carrying six bottles of port. I made it and we carried on our celebration. We'd had a great run – and only just missed. Why should we be downhearted?'

The same close team spirit and *joie de vivre* was in evidence as, a year later, in 1960, a *Topical Times* writer was shown around Mr and Mrs Duggie Reid's hostel in Portsmouth, home to fourteen 'young hopefuls' – groundstaff and young pros – who lived two or three to a room.

'They have hot and cold running water, central heating. A lounge with television. Radio. Two record-players – and the lads "club" together to buy all the latest discs.' Lancaster Gate was also apparently

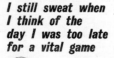

I still sweat when I think of the day I was too late for a vital game

SAYS BILLY HENDERSON

Glasgow Rangers and Scotland

IT happened to me. I missed a vital game because I was too late. I vow it will never happen again. It must be almost the worst experience a player can have. If I am in this game for as long as Stanley Matthews, I shall never forget it.

It happened to me in a European Cup match. It is still a nagging, nightmare memory.

I have had great moments even in my short football career, yet I sweat when I remember the night – Wednesday, February 14, 1962 – when I rushed into Ibrox and saw the lads filing out on the pitch to take on Standard Liege in the second leg of the tie.

I should have been going out there with them, although when I began the journey to Ibrox I was reserve to Alex Scott. But that didn't alter the urgency of my dash.

Like all other Rangers players, whether chosen to play or not, I knew that we had to be at the ground an hour before the kick-off. When I learned, in those last desperate minutes, that I had been picked . . . well, that made things worse.

Traffic, of course, caused the trouble, heavy, seemingly never-ending lines of it. Glasgow traffic—and a stalled engine. No motorist can have felt as frustrated as I did that night.

I had expected a hold-up in Glasgow, with such a game competing for road space with the normal evening traffic. But I didn't dream that it would be as bad as it was.

After fuming in the many hold-ups, my friend who was driving me to the game tried to start his engine again. It failed, and I had only a few minutes to get to Ibrox on time. I grabbed a cab.

Some of our reserves who saw me trying to get into the ground told me I was playing. But, as I have said, the lads were going out when I got there.

Rangers won 2—0, but that was not enough to rub out the Liege advantage in the first meeting, and so we were out of the competition. Not that I could have done anything to change that. I only know that nothing worse could possibly happen to me than to miss that game. I failed my team . . . and myself.

I suffered then. The only thing which made it bearable was the understanding way in which the boss, Mr. Scot Symon, took my story.

Now, a more pleasant memory — of the wonderful

Henderson at heading practice.

welcome we received at Renfrew Airport and in Glasgow when we returned from Russia after our close-season tour on which we were unbeaten in three games played.

It was like five Cup-winning receptions rolled into one! I feel it was so because we had far exceeded the expectations of most people by showing the Soviets that Glasgow Rangers knew a thing or two when it came to playing fitba'.

I don't think a lot of our supporters took kindly to that trip. They seemed to think that we might not do the Rangers' name much good, after a hard season.

But the lads were terrific in those three games. We won the first two, against Moscow Locomotive and Tbilisi Dynamo—the second match was played in heat none of us had experienced before. Then we came to THE match—against the Russian champions, Kiev Dynamo.

We should have made it three straight wins, but we didn't get the breaks. We drew, but the great thing was that yet another country had reason to know what the Gers could do. And the Russians gave us full and generous acclaim for our short but inspiring record among them.

None of us was prepared for what awaited us when our plane touched down at Renfrew. It seemed that the whole of Glasgow had either turned up at the airport . . . or lined the route back to the city. It was a tremendous homecoming and a sight I am never likely to forget.

Being a Ranger has meant for me a passport stamped for Russia, Sweden, Spain, Belgium, France, Denmark and Germany, countries I would not have seen but for football.

Yet it might not have been like that. I could easily have settled for what was my favourite club as a youngster—Airdrie.

For two years I was a ball-boy at Broomfield Park, four miles from my home at Caldercruix. That came about partly because so many up-and-coming youngsters were chosen for the job, and partly because my grandfather worked a turnstile at the ground.

I won caps at 15 against the home countries and helped Scotland to win the championship, but I could see no further than Airdrie where, from the line, I was more supporter than unbiased ball-boy on Saturday afternoons.

But the word had got round. There were several English clubs interested in the future of little Billy Henderson from Caldercruix. But Manchester United, Aston Villa and the rest from across the border were wasting their time.

My father would not agree to his offspring going so far from home to make his fortune. While I still thought of Broomfield, along came Rangers with an offer my parents could not resist even if they had wanted to.

So I went to Edinburgh Athletic, part of the growing-up process before reaching Ibrox.

From there on it has been pretty quick going—into the League for my first game against Clyde, the Cup Final against St. Mirren, and all those other big games, including the international against Wales at Ninian Park last October.

Ambitions? I want to try hair dressing as an outside trade, and I will get down to it seriously when I feel I can afford to devote the time to it.

Henderson . . . he smiles here, but he didn't on February 14, 1962.

58   59

helping them build a football library. What they all ate at Christmas 1958 was 'still the talk of the place: one turkey, four chickens, 10lb. of pork, 10lb. of beef, one ham, three Christmas cakes, six Christmas puddings, plus the usual sweets, oranges, &c. It's easy to see Portsmouth are all out to build up the stamina necessary for a footballer,' the piece concluded, although they still look a fairly skinny bunch, in their ties, pullovers and cardigans in the accompanying photos. But inside-forward Brian Yeo put on a stone in no time and, checking Wikipedia half a century later, made no appearances at Fratton Park before moving on to Gillingham – just like another couple of the trainees, Owen Paterson and Owen Dawson, who were both shipped out to Swindon. And perhaps Mrs Reid's dietary regime didn't agree with fullback Bill Williams either: he managed three appearances in three years, before also forging a career at the Priestfield stadium.

When not gathered round one of the Dansettes in the lounge, it seems Bill Williams, accomplished guitarist, drummer and formerly leader of his own swing group, led the lads in a nightly singalong. A few pages on in the same annual, Sunderland's 'singing winger' Colin Grainger talked about driving his Riley Pathfinder

> ROCK AND ROLL DIDN'T SIT EASILY IN THE PAGES OF CHARLES BUCHAN

to residencies at the Sheffield, Middlesbrough and Sunderland Empires. There were 'record takings' at Middlesbrough and Sunderland, apparently, TV shows with Winifred Atwell and a recording deal with HMV. Grainger even claimed his team-mates at Roker Park had bought his records.

Grainger's crooning ('a bit Vic Damone,' – Graham Sharpe) in the ballrooms of northern England could hardly be cited as evidence of the coming age of rock and roll infiltrating the pages of the sports press, but the *Topical Times* were at least a couple of years ahead of *Charles Buchan's Soccer Gift Book*. There, you might have John Thompson's successor, Pat Collins, predicting a great future for the 'the young ones who made him glad all over' but rock and roll didn't sit particularly easily in the pages of *Buchan*. There was an awkward WHAT . . . ! NO BEATLES? NO . . . ! NO . . . ! NO . . . ! spread in the '64–65 annual, featuring Ian St John, Billy Liddell and Ron Yeats holding electric guitars with, er, Ken Dodd; the Dave Clark Five somehow performing in the White Hart Lane dressing room; and half the Rangers first team in dinner jackets and bow ties 'swinging the Clyde blues'. All in all ' . . . we would imagine it's enough to make one emigrate to the rainforests of Malaya,' concluded the *Soccer Gift Book*

"HOUSE FULL" — OF FOOTBALL HOPEFULS

Pompey's Home From Home For Boys They Hope To Turn Into Stars

JOHNNY HAYNES. Jimmy Greaves. Bobby Charlton.

Three headline players. And all started as ground staff youngsters with their clubs.

There have been others—the late Duncan Edwards and Billy Wright, for instance. From schoolboys to the First Division a club setting itself out to take lads from school to the top of the tree is Portsmouth.

For years the Fratton Park people have been turning unknowns into internationals — Jimmy Dickinson, Peter Harris and Len Phillips (England), Jackie Henderson, Jimmy Scoular and Alex. Wilson (Scotland), Derek Dougan (Ireland). Several have moved to other clubs, but all were established as star material with Portsmouth.

JUST THE MAN

The Portsmouth club now has a special hostel to help them with the development of youngsters. It's only a couple of minutes' walk from the sea front at Southsea. Ten minutes from the ground. It cost between £5000 and £6000. It's a home from home for 14 ground-staff youngsters and young professionals at Fratton Park.

They live together. Talk football all the time. In charge is Duggie Reid, a Portsmouth topliner from the side that won the First Division Championship in successive seasons — 1948-49 and 1949-50.

Duggie combines the duties of hostel warden with groundsman at Fratton Park. He's assisted in the hostel by his wife, Mary. They are father and mother to 14 budding young footballers.

I went along to look at this football hostel. To discover what a youngster leaving school can expect if he decides to make football a career at Portsmouth.

It's a double-fronted house. Called Leverett House — after Sid Leverett, a Portsmouth director who was associated with the club from 1912 until 1959, from the old Southern League days to First Division Champions and Cup winners.

The lad who showed me round was Owen Dawson, a 17-year-old from Christchurch, near Bournemouth.

SING-SONG NIGHT

The Pompey hostel boys gather round for a bit of a sing-song — with BILL WILLIAMS on guitar. At right are Mr and Mrs Duggie Reid.

Owen joined Portsmouth straight from school. He was playing for Portsmouth Reserves at 16. He's rated a prospect sure to play for England—maybe even the full cycle of Youth, Under-23, "B" and "full" international.

The 14 youngsters share large bedrooms—two, in odd cases three, to a room.

They have hot and cold running water, central heating. A lounge with television. Radio. Two record-players—and the lads "club" together to buy all the latest discs.

LIBRARY, TOO

They have a dining-room, with a big dining table that can be turned into a billiard or snooker table quick as a flash.

In the dining-room and lounge are the trophies won by the Portsmouth Youth side—reminders of honours to come.

Also being established in the hostel is a football library. With the Football Association helping out in a big way.

It was felt the youngsters needed every book and publication on football they could lay their hands on. So the Lancaster Gate people are sending all spare football books to Pompey.

The lads come from all over Britain—Liverpool, Sussex, London, Wales and Dorset. I stayed for lunch—with the record-player sounding out pop music all the time.

Consider a typical day for Owen Dawson.

He reports to the ground at 9 a.m. Starts training at 9.15. The youngsters are coached by Reg Frewin, Portsmouth assistant manager, ex-Portsmouth captain and ex-England international.

They train until 11.30. Back to the hostel for lunch at 12.30, and then return to the ground at 2.30 to do various jobs. Owen Dawson, for instance, helps out in the office.

BIG EATS

Duggie Reid's double job of warden and groundsman means he has control of the lads the whole time, apart from when they are training.

They have to check in by 10.30 every evening. On Fridays they never go out on the basis that they are resting for the match the next day.

Everything is done to bring them up to accept the life of a footballer.

AWAY FROM THE FIELD

OWEN DAWSON does a bit of typing in the office at Fratton Park—to the dictation of manager Freddie Cox.

They stay at the hostel at Christmas and Easter. Just to bring it home to them that a footballer has to give up these two holidays.

Last Christmas the boys spent three days at the hostel. It's still the talk of the place how much grub they got through. Here's Mrs Reid's reckoning of it—one turkey, four chickens, 10 lb. of pork, 10 lb. of beef, one ham, three Christmas cakes, six Christmas puddings, plus the usual sweets, oranges, &c.

It's easy to see Portsmouth are all out to build up the stamina necessary for a footballer.

Brian Yeo, a Cockney from London, is rated a great inside-forward prospect. He arrived under-weight—and put on a stone in a few weeks.

The lads have their own "rock group." Bill Williams, a full-back from Esher (Surrey), plays guitar. He leads the lads in evening vocal sessions.

Before he decided to become a footballer, Bill ran his own swing group. Had a set of drums, bass, &c. He arrived at Leverett House with a guitar and a pair of football boots.

Every season Portsmouth run an "At Home" for parents of youngsters at the hostel. They are invited down for a Youth match and are given the freedom of Fratton Park. But at all times they can visit the lads in the hostel.

Instead of a wage the Portsmouth youngsters are given pocket money—£2 for a 15-year-old, £3 at 16, plus free living, laundry and accommodation at the hostel.

If they make the grade, they can sign professional at 17.

It's a scheme we'll all be watching with interest.

19

caption writer, somewhat stiffly.[68] A couple of years on and Des 'yes, we showbiz types enjoy our Soccer all right' O'Connor was looking back over his amateur days with Northampton Town.

There was a slightly more prescient coming together of the worlds of football and celebrity when Kenneth Wolstenholme, in his 1963 *Book of World of Soccer*, somewhat improbably proclaimed, 'If it's stars you want to see, the best thing to do is go to Brisbane Road. Here, east Londoners who make up the crowd are so used to celebrities that they turn towards the directors' box just before the kick-off and shout, "What's the team? Who are the celebrities?"' Hard though this is to fathom, it seems Orient directors Bernard Delfont and Leslie

Grade, when not being hugely successful West End impresarios, would head out east with whatever touring party was in town, be that Cliff Richard, Arthur Askey or Pat Boone. Tommy Steele and Sean Connery were noted as QPR regulars, and, interestingly, Alan Simpson, half of Galton and Simpson, the lugubrious writing team behind [Tony] *Hancock's Half Hour* and *Steptoe and Son*, was an ever-present on the terrace at Griffin Park, as Brentford embarked on a downward plunge through the divisions following their 1930s heyday in the first.

★

The streams of football, celebrity and rock and roll would fully converge later in the sixties. Before then football publications were becoming more self-conscious about the presentation of the game itself. In the fifties there had been the odd annual feature along the lines of SO YOU WANT TO BE A SPORTS REPORTER? In *Charles Buchan's Soccer Gift Book* these were invariably written by another hardened, moustachioed Fleet Street scribe, Clifford Webb.

In the 1959–60 article TRAVELS OF A SOCCER

68 Ken Dodd got six pages in the *International Football Book* of 1968, in a doomed attempt at light relief (the most entertaining part of which is his sudden adoption of a serious tone in the final paragraph, calling for an end to all the 'seat-ripping, bottle-throwing and window-breaking that seems to go on so often in the football excursion trains', especially as he's heard Liverpool fans have been involved. I point out the forced humour, ropiness and strange presence of Ken Dodd across a number of mid-sixties football annuals to Johnny Green. 'I won't have that,' he says. 'I'm a huge Dodd fan, a massive Dodd fan, and always was – apart from when he sings.')

Portsmouth stars of the future enjoy a sing-song at their club digs (left) and Colin Grainger (above) explains how he juggles his twin careers in football and showbiz, both featured in the *Topical Times Football Book* 1960–61

Following pages: Football and pop collide in *Charles Buchan's Soccer Gift Book* 1964–65. A similar spread appeared in the *International Football Book* in 1964, with the Dave Clark Five replaced by Pete Budd and the Rebels playing on a muddy Eastville pitch

WHAT..! NO BEATLES?

The Mersey Sound (left) . . . the Tottenham Sound (above) . . . and the Glasgow Sound (below). And we would imagine it's enough to make one emigrate to the rain forests of Malaya. Left, Comedian Ken Dodd does a noise . . . noise . . . noise with Ian St. John, Ron Yeats, of Liverpool, and former Anfield idol, Billy Liddell.

Above, Terry Dyson, Tony Marchi, Bill Brown, Mel Hopkins and Jimmy Greaves "change round" with the Dave Clark Five, of Dave Clark, Rick Huxley, Mike Smith, Lenny Davidson and Dennis Payton.

Below, Glasgow Rangers players swinging the Clyde Blues. Jim Forrest, Bobby Shearer, Craig Watson, Alec Willoughby, Ron McKinnon and Billy Ritchie performing at their Club Dance.

And not a Beatle in sight?

REPORTER unsuspecting *Gift Book* readers could have been forgiven for thinking they were in for a dissection of England's famous 1–0 setback against the United States, as Webb justified his placing with the England team, staying 'way up in the mountains, 300 miles from Rio de Janeiro in a small community which mainly housed the workers of the only British-owned gold mine – only in that way was it feasible that I could get any news at all of the English team without delay.' The road down from the gold mines to civilization, however, was little better than a mountain path: 'Bananas grew wild in great clusters, and it was strange to see them transformed into vividly red and completely unidentifiable fruits by the dust from passing transport . . .' The churn from the convoy of vehicles also turned the gourds of Brazil nuts hanging from the ample trees red, but the flowers were 'of such brilliant colours they even shone out above the coating of red dust'.

Over the page, and Clifford hadn't done yet: 'gorgeously coloured butterflies' flitted in and out of the undergrowth, football-mad gold miners travelled by mule – mules savvy with snakes hidden in the high pampas grass that is – in a dust-caked procession winding its way down through 'miles and miles of memorable and beautiful open country'. The gold miners made it to the game; the mule 'by the time its rider was at the match had the pleasure of "eating its head off" in some nearby corral'. But *Gift Book* readers never actually reached Belo Horizonte as, by the adjacent column, Clifford was travelling through the picturesque foothills of the Andes, to the Pacific coastal port of Valparaiso, 'one of the most colourful trips of all . . .' Over on to the next page, and he was visiting the Kremlin with his boss, Charlie, prior to the pair exerting undue pressure on the official driver to swerve out of the gridlock and into the empty priority lane – that way they might stand a chance of reaching Moscow Dynamo v Arsenal in time for kick-off . The driver, however, in fear of losing 'all her civil rights and quite possibly going to prison' refused. The pair got their way, only to be stopped, 'sure enough', at the next set of

The life of a TV football commentator. 'Sounds marvellous, doesn't it? A free ticket to all the big games,' wrote Peter Dimmock in the *Sportsview Book of Soccer* in 1964 but warned it wasn't 'all champagne and roses'. Tricky business like identifying all those trainers 'who often trot onto the field to attend an injured player' had to be dealt with. 'Managers too, pop up now and again . . .' Rules of the game had to be known backwards, and 'comments must always be brief and to the point'.

As a way of demonstrating all of this, Dimmock supplied a lengthy account of how Wally Barnes once heroically filled up 20 minutes on air, having been caught up in a late-running Italy v Austria fixture, the live BBC broadcast beginning just as the ref blew for half-time at the Prater Stadium. Barnes supplied a fulsome account of the first half, a look back at previous games played in the Prater, an impromptu interview with former Austrian legend Ernst Ocwirk, spotted by the camera man in the crowd, then plenty of footage of Italian and Austrian fans embarking on a massive snowball fight on the terraces.

How to become a football writer
– AND LIKE IT!

TRAVELS of a SOCCER REPORTER

By CLIFFORD WEBB

GOING to a football match in England, Scotland, Wales, or Ireland is not very difficult; or even very adventurous. One accepts the normal hazards of public transport—like overcrowded trains, or buses. At a pinch one can even walk, without any undue fatigue.

In the main, our Soccer grounds, especially in the provinces, are sited more or less centrally. Towns and cities, in many instances, grew up around the Soccer grounds.

This explains why many provincial Soccer grounds would be worth almost their weight in gold as building sites. But, because they were already established in their present positions as Soccer grounds long before cities and towns developed around them, there they remain—often to the chagrin of development speculators who can see what the sites would be worth industrially.

This is one of the things people are apt to forget when they grumble about our football grounds. In so many cases they may be out of date structurally, or from the point of view of personal comfort, but at least they are within reasonable distance of city centres and town terminals.

In my time as a football reporter, I suppose I must have visited most of the grounds in England — the grounds of the Football League clubs, anyway.

I can't think of any which present abnormal difficulties from a transport point of view. There's always a good local train service, a bus service, a tram service, or a comparatively easy walk.

But abroad it isn't always so simple. Soccer development in foreign lands has been of a more recent type. City centres have been established before Soccer got a hold, and so the football clubs have had to make do as best they could—and that applies even to those countries where the governments have had complete

control and could, one assumes, have taken over any site they required.

Still, these troubles concerning transport and travel in general have often provided — for me, anyway — fascinating sidelights to the matches in question.

The most unusual incidents always come to mind first, so let me begin my personal reminiscences with that extraordinary World Cup game in 1950 when, in Belo Horizonte, Brazil, U.S.A. beat England 1—o to set the cables buzzing all around the world. This was the one result nobody at the time believed possible.

I was a visiting reporter and, if it was at all possible, I always stayed with England's team. Only in that way was it feasible that I could get any news at all of the English team without delay, so that I could cable it back to my newspaper.

England's team stayed some 14 or 15 miles away from the little town, 'way up in the mountains 300 miles from Rio de Janeiro in a small community which mainly housed the workers of the only British-owned gold mine in Brazil.

The road down into the town was little better than a mountain path. It curled down in a series of hairpin bends that made any car journey a desperate adventure.

The surface was red dust, several inches thick. Any vehicle threw up thick crimson clouds of grit which got into one's eyes, ears, nose and mouth.

Only if you were in the first car of any convoy—and the cars usually travelled in convoy—did you have any chance to look at the natural beauties of this mountain roadside.

Bananas grew wild in great clusters, and it was strange to see them transformed into vividly red and completely unidentifiable fruits by the dust from passing transport.

There were huge gourds hanging from trees, each containing scores of Brazil nuts. There were weirdly shaped fruits and seed pods the like of which one never sees in Britain. There were flowers of such brilliant colours they even shone out above the general coating of red dust.

And there were gorgeously coloured butterflies flitting in and out of the undergrowth, and what we here would regard as rare humming birds hovering almost stationary in space, their wings moving so fast as to be almost invisible.

All this could be seen only when the car slowed down to round a particularly sharp bend. But it was nevertheless memorable and beautiful.

On the morning of the actual match, several hundred gold miners set out for the ground in the only way they had known since arriving there.

They mounted mules and took the short cuts across the mountains, over miles and miles of open country where the pampas grass was often three or four feet high and in which lurked poisonous snakes.

The mules, incidentally, were a safeguard where snakes were concerned.

They seemed to sense when snakes were near, and it was very rare for any mule rider to get into trouble from that source. The great thing was to let the mule have its head and not attempt to guide it in any way.

The mule knew the way to the town and knew, also, that all the time its rider was at the match it would have the pleasure of 'eating its head off' in some nearby corral!

Yes, going to a football match in Belo was quite something . . . .

The ground itself was small and the accommodation for spectators somewhat crude—nothing like the facilities in the giant stadium which had been opened only a few weeks before in Rio itself.

This is one of the sports wonders of the world—a completely circular stadium with room for 150,000 spectators, all seated. And going to a match with England's team in Rio was no ordinary journey.

As in all big cities, the roads leading to the stadium were completely inadequate to take the traffic, and at one time it looked as if England's team would be late for the kick-off.

The urgency of the situation was pressed on the driver, and he reacted immediately. It was a two-way road with a grass verge running down the middle and on the grass huge trees were growing at more or less regular intervals.

Sounding his horn loudly, the driver swung his big vehicle on to the grass and went charging down the middle of the road, scattering pedestrians and missing the trees by inches!

Going to a match in Santiago, Chile, was not quite so hair-raising, but was a memorable experience. In

the city itself there was sunshine and warmth, but as one approached the ground there was a scene of breathtaking beauty as the towering mountains of the Andes range came into view, covered in gleaming white snow for about a third of the way down from the massive peaks.

It was in Chile, incidentally, that I had one of the most colourful trips of all—a journey to the Pacific coast port of Valparaiso.

Much of it was through the picturesque foothills of the Andes where the roads twisted and turned so tortuously that warning signs were posted every mile or so—'Zona de Curvas' (area of curves).

Then, quite suddenly, we came on a fine, broad road that bore all the evidence of fairly recent construction. We hummed along at a fast pace for mile after mile until the road ended abruptly, right in the middle of nowhere!

Apparently the authorities had either come to the end of their finances, or they couldn't get the employees to proceed any further.

We plunged into rough cart tracks, went through dusty villages where South American Indian children sprawled over the roads without any thought of danger and where mules merely stood and stared with undisguised curiosity as we threaded our way past them.

And so to the Pacific Ocean—my first glimpse of it, by the way—and a big surprise for me was to see, instead of seagulls wheeling around, groups of huge pelicans.

We sampled some of the seafood for which that part of the coast is famous and went back to Santiago by a different route, this time finding it necessary to cross a river with the water above the car's axles.

There was a bridge, but the driver explained that it was doubtful if it would take the weight of the car!

Montevideo, in Uruguay was a pleasant port of call—a fine city on the edge of the ocean, with one of the loveliest golf courses I have seen anywhere outside England.

Here, the hotel was a surprise. The entire basement was a gambling casino!

There was everything that has made Monte Carlo famous, and the place was crowded every night, right up to the small hours of the morning.

The stadium at Budapest. The first time Clifford went there, there was some doubt whether his taxi would stay in one piece.

A panoramic view of the huge Central Stadium in Moscow. To see the Moscow Dynamos v. Arsenal match here Charles Buchan and Clifford Webb had to persuade their driver to break the law.

137

---

lights by a military policeman. An interpreter extricated them from tricky situation: once the policeman, 'a keen Soccer enthusiast', had been made aware of exactly who was in the back of the car, 'with a flourishing salute he waved us on'. Five thousand words further on and Webb was being driven about Budapest by Harold Needler, in the Hull City chairman's Rolls-Royce.

No one broke out into 'Land of Hope and Glory' but Webb concluded, 'Berlin, Rome, Milan, Lisbon . . . all have their Soccer memories for me. Perhaps you will be thinking about some of my travels the next time you make your way to a local game.' Perhaps, but then again perhaps not in the way Clifford imagined or hoped for – if you'd read this article during the gloomy Christmas of 1959 you probably did curse Webb on your way into Gresty Road in the rain, or stood outside Roker Park in a long queue as an icy wind blew off the North Sea.

In the '62–63 annual Clifford tackled radio commentary, recalling what a boon the advent of shirt numbers

> **'BERLIN, ROME, MILAN, LISBON – ALL HAVE THEIR SOCCER MEMORIES FOR ME'**

was. In the days before shirt numbering the *Radio Times* would print a grid of the pitch. 'All the squares were numbered,' wrote Webb, 'and the idea was that listeners would have this diagram in front of them when listening to commentary. George Allison ... [commonly acknowledged as the BBC's first sports reporter, and who, according to Webb, so made 'his acquaintances feel that they had squeaky, little falsetto voices that they hardly dared match against his rolling eloquence'] would describe a particularly exciting incident in the match and then, while he paused for breath, his assistant would quietly chip in with the number and square representing that portion of the pitch where the incident took place. It used to go something like this:

> "And now Stan Matthews has the ball. He's beaten the full-back, he feints to go left then weaves inside and – Oh! – a peach of a centre. Up go the heads – but no, Jones in goal makes a brilliant save. My word, what a let-off."
>
> And in would come the voice of the assistant – "Square four."

Left: Clifford Webb, 'one of Fleet Street's most experienced reporters' offers some career in advice in *Charles Buchan's Soccer Gift Book 1964–65*

Above: Webb's global football travels detailed in *Charles Buchan's Soccer Gift Book 1959–60*

See it again . . . a B.B.C. Sportsview film strip on one of football's most discussed incidents. Ollie Norris, Bournemouth's dancing Irishman, does his best to stop Tony Marchi (Tottenham) from taking a throw-in. It happened during Bournemouth's fabulous F.A. Cup run of 1957. Fair tactics—or foul? Gimmick—or gamesmanship? See it again . . . and judge for yourself.

58

59

But with the advent of regular televised football in the early sixties, football-annual writers began to latch on to the new medium. It was the beginning of what was to become a near obsession by the decade's end, when no annual would be complete without a behind-the-scenes feature from *Match of the Day* or *Sportsnight*.

First off the mark, unsurprisingly, was Peter Dimmock's *Sportsview Book of Soccer*, with a couple of features in their inaugural annual of 1958. In an article on the developing role of film in football – SEE IT AGAIN: 'If you weren't there at the big moment, or perhaps blew your nose at the most exciting moment, the cameras (film or television) were there for you' – readers are informed that Walter Winterbottom has started a library of film in the basement at Lancaster Gate, to be used for training purposes. Matt Busby was apparently a regular visitor, once requesting reels of film of Bournemouth in action, ahead of a Cup tie against the south coast club notorious for the antics of Olly Norris and his 'war-like dance' in front of the opposition keeper or a player about take a throw-in.

Film studied, Manchester United won 2–1.[69]

The feature also detailed some early set-backs with the new technology. Ahead of the Wales v England Home International of October 1955, the BBC's Ronnie Noble and his team proudly drew up to Ninian Park with *two* cameras in tow. '"Can't go wrong," said Ronnie. "This is going to get us all the goals we want for tonight."' Just ahead of half-time one camera ran out of film as, simultaneously, the other one broke down. Naturally this was the very moment Wales opened the scoring against England. Beads of sweat formed on numerous technicians' foreheads, but no one could get either camera up and running before Wales scored again. Half-time was long enough for film to be loaded into Camera One, just in time to catch

69 Actually, as early as 1955 Tommy Docherty was featured in *Charles Buchan's Soccer Gift Book* working out how to deal with Puskás after studying the Hungarian on film footage (he reckoned you just needed to push him out wide, away from the action – Scotland won). And the same was true for Len Graham, Doncaster Rovers and Northern Ireland full-back, who spent time watching Jimmy Mullen, the England winger on TV before a Home International.

Above: A controversial incident in a Spurs v Bournemouth FA Cup game gets replayed in *Sportsview Book of Soccer* in 1959

a third goal – a John Charles' own-goal was captured beautifully by the English TV team, much to the disgust of a nation of Welsh TV viewers.

On another occasion film of a Cup tie between Newcastle and Sunderland became exposed to light. The BBC showed what they could, Kenneth Wolstenholme apologising to viewers, '"I'm afraid our film was fogged."' Which apparently led to hundreds of irate Sunderland fans pointing out to the BBC that weather conditions had been bright and sunny, and jokes and cartoons about BBC cameramen in national newspapers.

Film could also rake up things that were perhaps better left buried, *Sportsview* noted, uneasily. Film footage had later revealed that Allenby Chilton had brought down Blackpool's Eddie Shimwell *outside* the area (the resultant penalty notwithstanding Man United won the 1948 Cup final anyway); and that in 1932 Jimmy Richardson's cross which led to Newcastle's winning goal in the FA Cup final had clearly crossed the line and so shouldn't have resulted in a goal.

In the same annual in a lengthy piece, FOOTBALL IN THE PARLOUR, Ronnie Noble took readers behind the scenes in the BBC's outside broadcast unit, 'the Scanner', a domain presided over by 'Chiv' (the producer Alan Chivers – 'if he says "jump" then everybody jumps. That's how it has to be') who is capable of making split-second decisions from deep inside the Scanner, parked *outside the ground*, because, it transpires, he was a Battle of Britain fighter pilot 'trained to think in split seconds at 350 m.p.h. flying Hurricanes and

> '"CAN'T GO WRONG," SAID RONNIE. "THIS IS GOING TO GET US ALL THE GOALS WE WANT FOR TONIGHT"'

Spitfires'. Not only could Chiv think faster than his opposing number in a Messerschmitt, he was a leader of men and even 'more at home with the television controls than with the "stick" of his Spitfire ... there sits Chivers, pipe puffing away ... watching four monitors from his four cameras and deciding which picture to cut to [simultaneously talking to commentators like] Kenneth Wolstenholme, from the same RAF stable. He got his experience flying bombers over Germany. He was a pathfinder ace with a couple of medals. So he too knows how to make a quick decision and keep his eyes open all around him ... ' Even in the fifties the favoured camera position was felt to be above the half-way line, but some folk it seemed, preferred the camera to be placed behind the goal 'so that you are looking right down the pitch, with one goal immediately in front of you and the other in the far distance, the way we do it at the Wolverhampton ground or at Arsenal.'

At the 1958 Cup final Ronnie Noble made history as the first 'radio cameraman'. He wrote, 'I was a bit doubtful. First of all it meant carrying the whole thing on my back, and with antennas and bits of metal sticking up in the air ... the whole thing weighed nearly half a hundred weight.' But with no heavy cabling weighing him down Ronnie could actually walk about – 'I was absolutely independent' – sending pictures sent by radio waves to Chiv in the Scanner, with whom he could also communicate by microphone. 'They told me I looked like a spaceman as I stood there waiting for the two teams to come on to the field.' Noble zoomed in on

An Outside Broadcasts Control Van   An interior view of the mobile control room

Above: The BBC outside broadcast team in action, as featured in the *Sportsview Book of Soccer* 1963

KENNETH WOLSTENHOLME WASTED NO TIME IN TAKING HIS BOOK OF WORLD SOCCER READERS BEHIND THE SCENES AT SATURDAY SPORT, A PRECURSOR TO MATCH OF THE DAY

Billy Foulkes, then Nat Lofthouse. He heard Chiv in his headset: '"Good man. Will stay on radio camera. Stand by camera one in case radio camera falls backwards." Chivers was quite right. The camera was weighing me down.' Then Ronnie heard Wolstenholme launch into soliloquy on Lofthouse looking confident. '"Radio Camera calling producer. Go off me for goodness sake. This thing's breaking my back," I called desperately,' as Ronnie began to wobble and Wolstenholme showed no sign of winding up.

Finally he got to put the heavy load down, and was about to take his headphones off when suddenly Harry Gregg was injured and Chiv was in the headset instructing him back down the other end, 'my assistant making technical adjustments with a screwdriver as we were trotting along the touchline'. Ronnie made it just before the bucket and sponge man, and was pleased with his shot obtained from poking the lens through the goal netting – he wouldn't have realised it at the

time, of course, but in getting his camera up so close Ronnie was starting to chip away at the exclusive domain of the football annual.

In the new decade, former *Sportsview Book of Soccer* contributor Kenneth Wolstenholme jumped ship to front his own annual. In his rather splendid, Pathé News-style delivery, he wasted no time in taking his *Book of World Soccer* readers behind the scenes at *Saturday Sport*, a precursor to *Match of the Day*, which also featured the day's rugby league and racing.

In the very early days he noted the BBC filmed the action in snatches, but, as the *Sportsview* team's experiences would testify, soon found 'it was very easy to miss goals or other vital incidents'. In the winter months the primitive light meters would struggle to cope too: a game might start in sunshine, only for the light to quickly fade; then there'd be a sudden explosion of luminosity as the floodlights were turned on – and presumably much fraught twirling of dials in the control van. Getting film to the processing laboratories, and then on to the programme editors, was also a complex and nail-biting affair, involving dispatch riders, 'dope' sheets being phoned ahead – 'Roll 1, 50 feet, disallowed "goal"' – league tables made up on 'fish and chip boards' and scalpel-wielding editors not only racing against the clock to make the film flow, but having to chop up the 'live' commentary to fit.

And the problems didn't stop there. Editor Lawrie Higgins' first day, 29 December 1961, saw him plunged into immediate chaos: 'Widespread fog cut the programme to ribbons. One camera unit was in the north of England going from town to town in an effort to find a match that could be played. It failed.' It was the same in the south: only Spurs v Chelsea survived the fog in the capital, 'yet some viewers wrote to complain that a London derby was chosen for coverage!'

The big freeze in the winter of 1962–63 caused the programme numerous headaches. Games were frequently called off with the outside broadcast lorry trundling into town, just a few miles away. On one occasion the fog in Huddersfield was so bad the editor in London, realising that Leeds Road didn't have floodlights, diverted the crew on to Manchester . . . only for the fog to lift by kick-off in Yorkshire. The fact that Huddersfield v Sunderland – deemed an 'important second division match' – was to be featured in the first place feels almost as antediluvian as a ground without floodlights.

Above: Kenneth Wolstenholme at the microphone in his 1969 *Book of World Soccer*

Right: Bristol Rovers' keeper Esmond Million at The Den in *Charles Buchan's Soccer Gift Book* 1963–64

Where have they got to? After the big freeze British weather got back to normal—lashing rain, and mud. Here is Esmond Million, goalkeeper of Bristol Rovers, keeping a weather eye open for Millwall raiders.

"ANYBODY THERE?

Early '60s annuals took a while to embrace the iconic design style we commonly associate with the decade. The *Boys' Book of Soccer*'s art department did produce fine work, such as the 1959 cover (below), and they eagerly tried to move with the times in 1962, grafting an action photo on to a sock. Surprisingly, it worked a treat.

The *Big Book of Football Champions* was published for the last time in 1961, with a great cover featuring Danny Blanchflower in balletic pose. But both it and *Football Champions*, its successor in truncated name and style, still felt like they belonged to the end of the 1950s rather than the new decade. The 1963 cover featured the England v Rest of World captains, Jimmy Armfield and Alfredo Di Stéfano, prior to the FA's centenary match at Wembley.

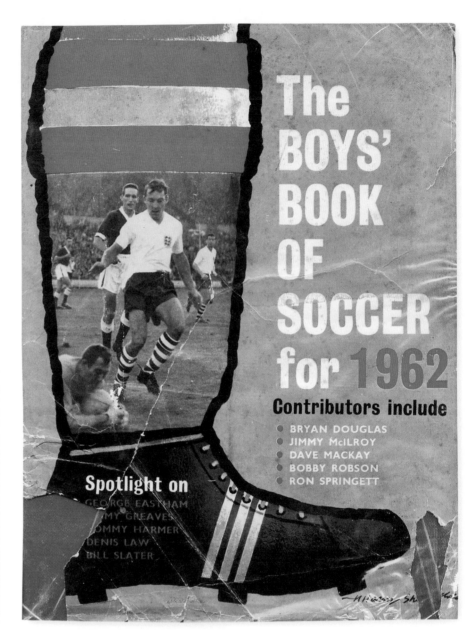

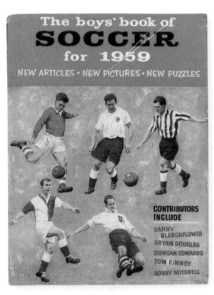

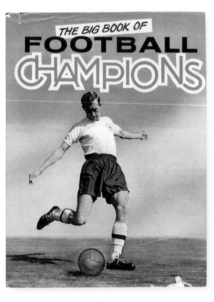

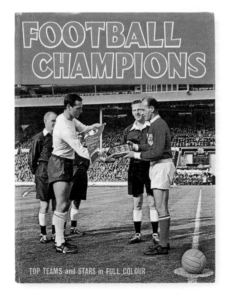

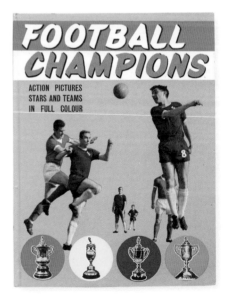

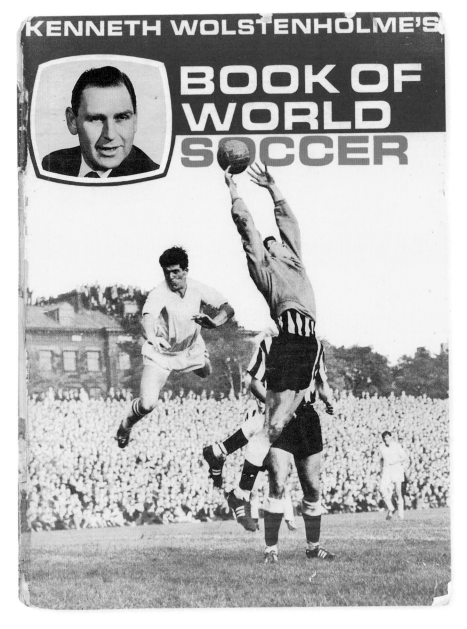

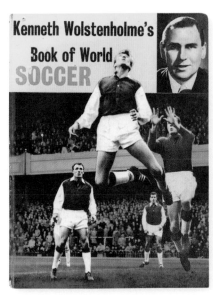

||||||||||||||||||||||||||||||||||||||||

Kenneth Wolstenhome's Book of World Soccer, first published in 1961 (top right), started using typography more typical of the period by 1963 (top left) and experimented with images overprinted on colour tints. In 1963 the usually staid International Football Book also used a font more in keeping with modern tastes.

The designers on All Stars Football Book, also first published in 1961, finally picked up the big bold condensed type letraset, albeit a little clumsily, in 1966. It was left to the The Boys' Book of Soccer, again, to make a firm declaration of design intent when it's 1966 cover featured hard postertised images on a rich green background. In doing so it finally started to embrace the visual aesthetics of the decade.

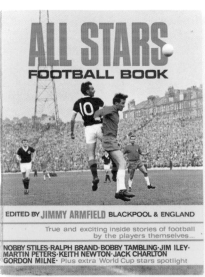

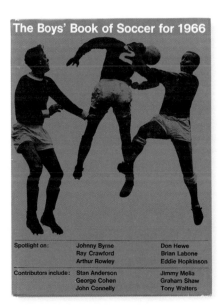

Rapidly fading light, wretched pea-soupers, violent thunderstorms, and goalposts standing in two or three feet of snow or floodwater ... as befits a nation forever checking the weather forecast, inclement happenings were never far from the pages of the football annual in the 1950s and '60s.

In the 1960 *Topical Times Football Book* sixteen-stone, six-foot-four Scottish ref, 'Tiny' Tom Wharton was lauded for instructing both the Dunfermline and Raith Rovers teams to retreat to the pavilion during a heavy storm that disrupted a league match in 1958. As deafening thunder and 'an almost atomic flash of lightning seared crazily around the ground' Wharton also thought of the fans, instructing the Tannoy operator to announce: 'Game abandoned temporarily – resume if weather improves.' The players did come back when the worst of the storm had passed, but after thirty-two minutes the match was abandoned 'with the lines disappearing under miniature lochs on all sides'. 'So what?' the reader of today might think, but Wharton's actions were pretty unusual by the standards of 1958 – the

normal thing to do would have been to have played on. Wharton is commended for remembering 'at the back of my mind that freak accident in the Army Cup final in Aldershot in April 1948' when two players were killed by lightning – a Sergeant Hill of the Royal Armoured Corps (it had been his goal that had got the RAC to the final) and a Gunner Broadley of the Royal Artillery 121 Training Regiment. The Dorset Tank Museum website describes a scene, early in the second half of the Army Cup replay, of darkening skies and a sudden 'shaft' of lightning knocking all the players and numerous spectators to the floor, not all of them able to get up again.

Back in the 1954–55 *Soccer Gift Book*, Spurs' Ronnie Burgess recounted the havoc wreaked by the weather during his time at White Hart Lane. A photograph of a lone ref in the centre circle shows the scene at White Hart Lane during a break in play in the third-round FA Cup replay against Leeds. Despite the whole pitch looking like 'the sea shore at low tide' play resumed after just thirteen minutes ... And in 1948, only a quarter of an hour into a home match against Nottingham Forest, Burgess

Above: White Hart Lane under water, pictured in *Charles Buchan's Soccer Gift Book* 1954–55. The game was delayed for a mere 13 minutes

Right: Tooting's pitch provides a stern challenge for Nottingham Forest in the FA Cup, as seen in *Big Book of Football Champions* 1960

recalled how 'clouds of fog began to billow in, smoke-like, through the opening between the Paxton Road and West Stands. It was almost as if a machine were pumping fog in.' The game was abandoned within minutes, but Spurs keeper Ted Ditchburn was later found, still wandering between his posts, wondering what was going on.[70]

The *Topical Times* in 1963–64 featured a piece on Chelsea players wearing smog masks to cope with the bad air on foggy days at Stamford Bridge; and a couple of editions later ran a story on FOOTBALL SPIDERMEN, recounting the day floodlight repairman Patrick Kelley and his team were called in as an icy storm seized Hampden Park in its grip. Queen's Park and Dumbarton played on, despite patches of darkness beginning to spread across the pitch, as bulbs, 210 feet up in the floodlights, exploded one by one in the heavy sleet. Kelly and his team shinned up the pylons, resting on ten-inch bolts for footholds, with no 'special shoes' or gloves: 'Our firm issues safety belts and helmets,' said Kelly, 'but the men find them an encumbrance. They prefer to do without.' They ended up replacing forty-one bulbs in all. (Assuming this was the

> INCLEMENT HAPPENINGS WERE NEVER FAR FROM THE PAGES OF THE FOOTBALL ANNUAL IN THE 1950S AND '60S

Scottish league division two game played at Hampden on 14 November 1964, unfortunately all was in vain, as the visitors won 0–1.)

In 1960 *the Big Book of Football Champions* had a feature suggesting a mid-winter break[71], illustrated with a photograph of the barely playable frozen pitch at Tooting, where the south London amateurs held the eventual Cup winners Forest to a draw in the third round of the FA Cup. The crowd is densely packed into shallow terracing, beneath a grey January sky punctuated with rows of council-house chimneys. It's a scene unlikely to be filmed today – even when a big Premier League club visits a fourth division side and, a few minutes before kick-off, the camera pans over the low roof of the stand opposite, it usually only picks up passing traffic on a busy suburban A-road, or the packed car park of a neighbouring IKEA.

'The Premier League is so sanitized,' says Laurie Rampling, who came across an annual recently that featured 'a great picture of Walsall v Notts County, and a player's foot had disappeared under the slush, right up to his ankle. Imagine Agüero in the slush like that today?'

---

70 This seemed to happen to quite a few keepers in the fifties: Ipswich's Roy Bailey, for one, who remembered in the 1962–63 *Soccer Gift Book* how he was left out alone in the fog for three or four minutes after a reserve match was abandoned at Selhurst Park.

---

71 Clifford Webb also called for 'sunshine Soccer' in *Buchan's Gift Book*.

A Midwinter Close Season?

COLIN BARKER

TRAVELS 550 MILES TO WATCH A HOME GAME!

Weather, of course, impacts greatest on the travelling fan. And, like today, those long, inconvenient journeys barely get a mention in the annuals of yesteryear – with one or two notable exceptions.

One of the first articles on a new generation of crazed super-fans featured fourteen-year-old Colin Barker from New Cross, who lived five minutes from the Den, but got up at 4.30 every morning to deliver newspapers in order to fund the rail fare to see his first love, Newcastle Untied. The Barker family were interviewed in the *Topical Times* of 1960, and presumably the world was a safer place back then, but attending every home game at St James's Park involved young Colin getting the five to midnight train north on a Friday night, arriving on Tyneside at 7 a.m. on Saturday, in good time for the match, only to endure a second overnight return journey to be back in London for Sunday morning and his paper round (his dad, a London docker, or his mates, covered for him at the newsagent's on Saturdays). Once, when asking Jimmy Scoular for an autograph, the Newcastle wing-half shot back, 'What kind of accent is *that*?' It's not reported what effect all this had on young

> ONE OF THE FIRST ARTICLES ON A NEW GENERATION OF CRAZED SUPER-FANS FEATURED FOURTEEN-YEAR-OLD COLIN BARKER

Colin's school performance, but when asked for her view of her son's lifestyle, his mum, Olive, said, 'Colin has always suffered from asthma. Until he was five we had to push him everywhere in a wheelchair. Even now he has to be careful. But he's been better since he started watching Newcastle. Maybe it is the open air he gets, but it has done wonders for Colin.'

Over the page, Stanley Bean of Rotherham was profiled. A member of the '92 Club' before the 92 Club existed, he travelled everywhere just to go to a different football match each weekend. The 1959–60 season was a typical one for Stanley: he 'covered a total of 12,770 miles and saw 70 first-class matches. All this – air and railway fares, hotels, meals and admission to matches – cost him £239 11s 1d. Every item is carefully recorded . . . He is single. He is a non-smoker. He never drinks intoxicants.' Stanley had vivid memories of FA Cups down the years: Manchester United overcoming Hartlepools 4–3, Crewe and Spurs facing each other, and 'a draw between York City and Bolton Wanderers'. The article concluded, 'Stanley Bean keeps a programmes of all the matches he sees. Tucked inside

Above: Colin Barker's travelling feats are recorded for posterity in the *Topical Times Football Book* 1960–61

each is his own account of the play. He will not be short of memories when he stops travelling – if he ever does.' His would certainly be a book worth reading, but today, Googling 'Stanley Bean football fan' or 'Stanley Bean, 92 Club founder member' sadly produces nothing. Hopefully Stanley didn't spend too much time alone in later years, reflecting on Port Vale v Aldershot from Christmas 1957; hopefully he found someone to share those recollections with.

Stanley Bean would almost certainly have read the feature – GOT ANY SWOPS, CHUM?[72] – tucked away at the back of the second *Charles Buchan's Soccer Gift Book*, in 1954, billed as an 'exciting article' on programme collecting, in which 'T.W. Dalton, well known authority on the subject reveals some interesting facts on a fascinating hobby'. Despite the billing, it's not a hugely revelatory piece, but there are tips on etiquette when

> OF PARAMOUNT IMPORTANCE TO THE COLLECTOR WAS PROTECTING THE PROGRAMMES FROM EXCESSIVE CONTACT WITH AIR AND DAMP

approaching other collectors and clubs for unsold programmes, and it's noted that there were 10,000 known collectors, with others – internationally even – joining the ranks every day. Of paramount importance to the collector – and Laurie Rampling would concur today – was protecting the programmes from excessive contact with air and damp and 'attic rooms not normally lived in'. Dalton advised wrapping each edition up in greaseproof paper (filing cabinets would be 'beyond the reach of most') and removing 'all paper clips from inside each copy, lest in a year or two an ugly, rusty gash appears down the centre pages . . . file your programmes according to your fancy [but] record each copy in a ledger or notebook, detailing the date, score, etc. This provides the necessary reference if you wish to make a check on possession of a particular issue. It also avoids excessive thumbing of your stock.' He suggested youngsters were drawn to programmes because of the increasing use of colour, and of photography; 'older collectors by the famous names in fading print.' He was talking of Alex James, and Charles Buchan, of course, but noted that a decent collection of programmes is each and every collector's 'personal soccer encyclopaedia', a record of the shifting sands of time, a portal

---

72 *The Eagle Football Annual* 1963 chose to profile 'Manchester storeman' Tony Daley, looking suspiciously younger than his stated twenty years, proudly revealing his 570 metal-pin club-badge collection from around the world, housed in a fine wooden display case his dad had probably knocked up in the shed. (Of the twenty or so letters he sent off per week to various clubs, seeking badges, English clubs were apparently the worst at responding.)

Thousands of boys throughout the world have enriched their collection of football programmes through the famous Readers' Exchange column of "Charles Buchan's Football Monthly." In this exciting article T. W. DALTON, well-known authority on the subject, reveals some interesting facts on a fascinating hobby.

Above: The programme collectors' art is revealed to an unsuspecting world in *Charles Buchan's Soccer Gift Book* 1954–55

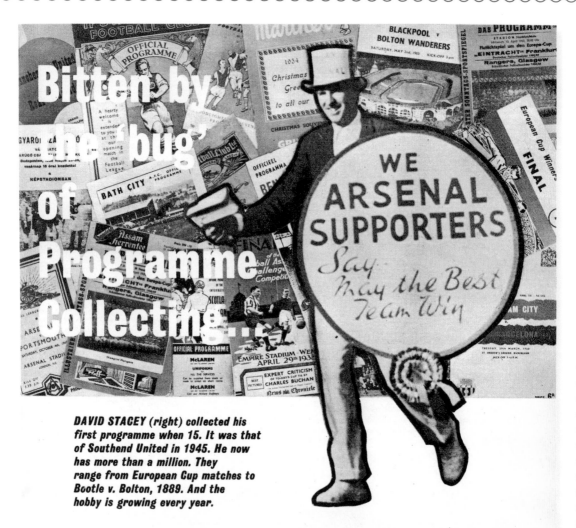

Bitten by the 'bug' of Programme Collecting...

DAVID STACEY (right) collected his first programme when 15. It was that of Southend United in 1945. He now has more than a million. They range from European Cup matches to Bootle v. Bolton, 1889. And the hobby is growing every year.

THERE are more than a million football programmes in my Wickford (Essex) home. Collecting them is my hobby. It is a hobby that is now shared by thousands of Soccer fans all over the world, and the numbers who take part in this fascinating pastime increase tremendously every year.

I got the "bug" when I saw my first League match. I was 15, and that first game was on the ground of my nearest club, Southend United.

It was Christmas Day, 1945. We were back to normal where football was concerned, after the war, and United met Walsall. You cannot put a price on some programmes and that is one of them.

It is just a single sheet of paper, but from that day I have kept the programmes of every match I have seen. The total is more than 1,000,000, made up of League matches, internationals, big European games, amateur and non-League games. Usually, you exchange to get

what you want. But often I have to buy a particular programme I need for my collection. With them I have collected old Soccer annuals, club histories and the like, so my Soccer library is a fair-sized one.

But it's the chase for programmes that is never-ending and always exciting. Often, people who have them will unbend enough to actually give them to you. They may be programmes they have as mementoes, but they are generous with their help when they know you really want them.

As an Arsenal follower in particular (though I prefer to believe I am a SOCCER follower first), I searched hard to find programmes for the Wembley Finals of 1932—against Newcastle, in the "was-the-ball-over-the-line?" match—and 1936, when Sheffield United were Arsenal's opponents.

It was a "Football Monthly" reader in Dagenham, Essex, who came up with them for me as the result of an exchange.

But try as I have, so far I have had no luck in my quest for a programme of the first Wembley Final of

103

In the 1963–64 *Charles Buchan's Soccer Gift Book* David Stacey revealed he had over a million programmes in his Wickford, Essex home. Pride of place in the recent acquisitions pile went to the gold-covered Oxford United programme from 22 August 1962, the occasion of their first league match at the Manor Ground, against Lincoln City. A midweek fixture, Stacey made it back to Essex at 4.30 in the morning; but the programme was 'a piece of football history ... well worth the trouble'.

to 'a glorious soccer past', enabling each collector to 'relive many a doughty battle and the highlights in the careers of old favourites . . . The football programme not only records the general history of the game, but also the rise and fall of clubs. To stress this point,' Dalton continued, 'I need go no further than season 1946–47 [a mere seven seasons previous] – Grimsby Town and Brentford were First Division sides, while Cardiff City were operating in the Third Division South; Gillingham and Colchester United were in the Southern League, Shrewsbury Town and Scunthorpe United in the Midland League . . .' and on and on and on, and further and further back he goes, taking in Workington, New Brighton, Arsenal as a third division side, Rochdale playing in the first division . . . along with Bury, Accrington Stanley and both Bradford City and Bradford Park Avenue.[73]

The rhythm of the old names, the distant echo of *Sports Report* on the radio, a world where Barrow v Aldershot is as important and as relevant as Manchester United v Everton, where Bedford Jezzard stands down as manager of Fulham, because, with the likes of Haynes, Hill and Robson, it's all getting a little out of control . . . it all puts me in mind of Laurie, retreating to his garage in Essex, surrounded by shelving, drawers, racks and a couple of fireproof safes: 'I come out here sometimes, and I just get totally lost. I shut that down [the garage door], put talkSPORT on, listen to *Hawksbee and Jacobs*, two totally obsessive football punters, Chelsea and Spurs, listen to the banter . . .' and

STANLEY BEAN

'EVERY ITEM IS CAREFULLY RECORDED . . . HE IS SINGLE. HE IS A NON-SMOKER. HE NEVER DRINKS INTOXICANTS'

Laurie pulls out his collection of cuttings, of people's old scrapbooks he's bought up at auctions (he shows me a meticulously stuck together fan's account of the 1913–14 season), of old programmes, newspapers and very early *Topical Times*.

Prior to the Christmas annual the *Topical Times* existed as a sports paper, a sort of *Playfair Annual*. Laurie describes it as the 'first mass produced football comic of its time . . . [full of] results. They're good for stats. Although there's nothing really riveting – the stats of the previous season, the fixtures of the next, out in the summer – but these were the forerunners.' There are profiles of all league and Scottish clubs, a few slightly rusty staples, and lovely faded, orange and green duotone covers. 'They cost me about a tenner a time; they're never in very good condition, the paper was pretty poor,' continues Laurie. 'People have chucked 'em in a box in the loft . . . mice have been at 'em, mice crap all over them . . . they've been in the shed, are damp, falling apart – saved but not necessarily loved or looked after. I dry them out, preserve them in proper bags in my garage.' Like Peter Morris, he's a fan of 'the lovely photographs of the players – they provided an album to put them in, in the twenties and thirties, up to the war.'

Laurie pulls out a *Sunday Empire News*, the *Sports Argus* – 'probably the bible of them all' – and a *Daily Worker*. Picking up the *Topical Times* published ahead of the 1923–24 season, I find a surprisingly irreverent definition buried in their dictionary of football terms: 'Policeman: a tantalisingly nimble biped who keeps moving about before the match starts, and at half-time, but is always in the way when a goal is scored.'

'That sums up the old bill, really,' says Laurie, who re-bags some of the more fragile publications, places them back on the correct shelves, or in their cubby-holes, and turns out the light.

---

73 A year later in the *Soccer Gift Book*, T.K. now 'Tom' Dalton updates us on the 'many programmes that have changed hands in Britain's fastest-growing hobby' and claims there are now 'nearly 20,000 known collectors'. He supplies a guide to which envelopes should be used for which clubs (given the difference in programme sizes): '6in x 9in at Bournemouth . . . 5½in x 8in for Workington . . . each season I try to obtain every Cup-tie issue from the First Round Proper to the Cup final, failing miserably each time. If I miss only a dozen of each tournament, I have done well. So if you have gaps in your collection do not despair. So have I!'

Above: The much-travelled Stanley Bean profiled in *Topical Times Football Book* 1960–61

Following pages: Another eye-catching spread in the *Topical Times Football Book* 1965–66 featuring Bobby Moore and the Murray brothers, both earning some cash from their off-field enterprises

Skipper of West Ham and England, here is BOBBY MOORE behind the counter of his
London sports shop.

The family market garden in Lanarkshire keeps the MURRAY brothers busy outside football hours. They are GEORGE *(left)* of Motherwell and CAMERON of St Mirren.

The sweet sensation of victory. Geoff Hurst and Ray Wilson chair England Captain Bobby Moore as he holds aloft the Jules Rimet Cup.

'AFTER THE FINAL GEOFF HURST WENT HOME AND WASHED THE CAR'

THE WORLD CUP

There's an account in an anthology, *The Thinking Fan's Guide to the World Cup*,[74] by the *McSweeney's* writer Sean Wilsey who, once the 2002 tournament was over, and still in need of a daily fix, started watching the 1970 World Cup tournament on a series of VCR tapes bought off ebay. 'Taking advantage of [his] American ignorance', he started watching the games in real time, as the tournament unfolded. Friends asked him if he 'wanted to place a small bet on the outcome', and in a successful *Likely Lads* scenario, he managed to make it to the end, in his 'own private 1970', Brazil's ultimate triumph providing him with 'several of the most rapturous moments I've ever had in front of a television screen'.

Reading the best of Hugh Taylor's *Scottish Football Book*s is a bit like that. Pick up *The Scottish Football Book no.16*, say, and it's not long before you're engrossed in Hugh's account of the Scottish FA Cup final in 1970, wherein Aberdeen, 'angry young men' at being written off beforehand, overcame the mighty Celtic, who 'reserved their worst performance of the season for the biggest game of the season'. 'So ruffled' beforehand were the Dons that they couldn't properly admire 'the beautiful golf courses, the magnificent scenery and the perfect service of Gleneagles'. Celtic, on the other hand, lost their composure on the pitch. A series

The question of whether the sixties would go down 'as the star-dusted decade' was one that 'dangles curiously'

of decisions – a surprise penalty, a disallowed goal, a not-given penalty – went against the green and white hoops and, 1–0 down, they became flustered: 'Never did they reveal the brilliant teamwork or the flash of genius that bejewelled their play on the big occasions so often.' Taylor faithfully reproduced the ebb and flow of the game, Celtic settling early, but the Dons surprising them by combining 'zest and style' with resolute defending. Aberdeen broke down the right, a 'classical move', a shot, a parry . . . then the rebound driven into an empty net by Derek McKay. Celtic strained, searching for a foothold, and— but then pages thirteen and fourteen have been ripped out of the copy I have.

Shamefully, being English, I didn't know the outcome[75], but somehow Hugh Taylor's weaving of significant match detail into a tense and enveloping narrative makes for a highly compelling read nearly half a century later. In the same volume Hugh bid FAREWELL TO THE SIXTIES, a decade that began, of course, with Real Madrid's dismantling of Eintracht Frankfurt in his own backyard and promised an era 'of glittering ball skills, fluid movement, exhilarating attacking play, an era, in short, of the gay football so beloved of the Scots.' The question of whether the sixties would go down 'as the star-dusted decade' was still one, in 1970, that 'dangles curiously'. Dazzling Celtic aside 'alas, the sixties contained more frustration than exhilaration'. There had been the Scottish national team's 9–3 slaughtering by England; the failure to qualify for Chile in '62, England in '66 or Mexico '70 – but also flashes of brilliance. 'A Phoenix

---

74 What would an 'unthinking' fan's guide read like?

75 Aberdeen went on to win 3–1.

Left: The photo that has subsequently become the most widely reproduced in the history of English football publishing, as seen in the *FA Book For Boys* 1967

FAREWELL TO THE SIXTIES

A decade dazzling or . . . ?

He helped make the sixties swing—Rangers dazzling winger, Willie Henderson

Hughie Taylor in his *Scottish Football Book* no16 concluded 'the sixties may not have been as dazzling as we might have wished but they showed that the old lion could roar in football, at least, even if most of the home play did not bring the sensation of the Pill, *Lady Chatterley's Lover*, the Rolling Stones or a visit to the moon.' Later in the annual he returned to his favourite theme: fair play, skill, expressive football and entertainment were rife in Scotland, unlike the dour fare served up south of the border, where 'winning the World Cup the way England did has had a corrupting influence'.

rising with bagpipes blowing and claymores flashing from the ashes of defeat and humiliation,' was Hugh's take on the Hampden Wizards' beating of England 2–0 in the April sunshine of 1962, 'a football lesson that should have been accompanied throughout by a roll of drums and a commentary by Olivier.' YouTube footage of the roar when Scotland's first goal goes in, and the swaying, dense thicket of human life crammed into the vertiginous slopes of Hampden bowl, sends a

shiver down the spine today. After a quarter of century of 'Hampden failure' in trying to overcome England, did this mean Scotland 'became a great international side at last?

'Alas no,' reported a Hugh. 'A month later the Scots lost 3–2 to Uruguay – at Hampden.'

Still, while Scotland may have lacked consistency, at least they continued to play the game how it should be played. Taylor quoted the journalist Malcolm Muggeridge, who said 'the sixties were a frenetic decade, having, however, more the character of a foolish dream than a nightmare.'

'So it was in football,' continued Taylor. 'For it was the decade of the robots, the faceless ones. The hired assassin in football made his debut, the player whose main job was to see the opposing stars were kept quiet. It worked. England became the first country to win the World Cup with a team of dour efficiency which made those who loved Matthews and Finney and Lawton shudder . . . '[76]

It's hard to imagine anyone airing such sacrilegious thought in a Christmas annual for kids today – even in Scotland. But back in the late sixties such sentiment was, if not exactly commonplace in the pages of football annuals, then certainly in keeping with a rather low-key and muted response to England's World Cup victory – or at least that was the case in both the lead-up and immediate aftermath of the tournament in 1966.

Getting into the mood early, the *Eagle Annual* of 1966 had a water-skier on the front cover[77], though inside Joe Mercer was quite prescient in saying that England didn't have players skilful enough to carve open modern-day defences. Rather, 'We must have method instead.' Unless you could admire the art of the retreating defence, funnelling play backwards, 'you might find the World Cup 1966 the biggest bore, instead of the greatest show on earth,' warned the Manchester City manager, an advocate of attacking football.

The *Topical Times* in 1964, just under two years ahead of the tournament, photographed 'one of England's more attacking hopes', Peter Thompson, strolling in the park with several dogs, looking relaxed.

But the main focus was on the preparations of

---

76 Hughie Taylor went on to note the demise of Third Lanark, but also a general increase in crowds – and violence, and reaffirmed the perennial wish for a stronger challenge to the Old Firm in the coming decade.

77 No pre-tournament hype here, but a fine pair of 1960s swimming trunks, and some kind of safety harness – presumably indicating travel at very high speed.

Joe Mercer, former England captain and England Under-23 Team Manager, takes a shrewd and searching look at Football's most exciting competition. And he tries to answer the big question . . .

Can England win the World Cup?

WHEN Jules Rimet, the man who started it all, handed the twenty-seven-inches-high solid gold statuette known as the World Cup to the captain of Uruguay in 1930, the streets of Montevideo were swollen with joyful throngs celebrating a national triumph.

Meantime, to show their anger at what they judged to be brutal tactics on the part of the home team, and one-sided refereeing by the official in charge of the Final, an Argentine crowd stoned the Uruguayan Consulate in Buenos Aires.

Eight years later in Paris, twenty-

June, 1962. Wilson (right) and Brazil's Garrincha fight for the ball in Chile

five nations assembled for the third World Cup competition. The world was on the brink of War, and Mussolini sent his team manager a telegram which read: "Win—or die!" Italy won.

It all seemed like a comic opera to us at the time, for the British team stood out of the World Cup in smug isolation until 1950 when Billy Wright led England in their first bid for victory at Rio.

Everybody expected England, Masters of Soccer, to put the rest of the world in its place, and our opening victory over Chile was no surprise.

But a sensation followed when England were defeated 1–0 at Belo Horizonte by a United States eleven so undistinguished that it had seemed a cheek for it even to enter.

England's humiliation was completed when we lost to Spain and so failed to qualify for the Final Pool of a competition we had travelled 6,000 miles to win.

Every four years since then England has striven to put the record straight and prove that we are indeed the Masters. Yet today we are no nearer to winning the World Cup than ever we were.

Or are we? For the 1966 World Cup competition is to be staged in England for the first time, and the man charged with the task of planning a home victory is Alf Ramsey who was a member

13

Down Mexico Way, Four Years From Now. . . .

THE TOP-OF-THE-WORLD CUP

THINGS move fast in football. So, with World Cup Tourney 1966 faded into the past, sights are already set on the next big world show—in Mexico in 1970.

Already countries are studying the problems it will bring, while searching for new players and developing new tactics.

Scotland, Ireland, and Wales, having seen their ways gone wrong, are doing the same as England did after the World Cup in Chile in 1962. No longer are they living on a day-to-day basis. Instead, they are gearing their programmes and training to hit peak at the right time for the period of the World Competition.

Brazil, for instance, have already started looking for a training ground in the same high altitude that will be experienced in Mexico City. The build-up has started all over again in Russia, West Germany, the Argentine, Ghana—even the unknown Far East countries. For new names will emerge in 1970, in the same way as North Korea did last time.

New rules could ensure an African country being in the final sixteen for the first time. And Mediterranean countries like Spain, Italy, Greece, Turkey, and Albania could be in the same group as, say, Algeria, Ghana, The United Arab Republic, and Nigeria.

With air travel becoming even easier, there is no longer need for groups to be worked out entirely on a geographical basis.

Mexico, of course, automatically qualify as hosts in 1970. As do the present holders of the trophy.

★ Background to the heading above is the fantastic, brand new Aztec Stadium in Mexico City.

7

Brazil and Dr Hilton Gosling, advisor to the Brazilian FA, who'd made several trips back home to check on the air quality ('smoke content') around Manchester and Liverpool, the road conditions and hotels. He was also running psychological profiles of the Brazilian squad – 'is he happily married? Does he drink?' – and 'somatotyping' them: running a kind of body–mass index of weight and height measurements, breaking it all down into specific analysis of fat on the thigh, the size of the hips, etc., and calculating optimum playing positions from there. England would give the Brazilians a run for their money, but it was clear who were the favourites, who was ahead in the game.

Printing deadlines also played their part regarding any low-key vibe afterwards. George Best in action for Manchester United against Spurs, and a neat circular cut-out of drama from Celtic v Motherwell make up the cover of the *Topical Times* annual placed under Christmas trees at the end of 1966. Inside, the first article breezily noted, 'Things move fast in football. So,

> **'Unless you admire the art of the retreating defence, you might find the World Cup 1966 the biggest bore'**

with the World Cup Tourney 1966 faded into the past, sights are already set on the next big world show – in Mexico 1970,' and fretted about altitude and oxygen in the dressing rooms, before moving on to the pressing issues of the day – namely Don Revie explaining in detail the workings behind his new colour-coded 'injury board', which looked like it could be useful for keeping the score in a game of bar skittles; a photograph of a swan on the pitch at Shawfield Park, Clyde; Millwall manager Billy Gray hiring ballet-trainer Doreen Armitage; and a feature on lanky scoring sensation Peter Osgood, picked up as a sixteen-year-old bricklayer playing for Windsor Corinthians after his mum wrote to Stamford Bridge.

The World Cup back then 'wasn't nearly as big as the Olympics,' remembers Richard Williams. 'It was probably to do with England not taking part in anything until 1950.'

Ros Pedley wrote in *BackPass* magazine of her trip down to the capital for the day, parking up at Stanmore

Top left: A blunt assessment of the creative options in England squads from future England manager Joe Mercer, *Eagle Football Annual* 1966

Top right: With 1966 long gone in the annuals' yearly publishing cycle, the *Topical Times Football Book* 1966–67 turned its attention to Mexico 1970

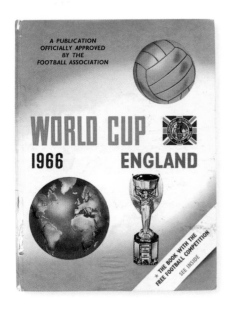

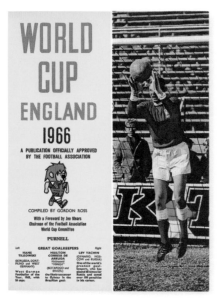

FLORIAN ALBERT, Ferencvaros and Hungary

FLORIAN ALBERT

Ferencvaros and Hungary

This great centre-forward was first capped in 1958, when he was only seventeen. He first blossomed as an inside forward. He scored the goals against England when Hungary won 2-0 in 1960.

FERENC BENE, Ujpest and Hungary

FERENC BENE

Ujpest and Hungary

Bene is a strongly built player with a fine burst of speed and is a cracking shot. He won his first cap on the wing when he was eighteen. He is likely to be the star of Hungary's World Cup team.

FA Chairman Joe Mears introduced this book with the exclamation 'The World Cup in England!' but the excitement didn't merit publishing more than 44 unnumbered pages. Many of those were given over to likely England players like Tony Waiters, Alan Peacock and John Kaye, who didn't make the final squad.

There was some pleasing use of colour in this still largely monochrome world. The title page featured Russian keeper Lev Yashin, in blue rather than his famous black, playing for a FIFA representative side. Inside, Hungarians Flórián Albert and Ferenc Bene lazed in the grass, while Italian and French star players were cut out on a typical black and white spread – both nations exited at the group stages.

CAN ENGLAND WIN?
YES, OF COURSE THEY CAN!

tube station and getting the tube down to Wembley. She remembers the ground covered by Alan Ball, the unselfish running of Martin Peters, the elation at the end, and the egg and chips at the motorway services on the way home. Only years later did the magnitude of what she and her fellow Wolves fan Liz had witnessed really sink in. 'Ramsey was quite convinced England were going to win. I don't think anybody else gave us a cat in hell's chance. It was here, in England, of course, and they kept on winning. But then Portugal in the semi-final – well, I don't think anybody expected 'em to beat Portugal; Eusébio at his peak. After the final Geoff Hurst went home and washed the car.'

'Will England win the World Cup? Nah, we're just not good enough,' was also the mood Laurie Rampling recalls in early 1966. 'We didn't have to qualify in '66 and a lot of people said – off the back of '62 – if we'd had to qualify we wouldn't have been there. We'll never ever know if we were truly the best, because we didn't have to qualify. I don't want to be a killjoy, but it's true.'

> **World Cup England 1966 annual had Brazil down as favourites, England as 'a definite possibility'**

I expressed surprise to Laurie about the lack of coverage – by today's standards – in most football annuals of the era. There was certainly no national newspaper printed and delivered to every home in the land on the occasion of England's opening match against Uruguay. Televised football – television itself – was still in its infancy back then. 'Only since the sixties has football gone totally global, become the most televised, consumed, enjoyed pastime – if you can still call it a pastime; now it's the biggest business in the world.'

There was, though, *World Cup England 1966*, a slim hardback annual which had Brazil down as favourites, England as 'a definite possibility' and West Germany as the 'dark horse', alongside plenty of lovely atmospheric shots of the likes of Flórián Albert and Ferenc Bene,

languidly posing in Super-8-hued photographs, their 'wine red' Hungarian kits against the hazy blue sky and faded green grass of the training ground, far-off apartment blocks shimmering in the heat-haze. A spread of photos, BRAZILIANS ON PARADE, featured Garrincha and Pelé sporting pale yellow, wide-necked training tops that wouldn't be out of place today on a fashionable Soho menswear rail. There was also a handy kit guide – although Portugal didn't play in white and blue – and numerous cool action shots of the likes of Russia's Valentin Ivanov (who didn't make the tournament), Argentinians Antonio Roma and José Varacka, Chile's Luis Eyzaguirre and Italy's Sandro Mazzola, with battered legs, socks round his ankles.

If Purnell books had the preview annual, then World Distributors of Manchester lucked in with *Kenneth Wolstenholme's Boys' Book of the World Cup, England 1966*, the 12/6 official annual of the tournament, published in conjunction with the FA. So no biting criticism of Ramsey's functionalism, obviously – the opening 0–0 draw was brushed away as a case of overly high expectation on behalf of a public ignorant of Uruguay's nous[78] – but plenty of information about the grounds, including fine aerial shots of White City stadium and the rest – and a nicely detailed write-up of the whole tournament. There were initial worries that Orange Day celebrations of the Battle of the Boyne – involving plenty of processions and pilgrimages to the seaside at Southport – would have an impact on the gate at Brazil v Bulgaria, but 'with the streets around Goodison Park gay with bunting' and a 7,000-strong Brazilian contingent 'complete with samba bands and banners'

---

78 Wolstenholme argued that some of Uruguay's football, though played at walking pace, was 'fascinating', as they still moved the ball at speed, and passed with 'bewildering accuracy'.

Top: *World Cup England 1966*, **the 'officially approved' pre-tournament hardback stays positive about the home nation's chances**

witnessing Bulgaria play their part in a match of 'splendid fluent football' (plus the odd brutal foul), worries of empty seats or a lack of atmosphere went unfounded.

One of the pleasures of reading this (and any other) annual today is trawling for the incidental, buried or lost, or simply atmospheric micro-detail. Things such as Ayresome Park only figuring because of Newcastle city council's failure to reassure FIFA over their lease renewal at St James's Park; Italy still managing to produce 'radar-controlled' passing against Chile, despite the rain pouring down at Roker Park; the Sunderland coach driver being seconded to the Russian squad for the tournament[79]; Brazil 'throwing caution to the wind' and putting in an inexperienced XI against Portugal to go all out for the three goals they needed ('they were going to win by the free, exciting, attacking Brazilian football or they were going out. They went out.'); Hillsborough's new cantilever stand apparently drawing gasps from visiting fans; Kenneth Wolstenholme agreeing with the Argentinians that they should have won it – but only had themselves to blame for their indiscipline which overcame their natural talent[80].

Needless to say the annual concluded with a lengthy match report of the final.

Steve Smith, the collector walled-in in his spare room in Bristol, surrounded by hundreds of thousands of pages of football history, firmly believes, 'The older annuals are better as they give a point of view of football as it stood then. If a book came out now, looking back at a particular era, it could still be limited and miss things out. If you get

RELAXATION—at the Pinewood Film Studios actress Viviane Ventura tries to see eye-to-eye with Jack Charlton—with the help of a high step!

a book that came out in 1951 that covered the 1950 World Cup, you'd get the 1951 viewpoint, fresh in the writer's memory.' It's a perspective not clouded by time nor distorted by the modern-day telling. Essentially, an unvarnished look, rather than a copy of a copy of a copy, of certain stories retold, some things looming into focus at the expense of others. The fact that Geoff Hurst took his chance against Argentina (while Jimmy Greaves was injured) has been magnified over the course of fifty years of football annuals to the point where no account of 1966 is complete without it; no school kid who ever picked up a football annual is unaware of this development; in fact, modern life today would not be as it is if Geoff Hurst had not come in for Greaves in the quarter-final. Greaves was distraught, but you hear a lot less about that.

Equally as interesting is the minutiae: Jimmy Armfield's account, in his *All Stars '67* annual, of the England party's trip to Pinewood studios after the underwhelming 0–0 draw against Uruguay, for instance. Sean Connery, Yul Brynner, Leslie Phillips, Viviane Ventura and Cliff Richard were all on hand to cheer up the squad: 'It took our minds off football and gave us a fresh start.' And on the eve of the final Alf and the squad filed into a cinema in Hendon to see *Those Magnificent Men and their Flying Machines*. Armfield was a squad member in the stand for the final, and those not on the bench had been told to make their way down to the touchline in the eighty-ninth minute. Germany equalized and Armfield and a few others were trapped in front of the royal box for the duration of extra time. Armfield also revealed that Ramsey had suggested a bonus of £500 per man, rising to £1,500 for those who actually played in the matches. But the first-teamers insisted it should be equal; Ray Wilson said he'd give his £500 to Armfield if there was going to be discrimination between the first team and the rest of the squad.

The earlier *All Stars* annuals could veer towards the bland, but as the series progressed into the

---

79 Actually a detail from the *Topical Times Book of Football* 1984.

80 Richard Williams is also of the opinion that Argentina would have won the tournament had Rattín not been sent off against England: 'Argentina should have won it – not a popular view, but it's always been mine. I once planned a piece I never wrote, in the seventies, about Duncan McKenzie, and I had a first sentence which was, "A Duncan McKenzie fan is someone who thinks Argentina should have won the World Cup in 1966."'

Above: Jack Charlton meets Vivien Ventura, totally spontaneously of course, at Pinewood Studios, from *All Stars Football Book* 1967 Following pages: The World Cup photospread in the *Topical Times* 1965–66 featured both the

Czechoslovakian Ján Popluhár and Yugoslavian Šoškic. Both nations were good bets for the finals in 1966 having made the final and semi-finals respectively in 1962, the editors no doubt thought. Neither qualified for the tournament in England.

The joy of goal-scoring. Geoff Hurst after heading the goal by which England beat Argentina. Behind him is Roger Hunt

Fly the poor North Korean defenders having to take the weight of this lot in the North Korea v. Italy game

The tension mage—and Eusébio weeps after Portugal's narrow defeat in that feate Semi-Final against England

|||||||||||||||||||||||||||||||||||||

Post-tournament tome *The Boys' Book of the World Cup* was entrusted to the publishers of *Kenneth Wolstenholme's Book of World Soccer* – the BBC commentator had also just coined 'that' World Cup final phrase. It contained no colour pages but did enjoy the pick of the images from the press photo pool, which gathered all the pictures officially taken at the tournament for collective syndication.

Included were: Geoff Hurst after scoring v Argentina, an aerial tussle between North Korea and Italy at Ayresome Park and Eusébio in tears after semi-final defeat. The back cover featured an eye-catching if brutal motif on a cyan-rich blue that suggested the designers had either been briefed to do something simple, or they'd run clean out of time.

A sometimes subtle distinction.

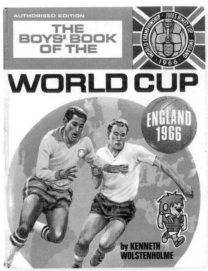

LEONEL SANCHEZ
(Chile)

JAN POPLUHAR
(Czechoslovakia)

LUIS SUAREZ
(Spain)

PELE
(Brazil)

FERREIRA EUSEBIO
(Portugal)

UWE SEELER
(Germany)

THEY'RE ALL WORLD CUP MEN

VICTOR PONEDELNICK
(Russia)

FLORIAN ALBERT
(Hungary)

SOSKIC
(Yugoslavia)

late-sixties and seventies there were some interesting articles[81]. Steve agrees: '*All Stars* didn't offer anything new. Content-wise there was nothing in there of substance – you'd open it up and think, "What have I got this for?"' Steve was far more likely to pick up the *FA Book for Boys*, or *Charles Buchan's Soccer Gift Book*, 'Something that will take you well beyond the Christmas holidays into Easter.' The *FA Book for Boys* he rates, in particular: 'Each year you get a good review of everything to do with the FA – schoolboy football, full internationals, the Amateur Cup, the FA Cup – a good account of everything. Then there's *Charles Buchan* for just nostalgia . . .'

As a kid, Steve concedes that, in the FA annual, the 'Charles Hughes tactical stuff', the Allen Wade drawings of 'triangles, matchstick men and dotted lines', and three-page instructional treatises on how to be an overlapping full-back 'went over my head, really. The two

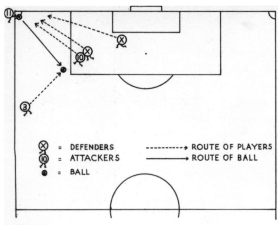

Figure 2

= DEFENDERS ---------> ROUTE OF PLAYERS
= ATTACKERS ————————> ROUTE OF BALL
= BALL

or three pages of text that related to the diagram didn't really make sense . . . I just played, and didn't worry about tactics.' Today, having forced myself through four pages of Alex Elder on the role of the full-back, at the point the Northern Ireland and Burnley star announces, 'And now for the throw-in . . . ' it's true, your eyes have long begun to glaze over.

Factually speaking Steve is right, the *FA Book for Boys* annuals were neat and comprehensive, particularly in reference to the amateur game. Laurie Rampling is also a huge fan.

Both the *Boys' Book of Soccer* (a new annual that appeared after the World Cup) and the *FA Book for Boys*, in their 1967 incarnations, had round-ups of the

81 A portrait of Harry Catterick, having been beaten up by 'young thugs' after a 2–0 defeat at Blackpool. Poker faced, the Everton manager disappeared early from the Championship dinner, but 'none of us had an inkling that it heralded the signing of Sandy Brown' wrote journalist Harry Stanley; the story of Bill Ridding who, struggling with injury at Old Trafford in the 1930s, was advised to undertake a lot of walking and climbing stairs regularly to build up his shattered knee following three cartilage operations – 'so for the next six months Bill followed the advice to the letter – by becoming a bus conductor with Manchester Corporation. "That did the trick," he said'; and Jimmy Armfield himself on the wolf whistles when Blackpool ran out for the 1953 Cup final in their new satin shorts.

The art and hobby of collecting Football Stamps

U.S.S.R. bequeathed philatelists this record of their victory in the 1956 Olympic Games at Melbourne

One of the most original and colourful designs for the 1962 World Cup Finals in Chile came from Hungary

Brazil, winners of the Jules Rimet Cup in 1958 and 1962, and England, the 1966 winners, issued special stamps

World Cup – printed in fetching red ink in the case of the FA publication. But it was all still fairly low-key, as if the editors were thinking, enough of that: let's swiftly move on with this article on commemorative football stamps around the world, and the piece written by Dennis Marshall, assistant secretary at the City Ground, concerning FOOTBALL LOCOMOTIVES IN THE STEAM ERA. (See right.)

Rather intriguingly the annual closed with a two-page history of the sock in football – from a bulky item of protective apparel in the days of hacking, through to the development of stretch nylon. I was looking forward to this: 'It is not beyond the realms of possibility,' concluded John J.H. Humphries, 'that a stocking will be designed embodying a complete lightweight padding. To date, however, no suitable material has been developed which would provide protection while fulfilling the requirements of flexibility and lightness so essential to efficient performance on the field . . . ' – but it was quite a shock to encounter the deadening language of the marketeer in a football annual feature. On reading the small print, it turns out John J.H. Humphries was managing director of 'Umbro international sporstwear, which has been worn by more English and Scottish Cup and League winners in the last thirty years than any other strip'. Charles Hughes may have been lurking in the corridors of power, about to inflict Position of Maximum Opportunity upon the world, but you couldn't say the FA weren't on the ball when it came to 'advertorial' content.

It could have been all down those restrictive print deadlines (going to press at the end of the May for the new season and that last-minute Christmas present from a busy uncle), but the tone of pleasing understatement around England's triumph in the football annuals of 1967 and 1968 shifts subtly in the run-up to Mexico '70. Clearly the squad were confident: Jack Charlton even professed, in *David Coleman's World Cup '70 Preview* annual, that a European team would win because European football 'from what I've seen and read, is far ahead of the South American game at the moment'. On other fancied sides, Alan Mullery considered West Germany 'a bit static, a bit predictable', and that 'England will always be Portugal's master'[82]. Bobby Charlton reckoned that England no longer needed to cower in the face of tricky Continental or South

---

82 Presumably at the time of the interview Portugal's qualification campaign hadn't disintegrated.

FOOTBALL CLUB LOCOMOTIVES IN THE STEAM ERA
by DENNIS MARSHALL
Assistant Secretary, Nottingham Forest F.C.

'Do you collect autographs? I expect so,' wrote Dennis Marshall in the *Boys' Book of Soccer*. 'Then the chances are that you are also one of a band of youngsters who also go trainspotting.' What followed was a lament for the days of steam, and especially the 22 B.17 class steam engines, usually found on LNER routes out of Liverpool Street station to 'East Coast resorts like Clacton, Yarmouth, Lowestoft and Southend', and named after various football clubs.

Trainspotting was still a national pastime in the mid-sixites, even if by 1967 diesel was king, and the *Nottingham Forest, Darlington, Barnsley, Hull City* and *West Ham United* had long been shown the blowtorch in the knackers yard. But the name-plates lived on, not only in the display cabinet at the City Ground, but also in the homes of a few diehard football-loving train enthusiasts willing to pay up to £200 to mount their own club's plate on the living-room wall.

American opposition: 'Skills don't worry us so much now because we've learnt to get on terms there . . . oh, yes, I've never been so full of confidence in any England side.' The relief is almost palpable as both Charlton brothers and Mullery comment on Argentina's surprise non-appearance at the finals, edged out by Peru. Geoff Hurst tipped Mexico for a top-three finish.

It's easy to mock with hindsight, but no one mentioned Italy, despite Gianni Rivera being in possession of the Ballon d'Or and Sandro Mazzola having been on fire as Italy won the European Championships in 1968. In the *Coleman* annual round-up of qualified teams it was claimed that Italy boss Ferruccio Valcareggi's 'major

---

If tactical diagrams and features on world football stamps – 'A complete collection would consist of over 500 stamps from 100 countries!' – were not enough . . . (left)

. . . the *FA Book for Boys* 1967–68 threw football and trainspotting into the mix: 'These two hobbies rank high in the list of outdoor pastimes of the schoolboys!' (above)

London's Young Hopefuls for Mexico 1970

Peter Osgood, Chelsea's midfield player, whose return to form in 1968/69 puts him right in line for a place in the England squad

84

Keith Weller, skipper of dockside Millwall whose consistent good form must put him in line for international honours soon

85

Young Hopefuls for Mexico 1970

Manchester City forward Francis Lee, who must be high on Sir Alf Ramsey's list of Mexico probables

26

Brian Kidd, another Manchester youngster with a fine chance of making the trip to Mexico

27

The *London Soccer Annual*'s 'Young London Hopefuls for Mexico 1970' photo-spread makes for poignant reading, especially for West Ham's Billy Bonds and Trevor Brooking, Arsenal's John Radford, Chelsea's John Hollins and Millwall's Keith Weller — none of whom made the final squad. Which left only Peter Osgood, who only got on as a sub in Mexico. Of all the 'Young Hopefuls' photographed in the *Northern Soccer Annual*, only Francis Lee made it on to the plane while Brian Kidd, Colin Harvey and Ralph Coates stayed at home; as did Jimmy Greenhoff, David Nish and Willie Carr from the *Midlands* edition. Other hopefuls Bobby Hope and Asa Hartford were Scottish anyway. Clockwise from top left: neatly cropped Osgood, Weller and Kidd; and Lee.

A car – A tent – A bacon and beans diet

HELENIO HERRERA is a top world coach. As manager-coach of Barcelona and Inter-Milan he's rated best in Europe. He has also been team manager of the French, Spanish and Italian national sides.

Herrera is in a position to pick almost any football job in the world. His knowledge of footballers is second to none. He rates none higher than the British player.

He's on record as saying, "I admire their vigour and purpose. Their competitive outlook, temperament and fitness. These are the factors that won England the World Cup."

Coaching has played a big part in bringing our football to the pitch that produces such compliments.

Until defeat by Hungary at Wembley in 1953, we were content with the approach that had served us for so long. And were convinced our way was best. Walter Winterbottom, then England team manager and Director of Coaching for the F.A., was as a voice in the wilderness.

When Hungary hit us for 6–3, everyone realised there was something wrong with English football. Our way was no longer best.

Well, if you see something you realise is better—why not make use of it? And, as far as English football was concerned, the ideal was to "marry" the best of the English style with the best of the rest of the world.

It took us until July 30, 1966, to prove we had succeeded in achieving that new pattern. Thirteen years between the Hungary defeat and winning the World Cup.

Now, thanks largely to coaching, there is a brand new generation of thinking footballers. Young players are learning new skills and tactics. It used to be skills came with experience. Now boys start learning them as 15-year-old apprentice professionals.

I was lucky enough to start thinking in terms of

By DAVE SEXTON

ARSENAL'S assistant - manager - coach, Dave Sexton, is one of Britain's top men at the job. One he began at Chelsea when he was only 30 — his playing career ended by a knee injury.

Dave took over at Highbury at the start of last season after a spell as coach with Fulham and as manager with Leyton Orient.

As a player he was a centre-forward with Luton Town, West Ham United, Leyton Orient, Brighton and Crystal Palace.

He holds the full F.A. coaching certificate and also played cricket for Sussex Second Eleven.

96

coaching as a twenty-year-old—which is usually the time you start to think about bettering your own game, rather than bettering other people's.

My good fortune was that I kept joining up with clubs that had "thinking" players.

I'd decided on football as a career—against a family background more inclined towards boxing.

Archie Sexton, my father, was a top middle-weight of the 1930's. He fought in the Hood-Harvey-McAvoy era, losing on a k.o. to Jock McAvoy for the British middle-weight title in October, 1933.

My grandfather, Jimmy Sexton, had been bantam-weight champion of the North-East. An uncle had fought under the name of Jim Blake. I'd won a brigade middle-weight title in the Army.

You can see how strong was the boxing background. But I liked football and cricket. Boxing was always an ordeal. I felt sick every time I went into the ring, and had to screw up the nerves and reflexes to get started.

The whole affair sorted itself out when I left the Army. I turned professional for Bury St Edmunds.

When I eventually signed for Luton Town, there were players around like Sid Owen, now coach with Leeds United; Wally Shanks and Charlie Watkins who were looking to the future and were keen on coaching. They talked me into going on a course as a 20-year-old.

And so to Upton Park, where there were coaching enthusiasts like Malcolm Allison, now assistant manager with Manchester City; Malcolm Musgrove, coach to

Off we went on....
THE FOOTBALL EXPEDITION THAT OPENED MY EYES

Listening to a tactics talk by coach Sexton are (left to right) TERRY NEILL, FRANK McLINTOCK, JIM FURNELL, COLIN ADDISON and IAN URE.

---

problem will be to motivate his players, who are used to receiving very large win bonuses'.

Sir Alf, meanwhile, was photographed with that famous reel-to-reel tape recorder, learning Spanish 'to conquer the boredom during the four-week acclimatisation period'. Ipswich chairman John Cobbold paid tribute to his former manager:

> It was the greatest day in 25 years of Ipswich Town football club. We had just clinched promotion to the first division. The boardroom was noisy, raucous. It was a heck of a party. I had just opened another bottle of champagne, looked around and asked, "Where's Alf?" I went out into an almost-deserted stand and there he was in this, his greatest hour watching Ipswich Boys play Norwich Boys. I said, "Alf, come and have a drink." He looked up and said quietly, "Not just now, thank you. I am working."

By Christmas 1969, the first forty-four pages of that year's *All Stars* annual were dedicated to looking ahead to the World Cup in Mexico. Or, rather, to taking a long look back – to Wembley glory in '66, of course, but also to the Haynes era, and Chile in 1962. If England had played the World Cup a year earlier, during their 'purple patch' in 1961, they'd have won it; if the pitch

'All of us suddenly realised football did not begin and end with an English first division game or an FA Cup tie'

hadn't been slippery against Hungary (in the opening 2–1 defeat in Rancagua); if Bulgaria hadn't settled for a point; if Peter Swan hadn't been ill; if Garrincha hadn't hit his peak at that precise moment ...'these [were] the sort of things that defeat all planning ... the luck of the game.' At no point was it suggested that England just weren't good enough.

More edifying, in the *Topical Times* of 1967–68, was the story of Dave Sexton (then assistant manager at Highbury) and pals travelling around Sweden in 1958 in an old Ford Prefect. Sleeping in a tent, moving from campsite to campsite, and surviving on a diet of bacon and beans, it was 'definitely a case of studying world football on the cheap – £70 a head for five weeks'. Sexton's travelling companions were Orient keeper

Above: Dave Sexton's journey of personal and footballing discovery, *Topical Times Football Book 1967–68*

RATTIN: TWO YEARS AFTER

'The Trophy comes back, in Mexico'

by ANTONIO UBALDO RATTIN
(of Boca Juniors and Argentine)

PEOPLE see me and say: 'We can't believe you were sent off at Wembley when Argentina was defeated by England in the World Cup!'

People believe what they are told or what they think is true. Everybody tells me that in the film 'GOAL!' I can be seen clearly uttering insults. Well, let everyone believe what they want.

The truth is that I shouted insults – of course I did. I sent everyone to hell. *But not the referee.*

Why should I insult the referee? I insulted the F.I.F.A. directive that took me from the field. I insulted it because it exasperated me to see the arbitrary injustice which meant my team was reduced to ten men without any reason.

Such a thing made me lose my self-control! Good gracious . . . ! If England won the World Championship it was because they were host team; because the match was played at Wembley; because everything was prepared to damage the opposition; because it was not fairly played, and everything was arranged beforehand.

I am not going to say it was a swindle or a

Looks like a sitter for Wednesday long-service man John Fantham – he's goalside of Wolves 'keeper Parkes (LEFT, TOP). But Fantham had his shot scrambled off the line! BELOW, another Wednesday striker, John Ritchie, goes on his knees to nod this one through the Wolves defence, but it went wide.

'*I am not going to say it was a swindle nor a plunder, but it looked like one . . .*

'*I dare to say England should not be World Champions . . .*

'*On a neutral pitch I am sure the Germans would win five goals to nil . . .*'

In the International Football Book of 1968 time had not proved to be a great healer. Antonio Ubaldo Rattin was still fuming

Pat Welton and Brighton's South African wing-half Eric Hodge. The trio had an epiphany witnessing Pelé, Garrincha and Brazil's 4–2–4 first hand: 'All of us suddenly realised football did not begin and end with an English first division game or an FA Cup tie.' Sexton also claimed that, post '66 and Celtic winning the European Cup, even Inter Milan's Helenio Herrera had come round to the English game. 'He's on record as saying, "I admire their vigour and purpose. Their competitive outlook and temperament and fitness. These are the factors that won England the World Cup."' Which sounded a bit like damming with faint praise. England had finally come round to '"marrying" the best of the English style with the best of the rest of the world,' Sexton believed, but didn't really elaborate, other than to add that rebuilding over the course of thirteen years since Hungary, with improved coaching, had led to a 'new generation of thinking footballers'.

A feature earlier in the same annual alerted readers to a Mexico '70 dossier at the FA offices 'covering such things as the best colour and material for kit and blazers to reflect the sun's rays, salt tablets to counter humidity, anti-dysentery pills, a training programme for high altitudes. Even the best type of sunglasses.' The FA's Dr Alan Bass had been experimenting with throat sprays and 'half a stone of boiled sweets' on the plane to a tournament in Canada to combat the problem of dry throats. It was also noted that 'the British Olympic Medical Commission recommend an acclimatisation period of five weeks in Mexico. But England reckon that would produce boredom . . . ' if those long, sunny days in Chile had been anything to go by.

A year later in the *Topical Times*, England revealed their new strip – all white; 'a light colour reflects the sun' – but it seemed the Yugoslavs (conquerors of England in the European Championships in '68) had been busy feeding statistics on everything from opponents' physical characteristics, previous results and supposed weaknesses in defence into a kind of early super computer. So while the Yugoslavs were mucking about with an embryonic Pro-Zone as early as 1967, England were fretting again over altitude and heat problems, and experimenting with boiled sweets. At least there was a realization that England couldn't really employ the methods they used in 1966 – 'tight marking and hard tackling. With players prepared to chase every ball' – even dressed in super-light white strips. 'England are now looking to produce ball-players. Fellows who can hold the ball and save energy for quick bursts into attack. "All South American countries specialise in this stop-start football – in which they build up slowly before a fast break," said Sir Alf Ramsey.'

Over in the *International Football Book* of 1968 time had not proved to be a great healer. Antonio Ubaldo Rattín was still fuming. Every morning, on his drive to Boca Juniors' training ground, he still worked himself into a fury. Of his dismissal in the quarter-final at Wembley, he claimed, 'Of course I shouted insults. I sent everyone to hell. *But not the referee* . . . if England won the World Championship it was because they were the host team; because the match was played at Wembley; because everything was prepared to damage the opposition; because it was not fairly played, and everything was arranged beforehand. I am not going to say it was a swindle or a plunder, but it looked like one.' And just in case we thought he was joking: '*Even further, I dare say England should not be World Champions.* In my opinion Germany was the best team in the competition.'

Above: Argentina's Antonio Rattin doesn't hold back in the *International Football Book* 1968

JOY: (Above) Chislenko, arms raised, has just scored for the Soviet Union (CCCP on their shirts) against Italy; (below) Players—and officials—of N. Korea hail the goal that made the most sensational result of the competition: Italy 0 N. Korea 1

CELEBRATIONS: 30th July 1966. (Above) The merry wives—Mesdames Moore, Peters, Hurst, Springett and Bonetti; (below) The fans—as England's coach leaves Wembley

fighting spirit have never been higher in my knowledge of the national squad. Privately, I'm even hoping that we might take the World Cup, which has only been won on our Continent before by Uruguay and Brazil.

Mexico has long been preparing itself for these international showcase events. As long ago as 1925 the then President Elias Calles created the National Roads Commission, and forty years later we have a network of 34,327 kilometres of paved road and a further 18,368 kilometres of gravelled road. According to Washington statistics, this places Mexico six-

teenth in a list of 145 nations' road systems—and a clear first in Latin America! The roads give comfortable, quick access to all the principal Mexican towns.

Principal among the playing grounds, of course, will be the great Azteca Stadium. It has a capacity of one hundred thousand people, and in size rates third on the Continent. Spectacular and modern, special care is given to its grass; the approaches are well planned, and the parking areas immense.

Most of the important World Cup games, including the Final, will be played there. The other stadia

There will be plenty to see other than football in Mexico . . . such as the ruins (below) of Teotihuacan, the ancient Aztec city. RIGHT, a magnificent aerial shot of the mighty Azteca Stadium, in which the 1970 World Cup Final is to be played . . . seating a hundred thousand and the third largest stadium on the American Continent.

Top: World Cup 1966 photo highlights in the *All Star Football* 1967 included the England players' 'merry wives' raising a toast to their husbands

Above: Visions of Mexico '70 in the *International Football Book* 1969. A landscape photo printed sideways on the page was a common design feature

He put England's victory on a par with Chile coming third in 1962 and Sweden reaching the final, only to be thrashed by Brazil in 1958. But he was equally hard on his own countrymen and women, continually deluded in thinking they were the best: 'Why can't we be more humble?' he asked. As for 1970 and England's prospects of retaining the trophy: not a chance.

In the same annual a year on Gianni Rivera, unlike Jack Charlton, predicted that a South American country would win Mexico '70 – not least because of '"*ambiente*" . . . environment, surroundings, atmosphere, background, acclimatisation'. Plus there was the small matter of 'sheer ball artistry and control and the use of imagination in those typical flashes of improvised genius', another bunch of requisite characteristics for the winners. A few pages on, Brian Glanville profiled Garrincha, looking back to the time he demolished England in the quarter-final in Chile at the 'delightful little Vina del Mar ground, where the sea mist swept in and the student band beat out samba rhythms [and] he scored two and caused another'. As a child, Garrincha 'wandered contentedly among the woods and fields around his village, watching birds, sometimes catching them and caging them. He accumulated birds, as later, he would accumulate daughters; seven of them by his first wife in Pau . . . ' But these days he cast the 'tense, inward expression of a lonely man, he expressed himself essentially in action'.

In what was essentially a Latin American special, the *International Football Book* of 1969 also featured Peñarol and Uruguay keeper Ladislao Mazurkiewicz, claiming that 'force, violence [and] a misplaced idea of "manliness"' were all wrecking football in his homeland. 'One enters the field in much the same frame of mind as troops heading for the trenches,' wrote Mazurkiewicz. And that was just the national team. Peñarol's and Nacional's stranglehold over football in Montevideo was such that it was extinguishing the life from smaller teams forced to sell their best players to the big two, who were simultaneously 'beginning to bore the pants off the public'. Oil-rich Venezuela was

Tofik Bachramov

Tofiq Bahramov, received the news he was to run the line in the final at Longleat safari park

also a bit of a mess, where people preferred baseball, and football was badly organized and often lawless – 'publicity seeking members of the National Liberation Front' had kidnapped Alfredo di Stéfano there in 1963.

Still, there was a fantastic aerial photograph of the Azteca Stadium, as majestic and impressive in scope as the accompanying shot of the ruins of the ancient Aztec city of Teotihuacan. And Mexican keeper Antonio Carbajal (a veteran of five World Cups) boasted of the 34,327 kilometres of 'paved road and a further 18,368 kilometres of gravelled road' in Mexico at present.

Over subsequent decades Alf Ramsey's decision to substitute Bobby Charlton, with England 2–1 up in the quarter-final against West Germany twenty minutes from time, has been raked over and widely held up as a catastrophic decision[83] presaging the end of an era and four and a half decades of subsequent failure. In *The Book of Soccer no.13, Edited by Bobby Moore*, there's a profile of Charlton celebrating his one hundred caps that noted his consoling of Eusébio after the '66 semi-final, talked of 'a shy modest hero off the field who shuns the spotlight, leaves the talking to others and finds praise an embarrassing experience' but semi-glossed over events in Leon only six months previously: 'England made the mistake of attempting to keep their lead rather than increase it. They surrendered some of their control in midfield and the lanky Beckenbauer made them pay for it.' A World Cup round-up hastily crammed in at the end of the book doesn't really add any depth of insight, but at least proved that by 1970 it was possible to feature a summer tournament in a Christmas annual.[84]

---

83 In Jeff Dawson's *Back Home, England and the 1970 World Cup* and in Brian Glanville's *Story of the World Cup* the decision to bring on the destructive but unshackled Leeds man Norman Hunter a few minutes later in place of Martin Peters is given equal if not more prominence: 'Thus, almost at a stroke,' wrote Glanville, 'the English midfield had been radically altered.'

84 Or at least that seemed to be case, though *Shoot!* were still struggling with this into the 1970s.

Above: Tofiq Bachramov (wrongly spelt with a 'c' in *Soccer the International Way 1971*) – the famous 'Russian' linesman was Azerbaijani

The 1966 World Championship referees entertained by the Marquess of Bath and his lions at Longleat. Bachramov is third from the left standing. The playful lion cub is in the centre of the picture – and enjoying it!

Soccer the International Way 1971 detailed the unlikely sounding incident of the assembled 1966 World Cup referees frolicking with a lion cub (photographic evidence above). The officials 'joked and played with a lion cub like schoolboys. Gottfried Dienst, the Swiss referee, wanted to take the cub in his arms, but as he moved somebody else pulled the cub's tail who instinctively scratched Dienst's hand. Then any further moves towards revenge by Mr Dienst, the lion club or the tail puller were stopped by a loudspeaker announcement: "Attention please. The Organising Committee of the 1966 World Championship announce that Dienst, Bahramov and Galba have been appointed for the final match."

Dienst became silent in mid-sentence. Galba smote with his fists the shoulder of his neighbour – and Bahramov nearly choked himself with a nut!' That *Fahrenheit 451* scenario digested, the article went on to perhaps protest too much that the ball crossed the line, even claiming that an unnamed German player approached Bahramov at the banquet after the final, saying: 'Excuse me, sir, you were right accepting the goal'!

A kids' annual today wouldn't be the place for an inquisition, and that was the case in the early seventies too. Far safer to stick with tales of Russian linesmen.

Soccer the International Way was Kaye and Ward and World Distributors' rival publication to the *International Football Book*, put together by one of their old writers, Gordon Jeffrey. The 1971 annual featured a striking cover photo of George Best in the green of Northern Ireland and a lengthy profile of Tofiq Bahramov, the Azerbaijani linesman from Wembley in 1966, who apparently received the news he was to run the line in the final while attending an official referees' visit to Longleat safari park in Wiltshire. (See inset.)

The Bobby Moore *Book of Soccer* did have a feature on Scotland in the sixties though, the gist of which was: so many great players yet such an abysmal record in qualifying for major tournaments. Frank McLintock put it down to the lack of days spent together as a squad and took a swipe at officialdom: 'The trouble is to be found in the administration. It's about fifty years behind the times . . . the player seems to be a second-class citizen. A mere cog in the wheel . . . too many people who aren't important and don't really know much about football, have far too much to say.' But looking ahead, the future was rosy. Such was the young talent for 1974, manager Bobby Brown reckoned, 'We have a very good chance of coming through as world champions.'

Football writer Ian Plenderleith's dad came down from Scotland to Lincoln and took up residence in the stand at Sincil Bank. Growing up in early seventies Lincolnshire, Ian had plenty of annuals for Christmas: '*Shoot!*, *Goal* and *Topical Times*, and I think I once got the *Sun* annual – presumably they decided to cash in too. It was the default Christmas present from the clueless aunts and great aunts. My heart would sink when I saw the shape of the package. Like all kids, I wanted to be surprised. It was either an annual or a 50p gift token to WH Smith. Once I'd reached the age of 12 or 13, I wised up, giving my mum a list of Subbuteo teams or facilities that I wanted.'

'We should DESTROY WEST GERMANY next time!' says Peter Batt

The Plenderleiths must have considered Bobby Brown's optimism for the World Cup in 1974 a little on the sunny side?

'I don't think so, not in my house. I just rewatched the Scotland games against Brazil and Yugoslavia at Germany '74, and they were a hell of a team – very positive, I was absolutely mesmerised; they had a lot of flair in the side: Willie Morgan, David Hay and Peter Lorimer, who actually attacked players. They took players on a lot of the time (though Dalglish was completely anonymous in both games, I don't think he did anything). To see a Scotland team that wanted to win and wasn't scared about playing the world fucking champions . . . They were clearly out to win every game, with that backbone of dirty Leeds grit to stop them getting pushed about too much. They deserved the draw against Brazil, at the very least, and outplayed Yugoslavia, who tried to kick them off the field. [In 1974] I was distraught and left the room after Yugoslavia scored, and never saw the goal – I went outside to play in the garden. Looking back now it's gobsmacking that they gave such a strong account of themselves. It was probably their best chance ever. Nowadays you get laughed at for saying they're going to qualify.'

The first *Sun* annual in 1972 had a feature on Scotland exporting all its best talent south of the border. 'A couple of seasons back Ayr United wanted to install lights,' wrote Bob Hely. 'But what about the cash? Simple! Off goes Alex Ingram to Nottingham Forest for £35,000, and Somerset Park has its floodlights.' Hely, only half-jokingly, went on to suggests a law preventing moves south: 'We could have Billy Bremner, Frank McLintock and Denis Law turning out for Cowdenbeath, with Hamilton Academicals being able to field Alan Gilzean and Charlie Cooke . . .'

'Something I always took for granted back then,' recalls Ian Plenderleith, 'was that there were tons and tons of good Scottish players – Man United had McQueen, Macari and Stewart Houston; there were good players at Leeds and Liverpool – and it's to the credit of football annuals that they reflected strongly the huge influence of Scotland on the English game.'

'England's World Cup victory in 1966 had only reinforced the notion that it had nothing to learn from the rest of the world,' wrote Eamon Dunphy (sadly not in the *Midland Soccer Annual* but in *The Rocky Road*), before noting that was precisely the reason Sir Alf gave for not staying on in Mexico to watch the rest of the tournament once England had been knocked out.

WE SHOULD DESTROY WEST GERMANY NEXT TIME, SAYS PETER BATT screamed a headline in the *Sun* annual in 1972. Looking ahead to how the 'bracing air and lush green grass' of Munich would suit England, Batt acknowledged that while 'England were accused in South America of being stiff-waisted Europeans – all grit and determination and no flair' what other country could 'boast such exciting young attackers as Peter Osgood, Joe Royle, Brian Kidd, Charlie George, Alan Hudson and Ian Hutchinson . . . Ramsey will cherish and nurse his young starlets like a hen sitting on her eggs.'

It didn't quite work out like that.

Above: Peter Batt makes a bold claim in the *Sun Soccer Annual* 1972 after England's World Cup '70 quarter-final defeat in Mexico

Right: England manager Alf Ramsey relaxes in training with some of the key members of that 1970 squad, *Topical Times Football Book* 1968–69

Team talk. By Sir ALF RAMSEY (*back view*) to his England trainer and players. The audience (*left to right*) are—HAROLD SHEPHERDSON (trainer) ALAN MULLERY, NORMAN HUNTER, ALEC STEPNEY, GORDON BANKS, ROGER HUNT, PETER THOMPSON, BOBBY CHARLTON, BRIAN LABONE (*back view*)

George Best on duty at his boutique

SUCCESS BREEDS SUCCESS BUT FAILURE ONLY BREEDS MISERY

◇◇

POST '66

◇◇◇◇◇◇◇◇◇◇

LIKE COLLECTORS Laurie Rampling and Steve Smith, Alan Hodgkinson, former Worksop Town, Sheffield United and England goalkeeper was also one to shut out the world – in favour of his thousand-strong programme collection: 'I have laid out the collection in the attic of my house. Now I can spend hours going through my little library – remembering games and names, replaying my career in a way.' Glancing at the article, with Hodgkinson photographed in a shirt and tie, sitting in amongst piles of his programmes sprawled over a 1960s Axminster carpet, the piece could have appeared at any point since about 1952. That it appeared in the *Topical Times Football Book* 1971–72, and had Hodgkinson claiming that you 'very seldom get any match programmes abroad' (he was probably referring to his England days in the late fifties) renders it pretty fusty for the kids listening to Roxy Music and War.[85]

There's nowt so queer as folk, goes the saying. To which you might add the rejoinder: there's nothing so odd, viewed through the lens of the twenty-first century, as footballers and their hobbies – or, more pertinently, footballers photographed 'relaxing' at home, especially in the 1950s. The gents at *Charles Buchan's Soccer Gift Book*, in particular, were obsessed with this photo-opportunity. In the 1954–55 annual they snapped a couple of Cardiff City players at home in their living rooms, in the bosom of their families, and also ran a double-page spread, AWAY FROM IT ALL . . . WITH

SHEFFIELD UNITED PLAYERS. Ever-present wing-half Joe Shaw is seen rather awkwardly grappling with a bag of flour, helping his wife with the baking – and wearing a tie[86]. The toddler of Irish international Alf Ringstead looks terrified as mum and dad suggest an impromptu kick-about in the living room. And, best of all, goalkeeper Ted Burgin and his wife Heather appear to have installed a snooker table in their kitchen. A year later scenes of domestic bliss appear to have been replaced by strange goings-on in the Leeds United changing room. Raich Carter is sitting in a bathtub full of brine solution, giving John Charles (fully dressed and crouching by the bath) a strange look; and keeper Ray Wood is trapped immobile inside a 'radiant heat cabinet' with only his head visible – wing-half Ronnie Mollatt is on hand to administer a cup of tea. But over the page Grenville Hair and his wife are making a rug.[87] The photographer also made it behind the scenes at St James' Park; it's unlikely a *Match* annual of recent vintage would feature an equivalent BATH TIME FOR TWO shot of Jimmy Scoular and Bill Punton.

In the 1956–57 *Gift Book*, Everton's Eddie Wainwright, pondering his wife's car accident while he lay in hospital with a badly broken leg, lamented, 'There is a lot of strain in soccer, but I have a hobby which helps me overcome it – I grow chrysanthemums!' Which was perhaps not as outré a pastime, in dressing-room terms, as the marquetry practised by Manchester City's Roy Little. Why Little couldn't have been content with a budgerigar, like everyone else,

---

85 Until that is, you open the 1973–74 *Topical Times*, and there's Alistair Donaldson, Falkirk keeper, photographed with his 800 medals and badges representing football associations from all over the planet, and his bemused-looking daughter. Which in turn is perhaps less strange than Sandy Davie, the Dundee United keeper featured in the *Topical Times* a decade earlier with his collection of over 300 portraits and action shots of Spurs keeper Bill Brown.

86 Until about 1965 it seems all players photographed on the treatment table were obliged to wear a shirt and tie – no matter that they were only wearing pants and socks below – or, in the case of Leeds' John Scott, a fine two-tone cardigan, shirt, tie, underpants and a leg brace. Wolves' Jimmy Mullen, snapped reading his kids a story in his front room while dressed in an official club blazer, is entirely within keeping.

87 Hair died tragically young of a heart attack, at 36, while supervising a coaching session at Bradford City.

Left: By the end of the sixties George Best had the world at his feet, a boutique in Manchester called Edwardia and an eponymous annual, *George Best's Soccer Annual* 1971

I'm a Numismatist

Hutchinson's coin-dealing spells something subtly different from the days of hill-walking, budgerigars and marquetry

◇◇◇◇◇◇◇◇◇◇◇◇◇◇◇◇◇◇◇◇◇◇◇◇

Brom sitting in his front room, antimacassar over the back of the chair to avoid any trouble with the pomade, with Pip the budgie perched on his forefinger. 'Rapt audience is Mrs Evelyn Dudley, [daughter] Janice, Twinkie the dog, and Rip the cat.' Janice looks terrified; Rip looks interested, pondering dinner; fluffed-up Twinkie could probably do a star-turn at Crufts.

A year later, Eddie McMorran of Doncaster Rovers, and his wife Muriel, are photographed in their front room trying to teach a budgie to speak. And, as we've seen, even the great Johnny Haynes wasn't immune from this mania: '"My budgie is a smart bird," confided Johnny. "My hobby is teaching him to talk – he already says, 'Come on, Fulham'."'[88]

The same photo-spread that featured the McMorrans also snapped Eddie Lowe of Fulham, caught red-handed sticking stamps into his album (although the fact he's wearing a shirt and tie suggests he too knew the photographer was due to call). As late as 1969 Middlesbrough boss Stan Anderson had no problem telling the *Northern Soccer Annual* that he'd started a stamp collection for something to do during the long winter evenings. In the intervening years the *Topical Times* in 1966 had outed Southampton's Terry Paine as a poodle enthusiast, while 'rabbit fancier' Ray Savino of Bristol City is snapped in front of a noticeboard of coloured certificates, clutching a petrified-looking bunny, 'one of the "stars" which have helped him win all these prize tickets.'

The Book of Soccer, Edited by Bobby Moore (no. 13; the 1970 edition of the series once overseen by Billy Wright) went one step further. In an eight-page feature entitled I'M A NUMISMATIST Chelsea's Ian Hutchinson talked about his thousand-strong coin collection, and his sideline in rare coin dealing. Across the page there's Alan Hodgkinson again, sitting on the carpet with his programmes, and many other players' hobbies are discussed: Sunderland's Len Ashurst has taken up home

remains a mystery. Any budding twenty-first-century historian flipping back through the collected football annuals of the 1950s will be surprised at the prominent role the budgerigar played in footballers' lives. People had budgies; footballers lived on the same streets, so why shouldn't they? There's Jimmy Dudley of West

---

88 As late as 1963 the *Eagle* annual had Nobby Lawton of Manchester United pictured with a budgerigar.

Above: Chelsea's Ian Hutchinson proudly shows off his coin collection in *Bobby Moore's Book of Soccer* **1970**

Right: Barry Bridges makes himself useful at the New Wilmington Hotel, *Charles Buchan's Soccer Gift Book* **1965–66**

brewing in his kitchen – mostly beer but by 'varying the recipe Len can produce stout, brown ale or lager . . . a pint of "Ashurst Ale" works out at about 3d. There is no record of what Mrs Ashurst had to say about the transformation of her spruce kitchen into a brewery'; Wolves' John Holsgrove 'drives his wife Janice round the bend' with his Shadows-like guitar playing; Chelsea's Alan Birchenall has taken up the baton from Colin Grainger and sings and plays guitar and 'was once offered a nightclub contract in Hungary'; West Brom's Asa Hartford is a soul boy; Ian St John DJs on Radio Merseyside; while Hull's Ian McKechnie 'prefers classical records when not pursuing his other hobby – reading the history of the Second World War'; and, back at Stamford Bridge, Peter Bonetti, no doubt inspired by Nobby Stiles, has apparently been collecting dolls in national costume 'for his wife'.[89]

But it's Hutchinson's coin-dealing that spells something subtly different from the days of hill-walking, budgerigars and marquetry. Hutchinson has nothing to be embarrassed about – nor is he simply filling time or getting misty-eyed about the past: 'There was a survey which proved that, weighed alongside bank or building society interest or stocks and shares, coins appreciate in value the most. I've sold some to Peter Osgood and

Peter Houseman as an investment for their children.'

In fact, while Rodney Marsh's interest in art and history, and Ron Davies' talent with a sketchbook are touched upon, much of the article tips over into players' sidelines and small businesses rather than simply hobbies: 'John Cushley of West Ham is a qualified linguist who teaches part-time at a local school'; Aston Villa's George Curtis runs a fish and chip shop; Motherwell's Joe Wark 'makes custard pies', Orient's Peter Brabrook is a butcher; 'QPR schemer Terry Venables has an electrical shop'; Peter Shilton 'designs sweaters'; Brentford's Chic Brodie drives a taxi . . . and on it goes. It seems that by the mid- to late sixties no player was fully set-up without their own business. *Charles Buchan's Soccer Gift Book* for 1965–66 had run a photo-strip of Chelsea's Barry Bridges standing with his Vauxhall Cresta outside the New Wilmington Hotel, peeling spuds in the kitchen, sweeping the steps and changing the bed linen of the new hotel he's opened with his father-in-law[90]. And the same annual featured Liverpool's Peter Thompson informing readers of his new 'caravan-hire string' business, and hoping that 'by the time you read this I will have combined it with a petrol station, and be operating in Liverpool instead of Preston where it

---

89 In fairness to England's doll-collecting footballers, by the seventies plenty of the nation's sideboards contained a Spanish doll and a pair of castanets.

90 A year later in the *Topical Times* Bridges appears that bit older and fractionally less cheery, manning the reception desk with his bee-hived wife Irena. Four years on from that, in *Denis Law's Book of Soccer*, now sporting a moustache and at QPR, he looks far happier leaping into air to celebrate scoring a goal at Loftus Road.

THE HANDY MAN!

There comes a time when the shooting has to stop and Barry Bridges, who is very useful in that line for Chelsea, is getting ready for that day—and turning himself into a real handy-man-about-the-house.

In partnership with his father-in-law he is running a hotel at Eastbourne—and doesn't mind doing some of the chores.

Top, checking in. Left, getting down to some spud-bashing.

Top left, lending a hand with changing the bedding. Top right, a clean sweep. Left, "Cheers!", but with a cup of tea, in the bar.

In a photograph captioned 'opening day at Peter Thompson's garage in Anfield' (in the *All Stars* annual of 1967) it looks as if a rave is about to break out on the forecourt. Thompson, smartly turned out in a 1960s mechanic's overall, is smiling amidst 'a fine show of support from his Liverpool club-mates and his fiancée' – who is sporting a fine bouffant hair-do and sitting on the bonnet of a Ford Cortina.

Three years later in the *Northern Soccer Annual* of 1970, a caption reads, 'Peter Thompson, Liverpool winger/businessman unloads a consignment of his own autographed footballs. Daughter Karen looks on.' Thompson is retrieving the job-lot of plastic footballs – the ones that blow away on the beach – out of the back of his car, no doubt about to flog them to one of those bucket and spade shops. Daughter Karen seems fed up – it might just be the stone grey cloud coming off the sea but, somehow, the scene looks darker.

◇◇◇◇◇◇◇◇◇◇◇◇◇◇◇◇◇◇◇◇◇◇◇◇◇◇◇◇◇◇◇

began.' When Thompson started in caravans he 'wasn't looking ahead so much as kicking against a dreary routine of trying to kill time, sitting in cafés, drinking endless cups of tea, going to "the flicks" – anything to pass time.'

While over the next few years there is a barely an annual photo-spread that doesn't feature the Liverpool winger manning the pump, cheerily filling up the rear-end of someone's saloon, you can't help but wonder that it doesn't all feel a bit downbeat for someone gearing up to play in the first World Cup on home soil.

The *Buchan Soccer Gift Book* of 1966–67 featured a lovely full-page black-and-white photograph of Sheffield Wednesday and England keeper Ron Springett, playing football on his sun-dappled lawn with his young daughter Terry. Springett is dressed for the office – shirt sleeves, tie, neatly pressed slacks and loafers. England's keeper since the Chile World Cup, Ron was about to lose the FA Cup final with Wednesday in spectacular style (to Everton's remarkable 1966 comeback) and win what would turn out to be his final England cap, just ahead of the World Cup. A few pages on, there's another full-page black-and-white shot – George Best is measuring the leg of a model in leather trousers in his new boutique. The times were changing, and not only for *Charles Buchan's Soccer Gift Book*.

I N THE 1968–69 *Topical Times* annual Mike Summerbee, full of the joys of being a Championship-winning centre-forward for Manchester City, revealed, 'I'm just a "village" kid at heart. A very special village, of course. That "with it" area just off Manchester's main shopping thoroughfare . . . see me roll up in my midnight blue 3-litre Daimler saloon. Out I'll step, wearing one of my expensive suede coats over my jacket and slacks. Cut in the French style I like so much.' He was talking about dropping in on the Manchester boutique he ran with 'a buddy of mine, George Best', in the 'village', the swinging centre of Manchester, full of boutiques, hairdressers, 'a restaurant, a record shop . . . everything for the modern youngster.' In an incident his co-owner would be proud of, Summerbee fondly recalled the time he turned up at a black-tie do in a camel coat and slacks. 'Oh, what a swinging life it is for Michael George Summerbee.' All a far cry from the grey days at Swindon Town, where the vibes were a bit more down in the flat he shared with Ernie Hunt ('now at Coventry') and the pair just stayed in and talked about

'See me roll up in my midnight blue 3-litre Daimler saloon. Out I'll step, wearing one of my expensive suede coats. Cut in the French style I like so much'

football all week. 'It was a bit of a strain. If I had a bad game I thought about it all week. There was no chance to relax.'

City were League champions, and by the end of the season United had won the European Cup at Wembley. Pity then, poor Stockport County and Oldham Athletic, having to cope with these two noisy neighbours. 'It is rather like a cinema showing silent movies trying to live in the same street with Cinerama,' suggested Stockport chairman Victor Bernard.

At least back then there was a football annual providing much needed, in-depth coverage for such sentiment. In 1969 Millwall footballer (and soon to be author

Above: Mike Summerbee talks shop in the *Topical Times Football Book* 1968–69, whose designers pushed back the graphic boundaries with arched type around a circular photo

Following: Two full-page pictures from *Charles Buchan's Soccer Gift Book* 1966–67. Ron Springett in formal attire while George Best in 'mod gear' measures up a 'fair model'

BETTER THAN DAD!

It's a busy time for footballers these days. Here is Sheffield Wednesday Goalkeeper Ron Springett doing his best against his 3½-year-old daughter,

The fellow in the mod gear taking the measure of this fair model is usually doing just that to Man. Utd.'s rivals. It's George Best with a new line — the Boutique he now runs.

of the fêted memoir *Only A Game?*) Eamon Dunphy teamed up with swinging writer-about-town-cum-nascent-football-agent-impresario Peter Douglas[91] to launch the *Northern Soccer Annual*, along with its regional counterparts the *Midlands Soccer Annual* and the *London Soccer Annual* (expanded in 1970 to take in clubs such as Ipswich, Portsmouth and Brighton) upon a public thirsty for insight into the lives of not only rock 'n' roll footballers, but also life behind the scenes at their own club, be that Mansfield Town [see inset] or Queens Park Rangers.

FRIDAY NIGHT IS FOOTBALL NIGHT AT STOCKPORT ran the headline in the first *Northern Soccer Annual*, the switch to floodlit football hopefully providing the answer to chairman Victor Bernard's problems: 'The club's own bingo brings in £25,000 a year,

the programme has been brightened up considerably, and there's even a slogan – GO-GO-GO-COUNTY.' Progressive ideas – 'we were the first with the car stickers idea. In this area at any rate' – was what Bernard was all about. However, added the chairman '. . . the prime object of a social club is to make money, but we would not worry if it did not make a penny. If it does nothing more than break even the club is providing an extra facility for the fans – and that is the main thing.' Amongst the regulars there had been a bit of grumbling over the club's strip change, the locals struggling to deal with anything other than the 'straightforward' white shirts and black shorts worn by the Edgeley Park greats of yesteryear, Jack 'Tiger' Bowles, Alec Herd and Ron Stainforth. Royal blue had soon become white with a horizontal blue hoop – perhaps okay for the likes of new signing Alex '*Golden Vision*' [see p199] Young of mid-sixties Everton vintage, but no doubt

---

91 He even looks a little like football's Andrew Loog-Oldham.

◇◇◇

Fifteen Men – and a Prayer

Tommy Eggleston discusses Life at Mansfield

Mansfield Manager, Tom Eggleston

36

MANSFIELD Football Club have the distinction of maintaining the smallest professional staff in League soccer, and it was this problem I was most anxious to discuss with manager Tom Eggleston (ex-Sheffield Wednesday and Everton) in his spacious, pleasant office overlooking the newly laid-out training pitch.

'Let me make one thing clear from the start,' said Eggleston, 'this club is far from struggling. Gates are up 2000-3000 on last season, and I have the backing of a young and enthusiastic board of directors.'

Certainly the Field Mill ground has an air of being cared for. The whole of the property is freehold and owned by the club; main effort at the moment is being concentrated on developing an area under the new main stand, erected in 1965, into a fully equipped indoor training area.

'We are well placed for outdoor training facilities,' explained Eggleston, indicating the large practice area that only twelve months before had been reclaimed from virtually waste ground. 'This area has now been completely drained and laid out and we have erected a shelter for officials (an old bus shelter, converted for the job) and are putting up poles to carry nets. We can now do all our training on the spot, without the necessity of travelling away by coach – worse still – coming back soaking wet to get a hot shower or bath.'

Eggleston gathers a third of his playing staff around him!

The new training area leaves the main pitch free for match days. The stands are not over-large and the ground can accommodate some 25,000 spectators in comparative comfort. The car park is enormous – so large in fact that the club were able to sell a piece of it recently to a cement company.

'We are now finishing off the tarmacing of the park – look, you can see where we had to leave off as we did not have the money to spare at the time' – indicating an area some ten feet wide, which still remained to be covered.

The club are very conscious of their influence on

37

◇◇◇

Tiny Mansfield had a squad of fifteen. In the 1969 *Midlands Soccer Annual* manager Tommy Eggleston gave an insight into the make-do-and-mend policy at Field Mill: there was a new training ground reclaimed from wasteland, that featured a converted bus shelter 'for officials', and the daunting task of tarmacking the vast car park (a car park so huge they'd recently sold off a large part of it to a cement company). The receding hairlines of centre-forward Nick Sharkey and midfielder Bob Ledger, and photographs of Eggleston in a beany hat with pom-pom, and then with his players, looking relaxed and happy in front of a corrugated shed, do little

to dispel the Sunday league atmosphere. 'A mining area Mansfield is good hunting ground for promising youngsters,' said Eggleston ... I'm against this practice of mums and dads auctioning off their sons to the highest bidder (a completely illegal practice). Even if the club could afford to join in this scramble, it is something I would never wish to be part of.' Having said that, the Tuesday and Thursday night sessions for local youngsters had uncovered eighteen-year-old Kirkby-in-Ashfield fast-bowler Stuart Boam, a defender who became a staple of the Christmas annual in the coming decade at Middlesbrough.

◇◇◇

awkward-looking on the recently departed Jim Fryatt, with his 'Good Old Days sideburns'. Decent intentions regarding the social club bar takings notwithstanding, Bernard had come across as a bit of a market-stall holder in the Charles Buchan Soccer Gift Book a couple of years beforehand, unduly proud of his 'go-go-go with County' catchphrase and ruminating on the need to run a club along the lines of an efficient business, clearing out the dead wood and restocking, 'competing as entertainment', while seemingly borderline obsessed with building a 'sporting club' complex adjacent to the ground. In Bernard's first eighteen months of overseeing life at Edgeley Park debts of £12,800 were wiped out and the club rose from the very bottom of the fourth division to being a contender in the third. In the spring of 1970 they finished a catastrophic seventeen points from safety and were back in the fourth – where Mike Summerbee had had a change of heart, playing out his final days between 1976 and 1979 – having told the International Football Book in 1973, 'I don't feel there is any point in going into a lower division and looking for something that isn't there. When the writing is on the wall, I'm sure I'll see it and get out – but my last game will be for City.'

A few miles anti-clockwise round the old Manchester ring-road the Northern Soccer Annual checked in, a year later, on Stockport's third-division neighbours, another club with a fine supporters' club bar. Under the heading OLDHAM – THE FIGHT BACK, the article began, 'If you thought Ken Bates, former chairman of Oldham, was a forthright man, try talking to present man in charge, [Harry] Massey. He is an ex-builder, and as blunt a Yorkshire man as you could wish to find.' The club had followed Chelsea's lead in pioneering private boxes – the boxes themselves were 'very comfortable with private seats, private heating, a Tannoy system that gives the half-time and full-time results and refreshments provided free of charge during the half-time interval' – and giant air ducts which 'pass under the stand to provide fresh air without having to open the windows [of the supporters' club lounge]'. Furthermore, the boardroom, 'tastefully furnished in modern style, has an acre of rich green carpet that would not disgrace a West End hotel.' That said, chairman Massey wasn't too happy with his bearded predecessor's attempts to turn the Boundary Park boardroom into something resembling a cross between a scale model of the nuclear bunker at Kelvedon Hatch and James Bond's Q section HQ. Massey pointed disdainfully at the telephone system installed by Bates: 'We

The Oldham supporters' group had bought an old cinema and turned it into 'a flourishing social club which had all the signs of being a moneyspinner'

◇◇◇◇◇◇◇◇◇◇◇◇◇◇◇◇◇◇◇◇◇◇

have three telephone lines, two of them ex-directory and a fantastic inter-com system. From here I can ring the offices, the club, the Tannoy control centre, the treatment room, the dressing room, everywhere. It's all too ridiculous for a club of this size.' Massey turned to the chair at the head of the boardroom table: 'Even that . . .[92] chair cost £70. Now what club in the third division needs to seat its chairman in such luxury? To me it's spending gone completely mad.' Especially for a club struggling to find players: with no transfer budget so to speak of, Oldham were dependent on local youth, but, as Massey pointed out, in the surrounding area, he didn't 'know of a single pitch that doesn't get bogged down to nine or ten inches of mud during the winter period simply because they are not well drained.' The Oldham supporters' group had bought an old cinema for £45,000 and turned it into 'a flourishing social club which had all the signs of being a moneyspinner. Then an alteration in the road scheme in town meant that the

---

92 Ellipsis in place of the expletive presumably edited out.

Above: Innovative Oldham Athletic enjoy some modern luxuries in the Northern Soccer Annual 1970

buses that brought patrons to their door were suddenly cut off and, within months, the whole place had folded up.' A year ahead of Stockport, in the spring of 1969, Oldham too had finished bottom of the third division, but that was the beginning of a slow upward curve, culminating in the days of Mike Milligan, Denis Irwin and Earl Barrett. Stockport, of course, eventually ended up heading in the other direction.

IT SURE WAS TOUGH, SAYS BRIAN CLOUGH

Derby County Manager

Even when up on the roof, Clough 'reckoned to answer at least 1,000 calls a week'

Other small clubs in the north were struggling too.[93] Brian Clough spoke, in the *Topical Times* in 1967, of the problems of trying to answer the telephone while up on the roof of the stand doing a bit of repair work at Hartlepools United: 'Just a few months ago we had one of the enclosures re-roofed. The iron sheets didn't arrive until a few days before a home game. I spent an afternoon humping 150 sheets of metal from a lorry into the ground,' wrote the young first-time manager, before regaling readers with tales of arriving back in the north in the middle of the night after long trips from Exeter or Torquay – on one occasion, they were caught in a three-mile traffic jam outside Huddersfield following an accident, and you can hear the relish in his voice when recalling 'at three o'clock in the morning the team and the directors were sitting drinking tea in the dirtiest transport café you ever saw' – and of travelling around the pubs and clubs of Hartlepool with a collection bucket in hand raising funds. 'At the Victoria Road Ground we had no full-time secretary. That meant I had to answer every phone call coming into the ground.' Even when up on the roof, Clough 'reckoned to answer at least 1,000 calls a week. The press boys were on every day. Other managers came on asking about players on the transfer list or just swapping views on a player they were thinking of buying. Fans rang up about tickets, recommending their nephew for a trial – or simply asking about the gloves they left at the last game . . .' A thousand calls a week to the Victoria Ground? That would be 200 a day.

93 And in Scotland. *The Topical Times Football Book* 1971–72 featured a piece on 'the Toffeemen of Scotland', detailing Stenhousemuir's woes: 'Everton's average gate [in 1969–70] was 49,000; Muir's was 537.' The problems went back to the 1950s, when the club was saved from oblivion by supporters each donating a shilling a week. Greyhound racing and 'horse-trotting' took place on the track around the pitch at Ochilview Park; whist-drives were a weekly event and boards were laid on the grass for dances. Floodlights were paid for by the local butcher, but sadly could only be used to light up the dancing couples of the Forth Valley, as they were deemed not powerful enough for Scottish league action.

Above: Derby manager Brian Clough gets handy with a hammer, *Topical Times* 1967–68

Right: A highlight from Scunthorpe's summer tour of Spain, *Midlands Soccer Annual* 1969

Hartlepools were a club in the fourth division in 1967. The *Topical Times* were perhaps on to Clough's taste for hyperbole early.

Down at the Old Show Ground they'd found a novel way of promoting Scunthorpe. Travel agent and pre-season-tour fixer for the likes of Brighton, Coventry, Crystal Palace, Norwich and Swindon, Arthur Whaley wrote in the *Midlands Soccer Annual* of 1969 about TOURING SPAIN WITH EL SCUNTHORPE UNITED. It seems there had been a bit of a kerfuffle beforehand, wherein the Spanish hosts of the tour, Ibiza and Hercules of Alicante, had been 'very tardy in concluding the fixtures and still suggested a stronger club would help.' They'd let it be known 'they would not object, for example, to Manchester United or Liverpool . . .' but the Iron men of the fourth division it was who departed in July 1968 for Ibiza. Villarreal stepped in for Hercules, who had their own financial implosion going on (or at least that was their excuse), and all seemed set for the opening game. At which point, wrote Arthur: 'the players had enormous appetites and were ready for meals long before the Spanish hotel's normal time of 2 p.m. for lunch and 9 p.m. for dinner.' Whaley was further dismayed to discover the head chef was preparing his signature dish of paella: 'Much as I like this national Spanish dish – composed of rice, fish and chicken – it did not seem to be the ideal meal to precede an energetic football match on a hot day.' Arthur had a word with the chef and, at the sensible time of 1.30 p.m. (perhaps midday just couldn't be swung), the Scunthorpe players and officials, with the temperature in the eighties, sat down to steak and chips.

Still, it didn't seem to affect them. Speedy winger Bill Punton (last seen in the bath with Jimmy Scoular in the *Soccer Gift Book*) 'played a wonderful game – his bald patch soon had the locals shouting, "Bob-bee Shal-ton"' and Scunthorpe acquitted themselves well to draw 1–1. The same result followed a week later in the second leg, but Ibiza were now wise to the likes of Punton and his counterpart on the other wing, John Colquhoun, who were both marked out of the game in a tight 'anti-climax' of a match. Whaley grumbled about the whistle-happy ref, and the 'Spaniards' funny ideas about the use of substitutes' – Scunthorpe had believed both sides would just have one extra player but Ibiza brought on several youngsters; in Denia, later on the tour, multiple substitutions appeared to be taking place behind the ref's back – but 'Skoon-tor-Pay' triumphed in a novel penalty shootout, centre-half Frank Burrows burying the winning spot-kick.

Scunthorpe players and officials, with the temperature in the eighties, sat down to steak and chips

◇◇◇◇◇◇◇◇◇◇◇◇◇◇◇◇◇◇◇◇◇◇◇◇

British holiday-maker kicks-off

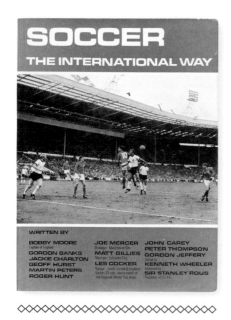

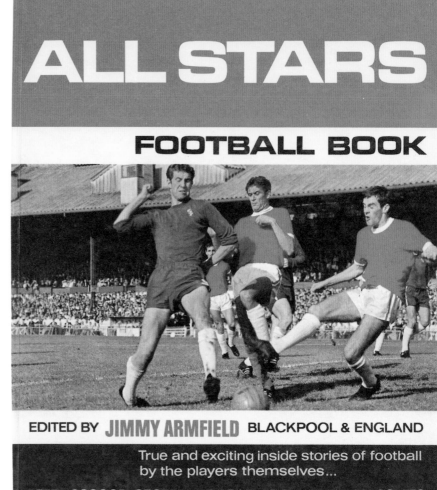

Football annual covers may have been a little slow to embrace the graphic trends of the sixties – certainly compared to, say, literary book jackets and film posters – but they did move with the times. *All Stars Football Book* and *Soccer the International Way* both arrived at a relatively clean graphic style and the same extended Eurostile typeface in their mastheads.

Bobby Charlton's Book of European Soccer and *The Boys' Book of Soccer* (both 1969) also kept it simple with period type placed on a single image. *Jimmy Hill's Soccer '69* meanwhile bravely deviated from the almost universal preference for action photography on front covers.

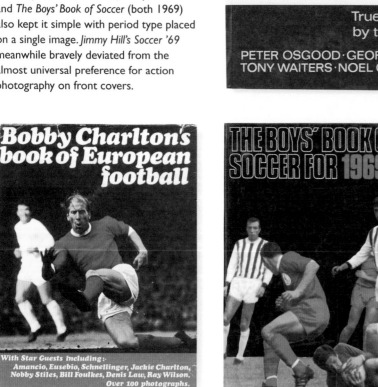

FOOTBALL
DAVID COLEMAN'S WORLD OF
FOOTBALL

By the end of the decade annual covers were in a state of confusing flux. *David Coleman's World of Football* kept it clean for its first issue in 1970, but the repetition of the word 'football' and use of beige-brown type made for a mildly curious masthead. After a couple of editions it switched to a *Superstars* style 'S' logo.

Other titles battled gamely with prevailing graphic trends but, as was the case with *Lancashire Soccer* and the *International Football Illustarted Annual*s, tended to try to squeeze a little too much in. *Soccer '70* is undoubtedly a period gem but, like *David Coleman's* 'S' logo, its distorted type had a firm underlying message: watch out, everyone, here come the seventies . . .

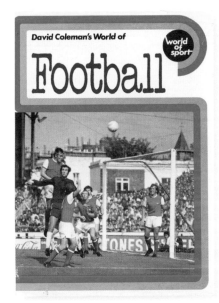

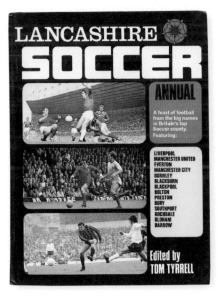

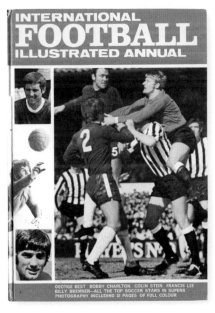

That Night Promotion Came

Lap of honour — Coventry style. On top of the world about making Division One, Manager JIMMY HILL gets into huntsman's rig to lead a Rolls Royce round the ground. It is driven by its owner — Chairman DERRICK ROBBINS. Riding high in it are players MICK KEARNS and GEORGE CURTIS, the skipper. Both Kearns and Curtis have helped the club rise three divisions in nine years.

Go-ahead Coventry City, under the pioneering Jimmy Hill (pictured in *Topical Times* 1967), were a staple of 1960s football annuals and widely seen as the model to follow for prospective club owners keen to drag football into the twentieth century.

Mike and Bernie Winters' bid for control at Villa Park, in a consortium with 'several showbusiness personalities including Tommy Steele and Anthony Newley' was ultimately resisted, but the comedy duo wrote in the *London Soccer Annual* of 1970 of how they would follow the 'Sky Blue Revolution' at Highfield Road – the Sky Blue radio programme; the Sky Blue special trains to away matches (eponymous cocktail served in the buffet carriage, with 'meals, snacks on board, with a special record-request programme and bingo laid on' according to Coventry keeper Bill Glazier in a 1967 *Topical Times* interview); closed circuit television around the ground; even a Sky Blue swimming pool – but the showbusiness pair continued to be baffled 'even in this modern age' by football clubs failing to 'bang the big drum

loud enough or often enough. Happy and successful clubs are as vital to the entertainment scene as pantomime, bingo and penny arcades.' Midweek games, for instance, were never advertised. What was wrong with football? It was now a business, after all. Hill bailed out as manager in 1967, just as Coventry reached the first division, and was last seen photographed on horseback in full huntsman costume (in *Topical Times* 1967, above) with the chairman following him in a Rolls-Royce round the perimeter of the pitch, and Mick Kearns and George Curtis waving from the back in matching jumpers.

But not everything had panned out as planned. 'If Colin Stein had been a failure at Highfield Road, few people would have been surprised,' wrote the *Shoot! Annual* in 1974. Not that Colin lacks the skill to survive in the First Division, but Coventry City had, in the past, been a graveyard for centre-forwards. Tony Hateley . . . Neil Martin . . . Chris Chilton . . . Bobby Graham . . . all had been bought to solve the Sky Blues' goalscoring problem. One way or another they all failed.'

THERE MAY have been chipped marble flooring in the Bernabeu dressing rooms, but that didn't mean things weren't moving on a pace in the English first division. Burnley chairman Bob Lord continued his redevelopment of Turf Moor while relying largely on youth on the pitch – WE DON'T BUY 'EM WE BREED 'EM SAYS JIMMY ADAMSON in a *Northern Soccer Annual* piece illustrated with some bleakishly modern, gritty black and white photography: Burnley players, including a very young Dave Thomas, sitting around a Formica café table drinking tea; Ralph Coates thundering on to a ball in front of the concrete skeleton of the Cricket Field Stand[94]; building workers, who must have been standing on a plank behind wooden hoardings, watching not one but two great follically challenged

---

94 Lord must have settled for under-floor heating rather than wafting spectators with heated air currents. Although even under-floor heating, powered by an oil-fired air heater, was discontinued on cost-efficiency grounds after a couple of winters (according to Simon Inglis in *The Football Grounds of Great Britain*). As a fifteen-year-old, Ralph Coates told Jimmy Armfield's *All Stars '67* annual that he had two interviews on the same day in 1961: one for the position of apprentice fitter at the Coal Board; one at Turf Moor – 'it was not a difficult choice to make'.

'In days gone by the mill and mine workers would forfeit a day's pay to watch the Rovers at an afternoon game'

midfielders (Coates and Bobby Charlton) play.

The Needler family at Hull also put a premium on spectator convenience, investing £12,000 in their adjacent railway platform at Boothferry Park. Meanwhile Middlesbrough trumpeted that Ayresome Park is 'fully enclosed on all four sides with a very high proportion of seating for spectators. New offices, tea-rooms and a restaurant are just a few of the improvements that are being made.'

Back in Lancashire, there was trouble at the mill though. 'In days gone by the mill and mine workers would forfeit a day's pay to watch the Rovers at an afternoon game,' wrote Bryan Hamilton in the *Northern Soccer Annual*. 'With cloth cap pulled firmly down over

Above: Burnley's John Murray, Steve Kindom and Dave Thomas pass the time drinking tea and alarming amounts of Coke, *Northern Soccer Annual* 1969

101

the brow, muffler wrapped snugly around the neck and rattle clasped firmly in hand, Sammy the Supporter would put Rovers above most things in life. "Aye, must watch t'match. I've saved for weeks for this one," he'd say as he turned his back on the mills, factory and frustrated wife to launch out on the long haul to London or elsewhere.' Modern affluent society was blamed (again), along with Blackburn's disastrous 1960 Cup final defeat, for falling numbers on the terraces at Ewood Park – only the 'champagne clubs of Manchester and Merseyside, and on a smaller scale, Spurs, Leeds and Coventry can

cause such enthusiasm . . . success breeds success but failure only breeds misery.' Nearly two decades on from Billy Walker grumbling about the rival attractions of dog racing, ice skating and the cinema, there was still a fear that 'the comfort of a Saturday afternoon armchair in front of television is more appealing than a wet and windy terrace on a bleak November afternoon. There's also the bowling alley, the bingo hall and the motor-car to compete with.' He might not have been entirely right about his club, but Hamilton was ahead of his time. He deemed the future for clubs like Blackburn bleak: 'Will

ALAN BALL, Everton – with his wife, LESLEY

ALAN BALL
~ Milestones from my Scrapbook

BALL is the name — Alan Ball. A V-baby, me. Born four days after the war in Europe ended in 1945. First saw the light in my granny's house in Brookhouse Avenue, Farnworth. Dad was in the Services and also a player with Southport at the time. Now he's manager of Halifax Town. I have a sister, Caroline.

Down below—
Coming events. Me with a ball when only a few months old. Must be about a year old in that second picture with Mum. Getting on a bit in picture No. 3. I was at Farnworth St Peter's School when it was taken.

The *Topical Times* in 1968 ran an early, and rather excitingly groovy photo-strip, 'Alan Ball – Milestones From My Scrapbook', the highlight of which was a full-page colour photograph of Ball and his wife Lesley, drinking cocktails from plastic beakers in their Lancashire back garden, on the coast near Formby. Lesley reclines on a sun-lounger in an orange and pink bikini, wearing extremely cool white plastic sunglasses, the kind later sported by Kurt Cobain. A poodle grins at the camera; next door's fence could do with a coat of creosote, though.

they be able to compete alongside the millionaire clubs of the first division "super league"; the clubs who have improved beyond all recognition in the last half decade, who have been lining their bank balances and scooping up all the top class players in sight?'

This was also troubling Jimmy Armfield. Looking back over a decade of revolutionary change in his *All Stars '70* annual – European football; the growth of hooliganism, etc – Armfield, while not wishing to return to the dark ages, acknowledged an unwelcome side effect of the abolition of the maximum wage: plenty of the big stars and emerging young talent were leaving smaller clubs for more money and the bright lights at the bigger clubs. It wasn't a particularly healthy development, and Blackpool, being close to the avuncular Armfield's heart, merited attention, Emlyn Hughes

being only the latest off the Bloomfield Road production line to seek glory elsewhere. Bolton had 'lost' Wyn Davies and Francis Lee; and Bury were receiving a huge lump sum for Colin Bell. But it was Blackpool's failure to ever really replace midfield dynamo and World Cup star Alan Ball (above), described by Denis Law in his *Book of Soccer no.5* as 'that fiery-haired ball of perpetual motion who went to Everton for a six-figure fee', that perturbed Armfield most of all. Over several seasons the *All Stars* annual came to be fixated on Tony Green, the diminutive ball-playing trickster from Albion Rovers, picked up after being spotted in game against Cowdenbeath one sunny morning in May 1967 (new Blackpool boss Stan Mortensen was lurking in the shade of the stand for the early kick-off). Following a biographical piece in the *All Stars '69* annual, Green

Left: Boothferry Park, Hull, and its adjoining train station (top left), pictured in the *Northern Soccer Annual* 1969

When Lady Luck Smiled

TONY GREEN

IN MY FIRST DAYS AT BLACKPOOL THERE WERE TIMES WHEN I WAS ALMOST PHYSICALLY SICK

fight on their hands to keep hold of their man, who was now being courted by the big clubs.

The same annual also featured a tale of woe from Blackpool's previous 'next Alan Ball' – A WEARY TALE of stuttering form, fitness and sporadic first-team appearances interspersed with life in the reserves. 'So much for the £60,000 buy that was supposed to be Blackpool's Christmas present,' wrote Alan Suddick, in what can be read as an early clash between a gifted, natural but inconsistent ball player with long hair and a manager of a somewhat more old-school disposition (a generational conflict that would blossom into a mini-genre over the coming decade, be it Rodney Marsh taking the opportunity to have a lie down and sun-bathe in front of the directors' box at Craven Cottage, Stan Bowles breaking another curfew, or Tony Currie and Alan Birchenall sharing a kiss at Bramall Lane).[95] After a lengthy account of what appeared to amount to Mortensen toying with him – a few games played out of position, then back in the reserves – you can hear the relish in Suddick's voice when he recounts, 'Then 2 April 1969 saw manager Mortensen sacked in dramatic fashion when promotion was again out of Blackpool's reach.' Blackpool's relegation in the spring of 1967 had brought an end to thirty glorious years in the top flight. The Seasiders subsequently missed out on a return, even with Suddick finally leading the line, 'by 0.28 of a goal average'.

At this point you suspect Suddick could have gone on to write his version of *Only A Game?*, but he spent much of the seventies cementing his cult hero status at Blackpool, not least by establishing the world keepie-uppie record (over three laps of the pitch in under 20 minutes), and played out his days at newly non-league Barrow. Instead, readers of the *All Stars '72* football annual could catch up with Tony Green, reliving his season in hell, out injured and watching Blackpool get promoted as runners-up to Huddersfield 'without me'. Then, three minutes into his comeback, in a pre-season

is the subject of a second feature later in the same book: an in-depth comparison with Ball – the World Cup winner coming off better: 'Tony Green is a rising star, an entertaining player who will have the world at his feet when he has acquired more experience.' That sentence somehow rings alarm bells even before reading – a year later in the *All Stars '70* annual – that not only was Green struggling with injury, but Blackpool had a

95 In the *FA Book for Boys* in 1967 David Prole had railed about a boys' team he'd seen in a park match wearing 'off-white' kit and boots covered in mud. Their main offence, though, aside from their cocksure attitude, lay in the fact that 'at least two of their forwards could hardly see the goalposts for the mane of hair which flopped over their faces.' The smartly turned-out opposition, in pressed shirts and shorts, neat and trim in red, had sensible haircuts, clean boots and a good team ethic. We didn't win the World Cup with long hair was the gist of the piece. And, remember, when celebrating a goal 'you needn't let your joy carry you to extremes of kissing or hugging a goal-scorer: a few words and a pat on the back do the job of express-ing your feelings equally well.'

Above: Blackpool's fragile star Tony Green in *All Stars* 1969

Right: Alan Suddick tells his maudlin tales at the same club in *All Stars* 1970

friendly in Northern Ireland, he was injured again. By the time the annual was out Green had made a transfer request and was playing for Newcastle. By the time the next annual was out his career was over at twenty-five after being hacked down by Mel Blyth at Selhurst Park.

Four years previously Jimmy Armfield confessed in the *Northern Soccer Annual*, 'I am one of those fellows who rates happiness above ambition.' Content in the restorative sea air of Blackpool, Armfield was going nowhere once his playing days came to an end. And he wasn't the only Bloomfield Road legend enjoying the relaxed ambience of the Pleasure Beach and Winter Gardens in the late 1960s: Stan Mortensen apparently

Alan Suddick spent much of the seventies cementing his cult hero status at Blackpool, not least by establishing the world keepie-uppie record

loved the place too – 'at one time he had a gift stall on the Golden Mile' before moving into (inevitably) sports shops, bookmaking, and eventually the dug-out at Bloomfield Road. Other tangerine illuminati you could have bumped into, strolling through the pleasure gardens or enjoying a round of crazy golf, included hotel owners Stanley Matthews, big 'Jock' Dodds and John McPhee; newsagent Harry Johnston and 1953 FA Cup-winning goal hero Bill Perry, now the proprietor of an electrical shop. Then there was Ray Charnley, a decorator in the town; Hugh Kelley who ran a café; Gordon Milne, who could be seen in his chain of laundrettes; and Alan Taylor, a plumber around town.[96]

Yet, a year earlier, in his *All Stars '68* annual, Armfield had profiled one of the new breed, another budding entrepreneur in football boots in the northwest: 'Francis Lee has already made more progress in the world of business than many men have done by the time they are sixty-five, and are ready to retire . . . "Yes I'm a professional footballer – but I'm also a wastepaper merchant, operate a laundrette, and have an interest in a hairdressing business," said Lee.'

Lee and his laundrettes and 'wastepaper business' (toilet rolls) crop up in at least half a dozen annuals of the period[97] – almost certainly more so than the wreckage of Manchester City under his chairmanship did in *Match* or *Shoot!* during the nineties. In a parody in *David Coleman's World of Football* annual in 1970, the illustrator Paul ('You Are the Ref') Trevillion imagined the big football stars of

96 The *Eagle* annual of 1963 featured a piece on twenty-one-year-old Steve 'Mandy' Hill, lined up as a replacement for Stanley Matthews at Blackpool. It didn't happen for him at Bloomfield Road either, and despite reasonable success at Tranmere and Wigan, he ended up running a TV rental shop in Blackpool. (His grandmother had apparently started calling him 'Mandy' after the song 'Mandy Is Three'.)

97 And even more famously in Peter Kay's autobiography *The Sound of Laughter*. Aged sixteen Kay worked the evening shift at F.H. Lee Ltd, driving a fork-lift truck into a plasterboard wall before being moved over to work with the hardened factory women on the production line.

Following: The regular 'Action and the Man' spread from *Topical Times* featured Southampton's Ron Davies and Manchester City's Francis Lee in the 1970–71 book

ACTION

A FOUR - WAY picture to spotlight RON DAVIES, Southampton's high-jumping, goal-heading, Welsh international centre-forward. The all-go sequence on the right finds the camera focussing on FRANCIS LEE, Manchester City's much-capped attack livewire.

and the *MAN*

Tycoons in football boots

Bob McNab, Geoff Hurst and Peter Marinello modelling menswear . . . and Geoff also has a profitable menswear-designing business

Bobby Moore . . . and comedian Jimmy Tarbuck, giving his suede business a boost

Jackie Charlton . . . with what the best-dressed men in Leeds should wear, and where to buy it

Today's top stars are in the big business bracket

THE CHARLIE BLOGGS story tells it all, really. The story, that is, of an era long since gone when footballers entertained huge crowds for a pittance of a salary, and often, too often, ended up on the scrap-heap.

Charlie Bloggs' fate . . . an unsuccessful period as a player-manager in non-League football, times on the dole, and unskilled work on a building site . . . was all too typical of the bad old days.

It is, indeed, not all that many years ago that players would spend part of their summer breaks, working on the ground and redecorating the stands and dressing-rooms to supplement their meagre close-season wages.

Others did casual labour for firms of builders, or whatever part-time job they could find through the good offices of friends and relations.

And when it was all over, when the roar of the crowds had died away and those well-worn boots were well and truly hung up in the cupboard under the stairs, the most the majority could aim for, if they were lucky enough, was a public house or a small newsagents and sweet shop.

Tell that to Bobby Moore, Geoff Hurst, Francis Lee, Willie Morgan, Jack Charlton, Paul Madeley, Johnny Giles and a host of other top stars of today, and they will sigh with relief that they were born in an age when the footballer, like other professional entertainers, is able to gain a just reward for his talents and from all the fringe benefits that go with life in the public eye.

It is not unusual for those at the very top to earn more than the Prime Minister, such are the business opportunities open to star players.

Bobby Moore, for instance, is reckoned to pull in a cool £20,000-plus from his interests OUTSIDE football. And he is obviously one of the game's highest-paid players.

He has a sports goods business, is involved in advertising, newspaper articles, and modelling. But his biggest and most long-term venture is his clothing company, Harrison-Moore Ltd., that makes pigskin, snakeskin, suede and leather coats and safari jackets.

Francis Lee saw the danger signs of leaving football to secure his future when he was 20. Between playing for Bolton, Francis built up a waste paper business that has mushroomed into one of the most profitable paper empires in Lancashire.

And Lee has added a chain of launderettes that puts his earnings in the kind of bracket that neither he nor his accountant is keen to discuss.

Certainly it has provided Francis with a beautiful £20,000 thatched cottage in his home town of Westhoughton, near Bolton, and a worry-free retirement when he eventually stops banging in the goals for Manchester City and England.

Willie Morgan, of Manchester United, is another who looked to launderettes for business success. Since then he has added boutiques and a night club.

Jack Charlton runs a men's outfitters in Leeds and souvenir shops, his Leeds team-mate Paul Madeley is in the painting and decorating business, while Eire international Johnny Giles is an insurance broker.

But not all the ventures of Soccer's star men are individual concerns. Arsenal showed how money, big money, can be made by collective efforts when during the run-in to their League and FA Cup double two seasons ago, they appointed a marketing expert to handle their affairs.

Arsenal were reported to have received £12,000 a man in bonuses for that historic achievement. They also made around the same total each from an Arsenal record, a Gunners booklet, colour posters for petrol stations, photographic sessions for newspapers and magazines, endorsement of boots and advertising.

Neither is it always simply a case of pouring money into a venture and letting the technical experts bring in the rewards.

Geoff Hurst, for instance, went to the Tailor and Cutter Academy to study clothes designing and already it is paying off. Geoff is a director of a company that designs and manufactures clothes.

And Bob Wilson, Arsenal's articulate goalkeeper, has covered himself at all exits. He is cashing in on TV advertising and is already established as a sports commentator on television.

60 61

---

the day as Hollywood icons. Trevillion had Lee as James Cagney: always spitting, sniffing, 'he's got very tight lips – he's got no lips at all, Lee, he looks terribly tough . . . he harks back to Cagney . . . he could play the gangster roles. He could carry a gun and look good. On the pitch, he should play in black leather gloves.'

By 1970 *Charles Buchan's Football Monthly* was losing ground to a weekly football magazine edited in the office next door – *Goal*. Inevitably, *Goal* launched a Christmas annual, and there, prominent in an article entitled TYCOONS IN FOOTBALL BOOTS in the *Goal Football Annual, 1973*, is Francis Lee. His toilet-roll manufacturing empire is now 'one of the most profitable paper empires in Lancashire.' Once the laundrettes were taken into account, Lee's earnings were in a bracket 'neither he nor his accountant [were] keen to discuss'. The evidence was there for all to see though: 'a beautiful £20,000 thatched cottage [outside Bolton] and a worry-free retirement when he eventually stops banging in the goals for Manchester City and England.'

Goal's tycoons article also noted that the days of a footballer painting the dressing room during the summer break for a few extra bob were long gone. No

Francis Lee's earnings were in a bracket 'neither he nor his accountant (were) keen to discuss'

◇◇◇◇◇◇◇◇◇◇◇◇◇◇◇◇◇◇◇◇◇◇◇◇◇◇◇

longer was it the case that, '. . . when it was all over, when the roar of the crowds had died away and those well-worn boots were well and truly hung up in the cupboard under the stairs, the most the majority could aim for, if they were lucky enough, was a public house or a small newsagents or sweet shop.' By 1973 footballers were paid what they were worth, as entertainers. And failing that, someone of Bobby Moore's calibre could rake in '£20,000 from *outside interests*' such as advertising, modelling and newspaper work – although in Moore's case, this windfall came mainly from a clothing company specialising in 'pigskin, snakeskin, suede and leather coats and safari jackets'[98]. Sadly for Moore

---

98 Jimmy Tarbuck is photographed looking the business in a proto-*Professionals* leather car coat.

Above: Football's new breed of entrepreneur in *Goal* 1973, let's hope Peter Marinello's business decisions were better than his wardrobe ones

Right: Footballer-turned-comedian Charlie Williams makes light of racist abuse, in *Charles Buchan's Soccer Gift Book 1973–74*

the nation's fad for dressing like a member of the *Daktari* cast proved to be only fleeting, and it's unlikely the particular line of machine-head-on-acid tank-tops modelled in the accompanying photograph by Arsenal's Peter Marinello (with bow tie!) caught on either.

Without wishing to stretch the metaphor, it looks as though *Goal Football Annual* could have been printed on some of Francis Lee's paper stock. With the pages badly yellowed by comparison with other publications of the day, *Goal*, the annual, looks not unlike a weekly magazine glued between hard boards.

Charles Buchan's Soccer Gift Book, on the other hand, still looked good – minimal, neat and tidy, not too flash and with a restrained but effective use of colour. It had ridden the wave of the World Cup and the explosion of football culture post 1966, guided by Pat Collins, who'd moved into the editor's chair as John Thompson moved upstairs. A veteran of the *Daily Mirror* from before the war, and the *News Chronicle*, Collins was a seasoned pro. 'He never lost his love for football, and he wrote about it all through his working life,' says Patrick Collins, his son, today. 'He felt strangely protective towards footballers, whom he rarely criticized. His only harsh words were reserved for administrators.[99] He loved the *Gift Book*, worked very hard on it, and was thrilled by its

---

99 Pat Collins' opening piece to the final Buchan annual in 1974 is a heartfelt paean to Bob Stokoe's Sunderland and underdogs the world over.

instant, considerable success. An extremely modest man, he would bring home the first copy in a large brown envelope and we children would pass it from hand to hand – there were seven of us, so it took some time – each offering murmured approval. "I think it's getting better," he'd say. "It'll be better still next year."'

That murmured approval had echoed throughout front rooms on Christmas morning for the best part of two decades. By the early seventies the *Gift Book* had not really varied its mix of lengthy features, season round-ups and MEET MORE STARS photo-spreads – it possessed a slightly behind-the-times earnestness that, forty years on, is hugely endearing. But to some readers back then it seemed somewhat tame. The 1973–74 annual's nod to rock 'n' roll, for instance (also with Charles' name shrunk to six-point on the cover, and THE WORLD'S GREATEST SOCCER ANNUAL added to the title wording), featured Chelsea first-teamers snapped in the studio singing 'Blue Is The Colour' and an in-depth profile of comedian Charlie Williams talking about his days down the pit and his time as a wing-half for Leeds then centre-half for Doncaster Rovers. (No playing electric guitar in a fur coat and listening to the Beau Brummels here.) The Williams family had arrived from Barbados during the First World War, and Charlie was one of the first black players to turn professional (having been an amateur at Leeds). 'Even amid the hurly-burly of post-War soccer,' added the *Soccer Gift Book*, 'with reactions among both players and rival

Charlie Williams says

I WAS NO COMEDIAN ON THE PARK

TO THE devotees of Granada TV's "The Comedians"—the essentially North Country show which became an equally big hit at—of all places—the London Palladium, the catch-phrase "Eeh—Y've Got To Laugh, Ain't Ya" can only mean one thing—Charlie Williams is on stage again.

His show business success came years after he first came into the public eye as a wing-half, then a strong man centre-half, with Doncaster Rovers. And despite his happy-go-lucky, extrovert personality on stage (and to a degree off-stage too) Charlie is a somewhat reluctant star.

Reluctant because—despite his West Indian ancestry—he is above all things a down-to-earth Yorkshireman who still lives in a neat semi-detached house in Barnsley. If there is one thing that he hates it is any kind of airs and graces, wherever they are shown.

Because he loves people—and is happiest when he is making them happy. Hence the broad smile, the cheeky grin, the laugh in his voice.

"Despite the fact that I was a coloured kid in a predominantly white world I had a happy childhood. I can remember that even as a schoolboy I was always cracking gags and encouraging my pals to laugh. Which is, I suppose, where and how my career as a comedian really started."

Even amid the hurly-burly of post-war Soccer, with reactions among both players and rival supporters often bad-tempered—Charlie never felt that he was in any way an outsider.

"My father, both in Barbados, from where he emigrated to Britain, was never a rich man—but he had one great asset. He was a wise, deep-thinking man —with all that that entails.

"He taught me many lessons on how to live my life—but one thing which he was often at great pains to impress on me was perhaps the most important of all. 'Earn respect—and you'll always get respect' was his wise remark.

"I am absolutely certain that it was this saying, and the fact that I really tried to live up to it, that developed my sense of humour—and this has stood me in good stead ever since."

Charlie's two careers have followed strangely identical patterns, each starting in the semi-pro ranks. Along with most Barnsley lads, he went into coal-mining from school, first playing Soccer for Upton Colliery.

In 1947 he joined the staff of Leeds United as an amateur wing-half, moving to Doncaster the following year as a part-time professional. And during his early days he played in *every* position for Rovers' Reserve and "A" teams—including goal.

He also played in his favourite posi-

26

tion of wing-half behind the legendary Peter Doherty in the League side.

"What a player," says Charlie. "No-one could possibly have given me (or the rest of the players) more encouragement. Off the field he was forever advising me on strengths and weaknesses. On the pitch he relentlessly cajoled, called-out, instructed—it was a 90-minute Soccer lesson.

"I didn't finally give up my job and turn professional until 1954—and in the next season, when Rovers sold centre-half Patterson, I was given his job, which I held for five years before moving to Skegness. I later played (again as a part-timer) for Denaby United and for Grimethorpe."

By now it was back to the pits for Charlie-boy, but this time in an office job, and encouraged by the reaction to his efforts to entertain friends with gags he found himself taking on occasional dates in working-men's clubs.

"I did it chiefly to help boost my earnings, for I was now married with two kids. In fact I started off as a singer, slipping in the odd gag or two. The gags went better than the songs—and the comedian emerged."

With typical Yorkshire caution he clung to his daytime job for six years before becoming a professional entertainer. He just wanted to be sure.

So it was not until 1970 that Charlie Williams, professional comedian, began to make an impact far and away beyond the confines of the local miners' clubs.

But it was, of course, his being included in the team for "The Comedians" that his happy personality and clever timing of simple gags made him a favourite in almost every home in the land.

It is amazing that his act consists of so few jokes about football.

"I have never sought-out Soccer gags," he says. "The two jobs were poles apart. I was happy playing football—but didn't often try to be funny on the pitch. And being a comedian is equally as serious a job—I just seek material that will make people laugh—and be happy.

"But laughs are good for everyone—they relax tensions. And if en route to a match I could help the lads relax by telling a gag or two—I did so. But the actual playing was serious.

"I remember once we were due to

The odd spectator would call: "Get back to your own country", I replied: It's only three bob to Barnsley."

play at Bury, and when we arrived at Gigg Lane the ground had just thawed-out after a spell of frost, and looked to be covered with water.

"Just before we left the dressing-room I called out to our skipper, inside-forward Bert Tindall: 'If you win the toss Bert—play with the tide.' A simple gag—but it helped to relax some of the lads who were worried about the conditions, and we all ran out with smiles on our faces!

The Comedian . . . "my gags went better than my songs"

"I don't get too much time to watch Soccer these days, but if I did my team would be Leeds United. Not because I once played for them—not because they are a Yorkshire side—but because they play as a *team*! Every man is a grafter —they all work for each other.

"How much happier, and pleasanter life would be if, in all walks of life, everyone did just this—worked for each other collectively, all benefiting from the results.

"If I can contribute to this by making people laugh—I'm happy too!"

But modest though he is, Charlie must also have been happy on an occasion when he drew applause, not laughs, from two sets of battle-weary players. His Doncaster mates and Aston Villa rivals clapped him off cricket-style after he had given a magnificent display in an F.A. Cup replay at Maine Road.

Rovers, who survived extra time with only ten men in this third match, finally beat First Division Villa at the fifth attempt!

We never took much notice of conditions. One foggy day I put three crows in back of net!

27

The sort of line-up that can be seen at schools coaching sessions today.

CLYDE BEST — He could become one of the greats among coloured footballers.

supporters often bad tempered, Charlie never felt in any way that he was an outsider . . .'[100]

'Bad tempered' was one way of putting it. A year later, in the final *Soccer Gift Book* of 1974, there was a three-page feature bemoaning the Apartheid-era ban on South African footballers, looking at certain clubs who'd previously tapped into the 'stream of talent from the Cape', notably Liverpool and Charlton[101]. That old chestnut – sport and politics don't mix – was another way of putting it.

Which contrasted with a *Topical Times* feature from their 1970–71 annual that, at first glance, appeared to be about West Ham's new young sensation Clyde Best but was actually a feature on the future of the black footballer in Britain. In seeming good faith Ron Greenwood was enthusiastic about boys with 'roots' in the Commonwealth having the world at their feet, it was noted that Bradford City 'tried to organise a game between all-immigrant sides' and Coventry's manager Noel Cantwell claimed 'football will be multi-racial in ten years'. Today the language reads as wincingly dated, a whiff of 'empire' still lingers, and a cloud definitely obscures the sun when it's noted that 'Clyde Best faded a little when the mid-season mud developed' – but there's also a sense of inclusiveness, even excitement at this development: this is all for the good, and the game will be enriched by these lads. There's an accompanying photo of a team line-up in a school playground. More than half the boys, slouched in their PE kit, are black or mixed race. It's almost possible to glimpse a multi-racial, trouble-free future here. This text would have been written just a year after Enoch Powell's Rivers of Blood speech . . . and eighteen years before people were hurling bananas at John Barnes.

A couple of years after the Clyde Best piece Ade Coker, his West Ham colleague, was telling the *Topical*

---

100 He finished up at Skegness Town, and other non-league outfits, Denaby United and Grimethorpe, before finally making it out of the working-men's club circuit to the bright lights and big time. 'The odd spectator would call, "Get back to your own country," remembered Williams. 'I replied, "It's only three-bob to Barnsley."'

101 Liverpool wingers noted for their 'outlandish names' were 'Denny' (Harman) van den Berg and Berry Nieuwenhuys, known as 'Nivvy' to the Kop. Twenty years before Lucas Radebe and Phil Masinga followed in Albert Johanneson's footsteps, Ipswich's Colin Viljoen was mourned as the last of a long line of greats . . .

Above: Black players – good for the future of the game, ventured the *Topical Times*, 1970–71

178

Times, 'I've never felt conscious of my colour at Upton Park', but also felt it necessary to point out that he couldn't judge the pace of a pass in the mud (pitches in Nigeria having been either bone hard or unplayable due to flooding), but was working on it.

Difficult political issues such as race relations, and the increase of violence, both on and off the pitch, would crop up now and again in football annuals – generally between the late sixties and early eighties – but weren't exactly thick on the ground.

Ian Plenderleith would have been 'surprised at references to trouble and hooliganism in annuals. I thought pitch invasions were great fun; all part of the spectacle.' He remembers being on holiday and seeing a pitch invasion at Hibernian. 'I was absolutely thrilled. I couldn't understand why my dad always sat there shaking his head when lads ran on to the pitch. I'd hear him talk with his former landlord, an old-school Scot who was in his seventies – liked proper football, attacking football – and they'd talk about the terrible state of today's youth. I remember his landlord saying, "They shouldn't be at the game on Saturday afternoon, they should be out *playing the game* on Saturday afternoon." To me a pitch invasion was just like one massive game of British Bulldog – you didn't analyse it and think, "This is killing the game, or stopping other people watching the game." You just had the moronic mindset of a twelve-year-old.'

Most readers would probably not turn to *Charles Buchan's Soccer Gift Book* for an analysis of the social ills behind terrace violence – nor any football annual for that matter. While football violence was largely a concern for the BBC's *9'O Clock News*, rather than books purchased by Aunty Irene for her young nephew, by 1974 the *Gift Book* did perhaps look a little old school.

That said, there was a fine profile in the final *Soccer Gift Book* of 1974 by 'John Anthony' (actually a young Patrick Collins Jnr) of Millwall legend Harry Cripps. Born in Plaistow, Cripps had been a graduate of the

What about the workers? Training over there's no let-up for the energetic Harry. Here he has turned demolition worker to help out some friends and as always gets to work with a smile

'The crowd started to shout for Harry. He emerged from the dug-out. There was a roar. He peeled off his tracksuit. Bedlam'

same youth team as Bobby Moore, but was handed a free transfer from Upton Park at a young age before becoming a formidable presence at the Den. 'When you've spent a week humping sacks of cement, or hauling timber in the docks, it's not easy to sympathise with people who seem to scamper around on a Saturday and complain about the pressures involved,' wrote Collins, expressing a timeless sentiment, applicable to the Premier League today. 'But Harry they understand. If things had been different he might have been the fellow picking up those sacks alongside them.'

Cripps' blood and thunder approach – he wasn't the most cultured player – meant the Millwall management hadn't 'always shared the fans' faith in Harry' and a couple of replacements had edged him out of the team in previous years. 'But each time Harry returned almost by public demand and eventually [manager] Benny Fenton conceded it was a fruitless task' to not stick with his old-school left-back.

Collins recounted the events of one warm September evening at the Den, when Harry was on the bench again, for a match against Charlton. Millwall went a goal down, and 'Aitch's mates in the crowd were growing restless: '. . . the crowd started to shout for Harry. He emerged from the dug-out. There was a roar. He peeled off his tracksuit. Bedlam.' Charlton wobbled; Millwall snatched an equaliser. 'Pandemonium . . . and all directed at Harry. "Fantastic, 'Aitch, you frightened 'em," someone yelled from the crowd. Harry grinned and put his tracksuit back on and sat down again.

The piece carried an accompanying photograph of Harry surrounded by rubble, helping some mates clear what looked like a factory yard or vacant plot. It was probably one of the final affectionate articles on life at the Den. A couple of years later *Panorama* were putting together their infamous programme on Millwall's 'F troop' and 'the Treatment' – the latter filmed on a grey 1970s afternoon, standing on the terrace at Eastville sporting surgical masks; the former made up of the 'real nutters' who'd go looking for trouble in the home end,

Left: Millwall legend Harry Cripps in *Charles Buchan's Soccer Gift Book*, **1974**

179

'Football isn't perceived to be at the cutting edge of culture, is it?'

◇◇◇◇◇◇◇◇◇◇◇◇◇◇◇◇◇◇◇◇◇◇◇◇◇◇

and numbering 'Harry the Dog' and 'Billy the Wolf' among their contingent.[102]

The film is mind-boggling to watch today; in 1977 it was another planet to that inhabited by Peter Dimmock, Kenneth Wolstenholme or Charles Buchan. Or, perhaps, in the case of *Buchan*, it was more that the round-ups of Leeds and Celtic's ascendancy, the rise of Kevin Keegan, further articles on Ron Davies, Tony Currie and Asa Hartford – and the very dated-looking black-and-white PORTRAIT GALLERY of stars, which, minus the odd moustache and feathered haircut, could have been from 1960 – were no longer the sole preserve of *Charles Buchan's Soccer Gift Book*. Magazines such as *Goal* and *Shoot!* had stolen a march in the newsagent's, and their Christmas equivalents were poised to dominate the 1970s in the WH Smith's book department.

West Brom archivist Laurie Rampling recalls, '*Football Monthly* started to tail off when Charles Buchan passed away – it tended to lose its way a bit [as the sixties progressed]. I'd read it and think, "You know what? That wasn't very interesting..." It got very bland. That's when I stopped reading it, let alone buying it. Some of the *Shoot!* and *Match* stuff wasn't bad ... good

Hooliganism—the blot on the soccer scene in the sixties. (Above) the senseless damage to train coaches by 'fans' returning home on a football special. (Below) A hold-up in Spurs-Manchester City match whilst players pick up pieces of broken glass in a goalmouth—the lunacy is not, of course, confined to any particular set of alleged supporters

reading material ... they started going back to a more stylish football, more colourful.'

Johnny Green travels back in time to the mid-sixties, a kaleidoscopic moment of expanding teenage consciousness and beat groups – 'very working class, spotty individuals with bad hair and bad teeth' – in which autograph-hunting and the *Soccer Gift Book* soon came to be part of the old, black and white world: 'They are coming of age books to me, *Charles Buchan*. This mythical Charles Buchan, who sits on top of this empire that furnishes me with images of the game, he's the ultimate old-timer, isn't he? He's not showing me the modern world, really. If anybody is it's the *Topical Times* who are ringing the changes – the very name, *Topical Times* – and yet [at thirteen] I'm not sure I want that. I'm looking elsewhere for those changes, not looking to football at that point. I'm getting it from music, from fashion, but I'm not really getting it in my provincial home, from my primary source, which is *Charles Buchan*.

'The mug shots are still mug shots, and I like that – it makes me feel solid – and yet, there's no creativity going on, is there? There's no posed photos in them [nothing like] The Beatles posing in Edwardian bathing suits for Dezo Hoffmann on Margate beach. But footballers don't do any of that shit – they're not

---

102 Unfortunately the coach carrying the 'F troop' broke down that day, leaving Harry the Dog to make his own way to the ground and undertake 'a solo assault' on the Bristol Rovers home end. He got escorted back to the away terrace, where he was filmed standing by the rest of the troop – one particularly mesmerising gent is wearing over-sized aviator shades and a grey turtle-neck jumper beneath his pin-stripe suit-jacket. If it wasn't Bobby the Wolf it would have been 'Mad Pat' or 'Winkle'. He was looking fairly pensive as Millwall lost 2–0, but earlier in the film had seemed obsessed with northerners: 'And I won't take it from a northerner. I'm not going away [with Millwall] for some dirty northern ponce to spit all over me. If he spits all over me, I'll put a pint glass in his head,' he told the *Panorama* reporter with the reasoned calm of the true psychopath. There's also Mick, 'the caretaker of an experimental playgroup', filmed at work with kids running around in the background, and 'his friend Gary'; and affecting footage of a forlorn-looking Den, empty during a midweek afternoon, nestling in a hollow surrounded by New Cross wasteland, where the frizzy haired repeat offender Billy Plummer – academically 'aware of his limited horizons' (but who loved his mum) – was being interviewed in the pale sunshine, overlooking the ground. Manager Gordon Jago tries to reach out to the community with his Sunday morning street markets and open days for the locals to meet the players – but when an exchange with 'the Treatment' over declining numbers of away fans at the Den threatens to get heated, the camera suddenly pans away.

Above: Football hooliganism emerges on to the pages of the *All Stars* annual 1970: British Rail football specials – still smashed up despite Ken Dodd's pleas; Spurs and Man City players pick up pieces of broken glass from the goalmouth at White Hart Lane

posing on cars, that comes later. Football isn't perceived at the cutting edge of culture, is it? There's Best in his leather car coat, but nobody else in the Manchester United team looks like that. Bobby Charlton probably told him off [adopts Geordie tone]: "Look at the state of . . . you're not travelling like that, are you?" The top division footballers did start to blur into pop stars. Of course, everybody will say that moment came when George Best went out and beat Benfica, came back with a sombrero and was called "El Beatle", but those of us who lived with one foot in music and one foot in football had known that moment was coming for quite a long time, really. I was already living the life in a humble, provincial way, and football didn't reflect that. Much as I liked football, the books didn't drag me into it, they were not leading the way in a way that the media informs you of those changes now.'

For Johnny the thrill had been all about access to players, and annuals fed into that accessibility. Once, at his Aunty Peg's in Manchester, 'I can remember looking through the Manchester telephone directory (which they kept in their outside toilet for some reason) and finding "Law. D" in Chorlton-cum-Hardy. I knew he lived in Chorlton-cum-Hardy because I'd read it in the *Manchester Evening News* – and I rang the number and he answered the phone. I didn't know what to say. I just put the phone down. It was just to hear his Scottish accent – "*Hullo*." I just did it to see if you could do it – and you could.'

It was that spirit of enquiry that led John – via university, and an early seventies spent on the terraces at Bootham Crescent and Boothferry Park – ultimately to life with The Clash[103]. Where annuals had made him 'feel intimate with football', real life now flooded in. He sold his autographed set of *Buchans* to a collector at

'It was just like introducing a cancer into the team'

◇◇◇◇◇◇◇◇◇◇◇

a point when he needed the cash, but can't recall much more about it.

Richard Williams had also moved on from childhood sports annuals, and was aware that '. . . the average English footballer remained very conservative, pre-Beatles, until about '68 or so, while we were all changing, '63, '64, '65. And then Best came along – but it took a long, long time before the rest of the squad caught up. Willie Morgan, a tricky little winger, went from Burnley to United, and when he arrived, Best was already acting up and kind of pissing Busby off – and Willie Morgan did this photo-shoot, because they were starting to do that kind of thing then, and had his haircut, but in a neat Beatle cut, and he presented himself very explicitly as the anti-Best, you know: "I'm as skilful as Best, but I'm a good upstanding sort." It didn't work, but culturally it was interesting, I thought.'

As a youngster Richard had fallen in love with Billy Walker's Cup-winning Forest side of 1959. His first really big match was the second sixth-round replay against Birmingham at Filbert Street: 'It was packed. Somehow my dad got me down to the front and I sat on the wall with my feet on the pitch, and we won 4–1: a Roy Dwight hat-trick, and Billy Gray got the fourth, and they were fantastic . . . classic two wingers, just irresistible – it was beautiful to watch.'

Johnny Carey's side, a decade on, 'was even better'. Carey's neat and free-flowing Forest team finished runners-up to Manchester United in 1967, and were briefly in favour in the football annuals[104]. 'But it didn't last for very long,' continues Richard Williams, 'because Carey wasn't a strong man, and there was a strong, opinionated chairman, Tony Wood. It was the chairman who ruined the whole thing by buying Jim Baxter. It was just incredible, awful; Baxter had scored a great goal at the City Ground for Sunderland, on the

---

103 *A Riot of Our Own*, John's account of life as road manager of The Clash was published in 1997, illustrated by his partner in crime, the artist Ray Lowry. 'You know Mick Jones used to do this?' he adds, of autograph-hunting. 'A few years younger than me – QPR – one of those London boys who went round the stations and hotels with us.'

104 In truth, Forest featured in a lot of the photography around this period, but less so editorially. By this point the big clubs – or simply the league champions (Derby, for instance, a few years later) – were beginning to dominate column inches.

Above: Jim Baxter in his pomp at Ibrox; but he was past his best by the time he reached Forest. Hugh Taylor's *Scottish Football Book* 1970

volley from about forty yards, and the chairman bought him and it was just like introducing a cancer into the team. It wasn't a big squad and Baxter started taking them to the Hippo on Bridlesmith Gate – a nightclub – and you could gamble there, and he started taking the young players, and it [wrecked] a finely balanced team.'

George Best led the way, of course, but the more you scan the football annuals of the 1960s (and into the seventies) the more names there are, big and small – hot one minute; not there the next – that begin to fall by the wayside. Baxter was one of the first. It's not that his decline, nor Best's for that matter, is recounted in any great detail in any football annual of the day – drunken shenanigans, domestic trouble, or melancholy nights drinking alone, a barstool and a bottle of Bacardi for company, are hardly the stuff of children's Christmas reading[105] – but that one minute there's Hugh Taylor lamenting that 'elegant Jim Baxter of Rangers' is the only Scottish player on a journalists' best international XI of the last twenty years, the next Jim is throwing Wee Willie Henderson's fancy Continental shoes out of a hotel window – and then his following appearance in an annual captures him in a tight-fitting Sunderland shirt.

As we've seen, Albert Quixall was all over football annuals a few years before Baxter. A record signing, he arrived at Old Trafford the coming man – a foundation stone in Matt Busby's post-Munich re-building.

And then . . . nothing.

Until a small piece in the 1966–67 *Soccer Gift Book*, where it becomes apparent he's been let go by Manchester United – to Oldham. But at 31 he's adamant the 'ability which induced that £45,000 fee is still there. I've regained my enthusiasm for the game. And I feel that the one-time "Golden Boy" can show them all

His moment of triumph! This is when Manchester United won the F.A. Cup in 1963. And Quixall, grinning all over his face, is second from the right.

Quixall arrived at Old Trafford the coming man – a foundation stone in Matt Busby's post-Munich re-building. And then . . . nothing

◇◇◇◇◇◇◇◇◇◇◇◇◇◇◇◇◇◇◇◇◇◇◇◇◇◇◇◇◇◇◇

this season.' One season and thirteen appearances later, for Stockport County, he called it a day.

Johnny Green was a fan: 'Albert Quixall seemed like a quirk of the fifties left over in the sixties. The golden boy, his hair – the most expensive player, and yet he had quiffage. In retrospect I like that immensely. There was that very famous picture, on the ballet bar – whatever they call that. I remember thinking, "Wow, that's cool." It wasn't poofy, it wasn't girly; it was taking football into somewhere new – it wasn't just men running about in the mud and hoofing it, there was something very elegant about it, and he was presented as this rather elegant player, but [at the time] it seemed to me he'd been and gone before I'd ever *really* noticed him. Myself and Ray [Lowry] picked up on it, talking about quiffage, really: "Whatever happened to Albert Quixall?" For one minute and one minute only he was the fanciest player in Britain, and then he was gone. It's like that bit at the beginning of *On the Road*, where Kerouac says, I'm only interested in the mad ones, the bright ones, the ones that explode like roman candles and then they're gone, gone, gone. Albert Quixall probably had his hair cut once every two weeks, probably even by a woman . . . he was superseded by Denis Law – £53,000 – for all the Busby Babes bullshit about youth and all that, no one ever spent more than Matt Busby.'

A youth-team player on the books at Old Trafford in the early sixties, well placed to comment on life behind the scenes, was Eamon Dunphy. He writes in his recent autobiography, *The Rocky Road*, that '"Quickie", a dazzling wonder boy at Wednesday, could never come to terms with his price tag or the pressures that came with being The Man at Old Trafford.' He was nice, friendly and always had time for an encouraging word with the kids in the youth team, but wasn't respected by the first-team dressing room as they 'believed he didn't have the "bottle" for the big games . . . Albert Quixall

105 See Duncan Hamilton's *The Footballer Who Could Fly* for a poignant account of Baxter's time in Nottingham.

Above: Albert Quixall celebrates with his Man Utd team-mates after the 1963 Cup final, but the curtain was about to fall on his Old Trafford career, *Charles Buchan's Soccer Gift Book* 1966
Right: George Best, 'always out of reach' *David Coleman's World of Football* 1970

George Best on duty at Old Trafford

Footballers Have Brains
by George Best

There's no doubt at all that the life of the professional footballer has changed a heck of a lot over the past fifteen or twenty years. Changed in a lot of different ways . . . not least in the size of his pay-packet. I'm happy to say. I think back to the days when even the mightiest stars could only earn twenty pounds a week, and I feel a funny shiver go right down my backbone.

It's changed, too, in terms of the way the players look. On the field or off. I've got some pictures of the giants of the past and there they are, arms folded and faces grimly unsmiling – legs out with hefty shin-guards, boots fitted out with toe-pads as big as those that the hooligan supporters wear to kick each other to pieces.

And the hair-styles. Close-cropped, most of them. Sir Stanley Matthews, in his hey-day as a wing wizard, actually looked to have pretty long hair, but it was greased down and was most certainly 'respectably short' round the nape of the neck and over the ears. Incidentally, nobody seemed to criticize *him* when his hair flopped forward over his eyes.

But there's another difference – and that's the main subject of this article. In the so-called 'bad old days', a footballer seemed to do his talking with his feet. You never really heard a peep from him as a talker, an orator, a chatter-on-current-affairs, if you like.

Nowadays, though, the star player is asked his views on anything and everything. And, if you're caught on the hop and give out with a controversial answer, you can come in for a whole lot of criticism. I know . . . because I've had my fair share of criticism.

Not that I'm griping. I'm proud that the status of the professional footballer has increased so much. I'm glad that he is regarded as an intelligent member of the community and is actually allowed to have views on things other than how to kick a football into the back of the net.

Now some of the lads in the star department find it difficult to chat away. That's never really been my problem – put it down to being Irish, for we're known to have the gift of the gab. But I can understand why some players get a bit tongue-tied when they're suddenly interviewed on things like marriage, or religion, or the current political state of the country. It's nice to be asked, maybe, but it's not so nice if you get criticized for expressing your views.

That's what makes me laugh about the way the newspaper boys tend to work. 'We want some star names to talk about how they'd run the country – get a film star, an MP, a footballer, a bus-driver, Get on to Georgie Best . . . he's okay for a quote.' So I give it a bit of thought and think of something worth saying.

And the next thing wrong is somebody else on another paper is having a go. 'G. Best is a footballer and that's what he does well. Why on earth does he

9

---

died a slow death. He lasted five years at the club.' One of Quixall's last games was the 1963 FA Cup final, but victory there led to a 4–0 hammering by Everton in that August's Charity Shield. Quixall, along with John Giles and David Herd, were dropped. 'Quickie had a nervous breakdown shortly afterwards,' writes Dunphy.

In his *Northern Soccer Annual* of 1969 Dunphy reminded readers that George Best fled Manchester, back to Ireland, after just a week as an apprentice, such was the bewildering step-up for the shy lad from Belfast. But, added Dunphy, despite the formidable appearance of the 'large smoke-blackened buildings in the city centre and the decaying area around Old Trafford' Manchester folk were very warm underneath. Best, by 1969 the playboy, was quieter underneath too. The man himself was quoted as saying, 'The old playboy image was all right when I was a lad but now I think the time has come to change.'

As already noted (in chapter 2) you don't have to search hard through the football annuals of the 1960s to find George Best ruefully confessing his ways have to change. In the *International Football Book* of 1968 he admitted he liked parties and 'meeting pretty girls' but claimed it was all under control: 'Fact is I'm only twenty-two now and I think I'm learning enough' about

The *Northern Soccer Annual* ran a cheery piece on Manchester landladies in 1969 – no *This Sporting Life* darkness and repressed desire, of course, but still a few difficulties masked over, no doubt. 'Widows appear to make the best "mums",' said United scout Joe Armstrong. 'We had one lad who was vegetarian and we had no trouble in having his needs satisfied. In all cases we try to get the "mothers" to keep the lads off the greasy stuff.' On his return from Turin, Denis Law may have switched Manchester clubs, but not lodgings. On Best's return he shared digs with David Sadler, and considered their landlady's place a refuge from the 'hustle and bustle and league soccer and big business'.

'Mums make the best landladies,' says Crystal Palace apprentice Phil Hoadley

Above: George Best airs a few of the frustrations of stardom in his 1970 annual

'If you are an electrician I bet you don't spend half your time talking about ring mains, fuses and junction boxes'

◇◇◇◇◇◇◇◇◇◇◇◇◇◇◇◇◇◇◇◇◇◇◇◇◇

football to go on for years and years, keeping myself out of trouble and not burning myself out.'

Dealing with ludicrous amounts of fan mail, and attempting to put to one side the hate mail, the numerous poison pen letters ('they're poison, but who cares?') is also a preoccupation of Best's in the publications of the day. By 1970, and the third edition of Pelham Books' *George Best's Soccer Annual*, the bearded genius is getting fed up of being harangued in the street by people who always open 'the conversation with the remark, "Well, George, you must be sick of talking about football . . ."' and then go on to do precisely that. 'If you are an electrician I bet you don't spend half your time talking about ring mains, fuses and junction boxes,' wrote Best. 'Equally, if you're a butcher I bet you don't swop small talk about sides of beef over the occasional pint. And I'll warrant that you don't want other folk coming up to you and insisting that you do anyway.' A page on, after spending much of the article warning young aspirant footballers to watch out for 'back-slapping hangers-on', con-men wanting you to endorse their dodgy fare, he apologized, or hoped he was not 'proving something of a bore over this, or giving any wrong impressions.'

In the same year's *David Coleman's World of Football* annual, in his footballers-as-movie-stars feature, Paul Trevillion wrote, 'Watching George Best play football is like watching someone on the cinema screen. He's always out of reach . . . every girl looks at him and you're just never going to get him . . . he's the James Dean of football.'

In the *Coleman* annual a year earlier, a group of top footballers had been asked the question, 'To what extent could personal problems, or a bad mood, effect you when you go on the pitch?' Bobby Charlton responded: 'Your wife might have left you in the morning, and I think that you would find that you get on the field on a Saturday and you wouldn't notice it . . . the field is like an island.' Whereas Alan Mullery seemed to need everything 'nice and happy at home especially before a game'. Best was closer to Charlton, though: he recalled once slamming down the phone after an argument with a girlfriend at 2 o'clock on a Saturday afternoon, 'But as soon as I got out on the pitch I forgot completely about anything . . . nothing else matters.'

David Coleman's World of Football annuals could have a refreshingly critical edge. And Manchester United in the early seventies were fair game. A piece in the 1974 *Coleman* volume headlined THE DECLINE AND FALL OF MANCHESTER UNITED, no doubt furiously punched out on a Remington typewriter by 'United supporter Geoffrey Godbert, a marketing executive in London', featured a stinging attack on Matt Busby for hanging on to power too long at Old Trafford, questioned the wisdom of Frank O'Farrell's signings, described Ian Storey-Moore, Ted MacDougall and Wyn Davies as 'sub-quality attackers', despaired at the indulging of George Best (and his on-off retirement), before embarking on a major dismantling of Tommy Docherty's managerial record – his handing of the 1965 league championship on a plate to United while at Chelsea (following his suspension of eight key players who'd broken a curfew in Blackpool, in order to show them who was boss); his walking out on QPR after only a month; his raising and then dashing of hopes at Rotherham and Aston Villa. Docherty's track record was described as 'only slightly less frightening

THE DECLINE AND FALL OF MANCHESTER UNITED

A United supporter, Geoffrey Godbert, who is an advertising executive in London, wrote in this book four years ago about the team he worships. Or, did worship. He said that what made United unique was a sort of magic, or mystique, that came from tradition and individual character. Today, Mr. Godbert, like many United supporters, feels a little disenchanted. Here he sets out the disturbing history of United's last six years and puts the responsibility firmly on the shoulders of managers.

Above: *David Coleman's World of Football* 1974 pores over the details of Man Utd's post-Busby decline

than his very determined personality, which frequently got him into trouble. If any man was calculated to stir apprehension in the hearts of United's friends used to the calm of the post-war years, Tommy Docherty was that person. But the truth seemed to be that, with Busby still a very visible power in the background, no one else would take the job.' Still, at least the 'negative joylessness' on the pitch in recent seasons would provide good groundwork for life in the second division. 'Busby should retire from Old Trafford,' concluded Godbert. 'Docherty should be given one more season, particularly if it is spent in the second division, and then he should be sacked, especially if United win promotion at the first chance'!

Those 'calm' post-war years, specifically the handing of the baton to Wilf McGuinness, featured heavily in *George Best's Soccer Annual no. 3*, but there's a defensive tone to the writing, a selling of the appointment from within to a sceptical readership. By the time that annual was being wrapped up and placed under the tree, McGuinness was toast. A year later, in *Best's Soccer Annual no. 4*, he wasn't even mentioned.

In the *Shoot! Annual 1974* – a fine blue and red typographical style for the cover, very reminiscent of the football cards of the day – Best looked back to the days of his tough childhood on an ordinary working-class estate in Cregagh, Belfast. The small houses were divided by privet hedges, all the front doors were painted the same; young George was desperate to escape a life of drudgery in the shipyards like his dad's. But even as an apprentice at Old Trafford he ended up on a work

placement scheme as a messenger in a Manchester ship canal company – a job that mainly seemed to consist of taking lunch orders and buying cigarettes for fellow workers. The *Billy Liar* aspect of the tale is overpowering, and Best was at pains to point out he could now mix with anyone, no longer was he a wallflower: 'If I don't know what a particular dish is, I call over the waiter and have him explain it to me. Waiters don't scare me nowadays . . . well, not much.'

Elsewhere in the same piece, he recalled, 'Christmas presents were always something to do with football. When I finally learned to read (much earlier than the age of fifteen by the way . . .) various relations would give me football books and annuals. Little did they, or I, know that one day I'd be writing in an annual like this.'

Which does make you wonder exactly how aware he was that he'd already lent his name to five annuals by this point. *George Best's Soccer Annuals no. 1* to *no. 5* are not bad at all, generally full of Best's wry tone when it comes to dealing with celebrity lifestyle and people's perception of footballers. In one article he appeared to be arguing that Stanley Matthews was actually the first long-haired footballer, albeit with greased-down locks 'most certainly "respectably short" round the nape of the neck and over the ears', and pleaded the case for footballers to be able to express political opinions and even 'join in panel games on occasions'. Apparently, in a (presumably televised) general knowledge quiz between different football teams, Arsenal's Ian Ure 'went on and talked like he was a walking encyclopaedia' and people were 'amazed' by this. 'But why should

In the *Midland Soccer Annual* of 1969 there's a sense Eamon Dunphy isn't overly impressed with the blunt-speaking Tommy Docherty. Dunphy pressed him on his aggressive football, his win-at-all-costs philosophy, and what example this set to young people. 'It's possible to play attractive football at home,' replied the Villa manager before trotting out that old chestnut about people just wanting to see results – 'anything we can do to that end is justified'. When asked what he liked in a player, Docherty made noises about character and loyalty – to both team-mates and the club. Quick as a flash Dunphy responded, 'Talking of loyalty, you have left your previous two clubs after short stays. Does it bother you to leave without finishing what you set out to achieve?' and then accused him of crippling Rotherham with financial debt.

In the *London Soccer Annual* a year later, Terry Venables spoke of how Docherty's criticism – that he was mouthy and too involved at Chelsea – 'had sown the seeds of doubt' in his mind and caused him to take a step back at Spurs and to try to 'fit in without controlling everything'. It didn't work, and he didn't regain form and confidence until moving on to QPR, flourishing again under Gordon Jago.

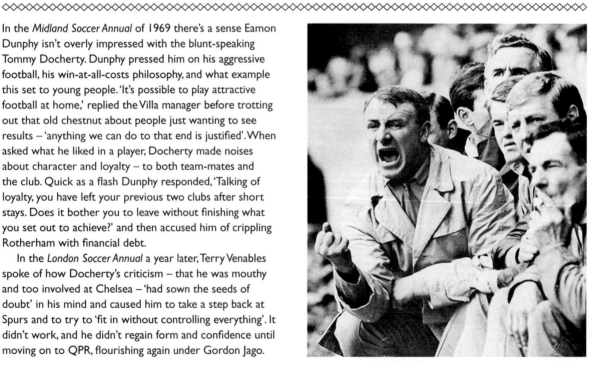

THE NORTHERN IRELAND TEAM

by DEREK DOUGAN

As I'm something of an old-timer in the Northern Ireland team, the only playing survivor of the 1958 World Cup squad in which I was by far the youngest, people ask me which I consider the best Irish team.

True, we don't have the likes of Blanchflower and McIlroy, we have no Bingham and no McParland, but we have the makings of a team that could go a long way in the World Cup in Munich. This is a considered judgement, not just an attempt to patronize the present side.

Sceptics often say: 'Take out George Best and Northern Ireland doesn't have a team, let alone a squad'.

They overlook the numbers of matches Northern Ireland has won without George, when he's been injured or unavailable through club commitments.

Let us look at the side in detail. I rate Pat Jennings, our goalkeeper, as the best in Britain and one of the finest in the world. I can't say 'the' best in the world because I've not seen all the world's top class goalkeepers, but Pat certainly stands alongside them to be counted. Gordon Banks is in a better position to dis-

play all his skills, as he plays in more top matches to justify his position. Think of what one great save, from Pele in the World Cup, did to his international reputation. It reaffirmed his fame throughout the world. In similar circumstances, Pat Jennings could become equally as famous.

For five years Pat's stature as a goalkeeper has been growing and I think he has the edge on Gordon.

Full-backs Pat Rice and Sammy Nelson, from Arsenal, are as good as any you will find in any national team. Pat has a direct approach to the game, is fond of overlapping and has a powerful shot, which gives extra firing power to the forward line when it's needed.

Sammy is the Terry Cooper type of defender, skilful and clever on the ball. Approaching the 18 yard area he often hesitates, perhaps feeling he's a little out of his natural depth. When he's mastered this touch of nervous uncertainty, there'll be no one to approach him.

Jimmy Nicholson, at right-half, is one of the most consistent international players to wear a green jersey. The reason he doesn't produce the same form in

Derek Dougan pictured in the Wolves dressing-room before a match

78 79

it surprise people? Why should they assume that a footballer's brains are stuck deep in his boots?'

Derek Dougan was a frequent contributor to Best's annuals, writing perceptively on topics such as the ever-changing nature of the game: 'Some people are nostalgic and yearn for the styles of those days [the golden era of Matthews, Mortensen, Doherty, etc.], but I think it is the personalities they remember more vividly than the way the game was played . . . but the players of any generation are, in a sense, pioneers; forerunners of new techniques, harbingers of change . . .'

Pelham also gave Dougan his own series – well, a couple of annuals. *Derek Dougan's Book of Soccer no. 1* was essentially a continuation of Eamon Dunphy's and Peter Douglas' *Midlands Soccer Annual*. Dougan opened the first edition in 1971 with, 'Jam yesterday, jam tomorrow, but never jam today. That is how soccer in the Midlands has seemed for the past two decades . . .' (with only a West Brom Cup triumph to shout about). The same annual contained a stylish full-page photo of Everton's Henry Newton (recently departed from Forest) practising golf in his front room, attempting to putt the ball into an upturned mug. (His wife was probably out shopping.) Paul Trevillion thought Dougan resembled Danny Kaye: 'an extrovert clown with a calculating'

'Jam yesterday, jam tomorrow, but never jam today. That is how soccer in the Midlands has seemed for the past two decades . . .'

nature. And Dougan was also capable of the odd backwards-looking outburst too: in *David Coleman's World of Football* (1974) the Molineux man and Terry Venables sat down to dissect a dire 0–0 draw between QPR and Wolves at Loftus Road that featured slow handclapping from the crowd. After a short exchange on whether Liverpool were a dour team who wore you down, or one attempting to play with a bit of flair, Dougan started slagging off his team-mates for their lamentable efforts to put in a decent cross during the QPR game, as well as Stan Bowles' performance ('he showed nothing, really'). He then proclaimed that young kids were far softer in the seventies than in the fifties, recounting how he was always saying to the physiotherapist, 'Bloody well don't treat them, clean the thing up and tell them to get back on the track and keep running.'

Above: The inimitable Derek Dougan pictured in his second *Book of Soccer* in 1972

Neatly segueing the '60s and the '70s were the Pelham titles. Their first books, launched in 1968, were player-led, fronted by the ubiquitous George Best and Denis Law. The first editions featured attractive cover images but rather conservative type. Then the designers hit on a new typeface, Futura Display (familiar to many from the titles to the TV series *Porridge*) which became the series' signature font.

In 1969 the publishers launched three regional titles (see facing page) but two years later reverted back to the star-name formula, adding Alan Ball and Derek Dougan to the roster. Best's and Law's titles lasted five years, Ball's and Dougan's two. Pelham sadly shut up shop in 1972.

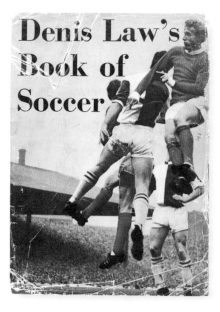

Pelham's three regional annuals were produced with pleasing design harmony. In 1969 the vibrant cover lines were set in pure magenta and cyan. These primary print colours were popular since mixing multiple inks to create red or dark blue could lead to blurred text, caused, as lithographic print officianodos will note, by misalignment of colour plates in the printing process. Oh yes . . .

In 1970 the cover lines were scrapped for a classic clean cover design, embellished with the trademark font. Sadly the series ceased at this point but if you can pick one up somewhere for less than a fiver, we guarantee you won't be disappointed with your purchase.

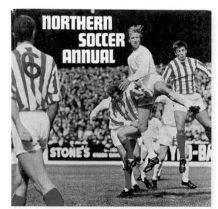

NORTHERN SOCCER ANNUAL

SPECIAL FEATURE ARTICLES BY:

Jimmy Adamson	Keith Farnsworth	Alan Kelly
Stan Anderson	Bryan Hamilton	Barry Mealand
Jimmy Armfield	Colin Harvey	Joe Mercer
Alun Evans	Peter Howard	John Morris

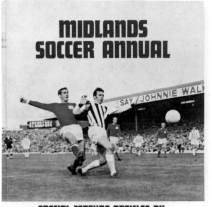

MIDLANDS SOCCER ANNUAL

SPECIAL FEATURE ARTICLES BY:

Terry Hennessey	Oscar Arce	John Dunn
Peter Shilton	Jeff Astle	Peter Knowles
Graham Williams	Gordon Banks	Stan Cullis
Ollie Conmy	Allan Clarke	Harry Gregg
	Tommy Docherty	Trevor Hockey

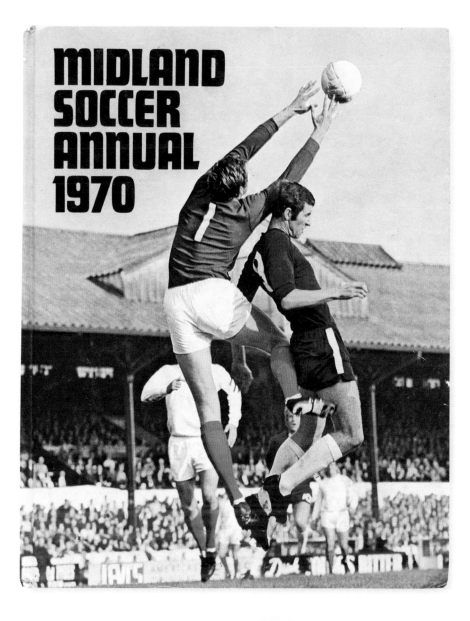

MIDLAND SOCCER ANNUAL 1970

LONDON SOCCER ANNUAL

SPECIAL FEATURE ARTICLES BY:

Peter Bonetti	Bert Head	Ian Morgan
Ron Boyce	Don Howe	Roger Morgan
Charlie Cooke	Joe Kinnear	Martin Peters
Eddie Firmani	Frank McLintock	Dave Sexton
	Ken Montgomery	

NORTHERN SOCCER ANNUAL 1970

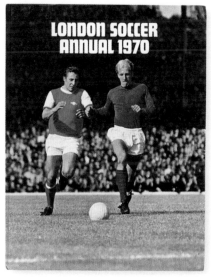

LONDON SOCCER ANNUAL 1970

Player-businessmen Les Barrett and Eamonn Dunphy have a look at their latest project

103

Soccer with the Stars was not a really serious attempt to impart soccer instruction by means of spoken word

◇◇◇◇◇◇◇◇◇◇◇◇◇◇◇◇

The Pelham stable of annuals included *Book*s of *Soccer* from Best, Dougan, *Alan Ball's International Book of Soccer*, a one-off from Billy Bremner, and also Denis Law's *Book of Soccer*[106] series. The look of the books was essentially that of the beautifully laid-out regional *Soccer Annual*s from 1969 and 1970, which featured a simple two-column grid of text and fairly extensive use of white space. Added to that was gritty black and white photography – Wilf McGuinness looking not unlike Alain Delon in *Le Samourai*, wearing a pencil-thin tie and white shirt, smoking anxiously in the dug-out; council-estate roofs glimpsed by the corner of a stand; Swindon Town players frolicking with the League Cup trophy in the choppy water of a utilitarian-looking communal bath; Burnley's Dave Thomas

sitting on the bonnet of his 1967 Vauxhall Viva; the abstract patterns on the wall and the continental dimple-effect on the bar of the new 'Glaziers Club' at Selhurst Park; the flat expanse of Essex countryside in the distance behind West Ham's Chadwell Heath training ground; wide-angled action shots of Spurs v Wolves simultaneously capturing individual faces and the enormity of the Shelf at White Hart Lane; Peter Osgood, his foot in plaster, playing blow football on the coffee table with his son; Martin Peters' wife looking like Audrey Hepburn as the 'merry wives' sat down to a meal on 30 July 1966[107].Viewed today the annuals, especially the *Northern*, *Midland* and *London* incarnations, could be mistaken at first glance for old copies of *Cahiers du Cinéma*.

In an article in the first *London Soccer Annual*, Peter Douglas (Dunphy's co-conspirator) set the scene in his Westminster flat that doubled as an office for 'Universal Productions', the company formed to exploit business opportunities for young footballers: 'As I look round and see piles of used newspapers, the overflowing ashtrays and wastepaper bins, tangled telephone wires, masses of paper and files, press cuttings and photographs, half-typed manuscripts and even a stale cheese sandwich (which somehow managed to get filed with incoming correspondence) I look back to the palmy [perhaps that should have read balmy?] trouble-free but much less exciting days before I went into partnership with two young footballers.'

The other young footballer was Fulham's Les Barrett, but the article, despite the enticing opening, doesn't really elaborate on the problems of why the recording of their first major project, the instructional LP *Soccer with the Stars*, featuring the likes of Bobby Moore and Peter Bonetti, led to, in the first instance, 'results that were not good'. A clue can perhaps be found in the reference to Les repeatedly turning up late for recording sessions. Douglas, though, is pretty

---

106 *No.5*, in 1970, featured a fiery sermon from Bill Shankly on courage, commitment, working to attain peak physical fitness, and avoiding temptation. After a few pages you feel like you've had a session in the sweatbox at Melwood. Larry Lloyd, in the *Topical Times* of 1971–72, testified to the semi-deranged, driven profile of Shankly evident in David Peace's *Red or Dead*: 'He'll watch a visiting team come in,' said Lloyd of his boss, lingering in the Anfield corridor on a typical Saturday afternoon. 'When they've all disappeared into the visitors' dressing room, he'll burst into ours: "They're midgets," he'll say. "Not a big bloke amongst 'em. Two points today, lads, it's a cert."' Apparently training games didn't stop until Shankly's team, of Paisley, Fagan, Reuben Bennett and Ronnie Moran were winning, the players on their knees. As for *Alan Ball's International Soccer Annual*, in the case of *no.2* (1970), *Alan Ball's Domestic Soccer Annual* might have been a more appropriate title. 'International' seems to mean George Best reassuring readers that every player feels honoured to wear their country's shirt, as well as Bally's own tribute to his boss, FOR SIR ALF AND ENGLAND, a piece so stilted I could only make it halfway through. It does include a fine photograph of a lone Jimmy Smith doing laps of the pitch in an empty, grim-looking Pittodrie, though.

---

107 Actually, the last two examples are from Jimmy Armfield's *All Stars* annual, laid out in a similar fashion.

Above: Eamon Dunphy and Les Barrett take delivery of their *Soccer With the Stars* concept LP in the *London Soccer Annual* 1969

Right: Manchester United manager Wilf McGuinness, star of French New Wave cinema, in the Highbury dug-out, *Northern Soccer Annual* 1970

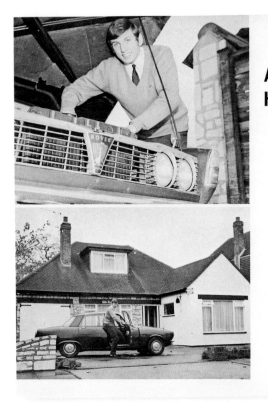

At
Home
with Martin
Peters

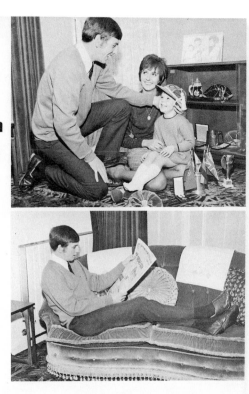

In an ideal world we could fill half of this book with photography from the Pelham publishing stable of annuals. The photographs here represent a small selection from merely the *London Soccer Annual* 1969. Clockwise from top left: Martin Peters climbing out of his Rover on the driveway of his swish Essex pad; Steve Kember, 'surely Mexico-bound in 1970', sitting on a rug in his front room with his younger brother and sister — the top shelf of the scruffy sideboard empty because he's got all his trophies out on the floor; London Weekend Television *Big Match* vans lined up at the back of Loftus Road in 1969; Rodney Marsh with short hair; 'mini-skirted interviewers chat up Crystal Palace fans in Croydon High Street to check on their views about the club'; and on and on . . .

The Big Match. London Weekend TV cameras in position for Q.P.R. v. Manchester United

London Weekend move in the morning of the game

The Big Match

Behind the Scenes at London Weekend TV

TV linkman Richard Davies introduces 'World of Sport' in the studio

London Weekend team have a go themselves, under the guidance of ex-Coventry manager Hill

frank about exploiting the Christmas market: '*Soccer with the Stars* was not a really serious attempt to impart soccer instruction by means of spoken word so much as to make a popular package that could be sold around Christmas time when mums, dads, aunts and uncles were looking round wildly for something to buy children.' Hence it wasn't long before the regional annual concept was born – a series of books with a strong behind-the-scenes footballing take.

What is striking from the Dunphy/Douglas annuals[108] is that footballers are now clearly individuals. Don Revie and the lads at Elland Road might disagree, but by the turn of the seventies the emphasis on the team game was under assault: after the functionalism of Ramsey and plenty of 0–0 draws, people – or football writers at least – were crying out for a bit of flair and colour.

In the first *London Soccer Annual*, Maureen Cleave of the *Evening Standard* interviewed a chippy twenty-two-year-old Rodney Marsh. Like George Best, Marsh had something of *Billy Liar* about him: 'I think clocking into a factory would be the worst thing in the world. All you could say to the man next to you is: "What's in your sandwich, Charlie?"' Marsh would rather talk about the Colosseum in Rome, Cardinal Wolsey ('he got away with a lot'), French impressionist painters, and the book he constantly has by his bedside: *Pears Cyclopaedia*[109]. He thinks he might have been a priest

---

108 It's not really clear what role Barrett played, although later he is photographed perched on his red Triumph Spitfire.

109 Not wanting to miss a trick, there is a footnote in the text of the original article: 'Pelham Books, 25s'.

if he hadn't become a footballer ('something different, something nobody else does'), and would also like an indoor forest in his house (so he could shoot rabbits at will, in private, without being harangued by animal-rights activists) and is upbraided by his wife of three days, Jean 'in her blue fluffy bedroom slippers', for not offering around the box of chocolates he's working his way through during the interview. 'Listen,' Marsh concludes, 'you've got to understand that most people are in a factory from nine to five; their job may be to turn out 263 little circles; at the end of the week they are three short and someone has a go at them. On Saturday afternoons they deserve something to go and shout at.' (A year later in the *Topical Times* annual Marsh admitted he enjoyed chess, a game 'some folks believe [is] for eggheads' and that he'd read a hundred books on British history and turned his hand to painting, but gave that up as he couldn't find the correct 'quiet frame of mind'.)

Meanwhile, for the same 1969 *Midlands Soccer Annual*, Peter Douglas ventured north: 'It was my first visit to the Villa, a dark red collection of buildings, and it rather felt like driving through the gates of a prison hospital instead of those of a football club; miles of harsh stone corridors being scrubbed by young apprentices in shorts and plimsolls added to the effect. Blue-and-cream walls, done in a thick gloss paint, heighten the impression.'

He was up there to interview Oscar Arce, Aston Villa's young Argentinian, out injured and struggling to establish himself anywhere near the first team. Arce complained he had 'lost his sun tan in the dank Midlands

AWAY FROM IT ALL –

Lovely scene, isn't it? Far from the City crowds and traffic, Bobby Kellard, of Portsmouth, with his wife Anne, children Bobby and Joanne, his painting – and peace.

For their 1966–67 *Soccer Gift Book*, Charles Buchan had dropped in on Portsmouth midfielder Bobby Kellard: 'We caught him working on a landscape he calls *Tranquillity*. It is one of three paintings he submitted to Southend art gallery. The others were *Tiger at Bay* and a seascape, *Eternal*.' Kellard could get the artistic call at any moment – sometimes when suited-up for a night out he just popped in to finish a bit off and then would 'get some paint on my sleeve or somewhere else and either have to do some hectic cleaning . . . or call the evening off.'

He always surprised his team-mates by strolling around galleries prior to away games, but couldn't paint on Friday evenings in case he became 'unsettled' by it and couldn't sleep before the match. At the time of the interview he was living on Hayling Island and 'thinking of heading into sculpture'. Kellard had a longish career that took in Leicester and a later return to Crystal Palace and Portsmouth, became joint manager of Harlow Town with Len Glover in the mid-nineties, then, according to Wikipedia, ran a taxi business in Southend, dealt in antiques and now lives in Spain. Sadly there's no mention of further exhibitions.

Oscar Arce

112

'Football My First Love' – Oscar Arce

by Peter Douglas

M Y last sight of Oscar Arce was of a rather sad figure, standing in the rain outside a West Bromwich hospital, his heavy leather overcoat slung over his shoulders, a voluminous Continental umbrella hanging on one arm. Following a pleasant lunch with Aston Villa's young Argentinian, we had offered to take him in the car to see a specialist for the final verdict on his cartilage operation, which up until a few days before had seemed to be a success but had now started giving trouble. Oscar directed us, but we ended up at the wrong hospital. He disappeared inside, to re-emerge moments later saying he had ordered a taxi to take him back into Birmingham to another hospital. He would not let us give him another lift and was profuse in his thanks – for lunch, for the lift in our car, for – it seems – even troubling to spend time with him.

Oscar is not the easiest man to talk to. His English is not good and he has an intensity about everything he says – whether on the subject of Argentinian football or the arrival of new-broom Docherty at the Aston Villa ground. It was my first visit to the Villa (writes Peter Douglas), a dark-red collection of buildings, and it rather felt like driving through the gates of a prison hospital instead of those of a football club; miles of harsh stone corridors being scrubbed by young apprentices in shorts and plimsolls added to the effect. Blue-and-cream walls, done in thick gloss paint, heighten the overall impression.

Oscar is tall and well-built, in the manner of John Charles. If I expected a dark man with a Zapata moustache, I was disappointed. He has fairish, thinning hair brushed forward. He complains he has lost his sun-tan in the dank Midlands air. He has to see the Doc about his knee and we wait until the interview is over. We then go to lunch.

Since he was twelve years old, Oscar tells us, he has been playing football. Every Argentinian club supports about a dozen teams and you simply have to work your way up through them. He ended up with Rosario Central. I asked him why he left it all to come to England.

'For love,' he replied simply, as if that was reason enough. His wife is a Glasgow girl he met when she was on a long study-tour-cum-holiday of Argentina – Oscar himself has a degree in art. They fell in love and Oscar bought himself out of his contract with Rosario and returned to Scotland to marry her. He is not sure what other ideas he had in mind, beyond a passion for English football, but through his country's embassy in London he got permission to work. Aston Villa were interested – and he signed with them at the start of the 1968 season.

His position is like any English footballer. He is a member of the League and can play for any club he chooses, by obtaining a transfer. His career at Villa was not spectacular. His injury, sustained during a match at Coventry, put back his progress. Add to this the complications of fluid on the knee when

III

'Arce complained he had "lost his sun tan in the dank Midlands air"'

air' and confessed that he didn't particularly mix well with other players, preferring to visit art galleries or a museum in London whenever he had a day off (he had a degree in art). 'I know we Latin Americans have a reputation for being volatile, but the truth is that after a game, football is quickly forgotten. We soon turn our attention to something else – a wife and children or a pretty girl you are hoping to dance with that night. We do not carry the disputes out of the club and into the streets like your English fans do – arguing and fighting and wrecking railway coaches.' The interview with Arce is a rare treasure today, however. An entertaining post on the *Heroes and Villains* website suggests Arce, 'allegedly an Argentinian under-23 international' running an antique shop in Glasgow with his newly married wife, thought he'd 'try his luck' and write to Villa. 'He hadn't played for two years, was unfit, but could juggle a ball like a circus act . . . his first game, a 2–0 defeat at non-league Bedford Town, culminated in him being sent off for spitting at an "over-zealous" opponent, eager to kick lumps out of this skilful foreigner.' He never quite recovered from a serious knee injury, 'sustained during a match at Coventry' according to Douglas; other internet sources suggest he never played for the first team and that Arce (perhaps less so his brother, whom Docherty signed at the same time), was

a late-1960s forerunner of Southampton's enterprising Ali Dia. But whatever Arce's playing pedigree, he has subsequently managed teams in Switzerland, Morocco, Côte d'Ivoire, Libya, the United Arab Emirates, Egypt, Burkina Faso (the national team), Tunisia, South Africa and Syria. That would be some book.

Possibly on the same trip to the Midlands Peter Douglas interviewed another 'character', Trevor Hockey: 'hair long, sideburns down to the chin . . . sleeves of his Birmingham City shirt stretched so that he clutched the cuffs inside the clenched fist of each hand. Slightly built and a bit on the short side, he worried the Millwall defence like a terrier dog having a go at a pack of sheep, and thoroughly enjoying every minute of it.' Hockey's reputation for off-the-field clowning earned him the 'George Best of the Midlands' moniker – photo-shoots with models; heavy costs pending after driving his Jaguar 2.4 into the back of a Birmingham Corporation bus – but in 1969 the midfielder was battling to be taken seriously

Above: Argentinian enigma Oscar Arce arrives in the *Midlands Soccer Annual* 1969

Trevor strums his guitar

25

Hockey is photographed strumming his acoustic guitar beneath a poster for a Bert Jansch gig

◇◇◇◇◇◇◇◇◇◇◇◇◇◇◇◇◇◇◇◇◇◇◇◇

and was studying for his coaching badges. He rued not paying more attention in school, especially in art and music, and was also struggling through an engineering course at technical college ('a pile of homework lies in the cupboard, untouched'), while Douglas commented that his two quiet daughters were 'the most well behaved children' he'd ever met. The Hockeys lived in a modest semi-detached in Marsden Green – 'warmly lit inside with deep oranges and contemporary furniture that make you feel instantly welcome' – and it's easy to picture Douglas sinking into a comfortable modish settee, settling down to discuss the matter in hand, namely Trevor's new folk record, apparently

Above: Trevor Hockey, 'the George Best of the Midlands', in his folk troubadour days
Right: Ron Atkinson throws a punch at the ref, both *Midlands Soccer Annual* 1969

already circulating amongst the official Trevor Hockey fan club after going down well when played over the Tannoy at St Andrew's. Hockey is photographed with a neat Beatle haircut, wearing a cool-looking cardigan, and strumming his acoustic guitar beneath a poster for a Bert Jansch gig (and another for the Folk '65 festival in Exeter). By the time the *Topical Times* got around to a feature on Hockey – by that point enjoying his hirsute heyday at Bramall Lane – he was recalling the pink piano at home, the velvet-covered car, and how he once took to the pitch at St Andrew's with daffodils stuffed down the front of his shorts[110].

Across the Black Country, the *Midlands Annual* profiled Graham Williams, the West Brom and Wales full-back whose love of ballet was so great that once, on the occasion of a Wales trip to Moscow, he became so enraptured by a performance of the Bolshoi that it was only as the lights went up that he realized he was sitting in a row of empty seats – the rest of the squad presumably having left for a beer some while before the end. 'It's not for cissies,' believed Williams. 'All I can say is go and try [ballet dancers'] routines. I think Rudolf Nureyev is the greatest . . .'

Lest we get too carried away with folk music, fine art, ballet and Rodney Marsh's reading of Cardinal Wolsey's role in the 1512 war against France, it's worth pointing out that the *Midlands Soccer Annual* of 1969 does feature a striking photograph of Oxford United's Ron Atkinson having to be restrained from punching a referee.

A NOTHER STALWART, not only of the regional *Soccer Annuals*, but across the board in late-sixties annuals, was Ron Davies – prolific in front of goal, and quite handy with a sketch pad and pencil too. In the *Topical Times* of 1966–67, in article devoted to his pencil

---

110 Something perhaps noted by twelve-year-old Steven Patrick Morrissey sitting in his bedroom across the Pennines, reading the *Topical Times* annual over Christmas 1972. The velvet-covered car was an advertising gimmick. Sadly Hockey died of a heart attack following a five-a-side tournament in his home town of Keighley, near Bradford, in 1987 aged only forty-three.

sketches and cartoons of Norwich City team-mates – i.e. another joke at the expense of Tommy Bryceland's height – the ambitious striker had signalled his intent. He'd like to reach the first division with Norwich, 'but most of all I would like to get there'. By the time that annual was at the printer's, he'd signed for Southampton.

If you'd received more than one football annual for Christmas 1970, the chances were you'd read a fair bit about Ron Davies. In Jimmy Armfield's *All Stars* annual for that year, Ron was railing at the people who said he was always after a transfer. Trained as an architect, Davies maintained he'd be equally ambitious in that line of work too, a footballer's life being too short: 'Each season that passes is another nail in the coffin of the professional footballer; there is that much less time left.'

Over in the *London Soccer Annual* of the same year straight-talking Ron, THE MAN ON EVERY MANAGER'S SHOPPING LIST, was grumbling about having to live with a £200,000 price tag – or, rather, an incident where some bloke sitting behind his wife in the stand 'had a few rude words to say' when Davies mishit a shot. But, said Ron, 'it does not affect my play at all. If they go into the net, great, they go in. If they don't they don't and there is nothing you can do about it.'

Similarly he made no bones about leaving Southampton if he didn't have a contract to honour: 'If Ted Bates came to me tomorrow and said I can go, then obviously I would.' Looking back over his career, Davies told Peter Douglas: '"Chester . . . that was a depressing time," Ron recalls with a laugh. "There were tiny crowds who used to throw everything at you as soon as we ran out on the pitch. I think the club had to apply for re-election virtually every year. I couldn't wait to get away."' He liked the mild winters down on the south coast, and considered Southampton 'a clean, pleasant town, maybe a bit lacking in social life'. He'd had a run-in with a local newspaper, though, who rejected a series of his cartoon drawings of fellow players because they 'were too personal'. Ron pointed out that the definition of caricature was 'personal'.

All of which would be familiar to readers of a third publication that Christmas – *George Best's Soccer Annual No.3* – where Ron appeared to be having something of an existential crisis: SO MANY GOALS BUT WHERE HAVE THEY GOT ME? The actual gist of the article was that, despite his prolific strike rate, all his clubs – Chester, Norwich and now Southampton – seemed to be always struggling, or perennially involved in relegation battles. 'People sometimes ask me if I feel I owe any loyalty to my club,' he wrote. 'I usually tell them that such talk is as out of date as baggy shorts and Accrington Stanley. I owe my club 100 per cent effort – nothing short – in training and in matches. I owe it to them to score goals. Regularly. This I try to do. But I don't think any club should expect more than that. This is business. After all, if I failed to score all season I'd soon be pitched out of the team. There would be no loyalty to me then. Neither should there be.'[111]

Davies' brutal pragmatism would certainly have struck a chord. Abolition of the maximum of wage, freedom of contract, the ability to cash-in and open a boutique (or a

Aiming for the TOP by RON DAVIES

I THINK IT'S IMPORTANT THAT, NO MATTER WHAT YOUR JOB OR PROFESSION, YOU SHOULD ALWAYS AIM FOR THE TOP

90

111 Davies drifted through Portsmouth, Man United and Millwall before spells at Los Angeles Aztecs and Seattle Sounders in the seventies. He studied photography, and used his draughtsman's experience to stay in America, working in the construction industry and living in a trailer park with his wife, only hitting trouble when he required a replacement hip: 'I was told it would catch up with me. It's my left hip – the leg I took off on,' he was quoted in his *Guardian* obituary, May 2013.

" Another one trying to get away. It gets more like Carrow Road every day."

Top: Ron Davies, prolific star of football annuals, *All Stars* 1970

Left: Ron's cartooning skills on show in the *Topical Times Football Book* 1966

West Brom's John Talbut was a short-head winner here from Geoff Hurst (West Ham).

car showroom) – these obstacles had been overcome. England had even proved they were the best in the world again, by winning the World Cup – how could the future be made up of anything other than rosy gardens (and sombreros)?

But along with the explosion of football annuals in the late sixties and their riot of colour – Bobby Moore on the Wembley turf in the sunshine; the ice-blue tracksuited Franz Beckenbauer; Florian Albert in the cherry red of Hungary; Tostão and Pelé in Brazilian yellow – came a creeping sense of despair, powerfully encapsulated in the very black and white world of Ken Loach's film *The Golden Vision*.

First broadcast as *The Wednesday Play* in April 1968, *The Golden Vision* follows the ups and downs of a fictional bunch of Everton fans – namely their escape from the drudgery of dead-end jobs in a tyre factory; arrangements for getting to the match on Saturday ('You'll be in the ale house. Where will he be?' yells young Johnny Coyne's mum at Bill Dean[112], the future Harry Cross from *Brookside*, when it's suggested the nipper accompanies his dad – and the lads – down the motorway in the back of a furniture lorry for the away trip to Highbury); and pub talk concerning the best Goodison XI of all time. Filmed largely in the misty, bleak slum terraces around Gwladys Street, it's a moving piece of kitchen-sink realism, less well known than *Cathy Come Home* or *Poor Cow*, normally considered vintage Loach from that period.

What's fairly unusual about *The Golden Vision*, though, is that real-life documentary footage shot behind the scenes at Everton is intercut with the goings-on of Bill Dean and his mates. Not only are the fans filmed amidst the throng on the terrace during actual matches at Goodison (and Highbury), the camera is also there to record Alan Ball, that bobbing run only ever being halted when he's hacked down, and Jimmy Husband burying one from the right into the corner of the net. There's mist, gloom, mud, and a lone fluorescent strip light is switched on at the back of the stand as it gets dark in the second half. There's also great *cinéma vérité* training-ground footage of Wilf Dixon explaining that ball work has now replaced

112 He took his stage name from Dixie.

Alex Young

'Is it all worthwhile?' Young wonders during long afternoons

◇◇◇◇◇◇◇◇◇

'lapping', and yelling at the first team – which would have been clearly audible in people's back gardens just over the adjoining brick wall.

While Bill Dean's gang are knocking back bottles of ale, perched on crates in the back of the lorry, the Everton players are on the train travelling down to London. Ray Wilson tells the camera, 'The game's got so big, results mean everything. Everyone wants to play West Ham now, simply because you know you're going to get a good open game.' Brian Labone agrees; people are going out there, playing under pressure, good football is being sacrificed for results: 'You go away from home, you've got a point and the idea is to keep it. It's for the home team to come and take it off you. You get a point away from home – two points at home; one away – Championship form.' Keeper Gordon West suffers from nerves before a game. Later, over the footage at Highbury, Harry Catterick says that fans don't know the half of it, that West is actually sick prior to a match because he's so nervous. West himself wonders how many in the first division actually enjoy the game: 'I don't enjoy playing at all on a Saturday. From 3 o'clock on till twenty to five I can't wait for it to finish.'

But the camera lingers longest over Alex Young, the fair-haired centre-forward, the 'Golden Vision' himself. He's fairly downbeat about the hard, gritty professional life that he's not sure he likes. 'Is it all worthwhile?' he wonders during long afternoons. It's just a job, ultimately, one with a lot of insecurity attached. He enjoyed life more when he was working down the pit part-time, playing semi-professionally for Hearts. There was a sense of freedom then. Now he just drinks endless cups of tea, waits to pick his kids up from school (in the family Mini), and worries about how he'll find work, some kind of trade, after football. Things aren't so bad on the afternoons when he gets to coach the local school-kids – that's something he enjoys, and seems to add real meaning to his life.

There's no sense of joy here, and with players of the calibre of Alan Suddick, Peter Thompson and Ron Davies beginning to infuse the pages of football annuals with a mild strain of ennui, all was perhaps not as well as it's fondly remembered on the surface.

The *Midlands Soccer Annual* of 1969 ran what was,

Left: Even in the late sixties colour pages in the main annuals were few and generally held for full-page portraits or action shots such as this West Ham v WBA aerial clash in *Charles Buchan's Soccer*

***Gift Book*, 1969. In the background a young Harry Redknapp hides behind a young Clive Thomas. Above: Alex Young, eponymous star of Ken Loach's *The Golden Vision*, *Northern Soccer Annual*, 1969**

Hateley was often to be found, explaining away yet another move after just a season – from Chelsea to Liverpool to Coventry to Birmingham, and back again to Notts County

◇◇◇◇◇◇◇◇◇◇◇◇◇◇◇◇◇◇◇◇◇◇

Towering Notts County and Aston Villa centre-forward Tony Hateley was a name too, but as the shadows of the late 1960s lengthened into the seventies, Hateley was often to be found, in the pages of various annuals, explaining away yet another move after just a season – from Chelsea to Liverpool to Coventry to Birmingham, and back again to Notts County. Relegation battles, lack of crosses into the box, short-passing teams, defensive-minded teams, and injuries were all cited. Still, at least *Kenneth Wolstenholme's Book of World Soccer* tried to put a spin on things in their 1970 annual with the headline THE AMAZING STORY OF TONY HATELEY, choosing to focus on his combined transfer fees up front, and dealing with the misery and false starts and 'people murmuring something about "expensive failure"' towards the end of the piece.

Perhaps less well known was the tale of 'much travelled' Hugh Curran, another one let go by Manchester United as a youngster, who ended up back at Third Lanark in his homeland, before drifting further afield, back down to non-league Corby Town where he supported himself by working in the steelworks and becoming an MC and singer in a nightclub. 'The money was really good. I was really settled there. I was planning to get married and get a home and settle down,' Hugh told the *Midland Soccer Annual* of 1970. But then Millwall came calling, and before long Hugh was on the road again – to Norwich, Wolves, Oxford and Bolton. 'I leave it to fate,' he said, 'it has looked after me so far.' Back for a second spell at Oxford, Hugh slipped into running a pub, and today (according to Wikipedia) works at a local Oxfordshire park and ride.

Then there was the journeymen's journeyman of the 1960s, Hugh McIlmoyle. In the *Topical Times* annual of 1972–73 McIlmoyle mentioned how 'pleasantly surprised' he was, back in 1960, when Leicester City picked him up from Port Glasgow Juveniles. And before he knew where he was he was in digs with Frank

in effect, a kind of lower-league, regional version of Alex Young's tale: OLLIE CONMY TALKS OF LIFE IN THE FOURTH AT PETERBOROUGH. Peterborough was described as 'a grey, flat town', and Ollie was interviewed in a local coffee bar-cum-bowling alley, a lunchtime hangout for Posh players. Despite the 'ready smile when you get him talking' he moaned about training, being played out of position, the extra work entailed in being an assistant manager (should he become one), and always being hassled while out for a quiet drink. Described as having 'a touch of the Blanchflower about him' – four seasons at Huddersfield, 'mainly in the reserves' probably knocked that out of him – Ollie reckoned: 'After a while, you don't play any more for the glory. It's a job, with money. I don't know what I'd be doing right now if I wasn't in football.' Even the supporters, faced with 'teams coming here and playing eight or nine men back' were fondly reminiscing about the good old days when Peterborough were thrashing everyone 6–0 or 7–0 in the old Midland League.

Ollie played for Peterborough 263 times, until 1972. But the flip side of the disillusion suffered by bigger names like Suddick and Davies was the journeyman's tale.

Above: Footballing nomad Tony Hateley pops up in the *Topical Times Football Book* 1968
Right: The equally well travelled Hugh McIlmoyle in the *Topical Times* 1971

McLintock: 'Yes, the same one. Captain of the "double"-winning Arsenal, Scotland internationalist and last Footballer of the Year. Even in those far-off days I could see Frank was destined for the top. We used to sit in digs at night talking about the future. He could see I lacked ambition.' Then came a training ground incident where manager Matt Gilles pulled Hugh up in front of the rest of the players to tell him he was dropped: 'I could feel all the lads watching me. They knew! It was only a little thing but it did a lot of damage to my confidence. Today, ten years later, I know I should have fought back. Instead, I hung my head and moped off. Mr Gilles was a fine man, but I felt he didn't understand me. However, that's my problem, not his.' Ten years of intermittent loss of confidence, contractual fuck-ups, managerial moves later and it was '. . . Rotherham. That was a strange episode. I signed on the Tuesday for Tom Johnson. He left on the Thursday' – and life between the reserves and first team followed. After Leicester and seven games at Millmoor, Hugh took in Carlisle (for the first time), Wolves and then Bristol City where, he recalled:

> Fred Ford was in charge. A big man. Big Voice, Big personality. Everything about him was big . . . It's a fact that most games we tried to play out of range of the dug-out. But, even there, it was impossible to escape from Mr Ford's booming voice. A great fellow for City. Who was suddenly sacked one Monday! It wasn't long afterwards I was on my way too. I saw Carlisle had transferred Willie Carlin to Derby for £30,000. I mentioned it to my wife. We reflected on how content we'd been up there.

He's played in every English division – and on every league ground too . . .

THE SCOT WHO'S ALWAYS ON THE TROT

By HUGH McILMOYLE

95

At that moment the doorbell rang. It was a City official asking me to phone Tim Ward, Carlisle's manager. I signed for them in October 1967, for £22,000 . . .and decided Carlisle was where I'd stay for the rest of my career. Everything started well . . .

But before long Ward's team embarked on a twelve-game winless run to welcome the Brunton Park faithful into the new season. 'The crowd turned nasty. They broke into the ground, put creosote all over the pitch, then wrote across it, in white paint – "TIM WARD MUST GO".' Bob Stokoe arrived and pretty soon Hugh and his long-suffering wife were persuading Middlesbrough boss Stan Anderson that he could, in fact, commute daily from the Lake District to Teeside, but 'people warned me I couldn't go on living in Carlisle and playing for Boro. Finally, I decided to heed them. I shifted home to Middlesbrough. More fool me. We weren't happy on Teeside and it showed in my play.' It was back to Leicester for McIlmoyle, then Preston, and a third spell at Carlisle sandwiched between two spells at Morton . . . Hugh was beginning to make Tony Hateley look like part of the furniture.

Five years earlier, in the 1967–68 *Topical Times*, classical music loving Southend goalkeeper Ian McKechnie had penned a feature describing how he'd been let go by the Roots Hall club and, in search of a trial (or better still an offer), had written forty-four letters to all the clubs in the top two divisions without receiving a single reply. It seemed some interest, originally shown by third division outfits Millwall, Crystal Palace and Brighton a few years earlier, had cooled, and he couldn't quite face taking up an offer to play in Australia (preferring instead to stay in Southend). So McKechnie was delighted when Dartford got in touch wondering if he'd play for them in a friendly, the idea being that he would sign after the match. Shooting out the door on his way to Kent, McKechnie realized he'd forgotten a handkerchief – heading back indoors he discovered a telegram asking him to contact Hull City urgently . . .

McKechnie had originally been converted from a left-winger to a keeper in his early days at Highbury,

'Rotherham. That was a strange episode. I signed on the Tuesday for Tom Johnson. He left on the Thursday'

often finding himself between the sticks on summer tours. Wikipedia claims his performance in a friendly against the Swedish national team in 1961 was so good, pulling off numerous acrobatic saves in the air, that he got the nickname Yuri (Gagarin had recently been the first man in space). That wasn't the half of it, according to McKechnie in the *Topical Times*: feeling flushed after his superb display, he decided to put himself at the head of the Arsenal team queuing to enter the post-match official banquet. 'I marched past my team-mates and everyone else in the party, past the flunky [a footman in ceremonial garb on the door] and into the packed room. With my hands raised high to acknowledge the applause. I'd only got a few steps into the room when George Swindin came dashing after me. "Where do you think you are going?" he asked. "It's the directors

who go in first . . ." What a bloomer. And Arsenal are so particular about the way their players comport themselves,' added the keeper dolefully.

Billy Wright succeeded Swindin, and considered McKechnie too fat. McKechnie's mum heard this, and reasoned it must have been the 'tattie soup I send the big yin' weekly to his digs in London from Muirhead. Wright's 'crash diet designed to take off surplus pounds' didn't help much' and McKechnie was released . . . which was more or less where the article began.

SO DESPERATE TO GET A CLUB...

44 TIMES IAN WROTE THIS LETTER

IT'S thanks to a handkerchief that I'm playing for Hull City, one of the top teams in the Second Division - instead of for non-league club Dartford.

It all came about when I was freed by Southend . . .

That was three seasons ago. And what a shock the club's decision was to me. I was enjoying playing for them. And my family liked the life there.

Still, I decided not to let the situation get me down. Especially when a number of clubs were on to me almost immediately to sign for them.

Brighton, Millwall and Crystal Palace all showed an interest, but I decided to hold out for a club in the First or Second Division.

By IAN McKECHNIE—Hull City Goalkeeper

McKechnie decided to put himself at the head of the Arsenal team queuing to enter the post-match official banquet

◇◇◇◇◇◇◇◇◇◇◇◇◇◇◇◇◇◇◇◇◇

BACK IN the 1950s and early sixties most players' tales of such buffeting at the hands of fate were relayed in a similar, rueful style. Where there was a lightness of touch and a shrug of the shoulders in McIlmoyle's and McKechnie's re-telling, increasingly, in England and also in Europe, there was a creeping sense of darkness.

Christmas 1970 saw the twelfth edition of the *International Football Book* and Red Star Belgrade and Yugoslavia's free-flowing and utterly mesmerizing lanky left-winger Dragan Džajić reach the same conclusions as Alex Young (now at Stockport). In an article entitled FOOTBALL FOR LOVE OR MONEY?, Džajić railed at the violence of the Belgians in getting him sent off during a World Cup '70 qualifier for retaliation – 'Behind all the increasing violence are the bigger and bigger bonuses being paid . . . *if you win*. This is the basis of professionalism' – and the huge pressure on players to be entertainers: 'Thirty years ago the players played for peanuts and enjoyed every minute of it. This is still true for youngsters today . . .' but, he added, professionalism was so rife, so many playmakers were being attacked, kicked out of the game, that football was, in effect, dying: 'It's a business – brutal and hard . . . the future of the game itself is really black . . . it's easy to burn down an art gallery with a petrol bomb but it takes real talent to paint the pictures.' Big money was ruining sport: 'Time after time I sit in the changing room after a tough game and I feel ashamed to be part of it.'

A few pages on Károly Sós, the Hungary manager, believed the days of individual stars – Best, Eusébio, Pelé, Di Stéfano – were over; replaced by an all-consuming emphasis on teamwork: 'Do simple things quickly, do them well and run, run, run . . . youngsters want to enjoy their lives and the emphasis is on seeking pleasure. They can find it too . . . but not in football.' Football was too much like hard work; like a job.

But the *International Football Book* had been preoccupied with bad news for a while – and took things

Above: The ever-persistent Ian Mckechnie puts pen to paper in his quest for goalkeeping work, *Topical Times* **'67**

JOHN COHEN

We're less human than we think

by PROFESSOR JOHN COHEN
(Head of the Department of Psychology the University of Manchester)

John Cohen . . . 'Misuse of energy'

the problem of
VIOLENCE

LEO HORN

Action from FIFA, not just words

by LEO HORN
(Holland's World-famous referee)

Leo Horn . . . 'Who backs referees?'

FOOTBALL is one of the most refined and sublimated forms of organised aggression that man has invented, because in theory violence is directed against the ball and not against man. But that rule is now being denied by events.

Where does all this human aggressiveness, in football or anywhere else, come from? Part is inborn. If Man had been completely devoid of any aggressive impulse he would long ago have become extinct.

In football the energy concentrated in the leg and aimed at the ball can, at the slightest encouragement, turn into a vicious assault against another player.

Football reveals how much less human we all are than we imagine ourselves to be. Take the injured player. He is, perhaps, in great pain, but in the crowd there is no feeling of compassion, only: 'We are wasting time!'

THE biggest contributing factor behind the present wave of violence in football is the attitude of the clubs. There isn't enough discipline anywhere, on the playing pitches or on the terraces. And when someone attempts to impose order and discipline, the general attitude is that they must be wrong.

Among the fans, the majority are younger than they used to be, many between 16 and 20 years. Every country has its share of hooligans but no one yet has done anything about them. The hooligans control the terraces and the players dominate the referees!

Referees today are not strong enough. Afraid of the big stars, they are too easy on the players. But it would be unfair to blame the referees for this state of affairs. I know very well that the present attitude is that if you send off a star player an influential

---

further than Ken Dodd's appeal for Liverpool fans to stop smashing up British Rail rolling stock. In 1968 they wheeled in professor John Cohen, head of psychology at Manchester University, and Dutch referee Leo Horn, to confront THE PROBLEM OF VIOLENCE head on, in a sort of down-the-page split-screen debate (a column each). There was violence both on the pitch and in the crowd, coupled with shoddy behaviour in FIFA circles. Horn pointed out that he had continually pressed FIFA president Stanley Rous to instigate professional referees and international co-operation between the officials of competing countries in order to observe and breed understanding between the different cultures of the game, but, Horn added, 'between 1962 and 1966 FIFA did nothing to solve the problems. Sir Stanley Rous talked of the problems often, but he did nothing. Nothing that is, except to see that for the 1966 World Cup finals the referees had a room each – and that Leo Horn was not on the list of referees.' This was considered a mind-boggling decision back in Holland, and Dutch folk badgered Horn about it long into his retirement. 'I could offer no explanation, but not long ago the Royal Dutch FA Vice-President told me the reason. "It would [have been] an insult," he said . . . "to Sir Stanley Rous."'

Since sex and aggression are closely linked violence will more readily burst out when a player is caught up body and soul in the heat of the game

◇◇◇◇◇◇◇◇◇◇◇◇◇◇◇◇◇◇◇◇◇◇◇◇◇

Professor Cohen, meanwhile, noted that human beings would have been wiped out as a race if they didn't possess inherent anger; football being 'one of the most refined and sublimated forms of organised aggression that man has invented, because in theory violence is directed against the ball and not against man. But that rule is now being denied by events.'

'Umm, for sure,' you can envisage a few *International Football Book* readers nodding sagely, no doubt recalling Jack Charlton kicking someone, before Cohen added, 'Sex is another factor. As Freud remarked, it may be that nothing important can occur in a person without in some way invoking a degree of "sexualisation". Since

Above: The *International Football Book* 1968 takes the football world to task and adds some Freudian twists for good measure

SPLENDOUR DEDICATED TO ANTI-FOOTBALL

'Fouls used coldly as instrument of policy'

by BRIAN GLANVILLE
(*Novelist, and Sunday Times football writer*)

WHAT with the disgraceful episodes of the Celtic-Racing World Club Final matches, and Pelé's professed intention not to compete in the 1970 World Cup, there have been signs that football may be set on a collision course; that international competition may sink in a welter of violence.

It has all long gone far beyond a joke, just as Soccer itself has long transcended – or fallen beneath – the limits of a game. The circumstances of Pelé's renunciation are worth examining, the more so as he himself has been the advocate of retaliatory violence as a means of pacifying aggressive defenders.

Vicente Feola, Brazil's team manager, advised him on these lines, he says, in 1959, and he has been grateful ever since. Yet his determination not to play in 1970 – my own feeling is that he will change his mind – indicates that the policy has been unsuccessful.

It did not, after all, prevent him from being kicked out of the 1966 World Cup, first by Zetchev of Bulgaria, then by the still more ruthless Morais. On each occasion, Pelé had pitifully little protection from a weak English referee. The Morais fouls will stick in the mind of all who saw them, either in actuality, or in the film 'GOAL!', when a 'frozen frame' allowed one to see them in all their brutal premeditation.

Spurs' Cliff Jones, bloodied, his head gashed, is helped off – 'There are signs that football is on a collision course,' says Brian Glanville.

'The violence involved is essentially motiveless, free-floating violence, looking for an outlet and an opportunity' – One such opportunity seemed to be afforded by this young Manchester United fan, being treated for a head wound at Bramall-lane.

Pelé himself was deeply influenced by the film; he has said that until he watched it, he was prepared to believe that the fouls had been unintentional. In that case, the poor fellow must have been the only man in Goodison Park that evening to think so.

As for the Racing-Celtic Finals, they were an example of what cynical provocation can finally achieve, when it goes to work on sufficiently combustible material. There can be no excuse, though there may be valid explanations, for the behaviour of some of the Celtic players in the play-off in Montevideo; for Hughes first punching then kicking the Racing goalkeeper, for Gemmell running up to kick an opponent, for Auld assaulting another.

But, by the same token, Cejas, the assaulted goalkeeper, had himself run forty yards to kick little Johnstone in the ribs when he was lying injured – under the guise of commiserating with him, while Johnstone, at half-time, was obliged to wash the spittle out of his hair.

This disgusting habit – one Racing player, Rodriges, early in the game in Montevideo, deliberately spat in the face of all four Celtic backline defenders – is proof enough that Racing were bent on provocation. And when one reaches this point, one asks oneself whether the game is worth the candle. What earthly object is there in playing these matches at all when certain countries approach them as they would approach a war?

Violence by spectators comes into another category; or rather, into two categories. One must differentiate between the sort of barbarism which has been traditional, say, at Rangers-Celtic matches throughout the century, the sort of violence which led to 44 deaths at a Turkish Second Division match in September, 1967, and the kind which leads spectators to set about one another on the terraces.

This last phenomenon has, in essence, nothing to do with football at all; it has simply chosen football as its context. The violence involved is essentially motiveless, free-floating violence, looking for an outlet and an opportunity. It might be regarded as the revenge of ungifted, 'underprivileged' youth on an affluent society which has no real place for them.

Peter Terson's lively and interesting musical play, *Zigger Zagger*, so well performed by the National Youth Theatre in 1967, summed it up perfectly. Zigger Zagger himself, half-Pan, half-Machiavelli, the malign sprite of the terraces behind the City

105

---

sex and aggression are closely linked violence will more readily burst out when a player is caught up body and soul in the heat of the game.'

The accompanying photos showed Arsenal's Ian Ure about to lead with his arm into Denis Law's face.

Then Cohen elaborated: 'The satisfactions which players derive from football seem to bear some likeness to the sequence of pleasures in sex. There is the foreplay, the mounting tension and finally an explosive climax. When a goal is scored there is a vast detumescent relief. No wonder the word "sport" once meant "amorous dalliance". Anyone keyed to a high pitch of excitement can fly into a fury if things go wrong.'[113] Cohen went on to pinpoint the loss of identity in a crowd as likely to lead to a mass orgy of violence too, and poured withering scorn on Rous's suggestion that tickets for big games 'should be issued through schoolmasters, youth leaders and sports organisers – only to people they know to be responsible.' That, Cohen argued, might lead the 'debarred' ones to 'take it out on the community as a whole'. If we accept that, like sex, violence is an innate human condition, we should be able to deal with it better, seemed to be the gist of the piece; hooligans were

just 'indulging in more emotions than they are able to bear [but] if people are treated like human beings they are more likely to behave as such'. That clearly fell on deaf ears, but still, Cohen concluded, 'My crystal ball tells me that the greatest days of football are yet to come.'

Those tales of Bert Sproston's kitbag and Bishop Auckland winning the Amateur Cup final again suddenly seemed a long way off.

Over the page Brian Glanville reported on the Racing Club Buenos Aires v Celtic World Club final, marred by violence and spitting (Rattín –'a splendid footballer dedicated to anti-football'), and illustrated with a photograph of a bloodied youngster/yob in a duffel coat at Bramall Lane (*above*) before referring readers to Peter Terson's 1967 National Youth Theatre play *Zigger Zagger* for further exploration and understanding of mindless terrace violence.

There were echoes here of a debate in *David Coleman's World of Football Annual* from 1969 when socialist, Methodist minister Lord Soper and Labour sports minister Denis Howell discussed whether football was actually 'a drug of the people'. Soper recommended watching football only once a fortnight: 'I think the addiction to watching football is part of the malaise of a spectator generation [a troublesome

---

113 Desmond Morris must have been taking notes.

Above: Brian Glanville explores mindless violence on and off the pitch in the *International Football Book 1968*

Right: *David Coleman's World of Football* 1969 wades in on football's contribution to an increasingly dysfunctional society

by-product of an increasingly affluent society, according to Soper, who bemoaned the coming new pagan age] . . . what really is insufferable today is the condition in which television, motor cars, motor cycles, money, are flung at people, at youngsters in particular, when they have no resistance to them.' Denis Howell thought we'd moved on from sport being the opium of the masses, but called for all-weather surfaces, and a shared leisure service that incorporated the use of school facilities for young adults in the evening: 'The nation that doesn't provide for its youth to get rid of its energies in a healthy manner surely buys trouble for itself.'

I N A separate article, a few pages earlier Howell (now sports minister but formerly a league referee) had paraphrased President Johnson's remark 'all the great virtues of our civilization appear on the back page of our newspapers' and stressed the need for the ball player in the modern game, 'because if the game is reduced to nothing but rushing and doing everything twice as fast, it's going to lose a lot, and you want someone who can hold the ball, and open up, and set the pre-arranged pattern of the game.'

The snuffing out of the creative playmaker was clearly a concern for all at *David Coleman's World of Football*. The same 1969 annual carried fairly revealing portraits of George Best and Chelsea's Charlie Cooke. Best offered a perceptive reading of the game

that some would no doubt have construed as arrogant. When asked how he beat people, he replied, 'I haven't a clue . . . it just happens,' before going on to express borderline contempt for the overly defensive state of the current game: 'If a fellow has to kick me it means he's not as good as I am. So, I feel sorry for some players. I could play the way some full-backs play against me. If someone said to me, "Go and follow him all over the place," I could follow someone around for an hour and a half and make sure they didn't get a kick. I think it's the easiest thing in the world to do. I feel sorry for people who are told to do it.' He claimed he didn't particularly admire any of his peers – in fact, there was only one footballer in his book: Alfredo Di Stéfano.

Charlie Cooke, 'being a "skill player"' also found himself 'rather disgruntled' at the close attention of the opposition:

Just the thought that some guy can go in there and do nothing, yet make sure that *you* do nothing . . . It seems terrible

'The nation that doesn't provide for its youth to get rid of its energies in a healthy manner surely buys trouble for itself'

◇◇◇◇◇◇◇◇◇◇◇◇◇◇◇◇◇◇◇◇◇◇◇◇◇◇

should be used by pupils in the daytime and the adult community afterwards. Administration has to be geared to it. The cry is that the playing surfaces suffer. Well, all-weather surfaces should be put down. And flood-lighting. It would be much cheaper in the long run than having all these wonderful conveniences shut down just when everyone wants to use them. The hour at which we close down our public parks is a nonsense.

A beer can, a frightened face, and a surge of police helmets . . . "Those who watch are escaping from the responsibility of playing."

Published by IPC Specialist and Professional Press Ltd, 161 Fleet Street, London EC4P 4AA, printed by Chapel River Press, Andover, Hants, and distributed by IPC Business Press (Sales and Distribution) Ltd, 40, Bowling Green Lane, London, E.C.1. © IPC

that all the work you may have put in over the years should be negated by some guy like that. So you've got to start working hard and get rid of the guy, tire him out, run all over the field and kill him, so you're killing yourself. And then you get the ball at your feet, and you're supposed to be good at doing this, but you've got no energy left to do it, you know . . .

Either David Coleman or Norman Harris (the latter variously billed as 'reporter' or 'researcher' on the annuals, but who no doubt wrote plenty if not all of the articles) wondered if being intricate and tricky 'without actually creating chances' might lead to a vicious spiral in which Cooke berated himself for his lack of goals, then suffered another loss of confidence and form. Cooke confessed he'd much rather give the ball to someone else: 'I'm, maybe, dodging the responsibility of putting it in the net . . .'[114]

A year later Cooke did, of course, supply the sublime ball – a slow-motion 1970 version of Daley Blind to Robin Van Persie, only with mud and yellow socks

114 '[If the football is] messy it doesn't appeal to Cooke any more,' wrote Paul Trevillion in his *Coleman* movie profiles, '. . . he is the matinee idol; the only man who can play football and not break into a sweat. He's the nearest thing we've got to Cary Grant.'

'A large part of [Leeds United's] success in the early days was attributed by some to what might euphemistically be called tough play'

◇◇◇◇◇◇◇◇◇◇◇◇◇◇◇◇◇◇

– to Peter Osgood that turned the FA Cup final replay round in Chelsea's favour just as, according to David Coleman's BBC commentary, 'Leeds were stifling the life out of it.'

Leeds United. 'A large part of their success in the early days was attributed by some to what might euphemistically be called tough play,' wrote Eamon Dunphy in the *Northern Soccer Annual* of 1970, adding that the cultured John Giles had become 'a harder player' since moving to Elland Road. Revie himself would usually be found in annuals of the day uttering sentiments along the lines of 'I am not saying we always behaved like angels on the field' while railing about southern

Above: Terry Cooper of Leeds and Everton's John Hurst in an uncompromising challenge on the endpapers of the 1973 *Goal* annual

bias to his 'close-knit family' and forever protesting that their reputation for defensiveness had been over-played – that that kind of thing was only necessary to reach division one in the first place.[115]

In the *Northern Soccer Annual* of 1969 Terry Cooper attempted to distinguish between a hard team (Leeds) and a dirty team (not Leeds). His line of defence consisted entirely of 'if you look carefully, our opponents always get up after a tackle'.

By 1971's *Soccer, The International Way* annual Cooper was feeling bolder, but was equally unconvincing when it came to backing up the claim BRITISH FOOTBALL IS BEST, (see inset) failing to provide any substance, depth or detail explaining exactly why all his Leeds mates and the England '66 team were 'the best'. In a lengthy list, he supplied a eulogy to the fighting spirit of the wee man Bobby Collins and informed us that while 'Nobby Stiles and Dave Mackay may not have won the hearts of fans all over the world, they, like my Elland Road colleague Billy Bremner, believe that football is a game for men – and they prove it by putting every ounce of energy into everything they do.' The best winger in the world who'd given him trouble? – Léon Semmeling of Standard Liège received a nod, but Mike Summerbee of Manchester City and Keith Dyson of Newcastle came out on top.

Still, the grammar-school boy who wanted a bit more first-team action and so fled big Don's coop – Jimmy Greenhoff – told the *Midland Soccer Annual* of 1970 that 'Leeds is a certainly a unique club when it comes to looking after its players' and that he particularly missed the pre-match bingo sessions with the Elland Road lads.

That uniqueness was perhaps a reference to Revie's hands-on nature, and the all-encompassing provision for players. *David Coleman's World of Football* annual reported that Revie commissioned 'experts to lecture the club's young professionals on subjects ranging from sex to etiquette' and the same feature included a sickly account of tears in the dressing room followed by a discussion of the meaning of the word 'loyalty' on the occasion of Don deciding not to jump ship to Roker Park because he couldn't bear to leave his boys behind. Such was the team ethic that all the players gathered in a vacant hotel

---

115 Which was not quite how Derek Hammond, author of *Got, Not Got* and *The Lost World of Football*, saw it: 'They were a hateful team – victory at any cost. Leeds did employ, very early on, the PR tactic of waving at the crowd and giving things away. That was incredibly cynical. Clough was right: they were a foul side who should have given their medals back. But they won . . .'

◇◇◇◇◇◇◇◇◇◇◇◇◇◇◇◇◇◇◇◇◇◇◇◇◇◇◇◇◇◇◇◇◇◇◇

Soccer, The International Way was more parochial than an annual purporting to have a world view should be, but did feature Brazil's Edu being asked if he thought it 'important that man should reach the moon' (answer: yes, God meant man to better himself), and whether he was in favour of the Vietnam war. Disappointingly, in true footballer-style-to-come, he dodged the bullet and observed the war 'was occasioned by boundary or frontier disputes'. He was appalled at racial discrimination in the States though, and was in favour of divorce and sex education for kids.

A few pages on from that Brian Glanville could be found, raging at coin-tossing and the away-goals rule to settle cup ties: 'That way, fiasco lies.' He also noted, in an article entitled 'On Falsifying Football', that 'a fashionable but rather silly method of decision is that of taking penalty kicks . . . better again than the toss of a coin, but what has such a contest *in parvo* got to do with the realities of the match?'

Completely impenetrable was a ten-page article 'Going Metric' – 'a glance forward and a longer look backward at football pitch dimensions and markings'. Tucked away at the back of the annual Leslie Page's discussion of the changes in pitch dimensions stretching back as far as 1863, and taking in the contrast between Cambridge and FA rules, really was one for those seeking to avoid any human contact after Christmas dinner (and perhaps for a while longer).

The 1971 annual did contain a great photograph of the crowd at Field Mill spilling on to the pitch and preventing Leicester's Len Glover from taking a corner (below) as well as a lovely double-page spread, 'A February Day In British Football', featuring action from Valentine's Day 1970: thick snow at both the Victoria Ground, as Stoke took on Wolves, and at White Hart Lane (Jack Charlton tugging at Alan Gilzean's shirt); and Ayr's game against St Johnstone was one of only two to survive the weather north of the border.

◇◇◇◇◇◇◇◇◇◇◇◇◇◇◇◇◇◇◇◇◇◇◇◇◇◇◇◇◇◇◇◇◇◇◇

'Bremner,' observed Ipswich boss Bobby Robson, 'is no longer trying to put people on the deck and as a result he is a better player than ever'

◇◇◇◇◇◇◇◇◇◇◇◇◇◇◇◇◇◇◇◇◇

The FOOTBALL COLLEGE at ELLAND ROAD

Walking into the club for the first time is a great moment. I came down from Scotland with Mr Revie. Seen here arriving on his own is new boy Bob Robertson.

And here's Bob having a chat with the boss. Mr Revie makes a point of an early yarn with all apprentices. Nice and friendly—it means a lot.

KEEP FIGHTING
HOME TEAM

Keep fighting. It could be our motto. The sign is above the home dressing-room door.

Apprentices are always made to feel important in the set-up. Here Billy Bremner and Johnnie Giles (right) pass on tips. I owe a lot to Bobby Collins for advice he gave me as a raw recruit.

suite the night before a game to play the bingo fondly recalled by Jimmy Greenhoff, as well as indoor bowls. Meanwhile back at Elland Road a hundred-strong workforce would be busy either removing or replacing the straw on the pitch between matches – all were 'paid 5/- an hour and treated by Leeds United to a Saturday evening dinner at a local fish and chip shop'.

Norman Hunter and Jack Charlton touched upon pre-match routines in the *Coleman* annual. In Hunter's case that involved picking up a ball and hurling it at Billy Bremner before every game: 'don't know why me, it's just that I did it once, and the Boss saw this, and he made me keep doing it, every game.' Charlton recounted a dressing routine (bandages first, followed by left boot, then right) that also involved leaving the match-day programme 'face down on the floor of the toilet if we're playing away, face up if we're at home'. On a winning streak the repeated patterns of behaviour could 'build up', and he reflected that 'yes, it could get to the stage where there is so much [ritual] to do you haven't got time to play the match!' It wasn't because they really believed in magic, just that it settled the mind: 'Otherwise you might worry about a mistake, and wonder if it was caused by something you hadn't done, and not feeling settled, and drive yourself mad with it . . . but as soon as we lose, then we start from scratch again.'

Between Leeds' first title win in 1969 and their repeat performance in 1974, opinion, in the annuals at least, did begin to soften, and respect was often more than grudging. Even a progressive thinker such as Gordon Jago, manager of going-places QPR, was won over, pointing out in *David Coleman's* 1974 annual that, having ditched their gamesmanship, they were now 'a delight to watch', and Joe Mercer, also known for the sparkle of his attacking side at Manchester City, praised their 'iron framework' which allowed for 'individual and self-expression. They've got consistency with flair.' 'Bremner,' observed Ipswich boss Bobby Robson, 'is no

longer trying to put people on the deck and as a result he is a better player than ever.'

But reading Jack Charlton's glowing account of his former team-mates' accuracy of passing, both long and short, you'd think he'd been watching Ajax. He spoke of Revie giving the team 'freedom to go forward at every opportunity' and of defenders joining the attack at will, others dropping back to fill in their spaces. 'This is the way I try to get Middlesbrough to play,' he added. Strange, then, that by 1977 he was fighting off accusations of overly dour football following another low-scoring season in charge at Ayresome Park: 'Only ignorant people call us boring,' he commented in the *Shoot!* annual of 1978, while defending an unadventurous 4–4–2 as the best formation for 'the players we have'. (The Republic of Ireland's European Championship and World Cup adventures under Charlton fall considerably outside the heyday of the football annual . . .)

THE CONFLICTING currents of the beautiful game (as practised by long-haired ball-players) and a brutal pragmatism course through the football annuals of the late sixties and 1970s, but are perhaps best encapsulated

Above: Eddie Gray, Don Revie and company welcome Bob Robertson into the Leeds United family, *Topical Times Football Book* 1970

Following pages: Leeds United – successful, innovative but not universally loved, *Topical Times Football Book* 1973

by Eamon Dunphy in *Only a Game?* The Millwall mid-fielder wrote of the joyless experience of playing Leeds – something that was particularly grim, airless and suffocating for a skilful ball-player such as himself. Leeds marked you so tightly you couldn't take a throw-in. But it wasn't long into his book, first published in 1976, before he was disabusing any dreamers of the notion that the midfield, in the second division in England in the 1970s, was any place for a playmaker – the intensity, the battle for breathing space, was so ferocious there was no time to dwell on the ball for a second. 'Take Johnny Haynes,' wrote Dunphy. 'They used to say, "What a great player he is at finding space." The reason he was able to find space was that when his opposite number had the ball, Haynes was nowhere near him. He was thirty yards away, waiting for the attack to break down so that he could have the ball. Of course he found space.' Dunphy then deconstructed eye-catching Wednesday playmaker Tommy Greig's contribution – 'if he had the desire, application and courage to go out there and play for ninety minutes, he would be a hell of a player. But he doesn't.' Greig wasn't willing to suppress his creative play to chase and harry, to concentrate on running and ball-winning – unlike Dunphy: 'I had a choice to make . . . and I chose to be a bit of a rusher around rather than a cool "put your foot on it" man. By Millwall standards I've perhaps still been a "put your foot on it" man, but for me the game is now 90 per cent effort and 10 per cent do it on the ball. I don't particularly love it that way, but that is the way it has to be . . . you cannot beat them, you have to join them.'

◇◇◇◇◇◇◇◇◇◇◇◇◇◇◇◇◇◇◇◇◇◇◇◇◇◇◇◇◇◇◇◇◇◇

Leeds weren't the only superstitious team. Ian Hutchinson (right) had revealed to the *Topical Times* in 1970–71, that the reason the Chelsea dressing room at Wembley in the 1970 FA Cup final looked 'like a hippy commune' was due to a long-standing vow the team had taken not to cut their hair following atrocious luck in a 5–2 defeat against Leeds in January 1970.

John Hollins made sure he was the one to pin the team-sheet to dressing-room wall before every match; Dave Sexton, when defiantly not replacing his jacket top button (lost during the third-round victory over Birmingham), was busy handing out 'lucky' wishbones before the semi-final at Watford; Peter Houseman wore his 'lucky' suit for the same occasion; and throughout the Cup run the players, when not fretting over the correct order in which they ran out on to the pitch, were insistent that right-back Irishman Paddy Mulligan was present in the dressing room whether he was in the squad or not, because he'd been there at the start and 'we looked on him as a lucky charm'.

Obviously the luck of old Paddy Mulligan won out over that of Don Revie's suit. (Mulligan was in the team that lost to Stoke City in the League Cup final a couple of years later, though.)

◇◇◇◇◇◇◇◇◇◇◇◇◇◇◇◇◇◇◇◇◇◇◇◇◇◇◇◇◇◇◇◇◇◇

Manager Don Revie

THE REVIE MEN

Allan Clarke

David Harvey

Mick Jones

OF LEEDS ★ ★

Johnny Giles

Peter Lorimer

Billy Bremner

Bobby Moore's *Book of Football* in 1970 opens with the tale of Joe Payne, 'boilerman at a Luton factory . . . hardly the sort of chap you would expect to find in soccer's hall of fame' who scored ten of the goals in Luton's Easter Monday 1936 trouncing of Bristol Rovers 12–0. More remarkable was the fact this was the first time he'd played centre-forward – and goes on to remember Ted Drake's seven against Aston Villa while injured; Dixie Dean's record haul in a season, as well as Johnny Summers (pictured), the Charlton left-winger almost dropped following a lean spell who changed his boots at half-time – Charlton were 5–1 down at home to Huddersfield on a damp and cold December afternoon in 1957 – only to re-emerge and score five in the second half. Charlton eventually won 7–6. Summers sadly died five years later of cancer, aged only 34.

◇◇◇◇◇◇◇◇◇◇◇◇◇◇◇◇◇◇◇◇◇◇◇◇◇◇◇◇◇◇◇

The regional *Soccer Annuals* were obviously lighter and fluffier than this – chances were you'd be more likely to find yourself reading an encounter with Terry Hennessey relaxing and playing his Tony Bennett LPs in his new bungalow in Rutland – but this emphasis on the midfield[116], and in turn a debate about the soul of the game, did seep through into the pages of the Pelham books (and others). In the *Midland Soccer Annual* of 1970 Noel Cantwell talked engagingly of Malcolm Allison's contribution under Ron Greenwood's progressive

set-up at West Ham. In the days before the fedora, camel car coats and cigars, Allison's enthusiasm and love of talking about the game spurred on a generation of managers, including Cantwell, Frank O'Farrell, Dave Sexton and, of course, Allison himself. But Dunphy pushed Cantwell into conceding that West Ham gambled too much, playing their way out of defence, and that as a manager Cantwell confessed he was more of a realist and less of an idealist, although he too encouraged players to be involved, talking tactics. He worried, though, that 'outside interests' turned players' heads and they didn't talk about and love the game as much as they used to. (Cantwell was probably fighting a losing battle – as routine modern-day footage of team coaches pulling up outside a ground, each player with his own headphones clamped on, would suggest.)

In that year's *London Soccer Annual*, Bobby Moore, wrote,[117] 'Show me a half-back and I'll show you a team.' In a thoughtful piece probing the balance between attack and defence in midfield – how to develop a sense of reading the game – Moore's ultimate message was: 'If the team do not control the middle of the field they will not control the game and therefore they will not win . . .'

A staple of many a football annual, especially from the mid-seventies onwards, was the GOALS, GOALS, GOALS (AND MORE GOALS) feature. Most people involved with football today will still hear themselves (or someone else) say, 'At the end of the day, if you don't put it in the back of—' at least once a week. But if you were looking for something a little less reductive, the football annuals of yesteryear contained plenty of insight on the other nine or ten positions on the pitch – especially midfield. Tony Currie told *Shoot! Annual* in 1974 that, while he idolized Jimmy Greaves, it was manager John Harris who'd made him a far better player by pulling him back into midfield at Bramall Lane; Peter Lorimer discussed the return of the winger in the *International Football Book* in 1973; and in the same volume Steve Perryman identified the great playmakers of Europe, Milan's Gianni Rivera and Jovan Aćimović of Red Star Belgrade. While Alan Mullery,

---

116 Over the page, Tommy Steele acknowledged goals were important, but, 'The thing is to go and see the thought that goes into midfield play. In these days of 4–2–4 and all that sort of thing, the midfield play is the thing, for my money, that's really exciting.' His man-of-the-people assertion that being subsumed in a 50,000-strong football crowd was far preferable to 'sipping champagne and having an occasional flutter with that horrible gentleman at the rails', or the stifling atmosphere of tea at Lords, beefs up any credentials weakened by the singer of 'I Puts The Lightie On' using the phrase 'that sort of thing'.

117 It was actually text reproduced from the *Soccer With the Stars* LP.

Terry's modern home at Ruddington

Dunphy pushed Cantwell into conceding that West Ham gambled too much, playing their way out of defence

◇◇◇◇◇◇◇◇◇◇◇◇◇◇◇◇◇◇◇◇◇◇◇

Jago still encouraged players to speak up, Dutch-style, and dismissed the need for an out-and-out ball-winner: 'There are more problems stemming in English football from lack of technique than anything else. You know, we in England had to become good tacklers because our technique and control are so poor. Players have had to win the ball back all the time … the joy for me would be one-touch football – because nobody would get a tackle in. The ball would be flowing all the time. But that's a dream that will never be realised.'[119]

Plenty of annuals also praised Everton's young trio of Howard Kendall, Colin Harvey[120] and Alan Ball, the midfield engine room behind Everton's 1970 league championship. Bobby Moore's *Book of Soccer* that year took readers through Harry Catterick's dismantling of the Cup-winning side of '66 and the bringing through of youngsters (Harvey) and marrying them up with signings such as Ball and Kendall (see Everton inset overleaf). That year's championship is usually recalled as Leeds' loss amidst a fixture pile-up, but apparently Don Revie was first to the post office with his 'heartiest congratulations. You are true champions' telegram. Catterick's response in the *Book of Soccer* was to the point: 'We have struck a blow for freer expression in the game and proved that you don't have to have assassins in your side to win success. We don't have anybody nobbling key players to get a result.'

It's tempting, but perhaps simplistic, to view West Ham and Leeds as opposing poles in the spectrum of 1970s football, forces for good and evil respectively. At different times Spurs and Fulham could equally slot into West Ham's shoes; the *Goal* annual in 1973 ran an article looking at how West Ham and Spurs were united in flair as a reaction to 'functionalism and work-rate' that

famous around that time for being the first England player to be sent off in an international – after kicking Yugoslavia's Dobrivoje Trivić in the groin during the European Championships of 1968 – hit the nail on the head in *David Coleman's World of Football* annual in 1969: 'You can be running around like a madman and doing everything, laying goals on, laying passes on, helping people back in defence and heading the ball off the line – and it's the person who knocks the ball in the back of the net who gets the mention.'[118] Both Mullery and Bobby Charlton – described in the adjacent article as 'the White Knight' ('something to do with purity … of performance and behaviour. And something to do with remoteness') – got as much satisfaction from helping the team with a great pass as they did from scoring.

And in the *Coleman* annual of 1974, Gordon Jago, widely considered to have brought a breath of fresh air to the first division with QPR's 'abundance of zest, flair and enthusiasm ' foresaw the death of the striker – or at least an increase in goals from midfield, and even from gifted defenders – three decades before any talk of false number nines. Despite replacing Rodney Marsh with Stan Bowles,

---

118 Andrea Pirlo was still making the same point half a century later: 'Without the final pass, there wouldn't be a goal, but I don't get angry if people forget that fact when they fill out their [Ballon d'Or] ballot paper,' he wrote in his autobiography, *I Think Therefore I Play*. 'The assist is a mere footnote.'

119 Jago took QPR to within a point of winning the league championship in 1976, before spending time at the Den then in America. In the same article he recalled the time the QPR kit-man packed the wrong kit – summer short-sleeve shirts – for a bitterly cold afternoon at Elland Road in December 1973. 'It was farcical because we'd even taken the precaution of taking gloves. You can imagine how ridiculous we'd have looked going out in short-sleeve shirts and gloves. We didn't dare.'

120 He collected Motown records.

Left: A photo of Terry Hennessy's modest abode brings the *Midland Soccer Annual* 1969 to a downbeat close

Above: 'Noel Cantwell – the quiet man of soccer!' says the ironic caption in *Midland Soccer Annual* 1970

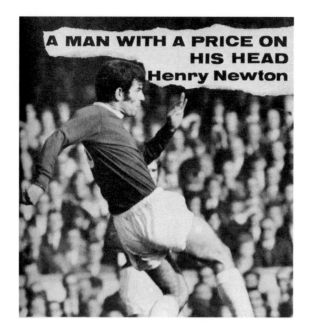

A MAN WITH A PRICE ON HIS HEAD
Henry Newton

Everton were frequently the toast of the heyday of the football annual. In an article in the *All Stars* annual of 1972, Henry Newton talked of leaving Forest to 'join the best team in the land' but found himself in and out of the first team at Goodison Park and playing out of position at left-back. Knowing other names were in the reserves – including Jimmy Husband, Keith Newton, whose left-back role Henry Newton had taken now and again, and even Brian Labone – 'I was able to melt into the overall pattern, so to speak, because there were so many players of great reputation finding that times had changed for them.' Which was an elegant way of putting it. (Another of Catterick's tasks was converting 'Chinese food addict' Joe Royle into a filled-out steak eater: 'I tried them, pushed them down. Now I'm off the Chinese. Steaks I love. And I AM stronger, fitter and better able to look after myself,' Royle told the *Topical Times* in 1970.)

worked through the personnel of both teams, past and present – winger Harry Redknapp was described as having the speed and trickery of Peter Brabrook; Trevor Brooking as the new Ronnie Boyce[121]; Martin Peters in possession of 'the same subtle qualities as Danny Blanchflower'. Ray Wilson's claim (on the train down to London in *The Golden Vision*) that everyone wanted to play West Ham is backed up in the football annuals of the time – best encapsulated by wild-eyed comedian Marty Feldman, who told *David Coleman's World of Soccer* annual in 1969 that he only went to watch attractive teams, advocates of intelligent play. Only the beautiful game would suffice for Marty: 'I'd sooner see West Ham lose by 8 than see Arsenal win by 1.'

Opening up a copy of the 1968 *International Football Book* readers would have come across Leeds' Billy Bremner, saying footballers like that Eusébio fella are all well and good (if only they could let go of the ball), but ask them to track back and you'll likely receive short shrift.

But after that preamble came the heavy stuff: a nine-page editorial on 'the Third Man Theory', hitherto kept under wraps but practised by the likes of Helenio Herrera at Inter Milan, Béla Guttmann at Benfica,

Albert Batteux of Rheims and St Etienne, and Ron Greenwood at West Ham. 'On the pattern elsewhere, it would therefore seem safe to predict that West Ham will win not one but *several* Football League Championships in the next few years,' they trumpeted[122]. Their theory had come to light after some forensic replaying of film: the BBC cameras at Wembley in July 1966 had picked up 'something interesting', namely that 'more often than not it was the West Ham men in England's World Cup-winning team who were directing the running off the ball by their team-mates . . .' employing specialist knowledge gleaned from their boss, a tactic only briefly glimpsed hitherto on these shores with Arthur Rowe's push and run Spurs side. The *International Football Book* pressed further, bringing up talk of 'the third man' in conversation with both Herrera and Batteux, but both apparently became 'vague and evasive' during interviews. It was noted that despite Béla Guttmann being

---

121 Forever the unsung hero – as on the pitch, so it was in annuals of the sixties: Ron was always there, in the background, stitching it all together. The *London Soccer Annual* of 1969 noted that Boyce tended to pass unnoticed, despite (or maybe because of) his versatility, and his phenomenal ability to read the game. He was also an avid reader of football literature on long away trips on the coach.

122 *International Football Book* italics. Perhaps Tony Stratton-Smith, editor of the *International Football Book* and founder of Charisma records, had been ordering too many 'flowers' on the Van der Graaf Generator expense account. In the course of researching this book I only found one avid reader of the *International Football Book*. Steve Smith's mum, in Bristol, was a Kay's Catalogue rep in the mid-1970s and the distinctive smaller format hardback became a Christmas staple from that point on. 'It would be in the book section at the back of the catalogue. I only read the English stuff, though,' says Steve. Which was, admittedly about 50 per cent of the annual at that point. 'Man City, Newcastle, Arsenal, Liverpool were all quite prominent then. I remember reading about Malcolm Macdonald, Dave Watson, Peter Barnes, that sort of thing.'

Right: An article by West Ham fan David Squires in *David Coleman's World of Football* 1970 bemoans his side's 'mixture of sheer genius and comic opera'

'already semi-retired' he attended the World Cup in 1966 'disguised by dark glasses', before saying to the *IFB*, presumably out of the side of his mouth, 'I will show you everything,' and cryptically adding, 'But I cannot let you see *with my eyes* . . . part of the secret is having players running off the ball to create space, but it's difficult to explain. It's better to show you in practice.' The editorial noted that running off the ball was hardly new – 'even FA coaches recognise its value, but don't really know how [best to employ] it', linking players together so that 'skilled players appear to be telepathic', just like the Hungarians of legend. *IFB*'s search led them to two coaching manuals written by Arpád Csanádi, 'a senior man in the Hungarian coaching system . . . but though both volumes were studied from cover to cover they seemed, initially, to contain no final, blinding truth about Hungary's football superiority.' Not so, said Ron Greenwood: 'It's all in the two published books *if you can recognise it.*' To paraphrase the denouement of this mystery thriller: essentially, where an English coach would interpret Csanádi's exercises as being for developing skill alone; in Hungary equal emphasis was put on the movement, place-changing, the developing of space *simultaneously*. Essentially, as the *International Football Book* chose to emphasise in capital letters, 'POSITIONAL SWITCHING, ONCE THOUGHT TO BE A HAPHAZARD ELEMENT, BROUGHT TO A DISCIPLINED ART. RUNNING TO TAKE THE PLACE OF THE MAN TO WHOM THE PLAYER HAS PASSED.' In other words an anticipation of total football, with overlapping full-backs often involved in a one-two-three,

with the third man moving on the blind-side, linking combinations of play. Martón Bukovi, in 1968 the recently departed Olympiacos boss, but who, while a coach under at MTK in Hungary, suspected a 'high degree of technical skill was not enough', was credited with implementing this as a routine into training. You'd catch it every other Saturday afternoon at Upton Park (and presumably every day at Chadwell Heath). Whereas elsewhere, the *IFB* continued, 'The tragedy for British football – even allowing for England's World Cup triumph and Celtic's memorable European Cup win – is that we took combination play little further than the wall-pass. Asked why the Third Man Theory had not been analysed and taught on FA courses, a senior coach said, caustically, they "didn't know". Now Europe's conspiracy of silence has been broken and the idea is there for all to act. The Third Man Theory could revolutionise football thinking in Britain.'

Ironically, elsewhere in that edition of the *International Football Book*, dark clouds had obscured the Continental sun: Johan Cruyff wrote of a creeping defensive tendency in Holland; Hungary's János Farkas and AC Milan's

'It would seem safe to predict that West Ham will win not one but several League Championships in the next few years'

◇◇◇◇◇◇◇◇◇◇◇◇◇◇◇◇◇◇◇◇◇◇

PROMISES, PROMISES

Terry Squires is a man with problems. He is 36 years old, an advertising executive, he lives in Chelmsford with his wife and two children, he has a government to support, and West Ham. As far as West Ham is concerned, there is no turning back now. Having supported them since the age of 12, he is now, as he says, committed to loving and hating them "till death do us part." He has come to terms with his life. This is his personal testament . . .

When I die, and my whole life flashes before my eyes, I shall remember the 1960's in particular. A large part of that period will be coloured by claret-and-blue flashes intermingled with a mixture of sheer football genius and deep gloom. Second Division Champions and promotion . . . defeat in the Cup by Swindon Town . . . F.A. Cup winners . . . defeat in the Cup by Mansfield Town . . . winners in Europe . . . and defeat in the Cup this season by yet another 2nd Division side, Middlesbrough – the final twist of the knife when your father-in-law is a Boro' man and an Arsenal supporter to boot . . . a jumbled mass of memories that will further rub salt into the wounds inflicted by the vagaries of Greenwood's Gremlins.

The last decade in the life and times of this fervent Hammers supporter has

been one long series of ups and downs. Next to Michael Parkinson of the *Sunday Times* and his beloved Barnsley, I must be the most frustrated football fanatic in the country. Unlike the present Barnsley side, West Ham undoubtedly have talent. But where the hell does it go most Saturday afternoons? To paraphrase Rex Harrison in *'My Fair Lady'* – "Why can't West Ham be more like Leeds . . . or Everton . . . or Liverpool . . . or . . ." But what's the use? They're not! They're a mixture of sheer genius and comic opera and, it seems, a masochistic desire for self-destruction.

Looking back to the late forties and the early fifties, and my first breathless boyhood days watching the 'Irons' . . . Archie McAuly . . . Ernie Gregory . . . Dick Walker . . . 'Rabbit' Parsons . . . John Dick, and so on . . . I suppose

18

'Possession of the ball is vital in football. Without the ball we can only defend and real football is based on attack'

◇◇◇◇◇◇◇◇◇◇◇◇◇◇◇◇◇◇◇◇◇◇◇◇

Swede Kirt Hamrin offered tips on how to break down *catenaccio*; and Dukla-Prague's Josef Masopust worried that 'soccer will not survive a period longer than forty to fifty years at most' in Czechoslovakia, if the 'concrete defence' continued to prevail.

Where Masopust was optimistic that physical perfection would 'bring enhanced technical perfection ... fast and tough, but also technical and intelligent soccer', Cruyff believed that, in Holland, only the Feyenoord–Ajax games were worth watching: '... the game flows from end to end. It's thrilling to watch, interesting and exhilarating to play in. This is the kind of football that should be offered every week, but we'll never be able to do it if we stick to our traditional national championships.' Cruyff was for opening up the borders to new ideas, genuine competition, basically a European superleague. Maybe then rigid football in England (and Italy) would loosen up and see that ball possession was vital in training to build up 'independence and individuality'. Tellingly, Cruyff noted, 'We haven't run around the ground in training for more than three years!'

Ron Greenwood could see that, of course. As long ago as 1968 he was telling *International Football Book* readers that 'possession of the ball is vital in football. Without the ball we can only defend and real football is based on attack.' Getting 'stuck in', in the typical 'manly' way of the British was all well and good, argued Greenwood, but once you've lunged in on the floor with your full-blooded tackle, what's happened to the ball? Generally it's either gone out into touch or straight to the opposition. You, meanwhile, are lying on the ground in the mud. Far better to follow the Continental model, where a player would look to harry and intercept and be upright so that when they win possession they can immediately spring forward.[123]

---

123 Half a century later, my teenage daughter, who plays at a decent level in England, has picked this up more by osmosis. than direct coaching I'm sure one or two on the touchline would still rather she 'got stuck in'. And *The Secret Footballer* feels it necessary to quote Xavi Alonso's views on tackling: it's overrated – a last-ditch measure, born of desperation; only in England is it considered an art-form to be developed.

HOW TO CRACK 'CATENACCIO'

by KURT HAMRIN
(*of A.C. Milan and Sweden*)

A LOT of water has passed under the bridge since that day in 1956 when as a 22-year-old amateur with A.I.K. I left my native Sweden and flew out to Italy to sign on as a professional for Juventus of Turin.

The Soccer revolution in Italy which was to impose the iron grip of the '*catenaccio*' defence on all tactical thinking had not yet begun. It is no coincidence that my best goal-scoring seasons during my eleven-year career in Italy were in 1958 and 1959, when I notched up 26 goals in each.

The effect of '*catenaccio*' tactics was startling, for although I have kept my position among the leading three or four in the annual list of scorers, my average over the past seven years has been between 14 and 18 goals.

Incredible though it may seem, this 14–18 goal average, which would seem trivial in a country such as England, has been just as productive in points for my club as those 'respectable' totals in 1958–59.

For under the present defensive system an extremely high percentage of matches are won with a 1–0 scoreline and 14 goals in a season can easily win more than 20 points in the final League table.

In fact I regard the 1966–67 season in which I scored 16 goals as one of the most successful I have had since coming to Italy.

Luigi Riva of Cagliari topped the list with 18 goals, followed by Inter-Milan's Sandro Mazzola with 17. José Altafini of Naples and myself were third.

But though the '*catenaccio*' severely restricts the number of goals scored, it has its weaknesses and I

'**mobility, speed, unpredictability**'

Five years later in the 1973 *International Football Book*, in lieu of the anticipated Upton Park trophy haul, Newcastle's Malcolm Macdonald was waiting in the shadows: 'So many people say that Ron Greenwood is the best coach in the business – and I'm sure he is . . . Yet I'm sure he'd love to get his hands on the league Championship trophy . . . (just as I would).' In *David Coleman's World of Football* in 1970 a West Ham fan, this time a 'PR consultant', had been let loose in similar fashion to the attack on Busby and a fading Manchester United. West Ham, he wrote, were 'a mixture of sheer genius and comic opera and, it seems [in possession of] a masochistic desire for self-destruction'. Peter Osgood, as far back as Jimmy Armfield's *All Stars* 1970 annual, believed that teams adopting negative Continental-style defensive tactics – 'stopping you scoring rather than trying to score themselves' – had led to 'automated almost machine-like football. Many people have maintained that this safety-first attitude has killed the modern game as a spectacle, but these critics must remember that it is success that counts, not entertainment. West Ham United are probably the best example of this – always attractive, always entertaining, but never in at the kill for honours.'

Above: Kurt Hamrin proffers a way to counter negative tactics in the *International Football Book* 1968

B Y 1974 Ron Greenwood had moved upstairs, and barely a year into the John Lyall era the FA Cup sat gleaming in the trophy cabinet at Upton Park. While smashed-up trains, dart-throwing, negative tactics, Leeds United, race relations, England's failure to qualify for a World Cup and the quantity of 0–0 draws[124] continued to be a cause for concern – now and again – in the football annuals of the seventies, it was definitely the end of the road for a certain type of late-sixties think-piece. In the coming decades articles entitled FOOTBALL – A DRUG OF THE PEOPLE?, or those in the style and tone of Spurs fan and Oxford don A.J. Ayer comparing the 'episodic excitement' of rugby with the flow and 'more continuous changes of fortune in soccer' (sample extract: 'I do not draw any close comparison between football and logic, though one of the things that attracts me to soccer is the aesthetic quality of the patterns that are created when it is played at its best . . . [but] I think the beauty and style of football are being threatened to some extent by an increase in aggression . . . and a growing emphasis on defensive play'[125]) came to be replaced by more pressing issues.

In *Shoot! Annual*'s FOCUS ON column, Everton's Kevin Ratcliffe revealed he would have been a lorry driver had he not been a footballer, and that 'chicken curry, fried rice and lager splash' was his favourite meal.

The roots of the modern-day annual (and modern-day football) were clearly visible in the early seventies. Jimmy Husband of Everton, after telling the *1971–72 Topical Times Football Book* that his first ambition was 'to make enough money to have a good life after football' and his second was to win an FA Cup winners' medal, wondered what a psychiatrist would make of the fact that he'd always 'gone in for fast cars', before going on to detail, at reasonable length, the vehicles he'd owned. From a Cortina to a Triumph Vitesse – 'I still rate it my favourite' – to a Corsair, a Lotus Cortina, an S-type Jaguar, a two-seater E-type Jaguar, 'and, right now, a 2-plus-2 E-type.' And there's Jimmy, wearing a stylish cardigan, perched on the bonnet. 'I like to know I can zip off somewhere quickly when I have to,' he added.[126]

---

124 Peter Morris is to be found complaining about this in late-period *Charles Buchan's Soccer Gift Books*.

125 From *David Coleman's World of Soccer*, 1969.

126 In fairness to Husband his preference was for a quiet meal with his wife. But, still, the days of 'Don't think too much of thyself. Tha've a long way to go and a lot to learn' were over.

Fulham: a 1960s soft touch. Under the heading 'One Way Love' from *David Coleman's World of Soccer*, 1969, were Honor Blackman's thoughts on life at Craven Cottage: 'One of the things I like about football is that one can go and just be part of the crowd. They know me, but people are very good-mannered at football, they don't pay any attention to you, they know that you go there to watch the game and that's that. At times we have been asked to go in the directors' box and all that kind of caper, and once we did, it's absolute torture, you can't say what you feel, it's all misery.'

The problem with Fulham, according to Honor, was that they were 'bung full of individuals' who failed to 'click together like a mechanism'. Honor saw things like Eamon Dunphy: Johnny Haynes, 'a *marvellous* player' in his day, got it in the neck again, for losing interest if colleagues did not make the most of those 'beautiful passes'.

If teams were happy to play West Ham around this time, they were probably ecstatic to visit soft-touch Fulham, who spent much of the mid-sixties flirting with relegation from division one before eventually succumbing in the spring of 1968. It must have been something to do with chairman, comedian Tommy Trinder, popping into the dressing room before a game and often cracking a string of jokes – as revealed by George Cohen in an 1965–66 *Topical Times* article which noted the 'wonderful, lighthearted approach off the field' at Craven Cottage.

TARGET~MUNICH '74

MIKE CHANNON
TONY CURRIE

MALCOLM MACDONALD
KEVIN KEEGAN

'I came to my senses and realised I was there to play football, not look at the scenery'

The Seventies

I always assumed the early nineties hip-hop band Marxman were so named because of their concern for social ills. The band members would have been the right age, however, to recall the 'Goals Incorporated' strip and short stories from *Striker* comic and annual. Marxman, looking a bit like Basil Rathbone crossed with Tony Hateley, and his trusty assistant Ferret (Peter Taylor) flew around Europe (though mostly the UK, for obvious footballing reasons) in a large pink helicopter, hovering over training grounds and park fixtures. One look at the action below would often be enough for Marxman to pronounce: 'Take her down! I think we've found ourselves clients . . . we're watching a first division club on the rocks.' Having swiftly negotiated a fee with a stressed-looking manager, Ferret would run film of 'Gorton Orient' or 'Stackport United' into the

helicopter's onboard super computer. The computer would 'clatter for about fifteen minutes' and then a remedy would be prescribed. In the *Striker Annual* of 1971 Gorton Orient were advised to abandon their overly defensive 4–3–3 formation and go for a more attacking 4–2–4. In training the attackers and defenders swapped roles, working along the lines of a total-football concept; and where television pundits forty years on still put their heads in their hands when debating whether to man-mark or defend zonally, for Marxman it was unequivocal: 'mark a zone rather than individual opponents'. There was to be no charging in, 'mad scrambles' or heading the ball with your eyes closed; victory over the defensively minded touring South American club 'El Plata' was achieved through the intelligent use of space, working the angles, and tricky ball skills. Where, in the sixties, the bearded psychoanalysts at the *International Football Book* had run with the thinking of Ron Greenwood over several pages of discourse, *Striker* annual had achieved similar results in a few frames of comic strip. Where previously managers had been known to laugh at 'the idea of a freelance football doctor curing all team ills and problems', Marxman would now be much in demand.

'**H**ow many people actually read *Shoot!*?' wonders Derek Hammond, author of *Got, Not Got* and *The Lost World of Football*. 'You flick through them, and people remember FOCUS ON – that worked because you could just dip into it; you didn't have to read a whole uninviting page about Archie Gemmill's debut for Scotland five years ago. There's no narrative arc to most football writing – none of the annuals were page turners. Whereas *Scorcher* and *Tiger* had stories. Comic stories spoke to me; they were books with a narrative arc, albeit short ones.'

Derek inherited a bunch of *Tiger* annuals, featuring the Roy Race strips, from his cousins. 'Melchester

Facing: Four players with World Cup ambitions in the *Goal* annual 1973 – only Kevin Keegan ever played in the finals and he had to wait until 1982
Left: Marxman comes to the assistance of Gorton Orient in *Striker* 1971

Rovers in a close season tour of Ju-Ju Island, playing the brave natives of Ju-Ju island – fantastic. Chris Donald of *Viz* also had the comics of his older brother – hand-me-downs, stuff from the fifties – and you can see that very much in *Viz*. The pre-1966 adventure yarn comic, that went missing a bit when things really kicked off with *Scorcher* – you know, they were much more standardized. Roy on Ju-Ju Island, that was from 1966 or '67, I think, but it seemed like the product of a bygone age when I got it as a hand-me-down in the early seventies. But these annuals . . . they *are* football annuals – *Tiger*, *Scorcher*, specifically, they made me the man I am today (laughs). Very rarely does a day go by without me considering my lot in life versus that of the Kangaroo Kid; they always stopped me in my tracks. I can just about remember the 1970 World Cup, and the stuff from those few years (the football cards, the teams) when I was at my most ultra receptive. That distant outpost of my memory is far clearer than stuff in the nineties – probably Man United v Chelsea in the Cup final; the decades slip by – whereas every week that went by in the early 1970s seems burned into my memory. In the same Roy Race annual I think he went to Canada and the baddie was called Abe Creel; and Melchester Rovers had a [pre-match] log-rolling competition against the local bully boys. That was much preferable to reading two thousand words on Bobby Charlton being so proud to play for Manchester United.'

Roy Race of Melchester Rovers led a dual existence in terms of annuals: there was the *Roy of the Rovers Annual* itself, which ran from the late fifties until the early nineties, and Roy also made regular appearances

'Very rarely does a day go by without me considering my lot in life versus that of the Kangaroo Kid'

in *Tiger Annual* – in 1976, for example, Roy had the Melchester squad dress up as motorway workmen in order to spring a 'surprise game' for rival Portdean City centre-forward Bob Dutton, who was struggling to overcome a fear of re-breaking his leg. But Roy was sharing column inches with 'A Horse Called Ugly', 'The Football Family Robinson', 'Johnny Cougar with Splash Gorton' (one minute the pair were out fishing from the back of boat on the placid water of the Florida Keys, the next they were being held hostage in the evil Neptune's undersea kingdom – a bit of wrestling from Seminole Cougar saved the day[127]), articles on speedway and colour photo-spreads featuring the likes of Clay Reggazoni tearing round Brands Hatch in the pouring rain ('three cars are almost hidden in the speedboat-like "wash" of Graham Hill's Embassy Lola'). As billed on the cover of the Fleetway annual, IT'S ACTION AND THRILLS ALL THE WAY, usually involving car crashes (when MARTIN BAKER MEETS SKID SOLO it doesn't end well for the driver of a brown Ford

---

127 Splash Gorton the beatnik swimmer, a cross between Shaggy from *Scooby Doo* and Dennis Hopper, and his companion penguin, 'Ice-Bird', turned up later in the annual, Splash playing records in a radio station, hosting a charity appeal.

A short story or a couple of fictional interludes were fairly common in the early days of the *Soccer Gift Book* and *Topical Times*. The stories were full of club chairman addressing people, 'Now look here, my good man', small-town clubs playing 'deplorably bad football', and characters like 'Fatty Hart', assistant to player-manager 'Sticks Stinchcome' – or schoolboy heroes such as 'Bats Belfry' who had to put up with being told to 'buzz off, kipper face' when breaking up a fight in the fourth-form corridor. By the 1970s such yarns were still a staple of *Tiger*, *Striker*, *Scorcher* and *Score* annuals.

The latter, in 1973, featured Sid, 'The Tin Talent Scout', a kind of tin R2–D2 figure who ran around on wooden castors, valves glowing in the dark while tabulating vital data on player statistics. Sid arrived at some surprising conclusions for team selection from the data he was fed, including playing the tea-boy-cum-kit-man 'Flagpole Flack' in goal, much to the hilarity of opposition and team-mates alike. Needless to say it worked out well for Larkfield Youth Club in the end – better, perhaps, than for some leading Prozone advocates in recent Premiership seasons.

Flagpole Flack was six feet seven inches tall, and he loved football. There was only one trouble . . . he was no good!

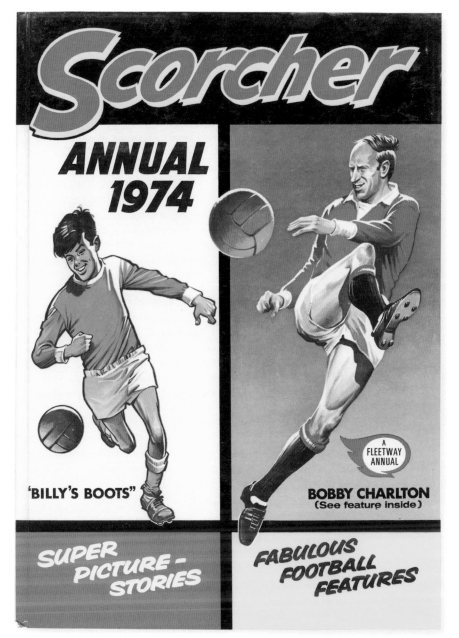

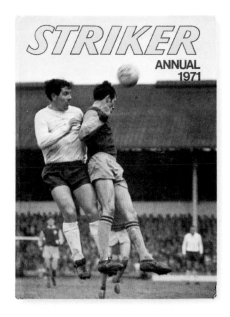

Since they were part fiction, part reality, illustrated annual covers posed something of a marketing dilemma for publishers. *Striker* kept to the trusted 'real' action, photo formula, *Score* went for illustration, while *Scorcher* attempted to bridge both worlds. The latter's 1974 jacket drew Bobby Charlton into the illustrated world usually inhabited only by Billy Dane of 'Billy's Boots' fame or Roy Race.

Roy's own *Roy of the Rovers* annual did fleetingly try real footballers on the cover in the sixties but the cover designers usually just had to ask: 'What shall we have Roy doing?' (Answer, invariably: 'Roy banging in the winner.') *Tiger*, in which Roy first appeared, covered all sports but is best remembered by football fans for 'Billy's Boots' and 'Hotshot Hamish'.

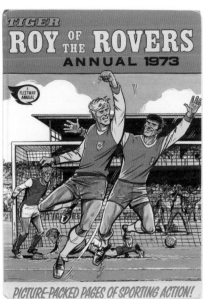

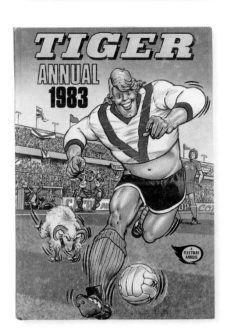

Escort), downhill skiing or secret trials for jet-powered army scout vehicles. All of this high-speed action made a ponderously slow Continental build-up, or a discussion on whether to go 4–3–3, seem, well, slow, and of the old world – a bit too much like a 0–0 draw.

Why have a plodding three-thousand-word recap of Chelsea's Cup run, say, when it's possible to capture it all, as *Shoot!* did in their 1974 annual photo-strip AWAY WITH CHELSEA. A few frames of photography took the reader closer behind the scenes than any bland player interview or profile would have done. 'Re-live the tension of the big-match build-up,' read a caption as Chelsea travelled to Stoke for an away fixture; the players spilling out on the platform in flared suits, wide collars and floral ties; not looking particularly tense; in fact looking like a bunch of chancers in a 1970s mob movie – a still from an embryonic *Pulp Fiction*. The puddles on the platform, damp from the leaky roof, date the picture as much as Eddie McCreadie's fine pair of heavy-framed glasses.

The photo-strip was a form that stretched back to the sixties: Jimmy Greaves' and Bobby Charlton's life

> *A few frames of photography took the reader closer behind the scenes than any bland player interview or profile would have done*

stories had both been committed to print by line drawing or photo-montage; and, as noted, in the *Topical Times* of 1968 there was Alan Ball, one minute in a school uniform, the next receiving an ornamental teapot at a Worsley council function to celebrate the local boy's contribution to the World Cup (finally, he was snapped standing by his 'TR–5 fuel injection sports car').

The same *Shoot!* annual that took in Chelsea's visit to the Potteries also featured AT HOME WITH DAVIE ROBB, the Aberdeen striker photographed digging the garden, hanging washing out, playing with his cat, playing draughts with his wife and about to place *The Richard Harris Love Album* on the turntable. The camera also got

Above: The *Shoot!* annual photographer joins the Chelsea squad for a trip to Stoke in 1974. The team's pre-match 'light' meal was steak

taken behind the scenes at Ipswich: head groundsman Stan Prendergast wearing a quilted anorak, painting the white lines on a misty morning; there was a spectacularly gloomy shot of the vast new cantilever stand at Portman Road; various serious-looking club officials, also in dark suits and heavily rimmed glasses, standing up in their offices, answering phones – it wasn't MI5 on the line, but 'a fan with a query about a souvenir'. Also, it was noted, the receptionists Una Dedman and Pat Godbold 'add glamour to a club now striving to establish a successful first division tradition'.

The *Scorcher* annual's photo-spread, a year later, of Leeds United staff putting together the match-day programme was comparatively light on information; slightly better was the trip to a grim-looking Mitre factory in Huddersfield, where it became apparent there was still a lot of hand-stitching going on when it came to manufacturing footballs. With all ninety-two league clubs having a new ball for each game – and presumably more than one? – the factory produced nearly four thousand footballs a season. That was a lot of leather to put through the moulding presses, which could reach

temperatures of 275°F (135°C). 'Which is pretty hot,' *Scorcher* informed us, in danger of patronising a readership who could most likely name all ninety-two league grounds and reel off a century of FA Cup finalists.

★ ★ ★

Another facet of the football annual that was slowly beginning to disappear was the comprehensive season round-up. No longer were annuals the sole repository of footballing fact and endeavour from the previous twelve months. Steve Smith was distraught when even the *FA Book for Boys* stopped listing Amateur results and the comprehensive review of the season. Across the board, as Steve describes it, 'the end of the directory stuff, the providing of solid info' came around 1974, by which point TV and newspapers provided all that fixture and result information, and annuals pretty much threw their lot in with features, puzzles and titbits. Once, where all the valuable statistics had been 'a source you could go to – "I need to find this or that about this club: I know an annual" – publishers were

Above: Aberdeen's Davie Robb shows off the trappings of ten years' success at the top of the Scottish game, *Shoot!* 1974

The photograph of Manchester City's Tommy Booth and his fiancée Janice watching TV in their front room is a high watermark

suddenly always keen to advertise "packed with colour" and tell you how many pages – usually 16 [were in colour].' We were on the road to the sorry state of the display stand at the end of the aisle in Asda today, which causes Steve to sigh ruefully every Christmas: '*Shoot!*, *Match*, *Chelsea*, *Man United*, *Liverpool* – all club annuals, any particular page the same – their corresponding annuals, even as late as the eighties, you'd know straight away from the layout which annual you were looking at.' Although it was a fine annual, Steve blamed *Topical Times* for 'leading the way with the breaking up of text' but approved of the fact that they were still running a fictional story pretty much until the end. 'Towards the eighties *Shoot!* tended to go the same way as *Match*, [even] less text and more pictures, or text boxes – that's what people wanted,' says Steve. '*Shoot!* from the seventies was exactly the same as the magazine. But if you keep producing the same thing year after year, but aiming it at the same age group every year . . . well, the reading habits of fifteen-year-olds change . . .'

Steve can distinctly remember his mum going on a daytrip to Blackpool and asking him, '"Do you want me to bring you back anything?" "Yeah, bring me back a football book." She spent nearly the whole day going in bookshops, and picked up the *Illustrated Encyclopaedia of British Football* from WH Smith, a collaboration with the Marshall Cavendish partwork *Book of Football*.'

This was the early-to-mid seventies[128] – around the time the very notion of an all-in-one yearly digest began to seem slightly jaded.[129] The football annual of the fifties and sixties began to splinter into myriad forms. Fact books, quiz books, and annuals that came to closely resemble their weekly publications, but glued between hard covers, were becoming the norm. Steve

---

128 Another fine repository found under the Christmas tree n the early seventies was *Football Facts*. The 1973 cover is an action shot from Plymouth v Bournemouth. Need the details of every League Cup tie from 1971–72 season? It's here.

129 With one glorious exception – *Soccer Monthly*, which wouldn't launch an annual for another six or seven years – see p.242.

would content himself with *Shoot! Summer Special* during the long close season: 'In the summer of 1977 I remember being away in a caravan with a friend's family. There was cricket on the old black-and-white TV with a coat-hanger aerial – you never got a very good picture – always cricket though . . . but *Shoot! Summer Special* – that covered you for the close season . . .'

None of this was a worry to writer Ian Plenderleith, who never read annuals anyway. 'Absolutely not, cover to cover. The thick text didn't interest me at all, unless it was about Man United. I'd be between eight and eleven years old. I also got *Shoot!* every week, and it was the same thing: my dad asked me if I wanted *Shoot!* on order – I think it was 5p a week, quite a lot of money at that time – so I was like, "Yeah, yeah, sure," and I used to read it in about two minutes. I didn't have the heart to tell him.

'Then I got *Purnell's Encyclopaedia of Association Football* when I was eight, and that was the greatest thing ever – it listed all the World Cup games and European competition games, every single one, and I would pore over those historical results. I still have it on my shelf now. So I loved history, but just in statistical terms, all those games – the East European teams – I had to work out which country they were from with an atlas.

'But I was too young to care about the culture of the game, or its social or tactical history . . . I looked at the photos, the cartoons, then I read stuff like player Q&As. You heard players' names on the radio, and it was great in a pre-Panini and pre-multi-media age to put pictures to names. And the other thing was pictures of foreign stadiums. Big open swathes . . . places like the Maracanã, these giant bowls: this was Britain, but that was what they had in fancy places abroad.'

Flipping through late 1960s annuals today, the gritty, realist black-and-white photography is an essential charm of many of the books. The photograph of Manchester City's Tommy Booth and his fiancée Janice, watching TV in their front room, reproduced in the *All Stars* annual of 1970, is a high watermark. Sunlight has all but bleached out the leading in the front window; framed on top of the TV set is a jug of chrysanthemums in water, a fancy glass ashtray and a model of Concorde sit on the windowsill; old fashioned wiring trails along the floor to the plug in the wall; and you can just make out Everton v Man City on the grainy screen. It's a beautifully composed shot which could easily be a still from a Tony Richardson film; or the sort of photograph

Right: A tender moment in the home of Manchester City's Tommy Booth, *All Stars Football Book*, 1970

Millions watch football on television—and footballers are certainly no exception. Here's Manchester City's Tommy Booth with his fiancée, J (for Janice) Royle, watching himself opposing Everton's J (for Joe) Royle

Photos and superlative heavy headlines from the *Tiger Book of Soccer Stars* 1970. This page, clockwise from top left: Peter Bonetti – 'Stamford Bridge Star'; Colin Viljoen – 'Pride of Suffolk'; Keith Weller – 'Roaring Lion'; Charlie Hurley – 'They reign at Roker Park'. Right: Nottingham Forest's 'Fighting Foresters'

pulled out for someone's fiftieth wedding anniversary to show young love in happier times. It was probably posed; it can't have been comfortable – Janice sitting on Booth's knee with the telly at an angle like that. But there's an unvarnished simplicity, an intimacy, and the last remnants of innocence here – all beginning to disappear from the pages of football annuals by midway through the 1970s, never mind the *Match* annual of today.

There was still one glorious series of annuals though – and in full colour.

The Tiger Book of Soccer Stars 1970 is a real beauty, and in some ways could be considered the spiritual touchstone of this book. I came across it in the late eighties in either a junk shop or car boot sale in south London, and had a Proustian rush on seeing the team line-up of Nottingham Forest: the very photo my dad had nailed to the door of our outside toilet, back when I was at nursery school. The *Tiger Book of Soccer Stars* must have been one of the first annuals to be printed entirely in colour – there's not a single black-and-white image. But what colour: it's Britain's equivalent of a William Eggleston collection[130]. The photography is a

---

130 I used to look at this annual over and over again – perhaps not what a young man in his mid-twenties should have been doing. I'd frequently take it (and before long a couple of others) into a colour photocopying shop on New Row in Covent Garden and get back to the office after lunch armed with glue and a scalpel to make an appropriate birthday card for a West Brom, Stoke or Coventry City fan. The blokes in the shop would pore over the pages, making their own copies of Spurs, Millwall or West Ham line-ups. My better half ended up with a home-made Valentine's Day card of Leeds' Gary Sprake, sprawled beneath an impossibly blue sky. (It was only years later I realised her childhood crush had been on Allan Clarke.)

The Tiger Book of Soccer Stars 1970 could be considered the spiritual touchstone of this book

mixture of posed action shots – Peter Bonetti sprawled like 'the cat', gripping the kind of yellow and black panelled ball you'd find in a beach shop; Keith Weller resplendent in Millwall white with a mod haircut, spinning the ball on one finger – and not-quite-right team line-ups, with players often photographed, judging by the numbers on the terrace, at five to three on a Saturday afternoon (John Toshack looks pretty pissed off at such a frivolous interruption minutes before kick-off at Ninian Park), or sometimes literally running out of the tunnel (Charlton at the Valley). You can smell the turf on the breeze, and ordinary life powerfully edges itself into pretty much every frame. The photography lets you in, behind the scenes; but it's the very ordinariness of it all that is most striking – in the background of the mugshots of Charlie Hurley and Jim Montgomery there's someone's bedroom window, caught in the gap between the stands at Roker Park; Sheffield United fans could have had a kick-about themselves on the moorland where Len Badger, captured in pristine kit, smacks a ball in front of a grass bank; likewise, in the misty field on the outskirts of Ipswich, where Colin Viljoen is trapping a high ball, you half expect to see a rambler by the far hedge.

THE FANS !

"OUR fans are magnificent", says George Best, "Our fans are an inspiration to us at Anfield," says Tommy Smith. "Our fans were marvellous", said Frank McLintock after Arsenal's wonderful Cup and League "double". No football club could live without its fans—especially the young 'uns. In the picture below left, it looks like this fan has had a long wait for autographs outside the Manchester United shop! Another United fan (right) going for a paddle at Fulham! The picture (below) speaks for itself! There's no doubt who they support!

The simple, unadorned strips are hugely evocative: there's barely a club badge, or any trimming, never mind a manufacturer's logo or advertising

Steve Smith recalls the *Tiger Books of Soccer Stars* fondly: 'They were wonderful photographs, lovely pictures – not reproduced in any other books.' And like with the *Soccer Gift Book*, there was 'nothing with any words projected on to the pictures – you had the whole picture to look at; the words were separate.'

The simple, unadorned strips are hugely evocative: there's barely a club badge, or any trimming, never mind a manufacturer's logo or advertising.

A year later, the 1971 *Tiger Book of Soccer Stars* annual underwent a bit of a reshuffle and was organised by player and position rather than the straightforward A–Z of first and second division teams. The mini-biographies were still little more than extended captions, and Scottish and lower-division teams (Celtic aside) barely featured – all, perhaps, an early indication of where football was headed; but all forgivable given the stunning photography, which was still beautifully expansive and unadorned; in fact, even more impressive than that in the first annual the year before. Squint, and that photo of Derek Parkin in action before the Molineux crowd could have been taken at a ground in Italy, Milan in a gold and black away strip. The same applied to a shot taken at shinpad level of Charlton playing Blackburn Rovers at the Valley: sunshine, clear blue sky, trees poking out of the top of the long East

Bank of terracing, a hint of brown in the blades of grass – the light suggests Spain or Greece (and then your eye catches the hoarding for Worthington bitter[131]). Even the photograph of Tony Book and Henry Newton, moving upfield, away from the old Kop at the City Ground, the roofs of the red brick town houses of West Bridgford visible above the packed terrace, feels hazy and slightly Continental somehow. Peter Brabrook is definitely wearing the kit of a Serie B side (rather than that of Orient), and there's an impressive full-page shot of John Aston in blue, jumping for a ball with a Benfica defender in the European Cup final of 1968. The bottom third of the photograph is made up of an expanse of green Wembley turf; the top third simple pale blue sky, only punctured by a flying ball.

By 1973 there was something more of an international flavour to the *Tiger Book of Soccer Stars* (action from England playing Scotland and Greece), plus more of a light-hearted feel – Gordon Banks faced a pot-bellied Ferenc Puskás in an impromptu penalty shoot-out before a handful of spectators on Arsenal's North Bank; Huddersfield youngster Steve Spraggs tied up in a goal-net by Frank Worthington and Roy Ellam; Alf Ramsey looking uncomfortable pretending to read the *Tiger* comic in his office – and plenty of stylish-looking menswear on display. Malcolm Allison, wearing a lilac tracksuit, was standing next to Joe Mercer. A stand at Maine Road was visible in the background, but this could easily have been an outtake from *The Italian Job*. Johan Cruyff lounged on the Wembley turf in a terry towelling top, reading what appeared to be a set of book proofs. And the annual kicked off with six pages of goalkeepers sporting vintage green shirts – it looks like Gordon Banks had got his from John Smedley.

---

131 Although even the wooden advertising hoarding looks like it should be at the side of a road in Sardinia, circa 1967.

Oxford United were the only second division team not included in *Tiger Book of Soccer Stars* 1970, but third division Plymouth (right) were in there for some reason – admittedly looking fantastic in all-white with a green and black hoop. Bury, relegated from the second in the spring of 1969 (along with Fulham and an old and tired-looking Johnny Haynes – the quiff flattened and losing its shape; the first signs of greying visible at the temples) were also photographed: an ageing Bobby Collins and the Shakers lined up before the blue and white painted stripes of the wooden stand at Gigg Lane, in what could have been a staff photo-shoot for a new ice-cream parlour or Punch and Judy show. Plymouth and Bury had swapped places at the end of the previous season, in the spring of 1968. But if the photos had been taken then that fails to explain the absence of Rotherham and Oxford,

who accompanied the Shakers and the Pilgrims, moving in opposite directions between the second and third divisions. Life can be mysterious like that.

Previous pages: A tribute to football's long-
suffering fans in *Tiger Book of Soccer Stars* 1973
Top: An atmospheric action pic from Charlton
v Blackburn at the Valley in the 1971 edition.

Above: High jinks with a goal net at Huddersfield
(left) while Johan Cruyff relaxes with some
light reading on the Wembley turf (right),
both in the *Tiger Book of Soccer Stars* 1973

'THE BOSS'

HE was famous as a player with Spurs—famous as manager of Ipswich Town—when they won Third, Second and First Division Championships between 1957 and 1962—and now he is one of the most respected men in the Soccer world. In 1963 Alf Ramsey became England team manager and built up the side that won the World Cup in 1966. A few months later Her Majesty honoured him with a knighthood, so to all of us he's Sir Alf, but to the England players he is always known as "The Boss". Above, Sir Alf is pictured in his office at the Football Association—with a copy of TIGER, as he posed for a special photograph which appeared in a Christmas issue of TIGER.

But it's the naturalistic photography that is even more affecting: Bobby Ferguson bearing down on goal in the fading winter light at Upton Park, the claret and blue in vivid contrast to the snow, ice, mud and slush; life-affirming scenes of wild joy as some kids, unable to contain their delight, spill on to the pitch and mob Jeff Astle after he's scored against Colchester in the Watney Cup final – even the policeman is smiling as he moves towards them (but in another shot Colchester captain Bobby Cram is the one in dreamland, lifting the Cup, as a young Asa Hartford stands behind him, looking pretty dejected after Albion lost on penalties); and a young Manchester United fan stands on the flooded bottom step of the away terrace at Craven Cottage.

Purnell's *Big Book of Football Champions*, not a particularly thick tome to begin with, became the somewhat slimmed down *Football Champions* in the sixties. It retained the spartan feel of its earlier incarnation – most photography was black and white, but when it came to colour, washed-out Super-8 hues replaced the cruder hand-tinting of yore – and remained, pretty much, a literal round-up of the previous season's champions, featuring plenty of photographic evidence of said victors.[132] The 1968 edition in our possession opened with another stunning sardines-in-the-crowd shot at Hampden Park, and a lovely colour line-up of Oxford United, division three champions in the spring of 1968 – Ron Atkinson

---

132 That said, the 1963 edition featured a section on the third division with an accompanying photograph of the Shay in the snow, and was captioned: 'Halifax goalkeeper Downsborough makes a flying save against Brighton. Both clubs were relegated from the third division.' Today you'd struggle to find such fantastically gritty action photography: QPR v Northampton in the mud, and Port Vale v Reading, complete with a beautiful old shot of Burslem Park.

**Left: Alf Ramsey looks nonplussed about being photographed for *Tiger Book of Soccer Stars* 1971, a copy of *Tiger* just happens to be on his desk
Above: A photo sequence follows WBA's Jeff Astle after scoring against Colchester United in the 1971 Watney Cup final. This goal made it 4–4 but the fourth division team went on to win the trophy on penalties, *Tiger Book of Soccer Stars* 1973**

Flipping through the 1973 *Tiger Book of Soccer Stars* feature on goalkeeepers one winter Saturday night, marvelling at the green jerseys, I looked up and caught David de Gea on *Match of the Day* wearing a purple shirt, pink shorts and yellow boots. A photograph from the 1970 *Tiger Book of Soccer Stars* featured a rare shot of a moustachioed Peter Shilton, crouching before an empty stand at Filbert Street, displaying the ball for the camera rather like you would a prize carp. Ever the perfectionist, he had been at pains to point out to Peter Douglas in the *Midlands Soccer Annual* of 1969 that it was, in fact, Shilts who had a Zapata moustache before Gordon Banks, and that he shaved his off when people started accusing him of copying the England no.1 keeper's facial hair, which perhaps said enough about the two famous goalkeepers' relationship.

The same annual featured a poignant photo-spread 'At Home With Gordon Banks', Banks mucking about in the back garden with his wife and two young daughters. By the time the nation's youngsters were pulling Christmas crackers and glancing through this feature, Banks' career was over, having lost an eye in a car crash one Sunday lunchtime in October 1972.

AT HOME WITH...
GORDON BANKS

WE thought that many of you—particularly regular readers of TIGER—would welcome a visit to the home of Gordon Banks, the TIGER Sports Star of the Year in 1971, so the Editor and one of our cameramen went along for a photo session. Here's the result . . . a super set of exclusive pictures of Gordon at home with his family.

At the time, Stoke's international goalie was living at Market Drayton, which is just a few miles from the Victoria Road ground. The number of his house . . . as you can see in the photograph above . . . very appropriately NUMBER ONE, and that's a title that football fans all over the world have given to England's master-keeper.

On the left, the Editor of TIGER talks over a few points about Gordon's latest article. On the opposite page, a spot of soccer practice with daughter Wendy.

seemingly twice the size of several of his team-mates. It's also heavily autographed – Ipswich's John O'Rourke, a young Brian Kidd at Manchester United, West Brom's Cup winner Graham Williams, Leeds' Jack Charlton and – ahem – George Best from Manchester United. As far as the annual is concerned there's not a great deal here not encountered before, or elsewhere – bar a good account of Leytonstone's 1968 Amateur Cup victory over Chesham. By 1970–71, man had walked on the moon

and the *Football Champions* typeface changed to reflect both this coming televisual space age and the Adidas-stripes-style logo of Mexico '70 (itself borrowed from the 1968 Mexico Olympics). Skelmersdale had beaten Dagenham in the Amateur Cup – all the more impressive a feat for doing it without FIND OF THE YEAR Steve Heighway, recently transferred to Liverpool and pictured in his gown (as he would be for much of the next decade, as football's honorary graduate, though here minus

THE AMATEUR CUP

In their second Amateur Cup Final Skelmersdale United won the Cup by beating Dagenham 4-1 at Wembley.

It was also Dagenham's second 'Final' appearance. Last year they were beaten by Enfield 5-1. It had also been Enfield who defeated Skelmersdale 3-0 in their first Final in 1967 in the replay after the Wembley game had been a 0-0 draw. Skelmersdale fans will remember how their team failed to score from a penalty in the dying seconds of the game at Wembley which would have won them the Cup. So this time they went all out to make quite sure the Cup would be theirs without any mistake. And they went about the task of bringing defeat to Dagenham in a cool, efficient manner.

Their centre-forward, Ted Dickin, scored three of his side's four goals. A superb effort.

Despite the score-line it wasn't altogether an easy Skelmersdale win. Dagenham were very much in with a chance up until the last 20 minutes of a tough, hard-fought final. The scoring was opened by Skelmersdale in the first-half when Dickin scored after heading in a cross from Clements. Twelve minutes into the second-half and they struck again. The scorer was Dickin with a flying header following a free-kick. A few minutes later Dagenham were back in the game after Bass scored. But Dagenham's hopes of an equaliser were crushed when the Skelmersdale substitute Windsor, who came on for Swift, headed home their third goal. Dickin scored their fourth after tremendous pressure from the Skelmersdale forward line. The Amateur Cup was well and truly won by the Northern side in their last season as amateurs before turning professional.

Skelmersdale's first goal scored by Dickin ▶

Skelmersdale players rejoice over their victory while hat-trick scorer Dickin kisses the cup

FINAL TEAMS:
Skelmersdale United: Frankish; Allan, Poole, Turner, Bennett, McDermott, Swift, Wolfe, Dickin, Hardcastle, Clements. (Substitute: Windsor).
Dagenham: Huttley; Ford, Dudley, Davidson, Still, Moore, Leakey, Fry, Bass, Baker, Dear. (Substitute: Smith).

10

11

---

his mortarboard). It was also noted that Liverpool teammate Brian Hall was a bachelor of science. And photographic evidence of Brian Godfrey chasing down Martin Chivers in the League Cup final confirms that while Aston Villa may have been newly relegated to the third division, their strip of this period was a design classic.

The late 1960s and early 1970s witnessed an explosion of heavily illustrated annuals. The *International Football Illustrated Annual* was a one-off, semi-embryonic *Tiger Book of Football of Stars*. And today, the detail of the captions, and the expansive photography still sucks you in to a world where Halifax and Swindon keeper Peter Downsborough has his page alongside an ageing Eusébio and Mario Coluna – the latter exchanging pennants before the 1968 European Cup final at Wembley looking, at thirty-three, as wizened and at ease as an old master of today, an Andrea Pirlo of his time. Dundee United looked magnificent in their new strip of tangerine with black trim; as did Northern Ireland in their dulled-emerald tracksuits. In a full-page photo also reproduced in the first *Tiger Book of Soccer Stars*, Terry Neill posed, mid-volley, in front of an empty stand at Highbury like it was 1955. Framed by the blue sky and lush green turf, the only give-away that this

By 1970–71, man had walked on the moon and the Football Champions typeface changed to reflect this coming televisual space age

was 1969 would have been the sideburns. Steve Smith in Bristol could recall an identical picture, somewhere in his vast library of annuals, of Stan Mortensen on the pitch, in full kit, striking the same pose in front of a similarly empty stand at Bloomfield Road. And any dads reading over their kids' shoulder on Christmas morning would no doubt have pulled up short at Bryan Douglas sharing a STARS OF THE PAST spread with Cliff Bastin and Ted Drake. Football keeps moving on and eating everyone up. Douglas, the tormentor of West Ham as recently as Christmas morning 1963,[133] stayed at Ewood

---

133 West Ham 2–8 Blackburn.

Above: *Football Champions* 1971 explores new typographic possibilities along with coverage of the Amateur Cup final

ALAN HODGKINSON

One of the smallest goalkeepers in League football, but one of the best. Alan joined Sheffield United about 15 years ago, after a short spell with Worksop Town. Since the 1956–57 season he has played in well over 600 games for United and has been rewarded with Under-23 and senior caps for England.

A charming personality and a fine sportsman in every way, Alan Hodgkinson has proved that height is not an essential to success as a goalkeeper. He has achieved fame with his studious approach to his job and the development of lightning-quick reflexes.

DUNDEE UNITED

Players in the group are:
left to right: (*back row*) Andy Rolland, Jimmy Briggs, Dennis Gillespie, Donald Mackay, Alec Reid, Doug Smith (Captain), Alec Stuart;
(*front row*) Jim Cameron, Dave Hogg, Alan Gordon, Kenny Cameron, Ian Mitchell, Ian Scott, Stewart Markland.

For many years after their entry into the Scottish League in 1923, Dundee United wore black and white, but in 1969 the "Tannadice Terrors" became the "Tannadice Tangerines" when they changed their colours.

62

Park his entire career, and now the wee winger of old was photographed sunk into an armchair, feet resting on a vinyl pouffe, white soles of his new slippers dazzling, a photo-annual or scrapbook on his lap, 'recalling some of his memories with his two sons Stephen and Graham'. Young Graham was wearing one of his dad's thirty-six caps. Time waited for no man.

Football Star Parade 'the picture-packed soccer annual [with] scores of thrilling photos' also started up in the 1968–69 season. For readers beginning to tire slightly of FA Cup résumés and reminders of the previous season there was plenty of photographic action, some of it in nice colour – QPR v Hull at Loftus Road, with people sunning themselves on the balconies of overlooking flats – but there was also a distinctly old-school forty-page directory at the end of the annual listing every league player, a WHO'S WHO IN FOOTBALL. The entries left Brian Glanville's twenty sketches in the *International Football Book* reading like *War and Peace*:

FLANAGAN, John (Partick Th). IF [inside-forward]. Skilful schemer. Signed from St Johnstone, 1965.

MIDDLEMASS, Clive (Workington). HB [half-back]. Originally a Leeds winger, converted to the middle line. 5ft 10in.
MURPHY, Barry (Barnsley). FB. This is his first club. 5ft 10in.

By 1970–71 *Football Star Parade* was 'the football annual by *Goal* magazine' but the format was essentially the same: Mexico '70, the full results, Brazil and Bobby Moore loomed large, of course, but also there were articles and photo-spreads on HUDDERSFIELD AND BLACKPOOL ON THE UP AND UP, and CHESTERFIELD A TITLE TEAM OF YOUNG LIONS. The colour spreads were printed in the slightly hyper-real colour of a Sunday newspaper supplement – Best, Morgan, Carlo Sartori, Paul Reaney and Jack Charlton in the mud in the FA Cup (*above*). There were still historical features, but now parcelled into 'Soccer's Strangest Stories' was the tale of WHEN ENGLAND GAVE THE NAZI SALUTE – skipper Eddie Hapgood objected, only to be overruled by an apparently sympathetic Stanley Rous 'for the good of peaceful relations' ahead of the 1936 friendly in Berlin. Rather sinisterly, in the copy we have, some youngster has scrawled 'England FC OK' over the photo of the

Above and right: The eclectic visual delights of the *International Football Illustrated Annual* 1970

During the summer Terry was signed by Hull City as their player-manager. They could not have made a wiser choice; the tall, elegant centre-half who spent 11 seasons with Arsenal is a true professional, dedicated to soccer and a born leader. Since 1960 he has played for Ireland on more than 40 occasions, captaining the side in many of these internationals. He was only 17 when he joined the Gunners from Bangor in 1959 but made rapid progress to stardom.

TERRY NEILL

Goalmouth thrills during one of those tremendous F.A. Cup semi-finals between Manchester United and Leeds with the action being provided by (from left to right) Terry Cooper (Leeds), Willie Morgan (Manchester United), Jackie Charlton (Leeds), Paul Reaney (Leeds), George Best , and Carlo Sartori (Manchester United)

players giving the salute[134]. There was also an account of the various disputes between the FA, the Football League and the BBC over radio commentary, including the famous story of a stream of 'banned' BBC radio reporters leaving Wembley at ten-minute intervals to relay what they'd just witnessed to the nation from a nearby makeshift studio – a sort of early version of listeners playing 'catch-up'. Terry Hennessey, looking not unlike James Gandolfini, hoped Wales would be at the World Cup in 1974, but worried about the way players' lifestyles were heading: 'You get used to having money and leisure too soon. So you gamble and gambling is the player's biggest problem.' Replacing the player directory was a fantastic GET YOU THERE GUIDE which advised, 'More and more people are travelling to big games by road these days. So don't let Dad get lost. Direct him to the ground with the aid of the *Star Parade* special maps, published courtesy of the RAC[135]. And here's a tip from *Goal*: always keep your eye in the

---

134 Devaluing, somewhat, the autographs of Peter Osgood and Dave Thomas elsewhere in the annual.

135 Looking curiously like RAC maps of town centres from the 1930s.

sky . . . and head for the towering floodlights pylons' – which was presumably aimed at the young *Star Parade* reader in the passenger seat rather than Dad behind the wheel.

In Scotland the *Daily Record* launched their *Book of Scottish Football* in 1970. A sort of Tartan fusion of *Football Star Parade* and *Football Champions* it had more than enough text to merit comparison with *Shoot!* or *Topical Times* – but focused, of course, exclusively on Scottish issues: that hardy perennial, the drain of talent south of the border; historical features (Hugh Taylor outed himself as a Third Lanark fan and contributed several pages on the centenary of the Scottish league); and plenty of player and club profiles from north of the border – three pages on Partick Thistle's glorious 4–0 thrashing of Celtic in the Scottish League Cup final of 1971, which featured 'one of the most composed defenders in Scotland', John Hansen, elder brother of Alan, at right-back – and was illustrated with a photo of captain Alex Rae, brandishing the trophy and looking like he couldn't get off the team bus fast enough to get to the party; his ma' overcome and weeping 'tears of joy' in the background.

The photography was pretty terrific: Morton striker

Above: A double page photo-spread in *Football Star Parade* 1970 catches an attritional midfield battle in a Man Utd v Leeds Utd FA Cup tie

Billy Osborne weaving through the Rangers defence in a blizzard; Airdrie in their classic white kit with the red V in the gloom at Ibrox, floodlights mounted through the roof of the stand, pale blue invalid three-wheeler cars lined up along the length of the touchline; Celtic's young Kenny Dalglish looking like a member of the Small Faces; a blurry close-up of Hibernian keeper Gordon Marshall, resplendent in red shirt and green shorts, smothering the ball from Ayr United's John Ferguson.

The first edition also had a remarkable (by today's standards) photo-spread entitled PUNCH-UP

The Book of Scottish Football 1970 had a remarkable photo-spread featuring QPR's Rodney Marsh kicking Rangers' Kai Johansen

featuring QPR's Rodney Marsh kicking Rangers' Kai Johansen (while he was on the floor) and then head-butting Bobby Watson as the Ibrox forward got involved. Across the page was referee 'Tiny' Tom Wharton (the ref who'd taken the Dunfermline and Raith Rovers players off during the thunderstorm in 1958 (see chapter 1) 'using all his 6 foot 4 inches and 15 stone to separate the players' in an Old Firm brawl in the mud. It put the reader in the mind of the *Topical Times* feature on 'the fine old Glasgow word "bawheid"' from their 1970–71 annual – 'bawheid' meaning 'the fumbling of a pass or other on-the-field ineptitude that will bring forth the cry, "Ya big bawheid", even though the culprit's head is of normal proportions and not abnormally round.' Three variations on the phrase included 'sodyheid' and 'boneskull' – or it could have been the case that someone had addressed one of the Rangers back four – or possibly Celtic's Bobby Lennox (who'd gone in hard on Rangers' keeper Gerry Neef) – as 'Ya daft tumshie-nut . . .'

★ ★ ★

Right: The *Book of Scottish Football 1970* catches tempers flaring north of the border, including 'Tiny' Tom Wharton, far right

The problem was, by the mid-seventies, there was nothing essentially new in a football annual. In the *Shoot!* annual of 1976 Billy Bonds was saying that West Ham would continue to play attractive football but would no longer be a 'soft touch'. A couple of pages on there was another photograph of White Hart Lane under water for that famous 1954 Cup tie against Leeds, alongside Ernie Hunt of Bristol City having ballet lessons from a member of the Northern Dance Theatre. Maybe Rio Ferdinand was to be found somewhere in a mid-nineties *Match* annual saying that, far from being 'gay', ballet is great training for footballers. Nothing changes.

Clearly, if you were ten or twelve, reading the *Shoot!* annual over Christmas 1975, you might not know much about Johan Neeskens or Barcelona – and that fairly unrevealing article behind the scenes at Radio 2, with photographs of commentator Peter Jones, might be interesting in terms of putting a face to the voice. But as Steve Smith pointed out, it's quite difficult to keep re-inventing the wheel for kids and teenagers with ever-changing reading habits and interests. Or, as Laurie Rampling in his garage off the A13 put it, 'How much longer are books are going to be around? In fifty years' time . . . a book with a cover, mate? The thing with technology: there's always victims. Ten-year-olds today will probably never ever buy a newspaper, so are fairly unlikely to buy many books.' And it's hard not to reach the conclusion that the basic template of the

The basic template of the football annual was firmly in place by 1974

football annual was firmly in place by 1974. From that point on everything was just a re-working, a copy of a copy; football itself was well on the road to becoming a commodified part of the entertainment industry; when West Ham's Alvin Martin told *Shoot!* annual's FOCUS ON column in 1983 that steak and lager were his favourite food and drink, and that the person he would most like to meet was Bianca Jagger, readers would have nodded wisely, expecting nothing less.

Still, looking back through the knowing lens of today, it's mildly interesting to note (from another FOCUS ON column in the same annual) that Spurs' Chris Hughton was a qualified lift engineer, and always had that as a fallback if things didn't work out, and that Cyrille Regis was working as an electrician on a building site in Middlesex when he was spotted playing for Hayes in the Isthmian League by West Brom's Ronnie Allen. History has generally lazily associated Ron Atkinson with 'the three degrees' at the Hawthorns, but Regis told *Shoot!* 'his career didn't quite take off under Atkinson. Yet when Allen returned to the Hawthorns in 1981–82 the goals started to flow as never before.'

In the same annual Justin Fashanu was invited to

240

I'M BACKING THESE BLACK ACES

Dave Bennett . . . excellent control and vision

says Jimmy Hill

THE PRESENCE of black players in our game has been felt for some time and, as the years have gone on, they have made, and are making, an increasing impact. There are now few clubs who do not have a coloured lad on their pay-roll and many black players have earned international recognition at different levels.

It is good that we are able to field black players in our national teams because they bring an added physical dimension to the game. They often possess outstanding pace, and are not lacking when it comes to winning the ball in the air. In addition, they seem to be able to acquire ball skills very readily.

Watching Cyrille Regis, Viv Anderson or Garth Crooks, you cannot fail to notice their graceful movement and a feeling of potential power.

A good measure of their ever-increasing place in our game was the 1981 FA Cup Final, in which three players entertained us in

vastly different ways — Chris Hughton in defence and Garth Crooks and Dave Bennett up front.

I nicknamed Dave Bennett the *Black Ghost* because he was extremely effective for Manchester City in an unobtrusive way. He has good control, excellent vision and a very gentle and accurate touch when he's laying the ball off. It is seldom that a movement breaks down on him and he achieves it all without flamboyance.

In that way he is different from Garth Crooks, who is equally skilful but far more expressive in the way he contributes to the game. He is older than Bennett and has taken time to develop into such an effective all-round player. I remember, when he began with Stoke, he was a nervous and weak finisher but now he relishes the responsibility of putting the ball in the net. The enjoyment he got from scoring for Spurs at Wembley was there for all to see.

Viv Anderson and Laurie Cunningham . . . England caps have rewarded their skills.

Chris Hughton, Tottenham's left-back, qualifies for the Republic of Ireland on the basis that his mother was born in Limerick. Chris himself was born at Forest Gate, in East London, and his father was from Guyana but he opted to play for the Republic rather than wait to see if England selected him. From what I've seen of him, I reckon that had he been patient he would have been good enough to win England honours. Instead, he may well set a new Irish record for the number of caps he wins.

It is England full-back Viv Anderson's extreme pace that makes him a formidable opponent in defence and such a threat in overlapping positions. He flew the flag and became the first coloured player to represent England in a full international when he played at Wembley against Czechoslovakia in November 1977.

Another coloured back, West Bromwich Albion's Brendon Batson, relies on

anticipation and calculation to rob opponents, rather than on sheer speed. I noticed, too, the performance of young Chris Ramsey, of Brighton, in their nerve-racking relegation struggle last season and he certainly didn't let them down.

I have high hopes that Danny Thomas, Coventry's right-back and midfield player, will follow in Anderson's footsteps in the years to come. Danny made a good start by being selected for England's Under-21 side against the Republic of Ireland last February.

Vince Hilaire, in the role of midfield-winger, is another coloured player to catch the eye and was rewarded with Under-21 honours again last season. It certainly wasn't his fault that Crystal Palace were relegated.

Up to now, we have seen few black goalkeepers in Britain but Manchester City have a young man named Alex Williams waiting for Joe Corrigan to come down from the extraordinarily high pedestal he has

---

assemble his SOCCER ALL BLACKS: four pages outlining a dream-team of 'ebony-skinned wonders, which if let loose against an all-white England Xl would offer the sternest test and could well triumph'. Unfortunately Fashanu felt it necessary to explain the historical absence of black and mixed-race players by adding, 'the trouble with most black footballers hoping to make a career in the British game in those days [the days of Albert Johanneson at Leeds – captured in a fair few Leeds portraits in the annuals of the 1960s, staring into the middle distance[136]] was that they bore all the physical attributes

---

136 There's a poignant photograph in the *1964-65 Topical Times Football Book* of Johanneson holding up his baby daughter Yvonne for the camera against some 1940s patterned wallpaper, his wife Norma looking on. There's no indication of what the future would hold here. In the accompanying article Johanneson confesses he was so nervous before his debut at Elland Road that Freddie Goodwin and Jack Charlton had to tie his boot laces for him. (After an agonisingly lengthy wait for the ball the tricky winger panicked and hoofed it into the mixer for his first touch – only for it to land on Jack Charlton's head before hitting the back of the net: cue Albert disappearing under a mass of joyous of team-mates.) That battle with confidence continued, though, and by all accounts led to one with the bottle. He died a lonely death in a flat in Leeds in 1995.

---

necessary to play professional football but had glaring weaknesses in technique and attitude. They often lacked commitment, they struggled to concentrate for a full ninety minutes.' He didn't cite any examples; and you wonder, in the middle of his Forest nightmare, how much input he actually had into the piece.

By the early eighties black footballers were, of course, commonplace, but not so unremarkable that Jimmy Hill, in the *BBC Match of the Day Annual 1982*, didn't offer a similar lengthy paen to the likes of Joe Cooke, Howard Gayle, Georgew Berry and Terry Connor. Both Fashanu and Hill credited the emergence of the black footballer with getting the turnstiles spinning again after a decade of hooligan blight, and both bemoaned the lack of black goalkeepers, Man City's Alex Williams aside. Hill only used the word 'coloured' once, argued that Chris Hughton should have waited for England to come calling (rather than the Republic of Ireland); and in Fashanu's detour into the introverted personality of Remi Moses it was momentarily possible to forget this was an article about race. Barriers were slowly being taken down, but then Hill concluded, 'I just wonder who is going to be the first black manager?'

**Left: Justin Fashanu picks a team of British black players in *Shoot* 1983
Above: Jimmy Hill assesses the impact of 'coloured lads' in *Match of the Day* annual 1982**

A question Tony Collins, manager of Rochdale from 1960 to 1967, must have found strange. Three decades on, such an article in the *Match of the Day* annual would be odd, to say the least, but maybe not so much has changed.

Football writer and author Jonathan Wilson shakes his head sadly as I show him the Fashanu article. 'I remember being in Austria in 2004,' he says. 'I think it was the first game England played after Euro 2004 and the centre pages of the local paper – I can't remember which one it was – had the headline BLACK POWER and there were pictures of the forty-eight black players who had played for England.'

Jonathan remembers having 'the *Topical Times* for three or four years [in the early-to-mid eighties]. I'm not saying it's the only one I got, though. I'd probably read it cover to cover over two or three days then read it again six months later. I read everything. Spent huge amounts of time reading, partly because I was weird, partly because I lived two and a half miles or so, quite a long way, from school. There were only five or six other kids [from the same school] who lived on my estate, but if you lived nearer school there were hundreds of people, so I spent a lot of time reading . . . there was no one to go out and play with.' Flipping through the *Topical Times Football Book* of 1984 he comes across a photograph of Sunderland's Shaun Elliott fishing: 'This is in Durham, just east of Durham as the river starts to go towards the sea, that's sort of the last main bridge, the weir just beneath it . . . Shaun Elliott was a genuinely great player until he got crocked by Graeme Souness in about 1981.

'You wouldn't get a Rochdale player in one of these now,' he observes, glancing over an article featuring Rochdale keeper Chris Pearce, who was apparently prone to turning up in the opposition changing room dressed in a Max Wall or Quasimodo mask (without the mask Pearce looked uncannily like Terry Christian's older brother).

I wonder if Jonathan picked up a tactical understanding, an appreciation of football writing, and a love of foreign football from hoovering up everything

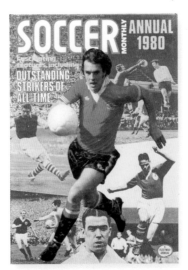

Smokin' Joe Jordan shared the limelight with a bunch of sepia-toned heroes of yesteryear

in football annuals; did that form the basis for at least two of his books, *Inverting the Pyramid* and *Behind the Curtain, Travels in East European Football*?

'Not really. The thing that awakened me to international football was the Subbuteo catalogue I used to get every year, which had huge lists. You sort of knew that Newcastle, Dunfermline and PAOK all wore black and white stripes.'

Jonathan was the last of a long line of writers to look at me blankly when I pulled a copy of the *International Football Book* out of my bag. I enquire if he didn't pick up this sort of retro item from car boot sales in his twenties? 'We had the internet, of course.'

He was interested in the *Soccer Monthly Annual* of 1980, though: 'This looks good. This just seems a much better thing, it's a lot of an older thing, I guess is what I'm saying.' The annual featured a South American photospread, Ricardo Villa waltzing his way through the defence at the City Ground – in the last frame turning away to celebrate at the same moment a heavily permed David Needham arrived in the box, the centre-half easing up on his run as if he'd just realized he wasn't going to reach the bus stop in time – and Alberto Tarantini of Birmingham City. 'Ah, you see Talleres de Córdoba far too infrequently [Tarantini's former club in Argentina]. It means workshops or studios, or somewhere an artist or a carpenter makes something with their hands.'

He approved of the cover too – 'Smokin'' Joe Jordan shared the limelight with a bunch of sepia-toned heroes of yesteryear: not only Denis Law and Jimmy Greaves, but Ted Drake, Dixie Dean and Liverpool's Billy Liddell. That would be like having Mark Hateley, Gordon Strachan and Bob Latchford lurking behind Wayne Rooney on the cover of the 2016 *Match* annual.

The *Soccer Monthly* annual led off with a dense eight-page feature tracing the development of the striker through the mists of time, and wrapped up that year's Christmas special with ten tightly packed pages from near-septuagenarian footballer writer Bernard Joy ambitiously chronicling the entire history of every London

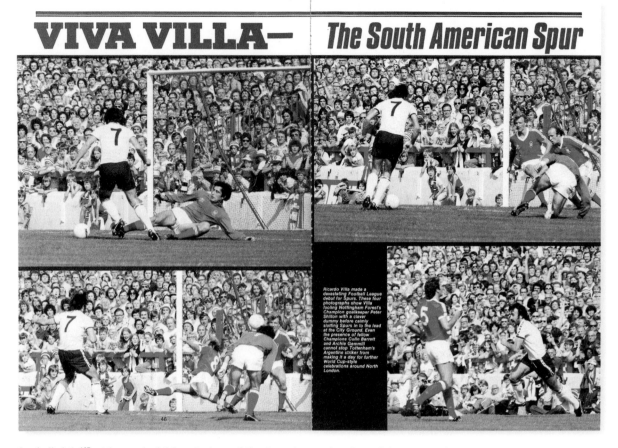

VIVA VILLA— *The South American Spur*

Ricardo Villa made a devastating Football League debut for Spurs. These four photographs show Villa fooling Nottingham Forest's Champion goalkeeper Peter Shilton with a clever dummy before calmly slotting Spurs in to the lead at the City Ground. Even the presence of fellow Champions Colin Barrett and Archie Gemmill cannot stop Tottenham's Argentine striker from making it a day for further World Cup-style celebrations around North London.

46

football club,[137] with wonderful descriptions of Alex James' 'puckish humour, long pants and "fluttering foot" dribble', Chelsea as an 'easy come easy go club', home to stars on the wane, that 'music-hall joke' (again), and the ball-bursting antics of Charlton's 1946 and 1947 Cup finals. All ninety-two league clubs were given several paragraphs in a lengthy HOW AND WHEN THEY BEGAN feature[138] and Don Revie ranted at length about the superiority of northern clubs (though he did concede London managers should have been paid more because of the distractions of the 'bright lights and high living').

'*Soccer Monthly* was aimed at the football supporter and the *Shoot!* reader who wanted that little bit more,' says Steve Smith, pulling the last of the short-lived run of annuals out of his extensive shelving. 'That's why they kept delving into the past, and you'd have three or four pages on a particular topic. The magazine ran from September 1978 to March 1980; unusually, the annual outlived the magazine. *Soccer Monthly* was different in that certainly by the eighties most annuals wouldn't normally be mentioning the war, or even 1966 that much; they'd perhaps only look back at the Tottenham double team from 1961 if Spurs were doing well, say.'

In the *Soccer Monthly Annual 1982* there was a progressive article by the England youth-team coach of the Greenwood era, John Cartwright, advocating ball-playing centre-halves, more training to develop skills at the expense of too many competitive matches, and a philosophy of attacking, entertaining football.[139] But

137 'For the replay, Chelsea switched Webb from right-back to the centre of defence, putting Harris on Gray with telling effect ...Tommy Taylor and Dennis Rofe were exciting discoveries, Mark Lazarus and Peter Brabrook good investments, and Orient returned to the second division in 1970 ... It was a surprise when Wimbledon were elected instead of Workington to the football league in 1977 ...' and on and on ...

138 Something this ambitious in scope hadn't really been attempted since the 1969 *Football Star Parade* player index.

139 Cartwright had spells of youth coaching at Crystal Palace and Arsenal and was last heard of in the *Daily Telegraph*, ahead of the 2002 World Cup, warning that 'the trouble with English football is that standards are set too low and players elevated above their true worth ... there are only 21 miles of water between our coast and France. So why is it that they can produce people like Henry, Vieira and Anelka and we can't? It can only be the development system. Yet I listened to someone on television the other day talking about a cup game. He said, "This match had everything. It had ferocity, it had passion, there was determination, there was atmosphere!" But he never once mentioned skill.'

Above: Spurs' Ricardo Villa makes an impact on his debut at the City Ground Nottingham, *Soccer Monthly Annual* 1980

by Christmas 1983 readers would have stumbled across that dreadful wording, 'the good news is that *Soccer Monthly* will combine with *Shoot!* . . . rising costs and decreasing revenue mainly through lack of advertising support in difficult economic times have forced us to reluctantly cease publishing . . .' *Goal* (annual and magazine) had been swallowed up by *Shoot!* Now *Soccer Monthly* with its lengthy histories of floodlit football, John Moynihan's fond memories of Christmas morning football fixtures (see inset), and features on the New York Cosmos – Dennis Tueart leaning nonchalantly on a Cadillac in the vast car park of Giants Stadium – was gone too.

★ ★ ★

In Scotland there was always still the *Scottish Book of Football*. *Number 24* was published at the end of 1978, and Archie Gemmill's goal against Holland in the World Cup adorned the front cover. But that was about as celebratory a moment as the tome managed. Hugh (Taylor) kicked off with a fine, wistful, eloquent, exasperated, opening account of the highs, lows and crushed dreams of the campaign played out before the Tartan masses at the foot of the Andes, WORLD CUP BLUES: 'Sometimes, I felt again, we Scots border on insanity as far as football is concerned . . . Why hadn't manager Ally MacLeod realised that Don Masson had lost form? . . . Why didn't the manager know enough about Peru?' And on – why didn't Scotland open the tournament like they finished it? They lost to Peru

3–1 in Córdoba, and Taylor was overcome by 'the smirk that turned the swarthy face of Teófilo Cubillas into that of a *bandito* who has just robbed a bank of a hundred million *pesos* [and] the whole, dismal story of the World Cup humiliation.'[140] Taylor elaborated: 'Strutting proudly with team-mates after the game [Cubillas] took time off from signing autographs and receiving kisses from Peruvian girl supporters in red ponchos and blue jeans which seemed to be sprayed on to tight bottoms to tell me: "Senor, it was a fiesta for me, this match, a holiday. Maybe I should be angry. Did Scotland think I am too old, that they ignored me?"

'It got worse,' continued Hugh. After the lackadaisical performance against Peru – Cubillas having been given 'the freedom of a street as wide as Sauciehall' – Taylor lambasted Ally MacLeod for his decision to pack the Scottish midfield with bull terriers or 'buzz bombers' (Macari in for Masson; Gemmill in for Rioch), and ditch the playmaker, which changed the pattern too drastically: 'We all felt, too, that while Iran were not the greatest they were probably the worst team Scotland could have encountered at a tragic time for Scottish

---

140 Looking on YouTube today I can't find free-kick maestro Cubillas smirking anywhere. He had a fine 'fro but was clean shaven rather than 'swarthy', scored a free-kick against Scotland to rival David Luiz's against Chile in Brazil, and, as for picking anyone's pocket, it seemed more the case that Peru were guilty only of beautiful free-flowing football, with Cubillas usually found at heart of the things in the midfield . . . (or that could just be the sumptuous four minutes of YouTube highlights soundtracked by Jimi Hendrix and remixed by P.M. Dawn).

Johnny Carey of Manchester United.

John Moynihan on football at Christmas, *Soccer Monthly* 1980: 'Foggy mornings along the Fulham Road, war scarred, blitzed, an abandoned piece of tinsel hanging sadly from a twig on a scruffy bombsite tree, men, hands in pockets, moving fast, working up their appetites for the match and the binge afterwards.' East along the Thames it wasn't quite the same: 'The Den at Yuletide was not always a place for merry rejoicing despite all those brown ale adverts in the club programme. One bright, Boxing Day morn, we were solemnly warned about our future conduct at the Den – "Don't Do It, Chums" was the headline: Don't ever invade the playing pitch – keep your seats and places on the terraces – keep off the grass. Don't throw soil, cinders, clinkers, stones, bricks, bottles, cups, fireworks or other kinds of explosives, apples, oranges, etc on the playing pitch during or after a match. Don't forget there are ladies and children in your midst. Don't barrack, utter filthy abuse, or cause physical violence to the referee and his linesmen . . . Think on this: "A bird is known by its chirp, so is a man by his conversation."' A photograph of John Carey accompanied the article despite only the briefest of passing mentions to him in the article.

WORLD CUP BLUES

The autumn leaves that fell sadly over the beautiful Mendoza Stadium in Argentina weren't a wreath for yet another World Cup funeral. They symbolized tears for yet another what-might-have-been, and I didn't know that cold evening of 11 June 1978 (which is autumn in that part of South America) whether to cheer or cry.

Scotland had just beaten Holland, who made it to the final only to lose to the host country, Argentina; and it was an epic victory. Once again Scotland had played with power and passion. They had the skill and the poise, the artistry and the all-out action, the pattern and the will to prove that they could have been a fine World Cup side, a side to bring pride to the nation.

They had decisively defeated one of the best footballing countries in the tournament and had the usually imperturbable Dutch jittery. They held the game in their hands for practically ninety minutes and they were within an ace of bringing off the miracle of this football century – a triumph by the three clear goals they needed to qualify over the giants.

I will never forget that sixty-eighth minute when the courageous Archie Gemmill scored the brilliant goal that made it 3-1. Scotland were well on top, the Argentinian crowd were right behind them, yelling for a Scottish victory, baying abuse at the boring disorganized Dutch.

It didn't last, of course. The pace was too hot, the endeavour too grim, the inspiration impossible to sustain for ninety minutes. Holland proved they had pride, were still a splendid team. And the magnificent Johnny Rep turned the glorious Technicolor of Mendoza into drab grey for Scotland with one of his fantastic goals to make it 3-2 ... and just when Scotland looked like adding another goal to that 3-1 total and making the next World Cup section for the first time.

So Scotland went home early. Their heads were high, though. For they proved they had the skill to play with the best, with performances from Gemmill, Bruce Rioch, the brave Joe Jordan, Martin Buchan and Tom Forsyth which will be talked about in Argentina in admiring, sibilant Spanish for years to come.

But still I cried. For this was the same old Scotland, the same old World Cup story. Why couldn't Scotland have played like that in the opening games which were vital – and in which Scotland were again a shambles? Why were we once again out of a World Cup on goal difference taking three points as Holland did to finish under the Dutch and Peru (who had five points) but with our goal difference 5-6 compared to Holland's 5-3?

Why did we have to ask the reasons why it's always too late for Scotland?

Sometimes, I felt again, we Scots border on insanity as far as football is concerned.

Behind me in the vast stadium, in the

Battle of the giants. Scotland's Joe Jordan and Holland's Rudi Krol clash in the World Cup.

11

---

soccer. They were spoilers, more likely to get a 0–0 draw against the best in the world rather than to beat Mexico, the worst of them all, by 1–0.

'Could Scotland rise to the occasion?'

'No, they couldn't.'

Hugh went on to describe the crowd of 15,000 in Córdoba 'laughing openly' as Scotland couldn't even find the net themselves (Iran scored an own goal in the 1–1 draw). 'All our fears were proved right. Scotland revealed themselves once again as a Brechin among the sophisticates of the world.'

And then, twelve pages in, there was Willie Johnston:

Surrounded by sympathetic team-mates he sat dejectedly in the vast dining room of the Sierras Hotel in Alta Gracia while outside SFA Secretary Ernie Walker, in dark spectacles which symbolised Scotland's humiliation, emotionally issued a statement which ranked as the most abject ever made in a Scottish World Cup history packed with disasters.

[Johnston's] crime was that from which so many professional footballers suffer – stupidity. His ignorance, his failure to appreciate what he had done, made me weep, for it was the complete unprofessionalism of it all that made Scotland the laughing stock of global football ... his explanation was that he took two yellow Reactiva tablets [stimulants] because he was feeling so low at one stage that he thought he wouldn't be able to play against Peru. He said he didn't think the tablets would have any effect on any doping test, so he didn't tell anyone,

All our fears were proved right. Scotland revealed themselves once again as a Brechin among the sophisticates of the world

although he'd been warned about the strict regulations concerning drugs in the World Cup.

As I said ... it's the stupidity of it all that makes you sigh for Scotland.

Before moving on to other topics – including of a discussion of how, in a Dundee shirt, inside-right Billy Steel, who 'flashed across the football firmament like a meteor: transient but brilliant' was probably the best Scottish midfielder ever – Hugh wondered why the Italian referee in the World Cup final wasn't wearing a blue and white shirt (Holland despite being the best team 'never really had a chance') and berated the hosts for taking 'such a girlish attitude to physical contact' on the pitch.

It's fair to say, by the mid-to-late seventies, for decent material north of the border in a football

Above: Hugh Taylor's *Scottish Football Book* assesses the national team's failure at the 1978 World Cup

STEVEN'S VERY SPECIAL DAY

There's one day in his life that nine year old Steven Challenger will remember for a long, long time—and that's the day he was West Ham's official mascot for their match against Southampton.

Steven and his father are met at Upton Park by Brian Blower, West Ham's commercial manager.

The boardroom—where vital decisions are made about the running of the club. Steven tries out the table for size.

Belgian and West Ham star Van Der Elst finds time for a chat with Steven before getting ready for the game.

Club officials show Steven and his father round the dressing room. A part of the ground few fans ever see.

A moment to remember! Steven sits in the dressing-room spot usually taken by West Ham and England's Trevor Brooking.

Time for an admiring look at West Ham's impressive display of trophies.

Then it's on with the famous West Ham colours.

annual, you'd have to pick up the *Scottish Football Book* or a *Daily Record* annual. Or possibly the *Topical Times*, published by DC Thomson of Dundee. Hearts fan and *BackPass* reader Angus Logan was bought the *Scottish Football Book number 13* and the *Topical Times* by his parents for Christmas 1967, aged ten. Angus still has both annuals today: 'Those two were marvellous acquisitions and I pored over them for months – the books really firmed up my interest in fitba'. I then started buying other annuals, if I could afford them – *Charles Buchan*, *All Stars* annuals, the *International Football Book*, further *Scottish Football Book*s numbers 14, 15 and 16. A theme I was conscious of in the late sixties, even as a ten- or twelve-year-old, was the dominance of British football in the 1966–70 era. Although the "Continental" had been perceived, we Brits would win out!'

Angus dug out a mid-60s *Scotsport* annual, recalling journalist Archie Aikman wondering, not unlike Johan Cruyff in the *International Football Book*, HOW LONG UNTIL A EUROPEAN LEAGUE? Unfortunately the article itself 'didn't actually discuss the headline' but did acknowledge that 'the biggest single influence in a revision of standards of play in this country has been the

brilliance of international sides like the Hungarians and the Brazilians and the skill of club teams like Benfica, Barcelona, Santos and Real Madrid.'[141]

★ ★ ★

Printed in Scotland, the *Topical Times* kept up with the interesting recurrent motifs of football annuals: fans, TV, the weather. Back in the 1970–71 annual, BBC's sports editor Sam Leitch berated people who wrote in to complain about an episode of *Match of the*

141 Angus can also recall Hugh Taylor, like Billy Walker and the *Northern Soccer Annual* before him, being concerned about rival attractions chipping away at football's fan base. From the *Scottish Football Book number 14* (Christmas 1968) Taylor wrote, 'In the old days, the average football enthusiast had to dash home from work on a Saturday, have a quick bite and then set out to watch his local team. Now he has Saturday off, has more money.' Hearts' answer was to build the fully-licensed Ace of Hearts Social Club into the back of the main stand to encourage, Angus remembers, 'the modern fan to bring his wife to supporters' dinner dances and provide useful income to Heart of Midlothian.' Simon Inglis in the *Football Grounds of Great Britain* noted 'it failed badly'. Built in 1969, it was sold to the Lothian Regional council in 1980. 'It became a bit of a 1970s white elephant,' remembers Angus, wondering if it was perhaps ahead of its time.

Above: The *Topical Times* makes young Stephen Blower's dreams come true with a VIP guided tour of Upton Park in 1984

Day from January 1970 which featured Huddersfield v Carlisle as the main game. 'It's important the programme reflects not merely the obvious box-office appeal of the Manchester Uniteds and Chelseas,' he explained, before pointing out the viewing figures were still 10 million that night[142]. (Which echoed another complaint on TV coverage from the same year. 'Mansfield seems to be caught in the twilight of publicity, placed as they are, between the Midlands and South Yorkshire,' wrote Peter Douglas in the *Midland Soccer Annual*. Defender Stuart Boam elaborated: 'We can get both Yorkshire and Midlands on our television here . . . and yet we never seem to get a mention on either channel. I usually watch Billy Wright and Simon Smith on the television before leaving for a game. If they've got time, maybe Walsall get a mention, never Mansfield. On Yorkshire TV it's all Barnsley and Rotherham.')

Conflicting ATV signals and 1960s regional variations of *Football Focus*, Peruvian girl supporters in tight jeans, Teófilo Cubillas and dinner dances at the Ace of Hearts Social Club – these are the nuggets to be trawled for in football annuals, part of the social and cultural fabric of the game in the mid- to late-twentieth century. As late as 1984 the *Topical Times* was still at it, following a young mascot around on a Saturday afternoon – young Stephen Blower, a nine-year-old in milk-bottle lenses, looking increasingly bewildered as he was thrust into the boardroom, the changing rooms

---

142 More than double the average today.

Left: An unlikely scoreboard message picture in Shoot! 1984

and eventually the dug-out at Upton Park in a series of behind the scenes photo-spreads that also involved a chat with François Van der Elst and John Lyall showing him the correct way to tie his boots – and a lengthy feature on Newcastle United super fan Jeannie Morrison ('even though she's a girl') telling the *Topical Times* that she had forty-four volumes of notebooks and prose extracts detailing the daily comings and goings at the club 'really for my own pleasure'.[143] The same annual also took the reader behind the scenes at the Football League HQ, a semi-detached house in Lytham St Anne's on the Fylde coast, shedding light on the problems of compiling the fixture list – QPR, Chelsea and Fulham obviously couldn't all be at home on the same day; Northampton always requested to play away at the beginning and end of the season due to sharing their ground with Northamptonshire County Cricket club; Doncaster and Chester didn't like to clash with race meetings. (This feature itself was an echo from of a photo-spread in *Kenneth Wolstenholme's* 1969 *Book of World Soccer*, the camera venturing as far as the 'spare programme department', in a Lytham St Anne's back room, where a cool-looking sixties woman is smiling, sorting through the programmes as if thumbing through albums in a well-stocked record shop.)

Meanwhile, over in the *Shoot!* annual of 1984, there was news of Watford's new electronic scoreboard (left). Which is where we came in . . .

'There's not an infinite variety of things that can happen on a football field, and that's what you run into with annuals,' says Derek Hammond. 'The actual game is the void at the heart of the football

---

143 The modern era was here: we were all awestruck kids.

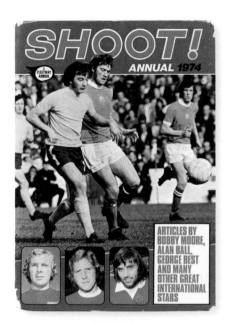

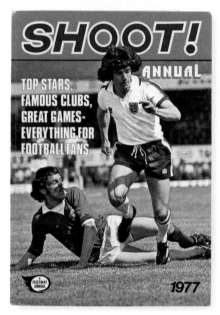

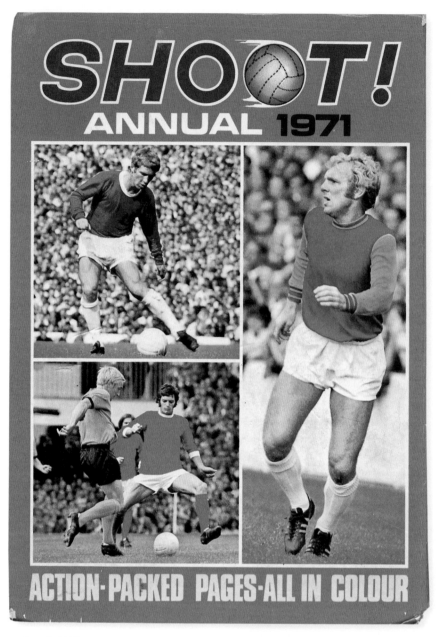

At the risk of making a sweeping demographic assumption, many readers in their mid-to-late forties may well consider *Shoot!* to epitomise the heyday of the football annual. Certainly it captured a new and colourful decade in all it's sometime garish glory but it would also inadvertently come to mark a period of almost terminal decline in English football.

The first *Shoot!* annual, launched in 1971 alongside it's companion *Quiz Book,* featured 1966 World Cup winning cover stars Alan Ball and Bobby Moore. Both were still at the top of the game and had performed creditably at the 1970 World Cup in Mexico. By 1974 the same players were reduced to inset pictures, alongside a waning George Best, and for the rest of the decade World Cups would take place without England.

Shoot!'s 1977 cover featured undoubted star of the seventies Kevin Keegan in admiral finery, but he was already set to leave Anfield for Hamburg. Liverpool continued to dominate domestic football, although their attritional (if successful) style in Europe wasn't universally admired. After leaving England Keegan was twice voted European player of the year.

By 1983 *Shoot!* carried its original style logo for the last time as England tasted World Cup football again in Spain, 1982. After a dramatic early goal by Bryan Robson the team petered out. Furthermore there were pockets of violence on the fenced terraces that did not augur well for the rest of the decade.

Shoot! annual publishes to this day, now a slick modern book unrecognisable from those produced in the title's first decade.

culture experience. You enjoy it in the moment and want Leicester [in Derek's case] to win, but there's not much mileage in that. The problem with all the things you enjoy – football, listening to music, sex, or whatever – it doesn't work as well just reporting it after the fact. Football is an exciting game, but the people who play it don't have to be. Why should footballers be interesting? It's almost like we've been blinded by the PR of the modern game, which dictates that players should be interesting, and have something to say in their twenties. But no one asks them any interesting questions. They're blokes who kick a ball around – they've been commoditized, fetishized by kids the world over. It's not really fair: why should Colin Suggett have an original thought?'[144]

Derek concedes that Eamon Dunphy and Peter Douglas generally had a good editorial eye, and the regional *Soccer Annual*s were readable. And that annuals became 'slightly more groovy, a bit more readable in the mid-sixties. The *Topical Times* was more accessible, there were snippets of facts that you were looking for . . .' Even *Shoot!*'s FOCUS ON 'gave you a little insight into the player, especially if the player was up for it, willing to have a bit of joke – but unfortunately the questions were dull. "So, Colin Suggett, what would you be if you were not a footballer?" "A PE teacher." . . . Plaice and chips, or steak and chips . . .

'It's a philosophical problem at the heart of this,' states Derek. 'Football culture gets me, not football; books about album covers rather than albums – it's the peripheral, the surrounding culture.'

In this light, the supplement that came free with the match programme in the seventies, the *Football League Review*, is an entry at the heart of Derek's first book, *Got, Not Got*. Peter Robinson's photography defined the *Football League Review*. Robinson was more interested in photographing the tea bar, the floodlights, a pair of hands on a ledge behind a walled-in ticket window, the gas works behind the corner of a ground, the entrance to the car park at the Valley, or Joe Mercer and Bill Shankly deep in conversation in a bare-looking corridor at Anfield. The very last thing he'd photograph would be a cropped-in, telephoto'd shot of the head of Cristiano Ronaldo or Steven Gerrard,

---

144 According to the *Midland Soccer Annual* in 1970 West Brom's Colin Suggett liked history and geography at school, his brother holidayed regularly in Belgium, he'd been unhappy at Sunderland and he could put two or three pounds on with his wife Susan's home cooking. He'd also bought a Jaguar from Bobby Hope's brother-in-law's garage ('he gave me a good deal').

'The annuals, there's something about the feel of them – that's football culture'

pensive before taking a free-kick. 'The way the football authorities see the game now is the way they want it reflected back to them,' Robinson observed in *Got, Not Got*. 'Fans in replica shirts with painted faces . . . this is the way football will be sold.'

There was a time when that wasn't the case; and football annuals were at the heart of an older, more reflective culture around the game. Even Derek concurs, 'The annuals, there's something about the feel of them – that's football culture, they're really nostalgic, full of that very old-school football writing.'

There's no question a lot of the annuals were full of guff and filler, that there was bad old-school writing – many player profiles and interviews were precursors, in a way, to the bland, reveal-nothing footballer autobiography – as well as good and charming. Equally, there's a fine body of football literature, bottling and analyzing with great depth, insight, verve and fine writing what happens on the pitch at any given time (maybe not quite as good as sex or listening to certain records, but much of it written by contributors to this volume, and found lining the shelves in Steve Smith's Bristol archive). It's just that back in the day the line between the two was blurred. Sifting through the mulch in football annuals, it isn't too difficult to find nuggets of insight. But at some point – and it's possible to sense the hardening; the draining away of the last bit of innocence during the 1970s – the football annual became just another line of product to sell in the club shop. Maybe, given the distance of another twenty or thirty years, it will be easier to pan for gold in the annuals of the eighties and nineties.

In the *Shoot!* annual of 1976 Alan Hudson glossed over the difficulties of his 'surprise move' from Chelsea to Stoke – 'many unpleasant things were said in the heat of the moment' – and recalled the day he arrived at the Victoria Ground: 'It was pouring with rain and blowing a gale. Not exactly picture-postcard stuff. Then I came to my senses and realised I was there to play football, not look at the scenery.'

Afterword

|||||||||||||||||||||||||||||||||||||||||||||||||||||||||||||||||||||||||||||

One sub-genre of the football annual that never fully blossomed was the football poetry book. *Gosh It's Tosh* appeared in 1976, a celebration of John Toshack's Liverpool heyday in poetry, prose and photographs. The Anfield striker was apparently inspired by Muhammad Ali's *The Greatest*, and there's a fair bit of ironic self-aggrandisement in the Anfield forward's couplet that rhymes Toshack coming 'in for Hall/Now we will see the Germans fall' in a poetic recreation of Liverpool's 1973 UEFA Cup triumph over Borussia Mönchengladbach, 'You Never Know'.

Mentioning this in passing to Dominic Bliss, responsible today – along with a team of three others at Stamford Bridge – for the Chelsea annual, Dominic recalls Chelsea lifting some of Eddie McCreadie's 1970s poetry for their yearbook. '"Winter's Coming" by Eddie McCreadie was full of this sense of existential depression,' says Bliss:

> December snows of winter,
> Colourful flowers now dull,
> Sleeping till Spring.
> People in heavy coats,
> Upturned collars,
> Rushing from the North Pole,
> And bitter cold winds,
> To the Equators of their homes.
> I have no coat,
> And if I had,
> I could throw it away.
> I tread the cold ice of reality,
> Happily slow.
> Thoughtfully and warmly,
> Remembering your eyes.

It could just be McCreadie's early seventies sculptured *coiffure*, but I can almost hear early Scott Walker solo records here, something like 'Montague Terrace (In Blue)' from 1967's *Scott*. Even more so in the lovelorn despair of McCreadie's 'It Might Be Cold Tomorrow': 'Let's fly to the Moon/What the hell if we hurt later . . . /I love you today/It might be cold tomorrow.'

Sadly, existential poets seem to be thin on the

ground at the Cobham training centre these days, and this year's Chelsea annual will feature the usual mix of word searches, quizzes, player profiles and fun facts and stats. Not that Dominic, also the author of *Erbstein: the Triumph and the Tragedy of Football's Forgotten Pioneer* (a biography of the Torino manager who died with the team in the Superga air crash in 1949) doesn't try to recycle the past and work in a historical perspective through fragments and snippets where he can:

'We try to introduce a historical double-page spread here and there. We might have something on the FA Cup in '97, say – the trophy before that was the '71 Cup Winners' Cup; the last FA Cup was 1970, so that [1997] was 27 years in the making, where Chelsea hadn't won any silver, which might be hard to believe for kids today. We did the same for the 2004–05 league title, which was actually ten years ago. Kids now might not remember that first league title under José Mourinho, with John Terry as captain. We rotate historical events: the 1970 FA Cup or the '55 league title could look a bit boring to kids today, those old cloggy boots, [but] you'd still do it because it's important. Although you probably wouldn't do anything that wasn't a trophy, if you were going that far back. You might work in some historical detail on pre-season tours, say, photos

Above: John Toshack gets some feedback on his verse from Emlyn Hughes at an Anfield poetry gathering, 1973, *Gosh . . . It's Tosh*

•

of kids in America, like you, supporting Chelsea – and then within that you might have a black-and-white picture of the first ever pre-season tour: Brazil, 1929.

Dominic was born in the eighties and grew up reading *Shoot!* annual: 'I used to peruse and pick out little bits, but that may have been because I was brought up with annuals that were presented that way. And perhaps it's because of that experience that I have the belief now that when we're putting together the annual we do things in short bursts: 300 to 500 words on a double-page spread; no more than 150 in one go.'

I ask him why he thinks kids' annuals are so much more, well, childish and clearly written for kids today than they perhaps were thirty or forty years ago. Back then, something aimed at kids would be less targeted and have a broader resonance too. Kids are perhaps more central in our society today: up until the 1960s and 70s, Little Johnny would be stuck outside the pub in a Ford Anglia with a packet of crisps, reading *Shoot!* while Dad was inside having a pint.

Dominic concurs: 'Today we address children directly. There's the 7–14s *Bridge Kids* magazine (which you get with your season-ticket); but by about age 11 your teenage ego takes over. We imagine talking to someone that age and adapt our writing style like that – you take on a spoken-word language. We do put a lot of thought into it. How many puzzles do we put in there? Is that patronising or is that fun? What did I want when I was an eight-year-old?'

But history has always been there. Dominic remembers picking up his dad's *Encyclopaedia of British Football* from 1978, 'in about 1990. It was full of records, league tables, club profiles – I was glued to the records, a bit of a *Rain Man*, taking notes on who'd won the most league championships.' He was also inspired by his dad's home-made 1963–64 scrapbook on Fulham, which included numerous articles cut from newspapers, such as a lengthy Johnny Haynes feature: a week in the life of a professional footballer, where Haynes talked the interviewer through his routine at Fulham . . . and we still try to do that now . . . "here's Petr Čech doing a reflex exercise in the club psychologist's room, pressing lights, knowing which one will come next, and he'll get a score"; then Hilário will do the same game, and you'll do a two-page spread of him and Ross Turnbull competing at this game and talking of how it helps them as goalkeepers, then a side-bar on training-ground tips if you want to be a goalkeeper – lots of kids do. It's still relevant now, I think, this desire to look inside the club, the training ground, behind the scenes, to see what

they do. It's one aspect that has definitely never gone away. Only a club annual can go behind the scenes nowadays anyway, which may be an answer as to why club-specific annuals [are so dominant]. You'd never let the *Match of the Day Annual* come and watch Petr Čech and Hilário do training. They'd have to come inside the training ground, everyone would be suspicious: "Who do these people work for? Who else are they going to do this article for?" Whereas if you come in to do an interview, you've got an appointment; you come in and wait in reception and the player is delivered to you. You don't go into the training ground, walk around, say hello and have lunch . . . but the staff do, and the staff make the annual, so they're able to get a different kind of access – it's the same for the club photographer.

Today, Grange Communications package and pub-

Ron Harris, Allan Harris (brothers) and Eddie McCreadie, of Chelsea.

Sadly, existential poets seem to be thin on the ground at the Cobham training ground these days

||||||||||||||||||||||||||||||||||||||||||||||||||||||||||||||||||||||

Right: Chelsea's very own Poet Laureate Eddie McCreadie (right) at a pre-season photocall in *Charles Buchan's Soccer Gift Book 1966*

'I don't think that kids are used to reading long articles about football any more'

lish the Chelsea annual, as well as those of all the usual big clubs, along with the annuals of QPR, West Brom, Aston Villa, Wolves and Hearts and Hibernian (the latter two possibly as Grange are based in Edinburgh). Dominic peruses a West Brom annual from 2009 that I have to hand. 'That's interesting how much copy is in there. I don't think that kids are used to reading long articles about football any more.'

'Grange do about 15 or 20 annuals, including Villa's,' says Dave Bowler, the man behind West Brom's annual. 'We get to about June every year and we've both got about six pages to fill. So we email one another and I pinch some of [the Villa editor's] ideas and he pinches some of mine. Hopefully there's no family with a Villa -supporting kid and an Albion-supporting kid . . .'

Dave Bowler is the author of critically acclaimed biographies of Bill Shankly, Danny Blanchflower and Sir Alf Ramsey from back in the nineties and, for the past decade and a half, has been the driving force behind the multiple-award-winning West Brom programme and the Baggies' kids' annual. He's under no illusion that he's swimming against the tide. A mere five years on, if Dave were to file a 700-word piece on the history of the Hawthorns today (the aforementioned article from the 2009 annual) he knows such a text-heavy missive would be back on his desk in no time. 'But,' argues Dave, 'if you keep giving kids easy stuff to cope with, what's the point? Sure, you don't want to set them a maths exam on Christmas morning, but at the same time you want a bit of a test, to try to drag 'em on

to something else.' It's one of the reasons the annuals are very light on captions, and there are none at all in the West Brom programme. The adult readership doesn't need it spelled out for them, and if the kids 'don't know who it is, or don't understand a particular word, they can ask somebody and start a conversation. They can ask their dad about Jeff Astle and 1968.'

I mention Dominic's raised eyebrow over the length of some of the articles in the West Brom annual. 'Ah, well, Chelsea are in the business of creating history, whereas some of us have already got it,' Dave retorts, before echoing Bernard Joy's music-hall jibe back in the 1980 *Soccer Monthly Annual*: 'When we were growing up [1960s] Chelsea were still a bit of a laughing stock.'

Among the word searches, player profiles and photo-montages of Scott Carson[145] in recent Albion annuals, you're as likely to find a black-and-white photo of a flowerbed in a park in West Bromwich, the FA Cup sown in chrysanthemums. That photo, included in the 2009 annual, was taken by Dave's nan: 'It was an old fashioned box brownie type of snap that we blew up. That was the sort of thing they always used to do in those days; there was always a fancy flower bed commemorating something or other.' And Laurie Rampling's archive has, of course, proved invaluable to Dave over the years: 'Without Laurie, God knows what we'd do. An unbelievable archive – we are lucky in the sense we've chanced upon something that most football clubs haven't got.' But, even so, Dave ruefully admits that most of the historical features involve 'a bit of glamour or excitement. There's not much point in talking about the exciting season in 1934 when we finished seventh.'

'Sometimes,' he continues, 'I just think about what you could do with all that history if you were putting together the Manchester United annual. But they don't really care about George Best: "We'll just put a statue up." Because for Man United, Man City and Chelsea it's all about now: this team, the owner, and the future. Whereas for us, let's face it, we've got no now. The now for all but about five clubs in the Premier League is: "Are we going to stay up this year? If we're lucky we'll get a Cup run." But, believe me, staying in the Premier League is much harder than most people think: it's a real achievement – but trying to laud the fact that you've finished twelfth for the fourth season running, that's difficult. That's the problem most Premier League

---

145 'When he went to Turkey we were worried. We thought it was going to be like *Midnight Express*.'

teams face, and it's been like that for fifteen years. The really interesting thing is the battle for fourth and who's going to go down. For the bulk of us it's about creating a different feel for your football club. So we can talk about the history.'

'Getting them young' is certainly a commercial factor in the production of a kids' annual for the Premier League giants – these days Chelsea are up against not only Spurs and Arsenal, but also the Manchester clubs; whereas in the Midlands, allegiances are perhaps less transitory, more firmly rooted in geography and a sense of place. 'It's more a case of getting 'em in the ground young,' says Dave, all too aware of West Brom's ageing fan base. 'I had to do a talk in a school a while ago, which was instructive. There was one kid, who said, "We're not interested in the old clubs like Albion and Wolves any more. We only really look at Man City and Man United." Which was an interesting observation . . . they're winning things; they're exciting.'

So, 'Bugger off with your flower beds and tales of the 1954 FA Cup,' the youngster might as well have concluded.

'Everything in society that kids get rammed at them is about winning, it's about celebrity; it's *The X Factor*, *The Apprentice*, all of that. Winning. And all the rest of you don't actually count. If you're not famous we shouldn't have any interest in you,' continues Dave. 'But club-centric annuals are great. They're why I've spent half a lifetime fighting for this shit [the historical angle]. It's that which connects you to your town and where you're from – it's about place and community and all of that. Let's face it, would you have ever heard of West Bromwich if it wasn't for West Bromwich Albion? Or Accrington or Darlington? The history roots you to where you're from. West Brom won the FA Cup five times, the championship once, they were

Above: The FA Cup in chrysanthemums in a park in West Bromwich. Photo courtesy of Dave Bowler's nan, as seen in the *WBA Annual* 2012

founder members of the league, the first team ever to go to China; they had some great players, not least the black players in the late seventies . . . we shouldn't let all of that go. We try to sow a seed with the kids, to make them go and look it all up again. But if we make it too simplistic it's no surprise when they think in a simplistic fashion . . . but I hope [the annual] is still enjoyable.'

How do you ignore the bad news, I wonder. The fact that Saido Berahino will almost inevitably end up at one of the Big Four if he carries on knocking them in?

'Well, you just ignore the existence of Nicolas Anelka altogether,' says Dave, which brings him on to the nightmare of transfer deadline day usually coming after an annual has gone to print. 'Last year's annual, he was the big summer signing: Nicolas Anelka. A two-page spread. Great. All ready. Going to print on Friday. Thursday, Nicholas Anelka retires . . . "STOP! Don't print anything." There was a mad panic and we pulled the two pages, bunged something else in, and it went to print. Then the following day he hasn't retired at all. He's coming back . . . but then, as it turned out, given what happened on Boxing Day, when they were all opening their annuals [the *quenelle*] it was probably as well that we took him out anyway.'

Thinking of Pat Collins Snr fielding questions from eager Brylcreemed footballers wondering when *Charles Buchan's Soccer Gift Book* would hit the shelves, I'm curious as to whether Anelka would have noticed his strange absence from the West Brom Christmas annual of 2014.

'God, no, he wouldn't have noticed anything,' says Dave. 'You could tell the difference with Anelka when he came. In fairness, he was a world star, a big name, he'd been there and done it – played for Real Madrid, Arsenal, Liverpool – and then he comes to us and he's the biggest thing we'd ever had, probably.'

So it's not like in Pat Collins's day when it comes to player co-operation with the annual?

'I drive Tony Brown everywhere,' says Dave. 'He must be the best documented footballer in the world now. We've been doing a column, 2,000 words, for fifteen years in the programme. Everything Tony Brown ever thought or did is in those programmes, but all through his playing career he hardly ever got interviewed. As a player, after a game, you'd just go into the players' lounge and have a drink then go home. You wouldn't be doing television – it was a big thing if they ever got interviewed, and a lot of them were quite nervy about it because they never practised. But now

'Would you have ever heard of West Bromwich if it wasn't for West Bromwich Albion?'

they're being interviewed all the while and they hate it.'

To illustrate his point, Dave outlines the scenario of (then) manager Alan Irvine doing about seven television interviews after a game: 'And by the time he gets to me [for the West Brom website] he's been asked pretty much the same questions seven times. And then when he's done with me he's got to go up and do the written press conference, only to be asked all the same questions again. You can understand – despite the salaries – why they get cheesed off with it. [Players] don't get paid for playing football, they're paid for being TV personalities. They get paid so much money because they're on Sky, not because they're footballers – the football is like a by-product.'

But, Dave adds, 'Our lot are generally OK. The bulk of them are self-aware enough to realise they're at a good club and doing well.'

★★★

Dominic Bliss at Chelsea perceptively comments that the golden age of football writing 'is whenever the writer was young'. 'Too right,' would be Dave Bowler's response. 'What an annual was then,' says Dave, flicking through the *Topical Times* of 1970–71, 'and what an annual is now, are just two totally different concepts. *They* were proper football books – *Peter Dimmock's Sportsview*, or whatever; the *Topical Times* – you could be reading that for three months, couldn't you?; *Shoot! Too*'; *David Coleman's World Cup '70 Annual*, England v Czechoslovakia (inexplicably in colour: 'Christ knows how because we didn't have a colour set until 1974'); *Good Morning, Mexico*, nipping home for more highlights during school dinner-time, and the moon landings all form a kind of psychedelic montage of happy childhood memories for Dave.

And football had an alluring otherness: 'Your world was small, but when you saw people from these exotic places, from Doncaster or Carlisle, it was like they were from another planet. I hate to suggest there's a sense of wonder over Doncaster, it's difficult to relate to these things ... [but these teams were] somehow

enthralling. I don't think things are as exotic as they used to be. If you had something in there [*Topical Times*] about Juventus or Bayern Munich, it was like being on another planet. Nowadays kids are much more clued up on football around the world, thanks to TV. That was why the World Cup used to be much more exciting than it is now. You'd see these players you've never seen. People are more blasé now.'

Dave remembers Valencia's Mario Kempes – a World Cup winner, no less – coming to the Albion on a freezing cold Tuesday night in December 1978. The night before the game Dave and his mate went up to Sandwell to catch the Spanish side after training and successfully secured Kempes's autograph as he left the Hawthornes. 'Now there's telly and everyone playing Football Manager on the computer. There's nothing exotic about that ... if you read about Arjen Robben, you've seen him play God knows how many times already, whereas Dino Zoff ... It's a problem with football writing: you used to be able to conjure up these people by writing about them – now you just switch the telly on, or go on YouTube ...'

Dave fondly recalls the days of football annuals when 'there would be a feature on Doncaster Rovers, then Bobby Moore on the next page', and argues that despite *Football Focus*, Sky Sports, Twitter, Facebook, Tumblr and all the rest of it, there's actually 'more scope now for books like the *Topical Times* than there ever was.' In the world of endlessly recycled player interviews, soundbites and self-evident platitudes that pass for punditry, Dave points out, 'I don't know anything about the Rochdale right-back, other than his is somehow a less worthy occupation. More on him would be interesting.'

Dave's recent school trip – to talk about how, as a son of the Black Country town of Wednesbury, he somehow escaped the designated 1970's life of working in a factory or an office to forge a career in writing – left him, on the one hand, depressed: 'You go into a school now and a lot of kids will say they just want to be famous.' But, on the other, most youngsters saw no limits to what they might achieve: 'And that can be a positive thing.' Maybe the wheel might turn again. 'I couldn't get away from 'em,' says Dave, of the kids. 'There were a lot of good questions – about writing, about the Premier League. When I was that age no one would ask a question. But they're all so bloody confident now. I don't know where that's come from.'

★★★

Right: Life's a 0–0 draw at the Goldstone Ground, visible from your bedroom window, the *Big Book of Football Champions* 1961

Brighton v. Swansea, March. Swansea centre-half, Mel Nurse, is sandwiched between his goalkeeper, Dwyer, and Brighton centre-forward, Windross (No. 9). This second division game ended 0-0.

Acknowledgements

Initial thanks to Doug Cheeseman, Andy Lyons and Richard Guy at *When Saturday Comes*, especially Doug, for phoning me up when life was at that euphemistic crossroads – one article became another, which led to this book, twenty years on from happy days working on *Shot!* and *This Is Soccer*. Huge thanks also to Richard Williams, Johnny Green, Dominic Bliss, Dave Bowler, Jonathan Wilson, Steve Smith, Laurie Rampling, Graham Sharpe, Sean Magee, Ian Plenderleith, Derek Hammond, Ros Pedley, Patrick Collins and Angus Logan, for their wise words and generous allocation of time spent recalling 'the past'. Steve Smith and Laurie Rampling also contributed hugely in opening up their vast archives – at least the past is safe somewhere.

In a similar vein, we're also indebted to Simon Inglis, for his near complete set of *Charles Buchan Soccer Gift Books*, and *WSC* staff past and present, especially Mike Ticher, Bill Brewster and John Duncan for leaving their football annuals lying around the *WSC* office for the last few decades. Thanks also to Daniel Tatarsky (for loan of his copy of *The Golden Vision*), Mike Berry at *BackPass*, David Dewar, Andreas Campomar at Constable & Robinson, for taking a punt in difficult times, David Lloyd for his sharp copy-editing and Allie Collins for proofreading. Also Jörn Kröger for going beyond the call of duty on the imaging work. And Clive Hebard, Nick Ross, Linda Silverman, Claire Chesser, Helen Bergh and everyone at Constable & Robinson and Little, Brown.

Personal thanks to Mo Fearn, who sadly didn't make it to the new season; Neil Woollatt, also much missed; to my mum, Joyce Preece, for some 1960s fact-checking and for giving birth to my brother (Nick), which meant my dad first took to me to the City Ground at an impressionable age – and to my dad, David Preece, who always preferred Allan Brown to Brian Clough anyway; to Edie Preece, one of the finest passers of a ball in u17s football; Thurston Preece, for his early photos of some of these annuals (even if his heart is on a skateboard); and to Angela Warren, for everything.

If it's not too indulgent, Doug would like to thank Ian Preece for taking up the project in the first place, undertaking the epic task of reading every annual in our possession and disseminating the content therein with dedication, skill and good humour. Personal thanks also to Tim Bradford, Matt Stone, Lance Bellers, Paula Bellers, Dom English, Boyd Hilton and Martin Hardwick for moral support over the years. Lastly to Sarah, Polly, Rosie and Joe for, well, just because.

Plendy, you can have those books back now . . . Cheers

Permissions